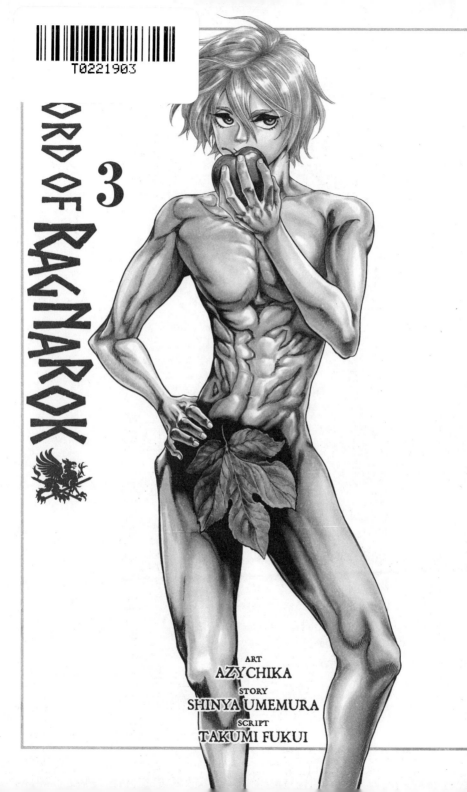

LORD OF RAGNAROK

3

ART
AZYCHIKA
STORY
SHINYA UMEMURA
SCRIPT
TAKUMI FUKUI

3

RECORD OF RAGNAROK

Chapter 10: Expulsion from Paradise

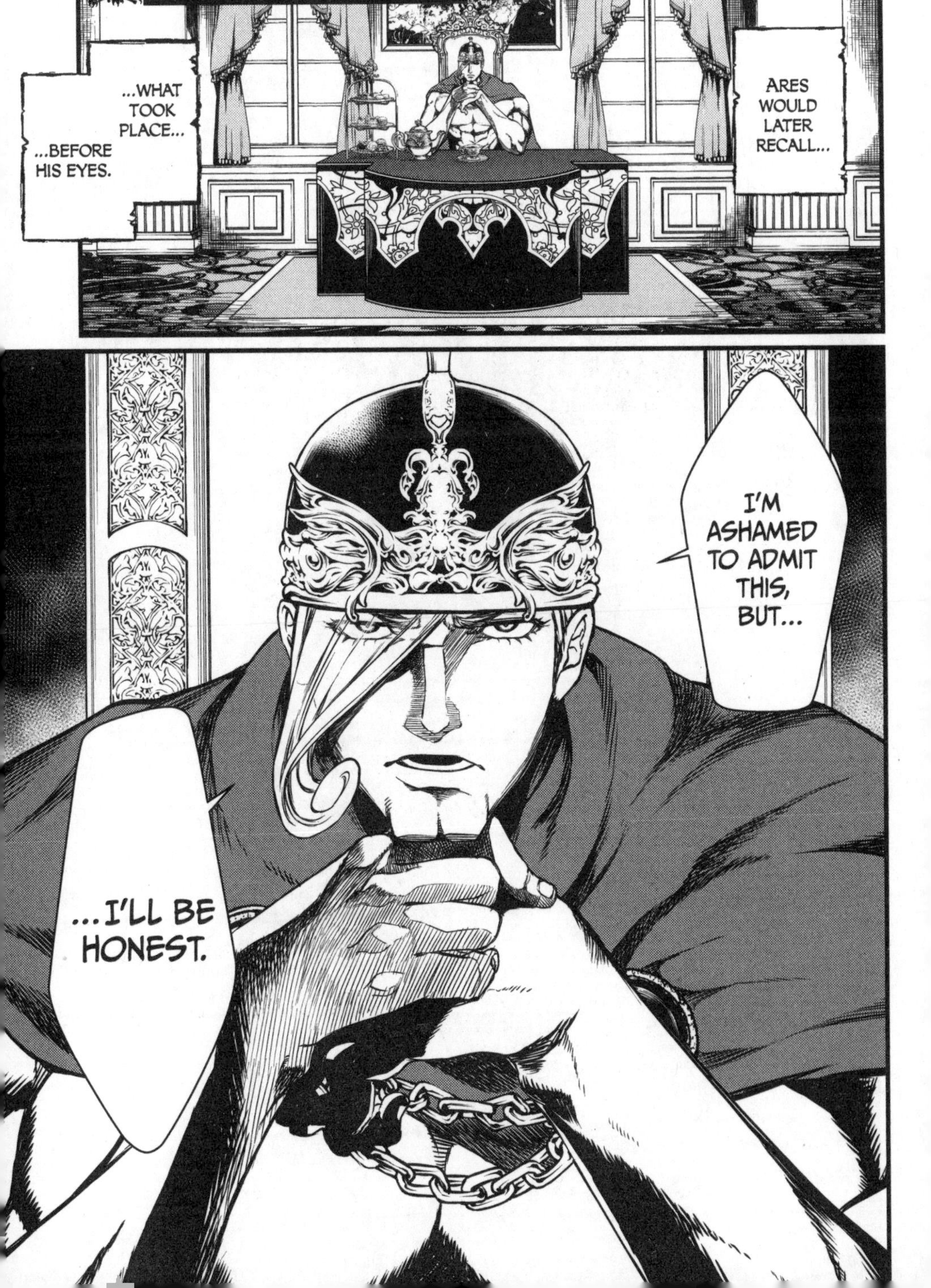
ARES WOULD LATER RECALL...
...WHAT TOOK PLACE...
...BEFORE HIS EYES.
I'M ASHAMED TO ADMIT THIS, BUT...
...I'LL BE HONEST.

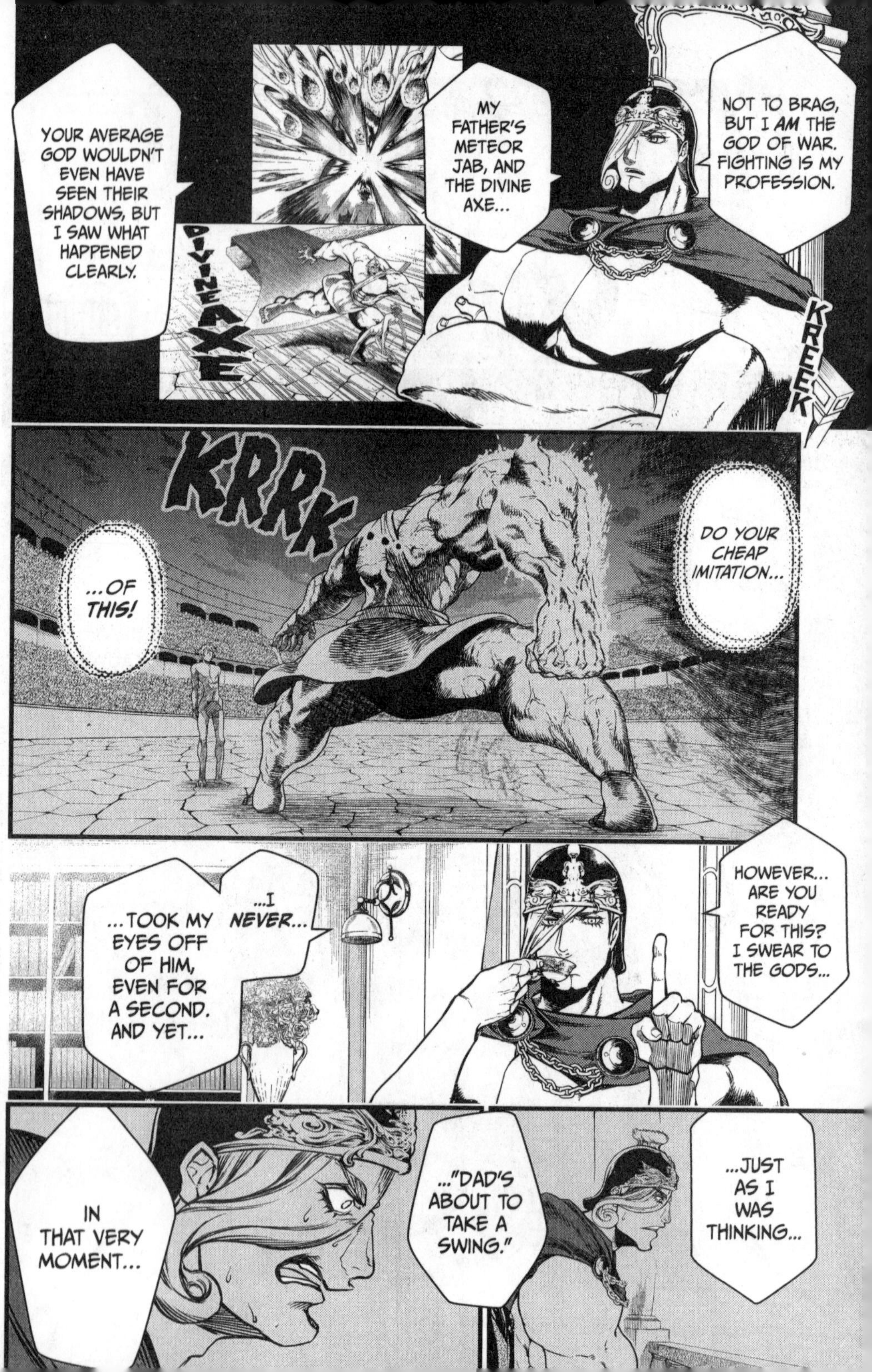
NOT TO BRAG, BUT I *AM* THE GOD OF WAR. FIGHTING IS MY PROFESSION.
KREEK
MY FATHER'S METEOR JAB, AND THE DIVINE AXE...
DIVINE AXE
YOUR AVERAGE GOD WOULDN'T EVEN HAVE SEEN THEIR SHADOWS, BUT I SAW WHAT HAPPENED CLEARLY.
KRRK
DO YOUR CHEAP IMITATION...
...OF THIS!
HOWEVER... ARE YOU READY FOR THIS? I SWEAR TO THE GODS...
...I *NEVER*...
...TOOK MY EYES OFF OF HIM, EVEN FOR A SECOND. AND YET...
...JUST AS I WAS THINKING...
..."DAD'S ABOUT TO TAKE A SWING."
IN THAT VERY MOMENT...

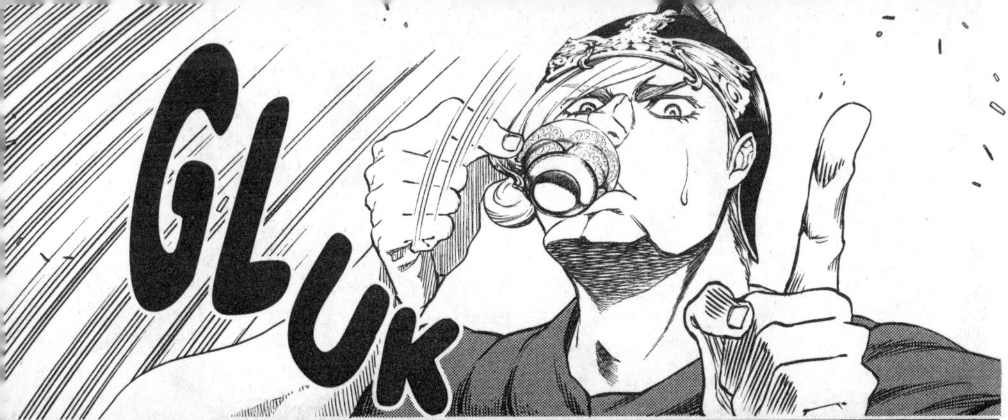
GLUK

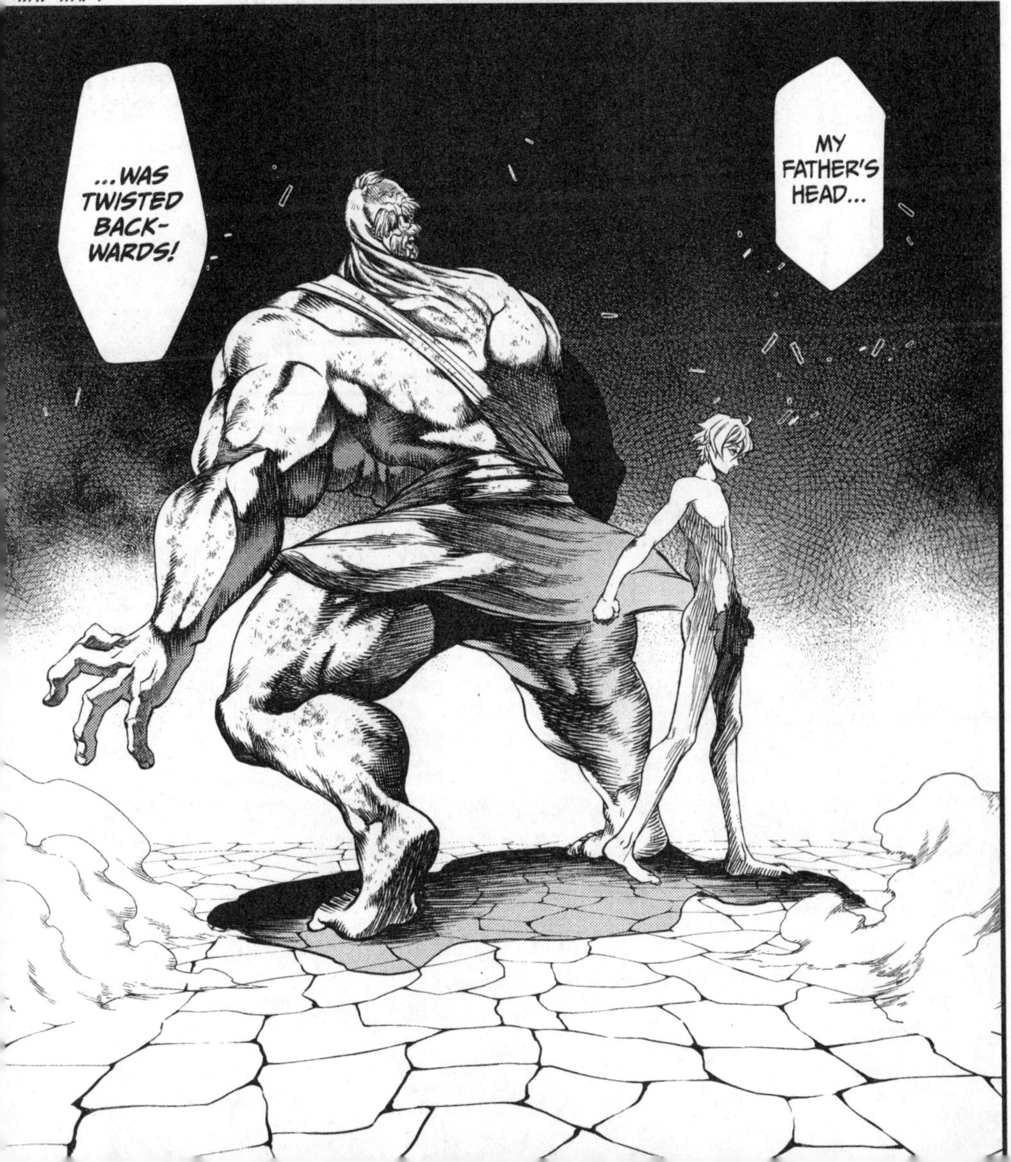
MY FATHER'S HEAD...
...WAS TWISTED BACKWARDS!

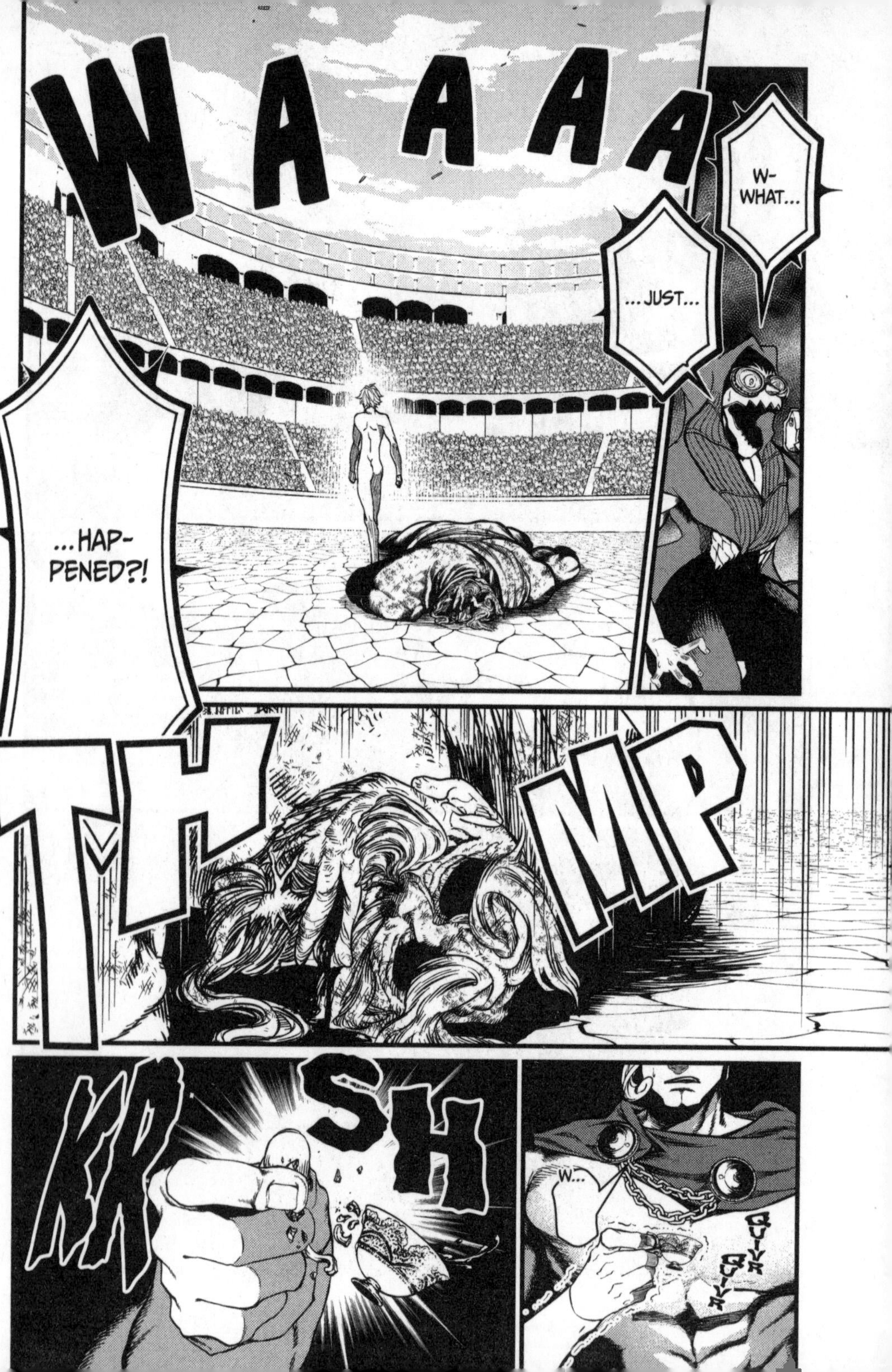
W-
WHAT...
...JUST...
WAAAA
...HAP-
PENED?!
THMP
W...
QUIVR
QUIVR
KRSH

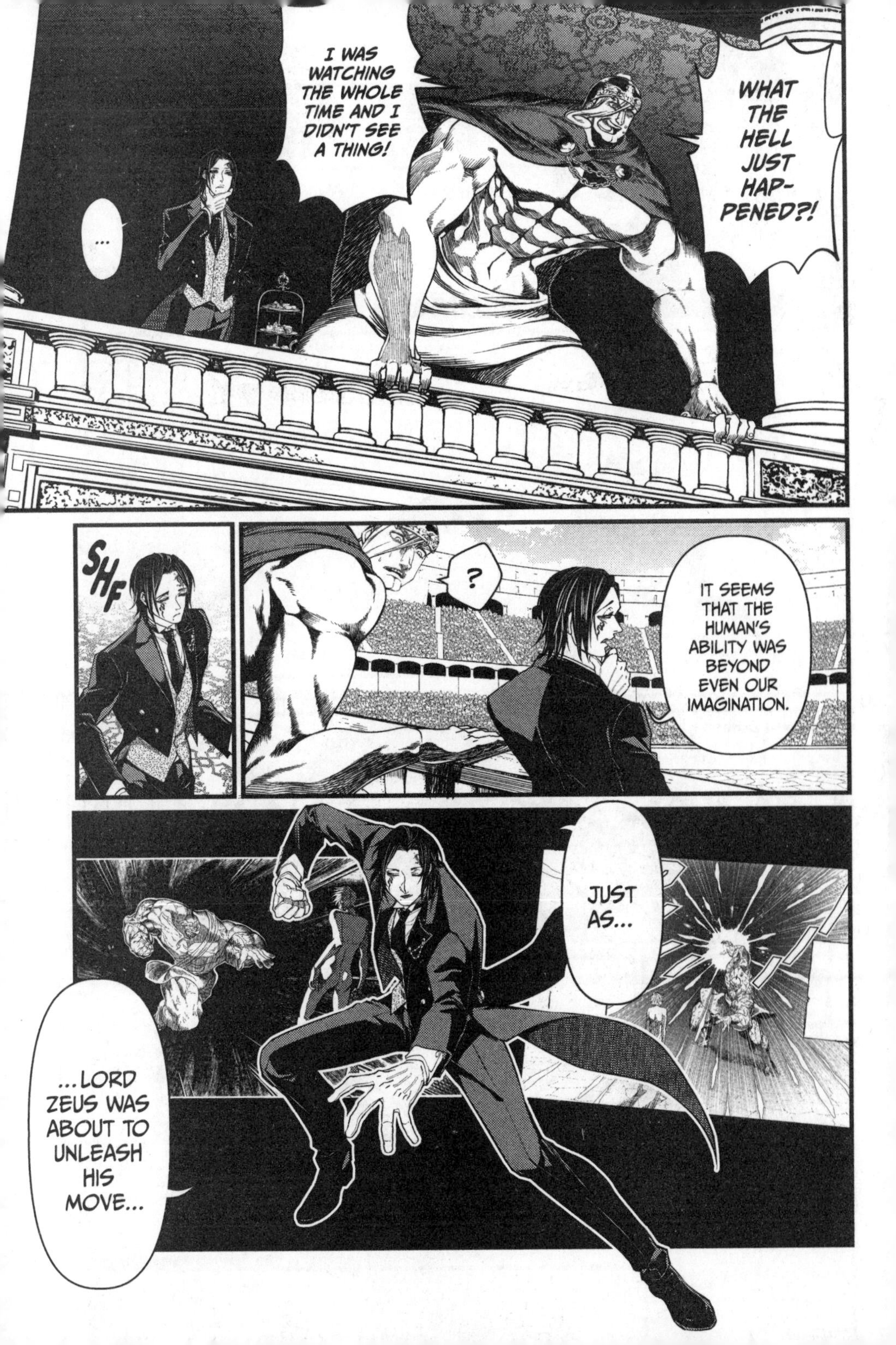
WHAT THE HELL JUST HAP-PENED?!
I WAS WATCHING THE WHOLE TIME AND I DIDN'T SEE A THING!
...
IT SEEMS THAT THE HUMAN'S ABILITY WAS BEYOND EVEN OUR IMAGINATION.
?
SHF
JUST AS...
...LORD ZEUS WAS ABOUT TO UNLEASH HIS MOVE...

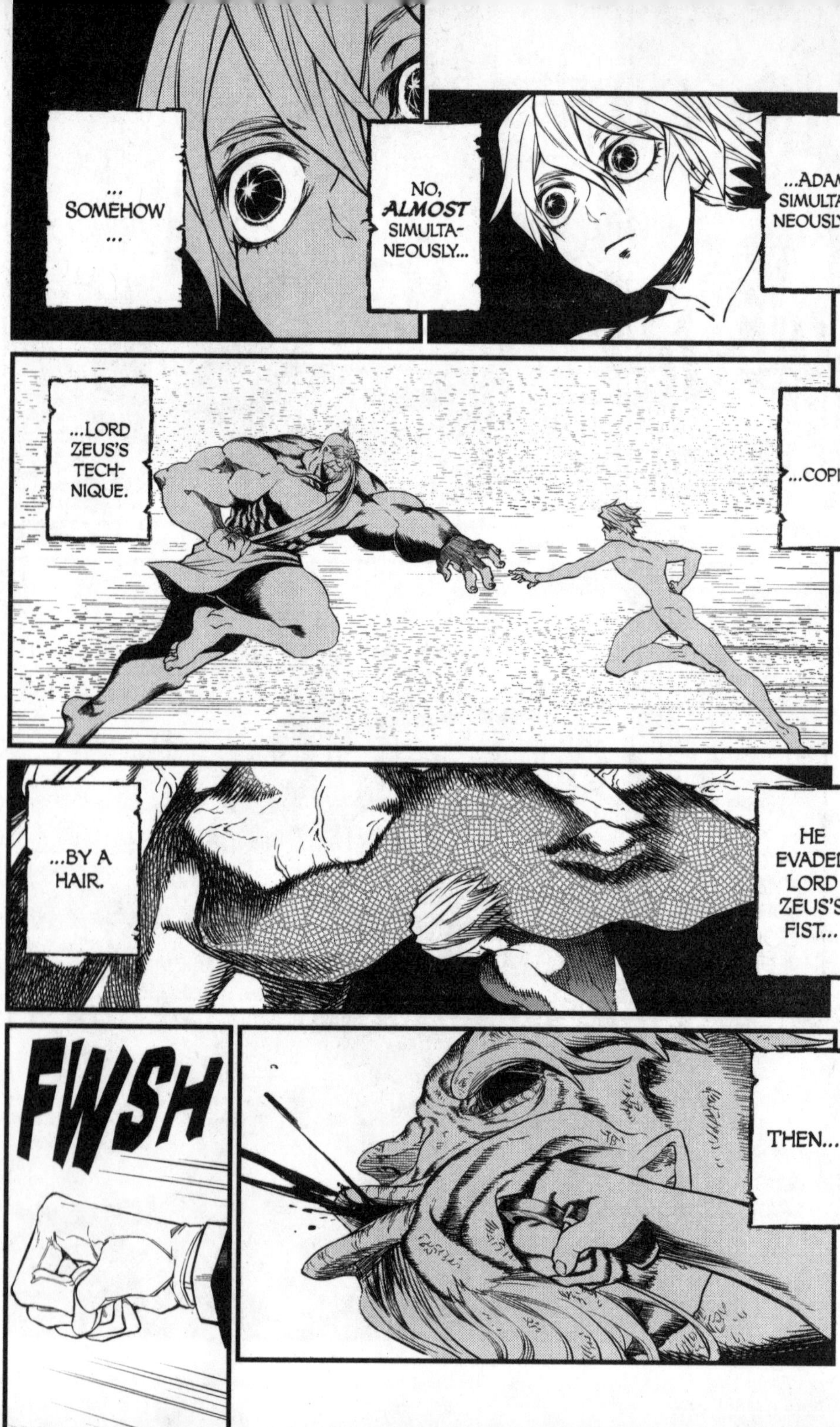
...ADAM SIMULTA-NEOUSLY~
NO, ALMOST SIMULTA-NEOUSLY...
...SOMEHOW...
...COPIED...
...LORD ZEUS'S TECH-NIQUE.
HE EVADED LORD ZEUS'S FIST...
...BY A HAIR.
THEN...
FWSH

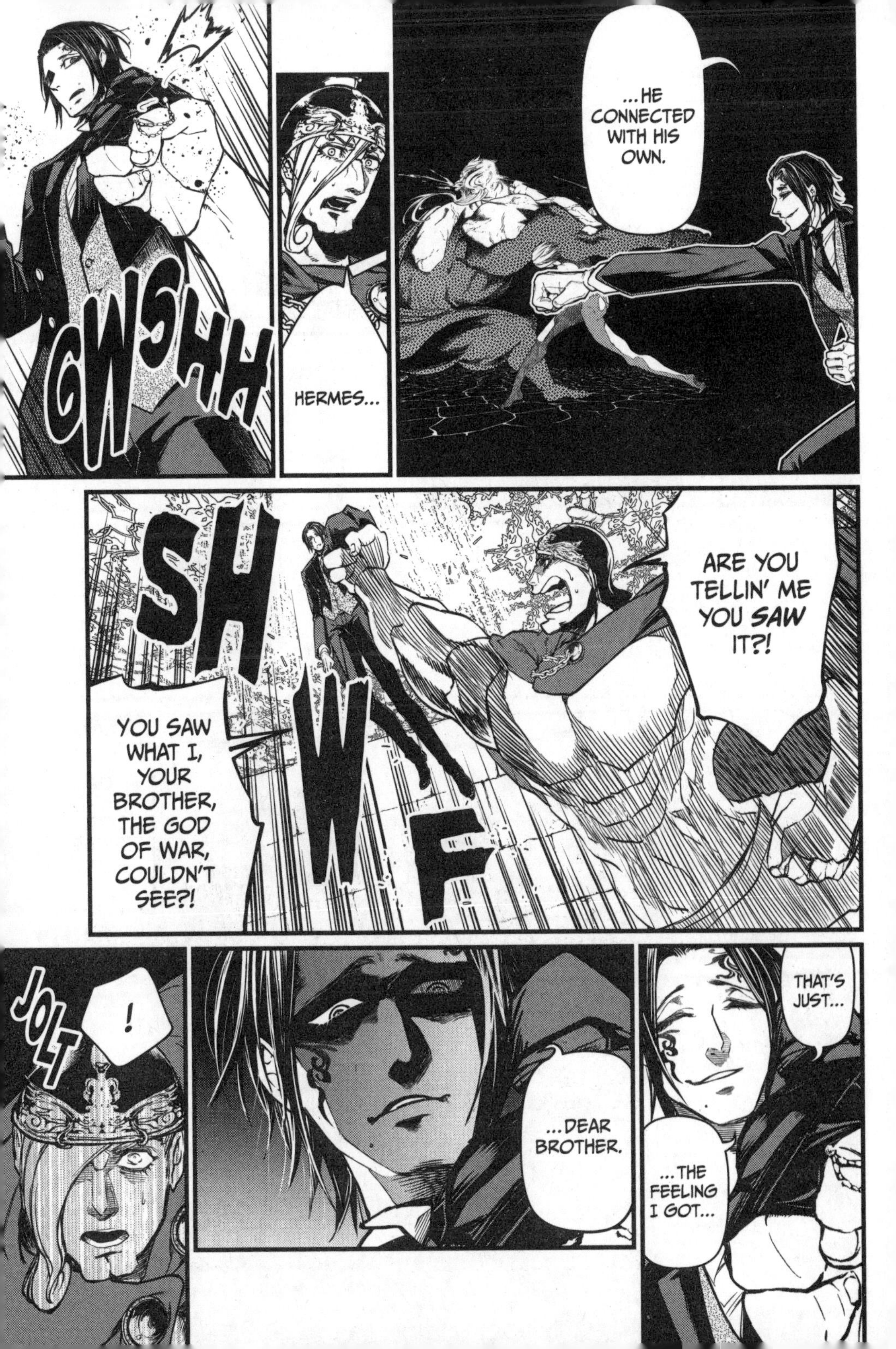
...HE CONNECTED WITH HIS OWN.
HERMES...
GWGHH
ARE YOU TELLIN' ME YOU SAW IT?!
SHWF
YOU SAW WHAT I, YOUR BROTHER, THE GOD OF WAR, COULDN'T SEE?!
THAT'S JUST...
...THE FEELING I GOT...
...DEAR BROTHER.
JOLT
!

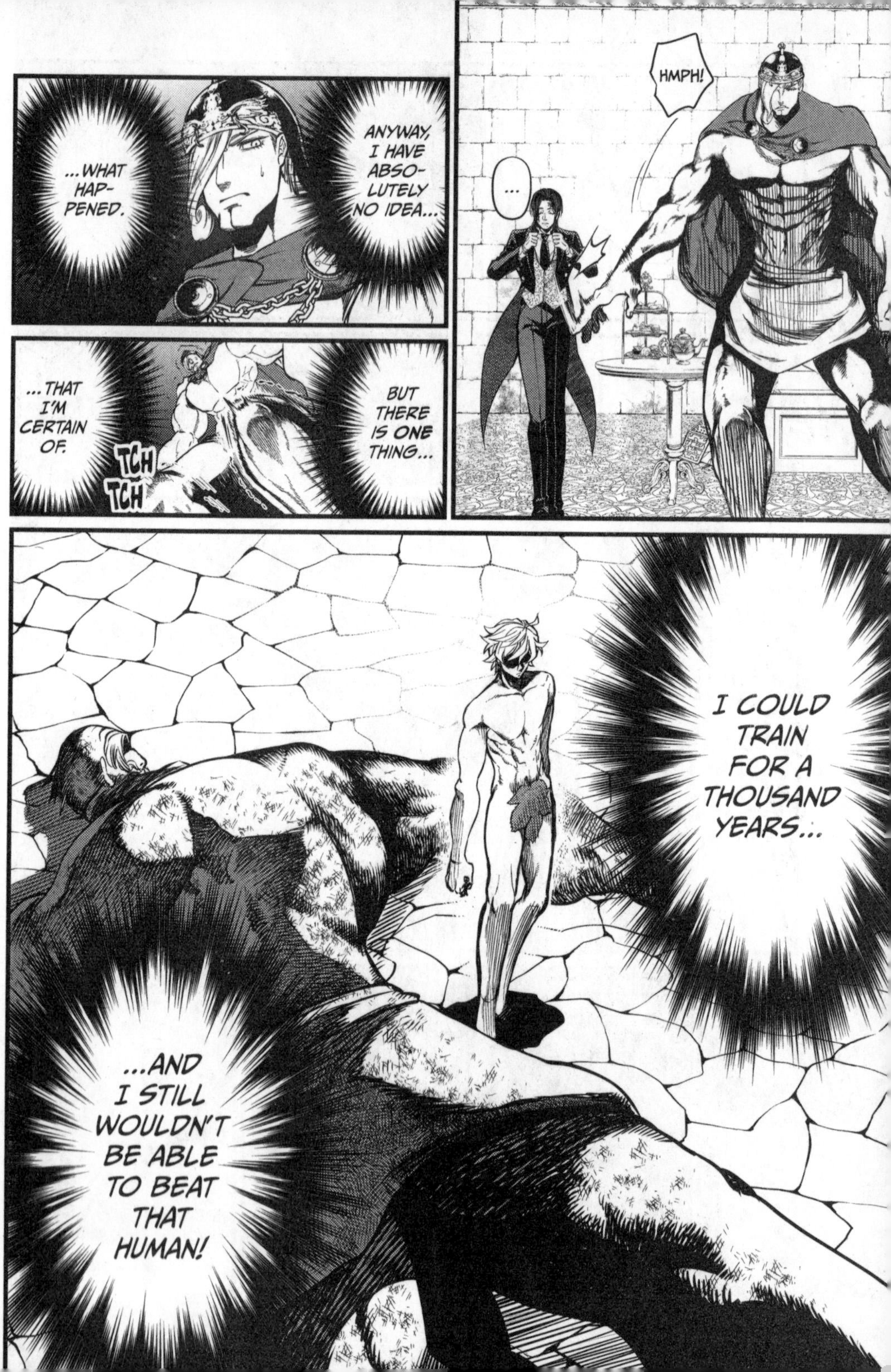

HMPH!
...
ANYWAY, I HAVE ABSO-LUTELY NO IDEA...
...WHAT HAP-PENED.
BUT THERE IS ONE THING...
...THAT I'M CERTAIN OF.
TCH TCH
I COULD TRAIN FOR A THOUSAND YEARS...
...AND I STILL WOULDN'T BE ABLE TO BEAT THAT HUMAN!

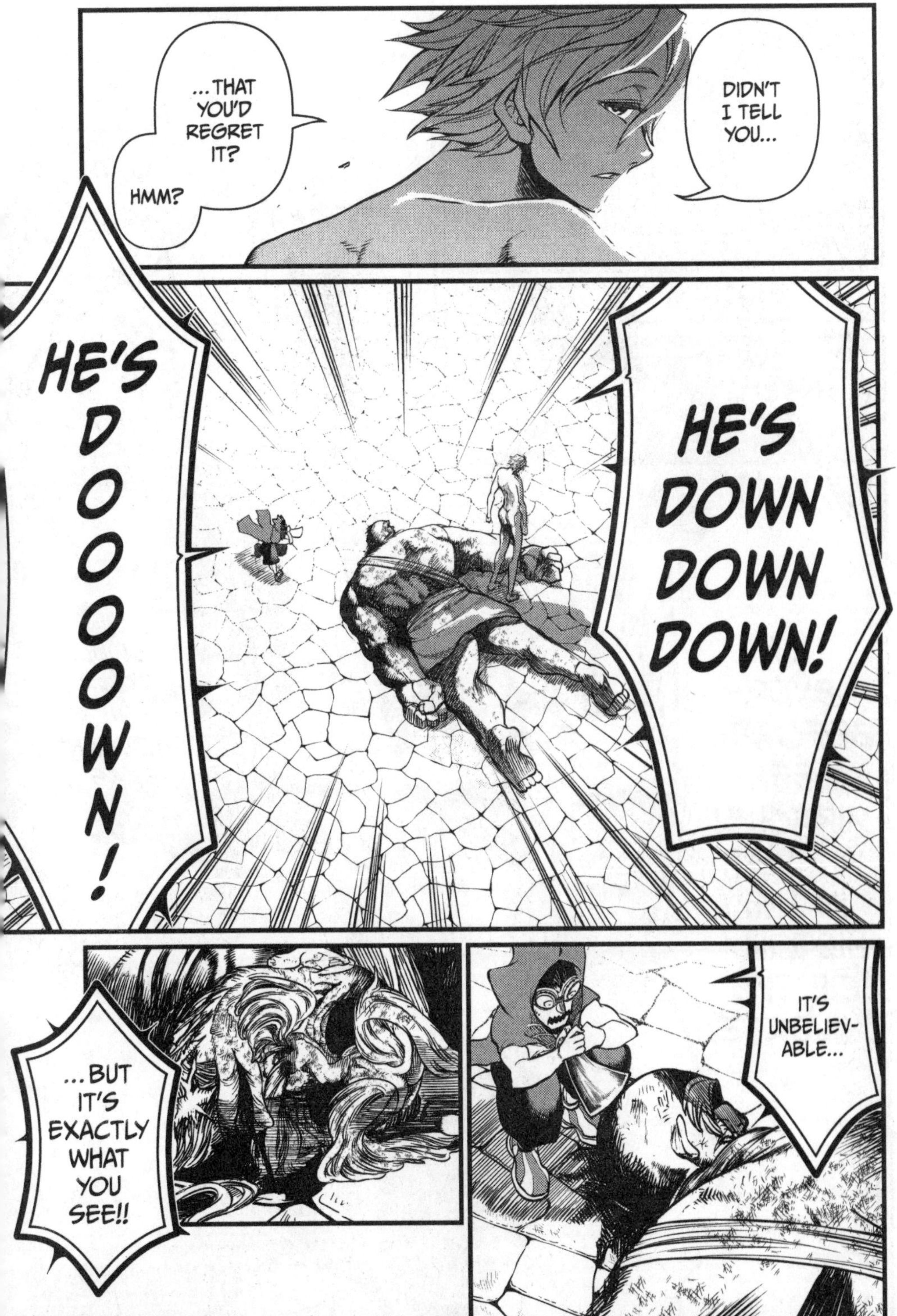
DIDN'T I TELL YOU...
...THAT YOU'D REGRET IT?
HMM?
HE'S DOWN DOWN DOWN!
HE'S DOOOOWN!
IT'S UNBELIEV-ABLE...
...BUT IT'S EXACTLY WHAT YOU SEE!!

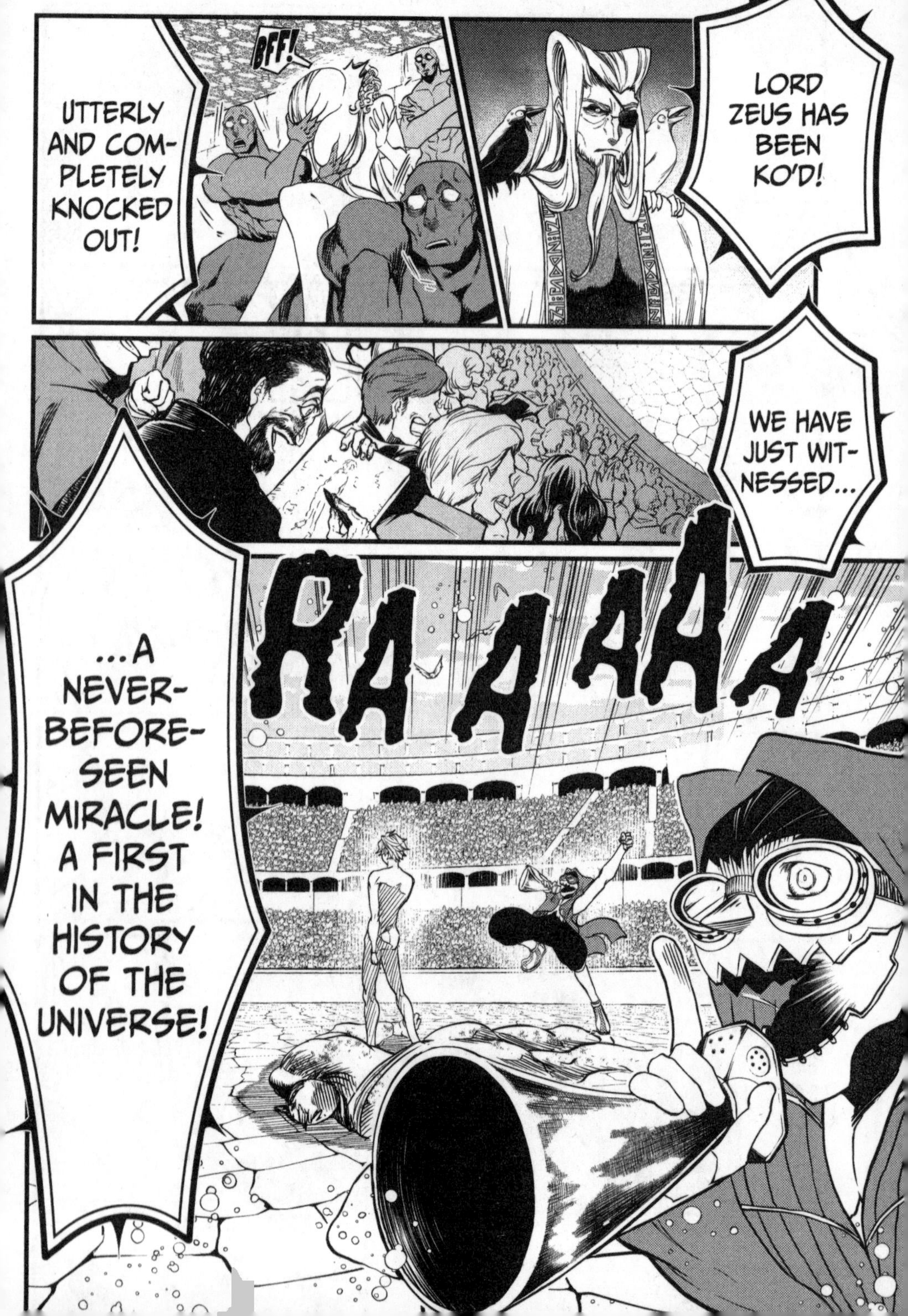
LORD ZEUS HAS BEEN KO'D!
BFF!
UTTERLY AND COMPLETELY KNOCKED OUT!
WE HAVE JUST WITNESSED...
RAAAAA
...A NEVER-BEFORE-SEEN MIRACLE! A FIRST IN THE HISTORY OF THE UNIVERSE!

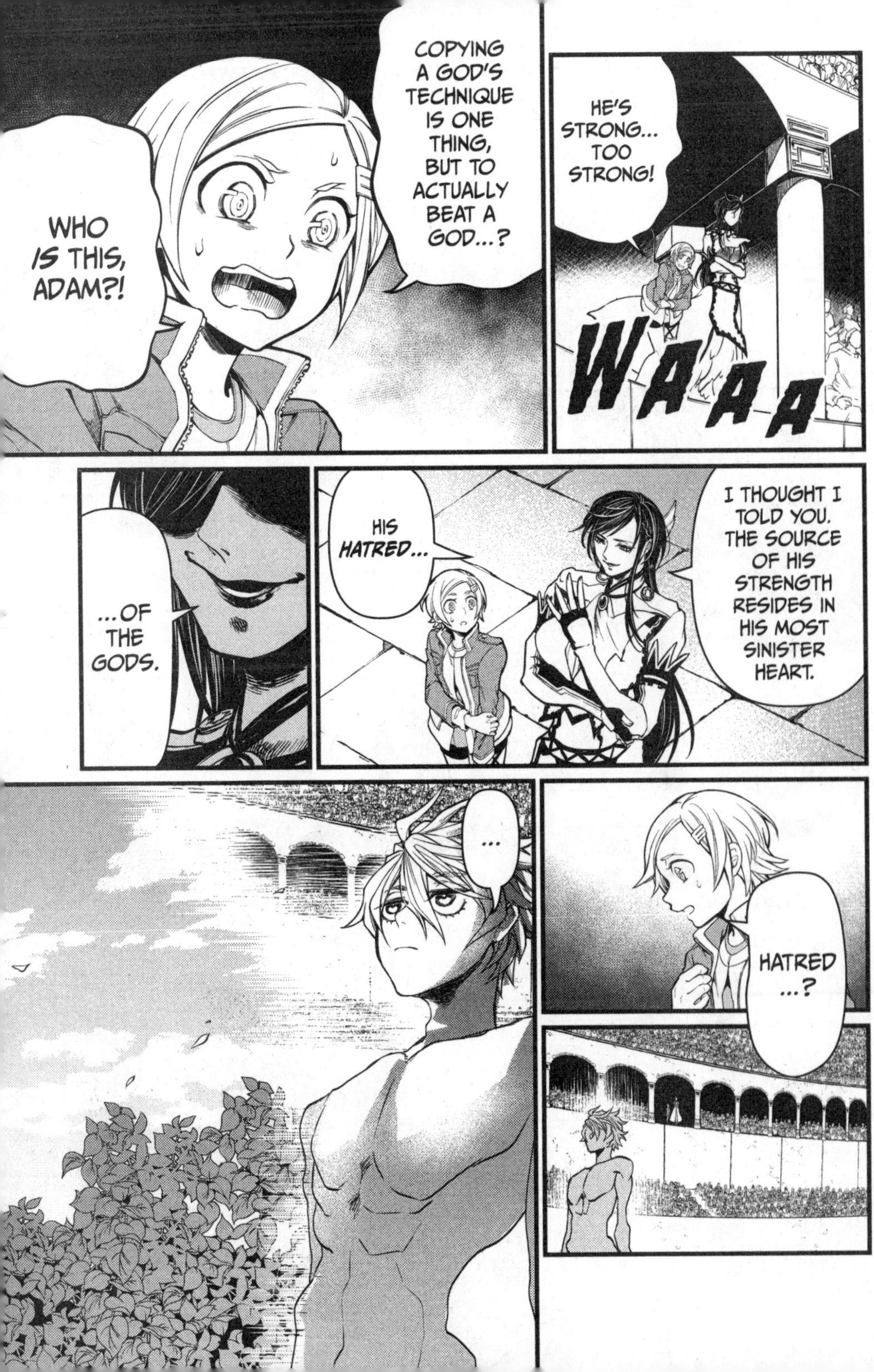
HE'S STRONG... TOO STRONG!
WAAAA
COPYING A GOD'S TECHNIQUE IS ONE THING, BUT TO ACTUALLY BEAT A GOD...?
WHO *IS* THIS, ADAM?!
I THOUGHT I TOLD YOU. THE SOURCE OF HIS STRENGTH RESIDES IN HIS MOST SINISTER HEART.
HIS *HATRED*...
...OF THE GODS.
HATRED ...?
...

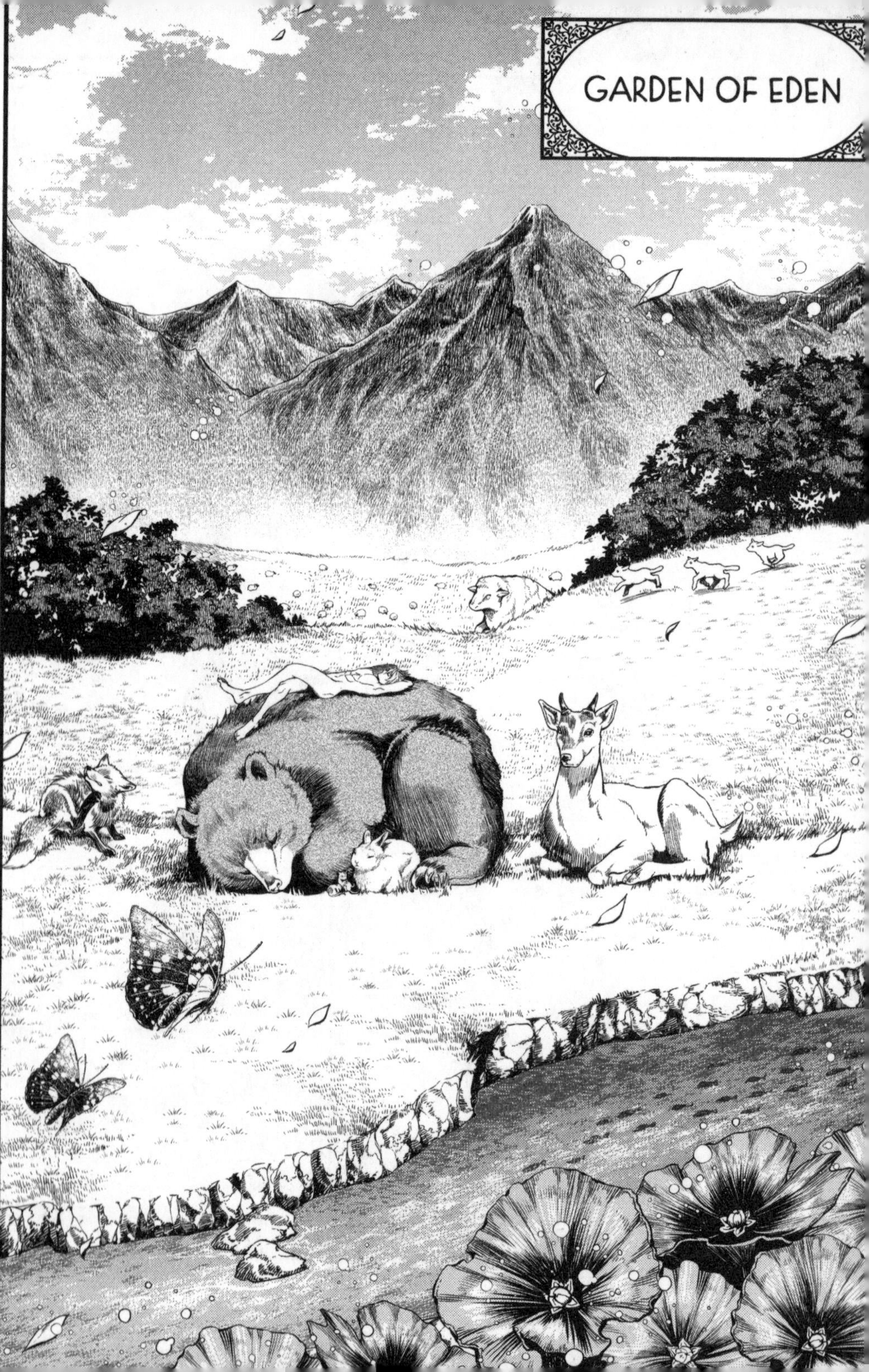
GARDEN OF EDEN

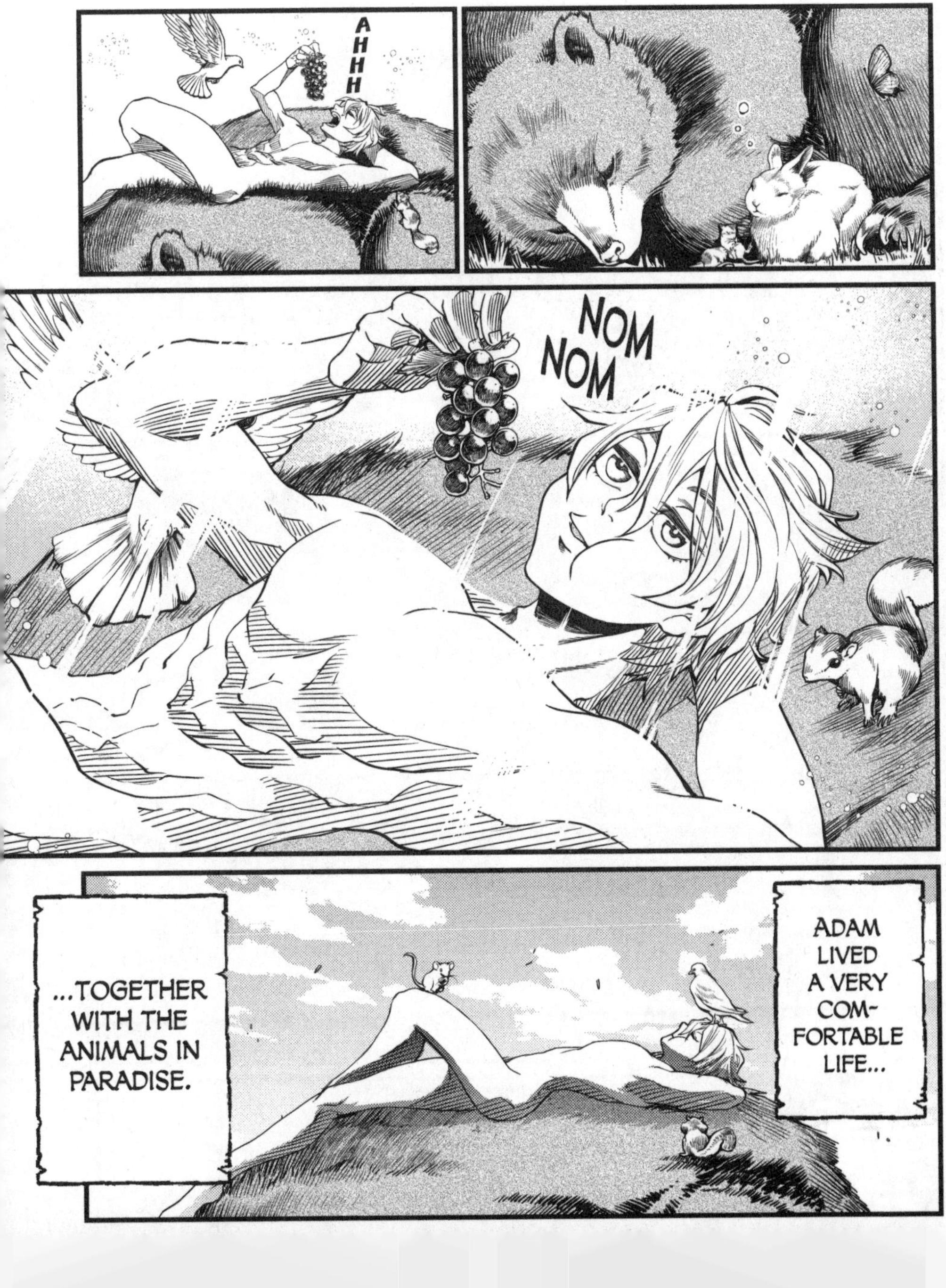
AHHH
NOM NOM
ADAM LIVED A VERY COM-FORTABLE LIFE...
...TOGETHER WITH THE ANIMALS IN PARADISE.

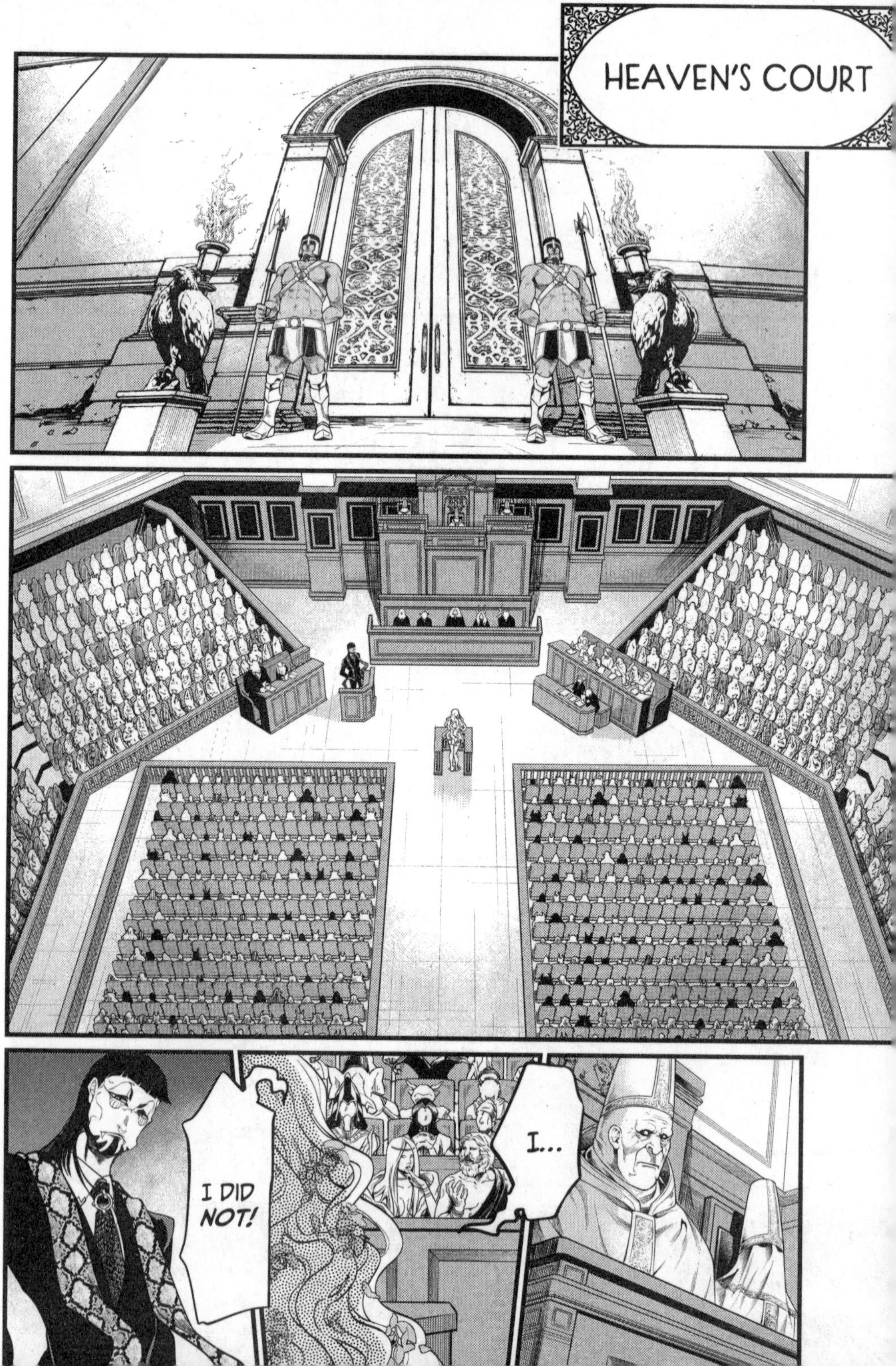
HEAVEN'S COURT
I...
I DID NOT!

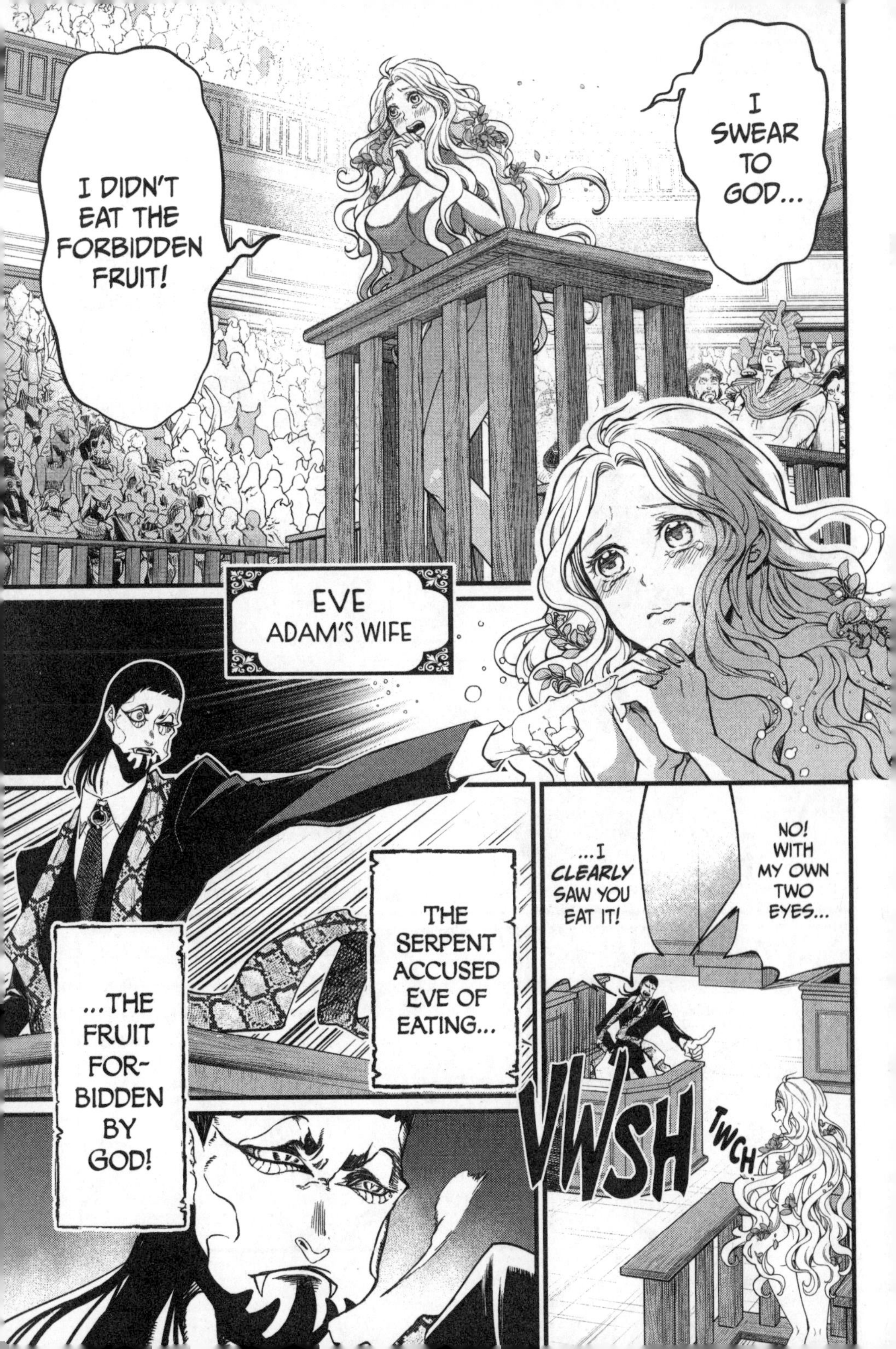
I SWEAR TO GOD...
I DIDN'T EAT THE FORBIDDEN FRUIT!
EVE
ADAM'S WIFE
NO! WITH MY OWN TWO EYES...
...I CLEARLY SAW YOU EAT IT!
VWSH
TWCH
THE SERPENT ACCUSED EVE OF EATING...
...THE FRUIT FOR-BIDDEN BY GOD!

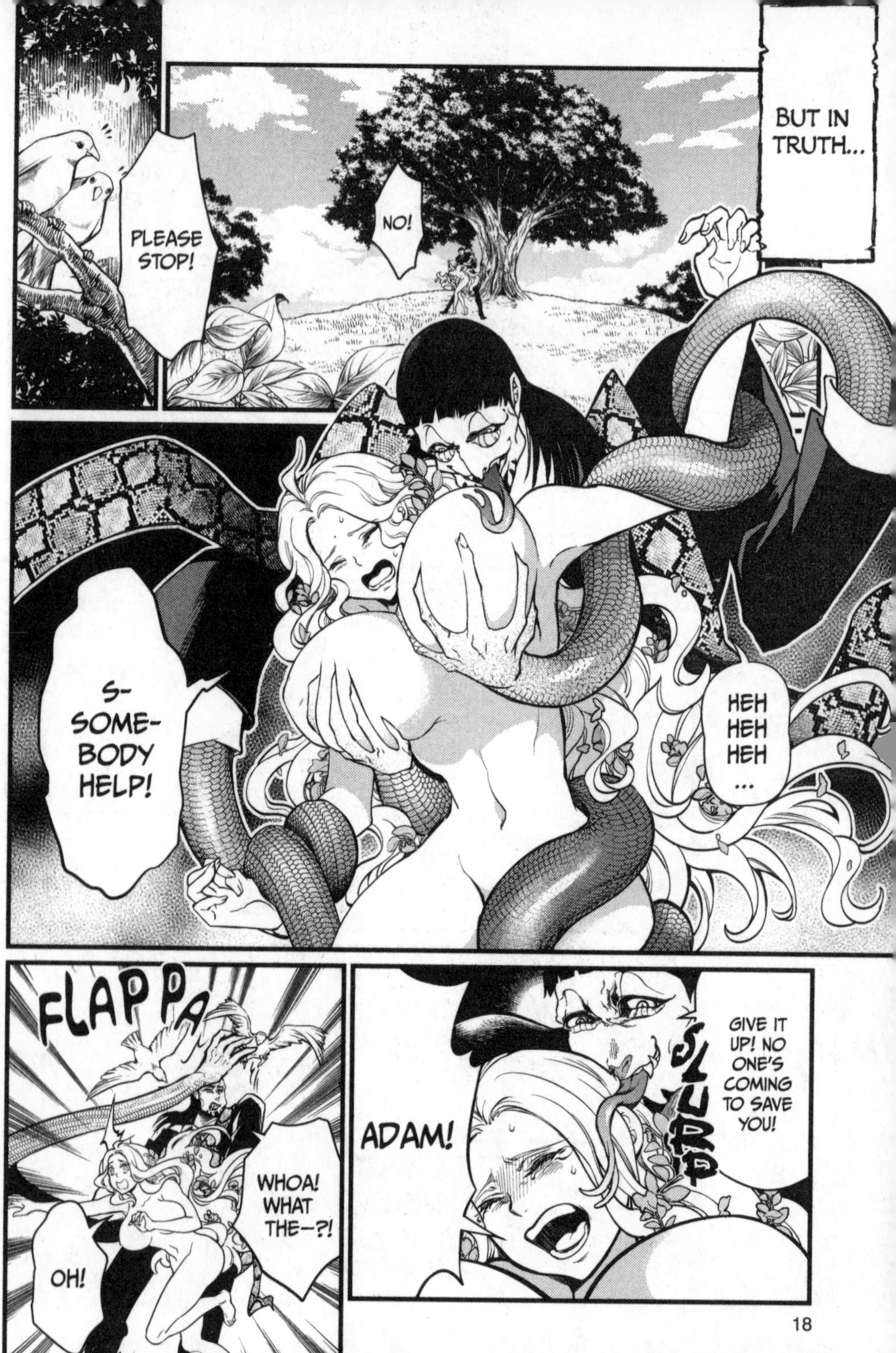
BUT IN TRUTH...
NO!
PLEASE STOP!
HEH HEH HEH ...
S-SOME-BODY HELP!
GIVE IT UP! NO ONE'S COMING TO SAVE YOU!
SLURP
ADAM!
FLAPPA
WHOA! WHAT THE--?!
OH!

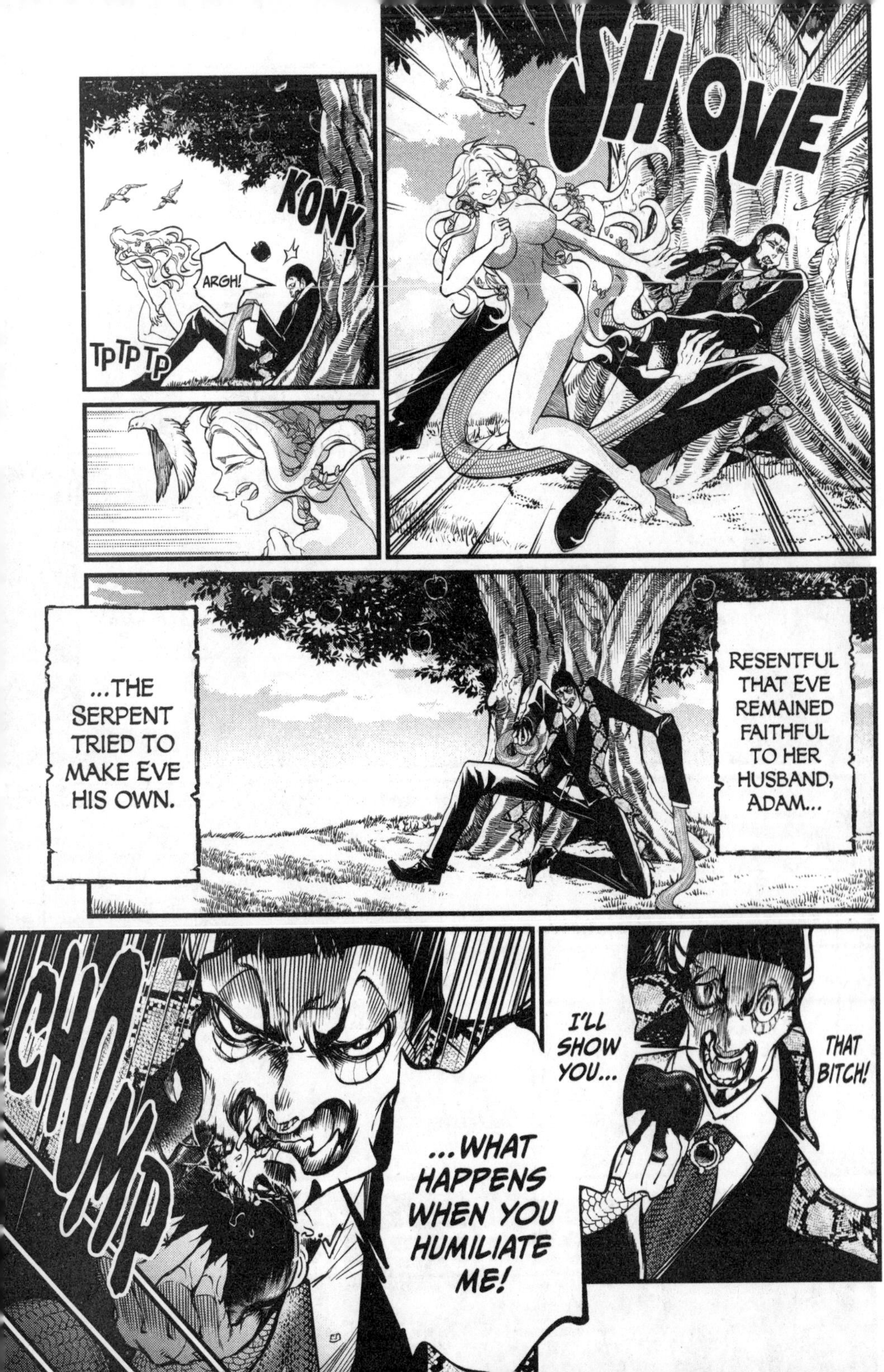
SHOVE
KONK
ARGH!
TPTPTP
RESENTFUL THAT EVE REMAINED FAITHFUL TO HER HUSBAND, ADAM...
...THE SERPENT TRIED TO MAKE EVE HIS OWN.
THAT BITCH!
I'LL SHOW YOU...
...WHAT HAPPENS WHEN YOU HUMILIATE ME!
CHOMP

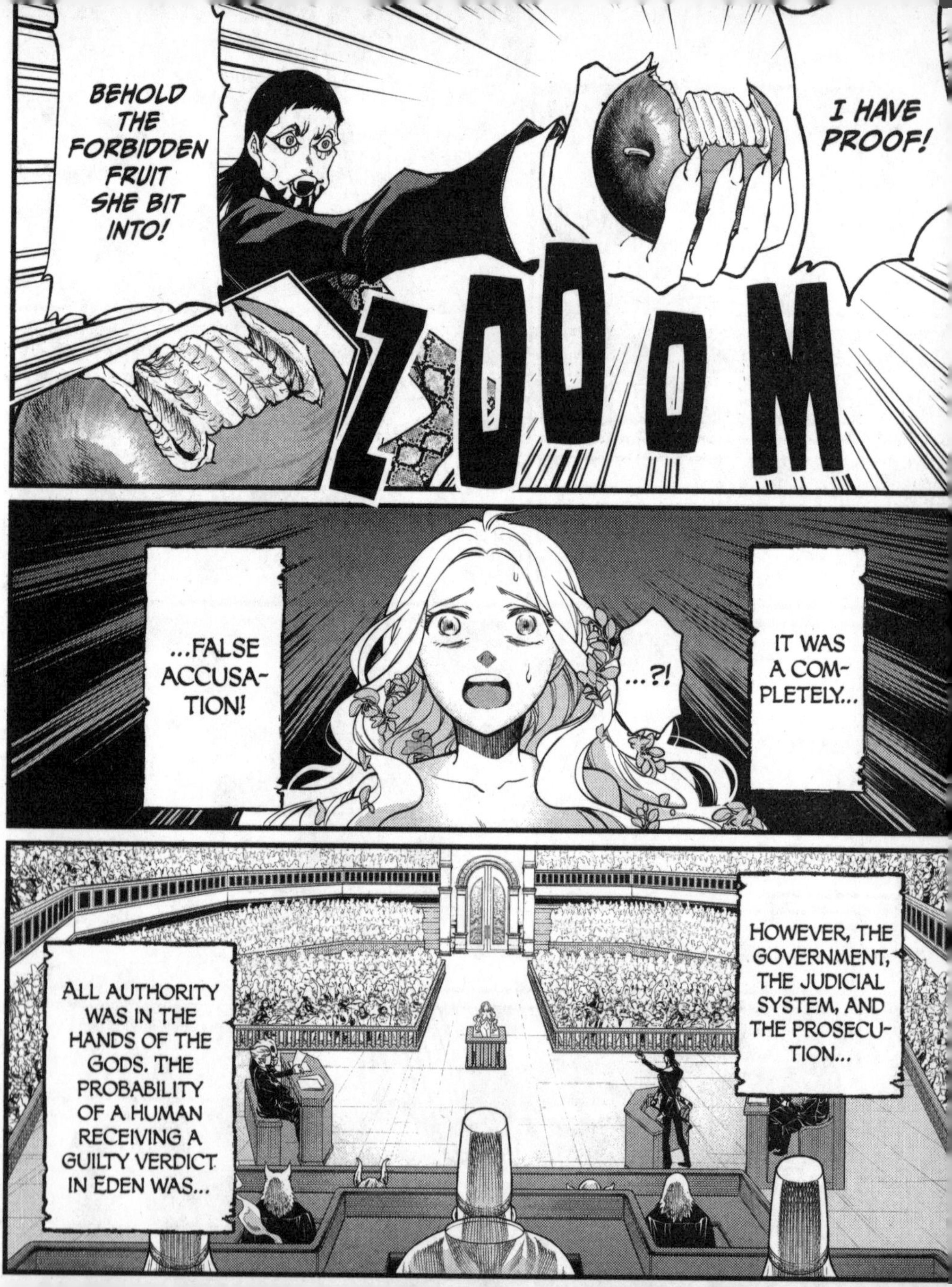
I HAVE PROOF!
BEHOLD THE FORBIDDEN FRUIT SHE BIT INTO!
ZOOOM
IT WAS A COM-PLETELY...
...?!
...FALSE ACCUSA-TION!
HOWEVER, THE GOVERNMENT, THE JUDICIAL SYSTEM, AND THE PROSECU-TION...
ALL AUTHORITY WAS IN THE HANDS OF THE GODS. THE PROBABILITY OF A HUMAN RECEIVING A GUILTY VERDICT IN EDEN WAS...

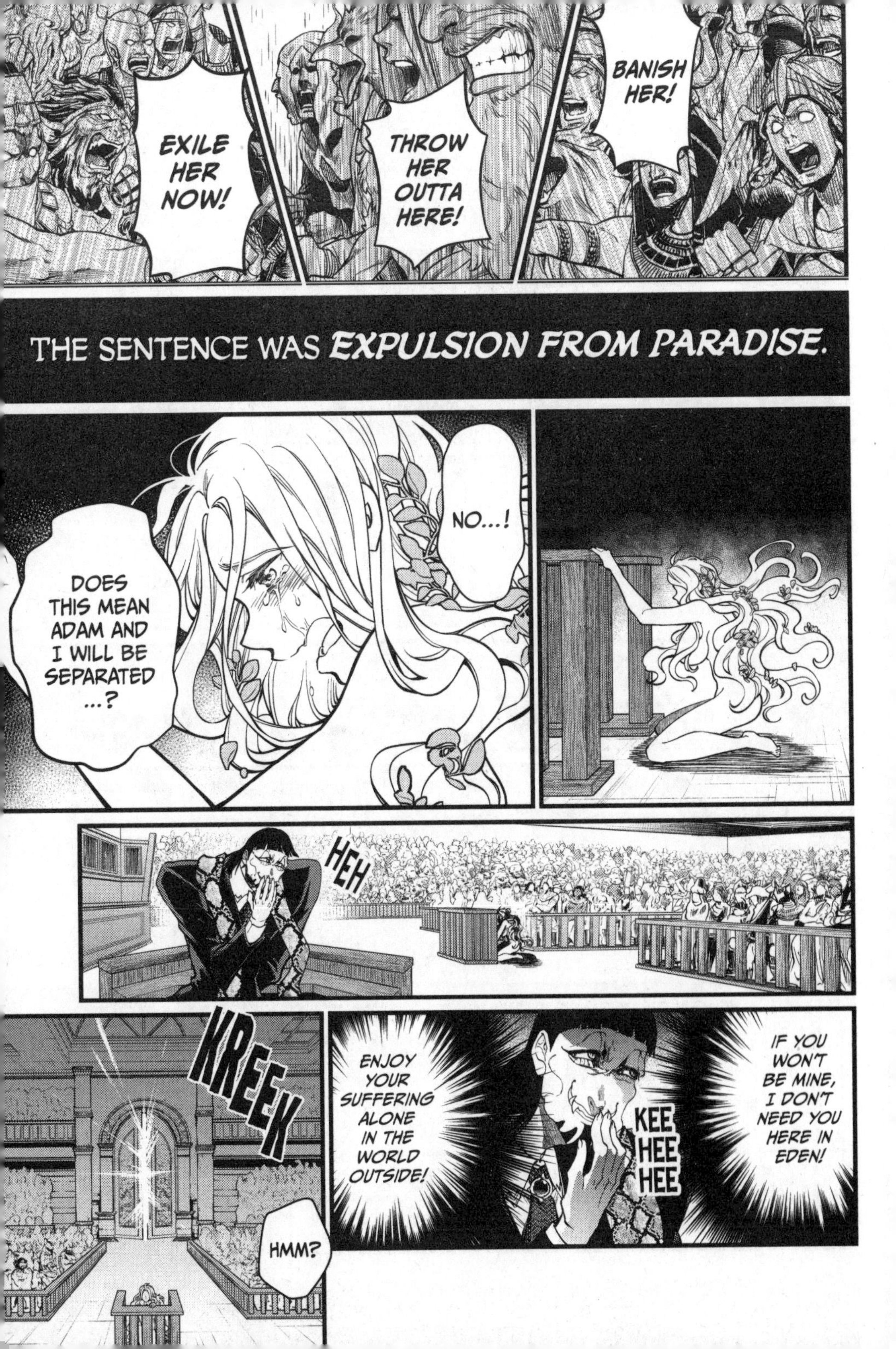
BANISH HER!
THROW HER OUTTA HERE!
EXILE HER NOW!
THE SENTENCE WAS EXPULSION FROM PARADISE.
NO...!
DOES THIS MEAN ADAM AND I WILL BE SEPARATED ...?
HEH
IF YOU WON'T BE MINE, I DON'T NEED YOU HERE IN EDEN!
KEE HEE HEE
ENJOY YOUR SUFFERING ALONE IN THE WORLD OUTSIDE!
KREEK
HMM?

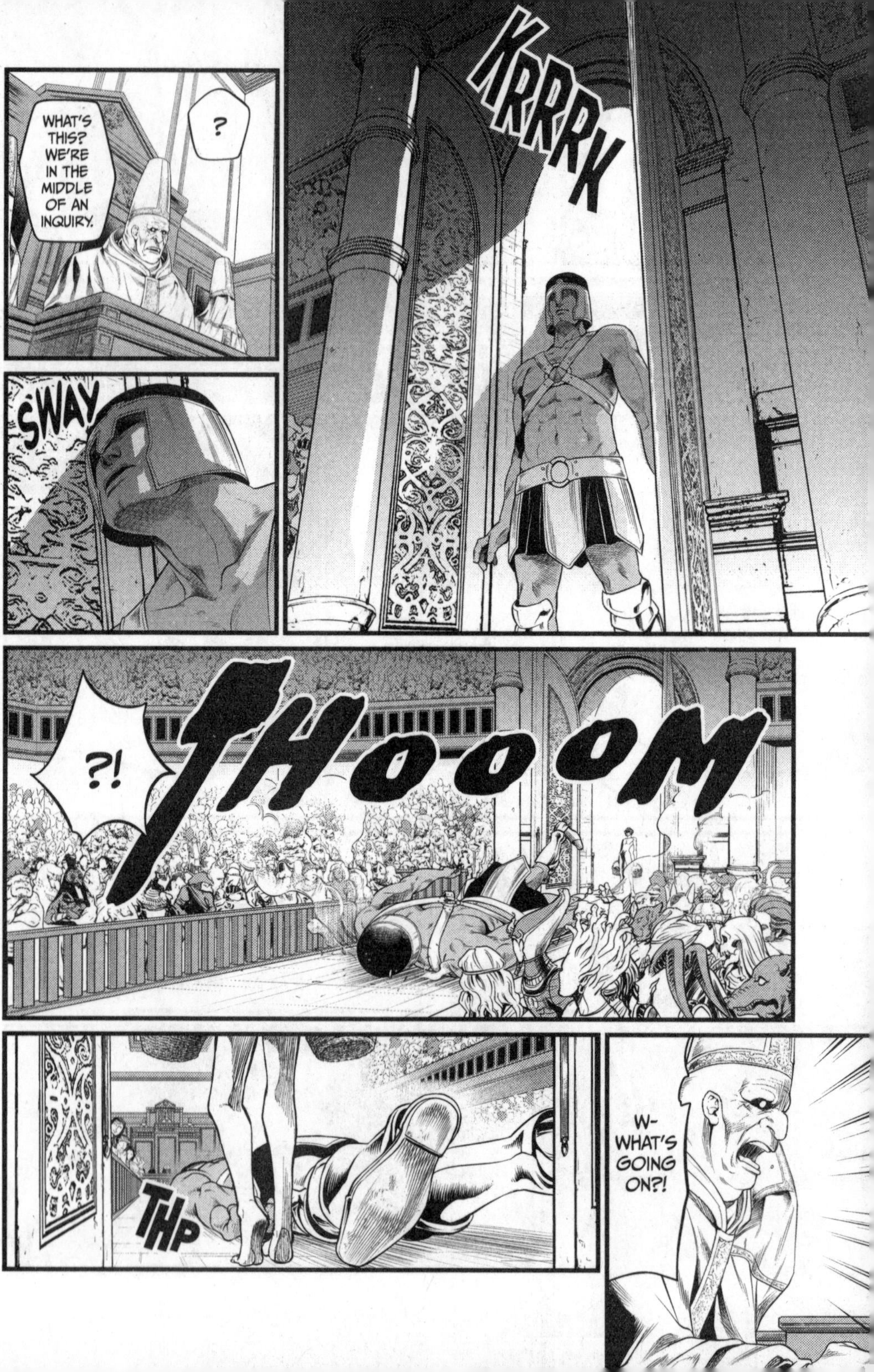
KRRRK
?
WHAT'S THIS? WE'RE IN THE MIDDLE OF AN INQUIRY.
SWAY
?!
THOOOM
W-WHAT'S GOING ON?!
THP

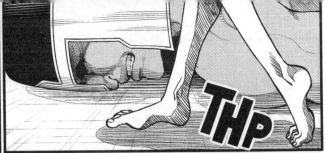

THP

WHAT
...?!

W...

DID HE
TAKE
OUT THE
GUARD?

I-IT'S
ADAM...

THP

THP

HUH...?

HEY...!
IS
THAT...?

ADAM!

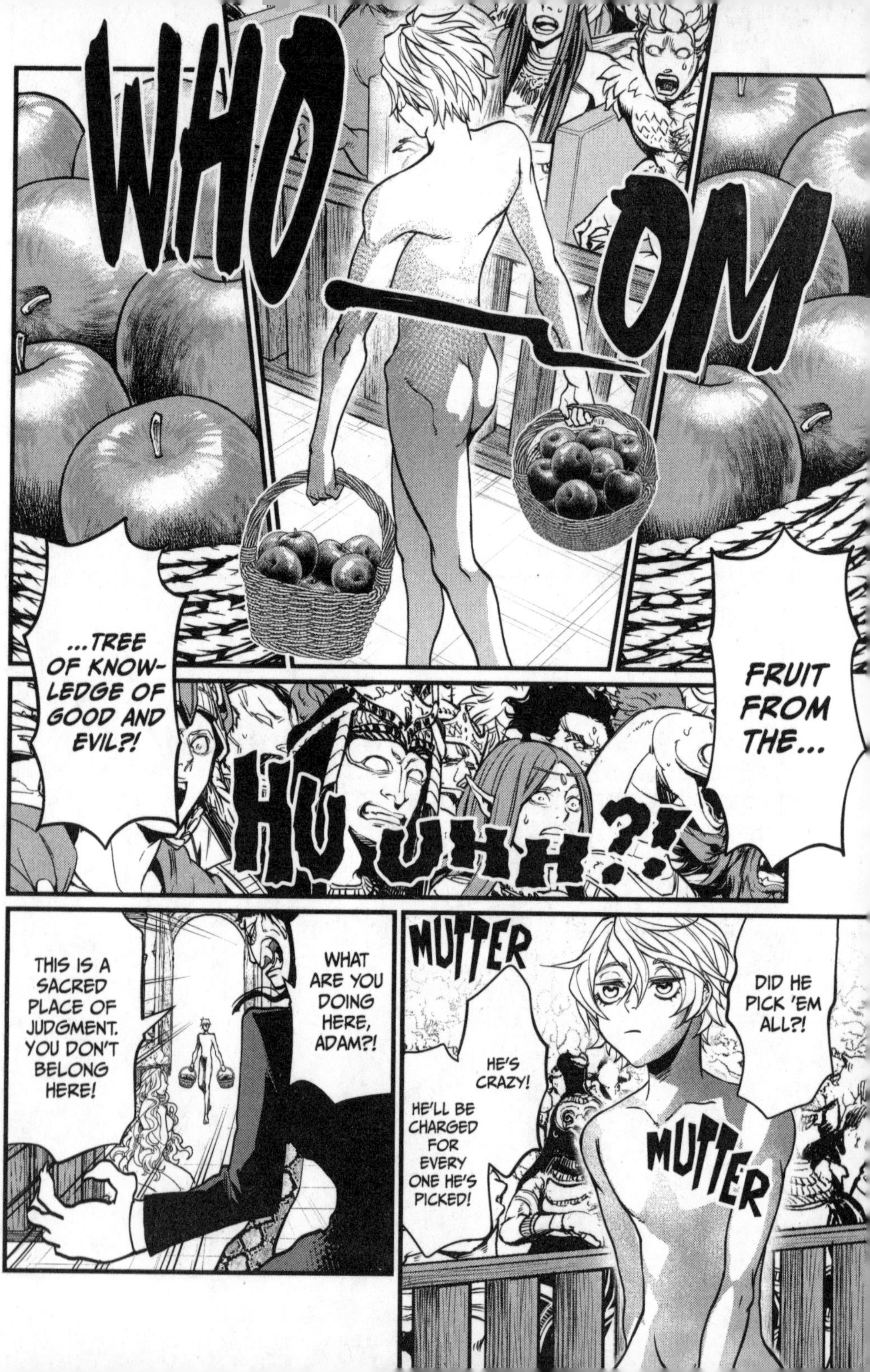
WHO—OM
FRUIT FROM THE...
...TREE OF KNOW-LEDGE OF GOOD AND EVIL?!
HU UHH?!!
DID HE PICK 'EM ALL?!
MUTTER
HE'S CRAZY!
HE'LL BE CHARGED FOR EVERY ONE HE'S PICKED!
MUTTER
WHAT ARE YOU DOING HERE, ADAM?!
THIS IS A SACRED PLACE OF JUDGMENT. YOU DON'T BELONG HERE!

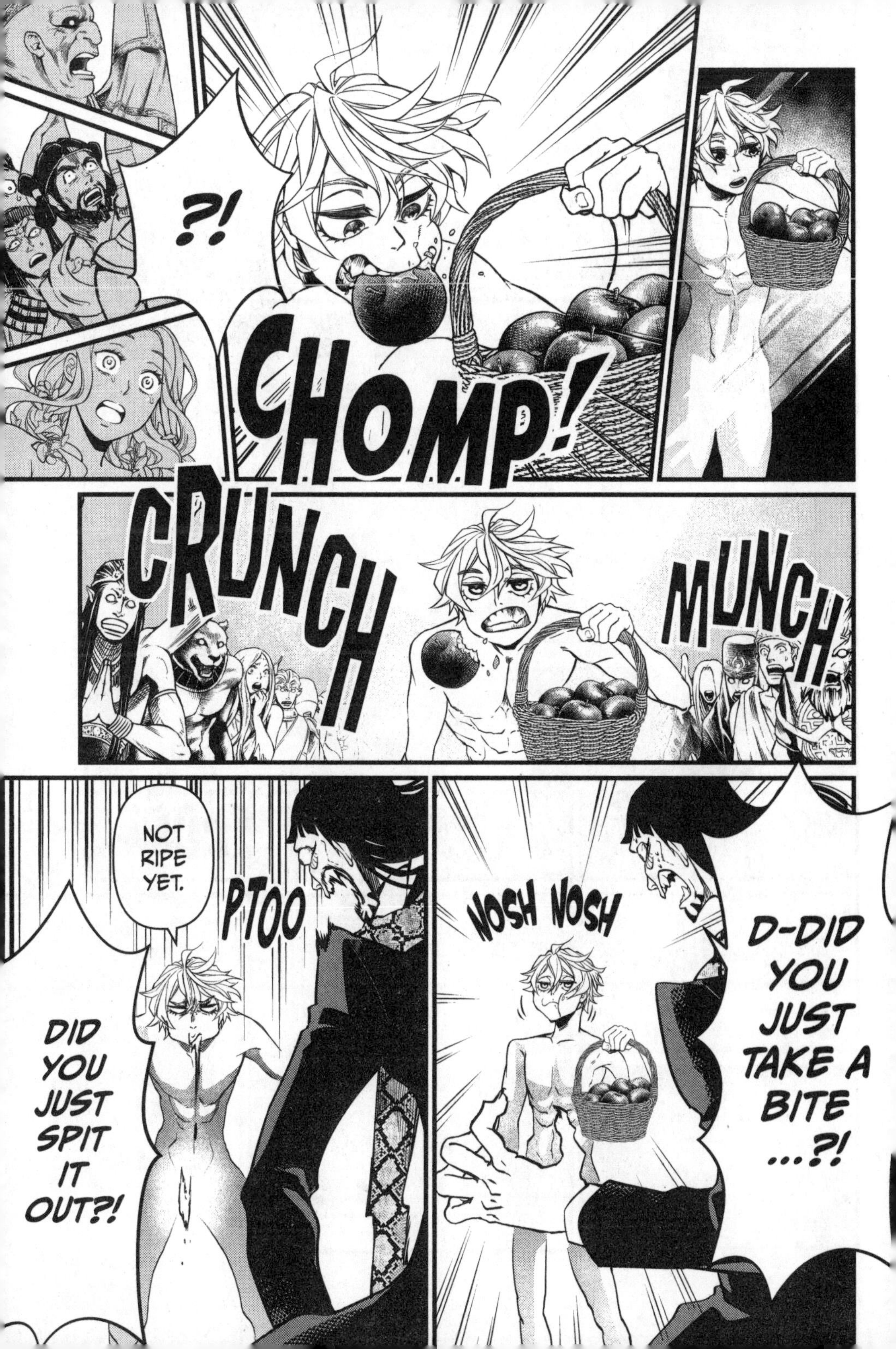
CHOMP!
?!
MUNCH
CRUNCH
D-DID YOU JUST TAKE A BITE ...?!
NOSH NOSH
NOT RIPE YET.
PTOO
DID YOU JUST SPIT IT OUT?!

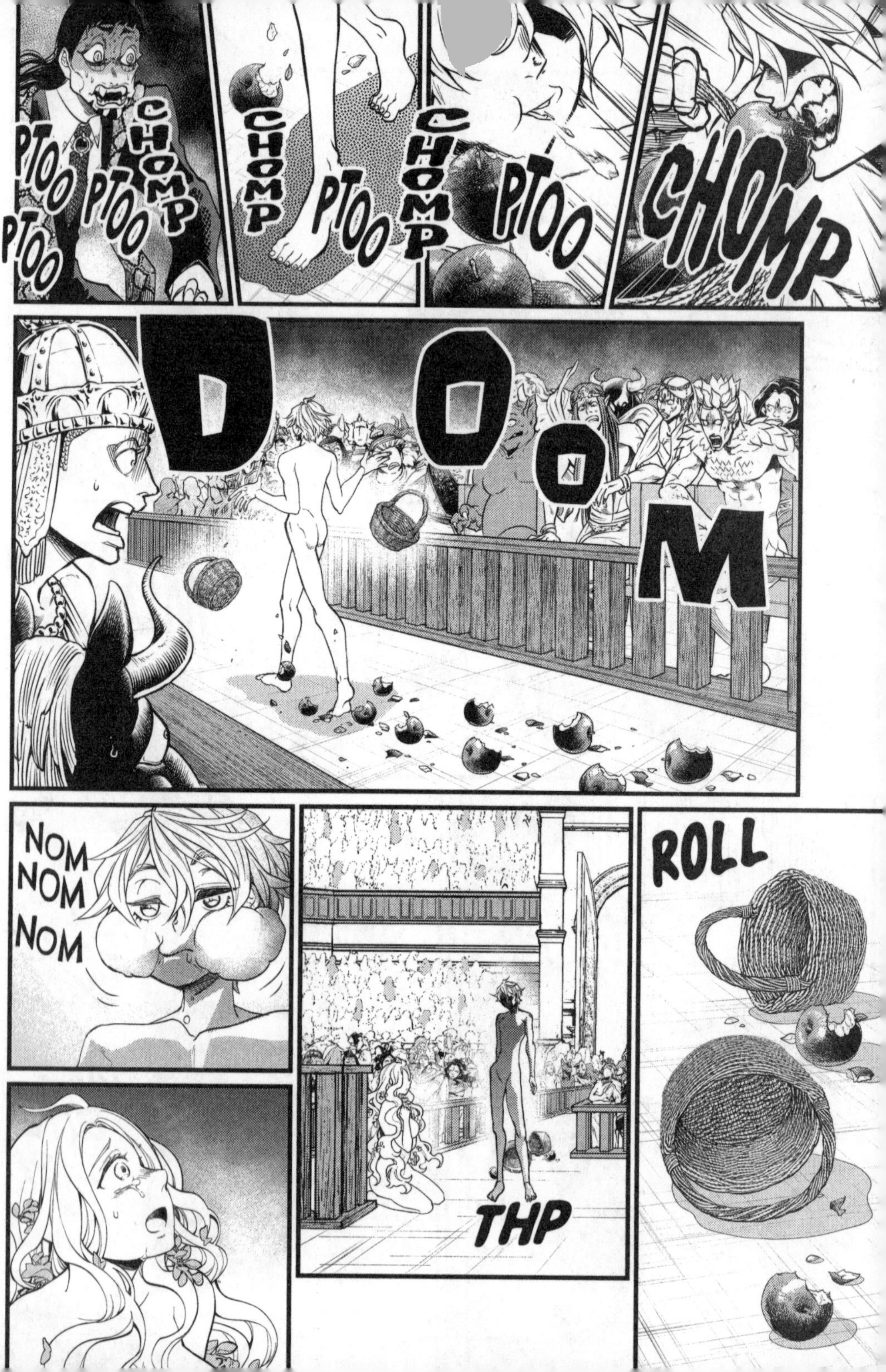
CHOMP
PTOO
CHOMP
PTOO
CHOMP
CHOMP
PTOO
PTOO
PTOO
DOOOM
ROLL
THP
NOM NOM NOM

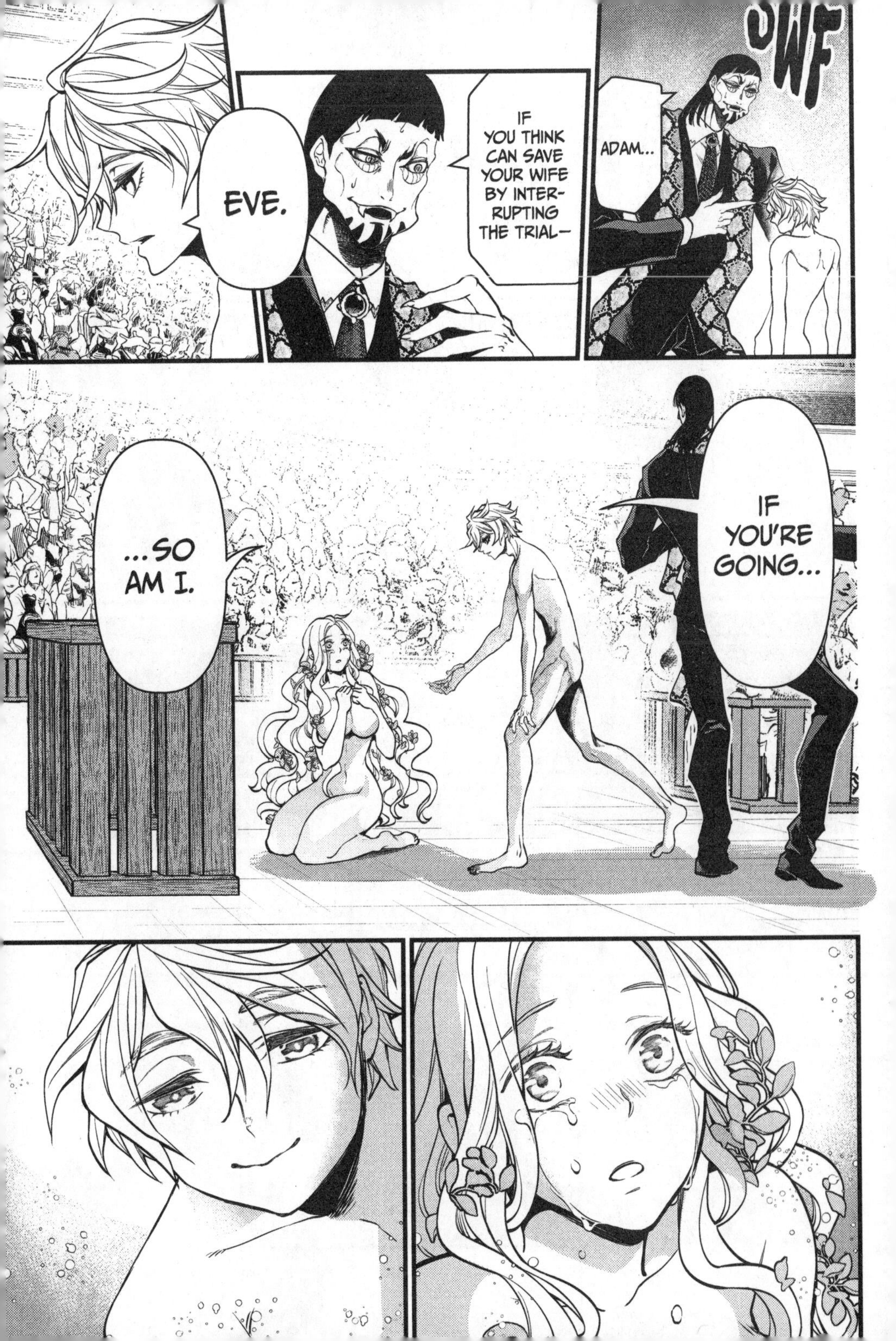
SWF
ADAM...
IF YOU THINK CAN SAVE YOUR WIFE BY INTERRUPTING THE TRIAL—
EVE.
IF YOU'RE GOING...
...SO AM I.

ADAM!

ADAM!

ADAM!

W-WHOA! WHAT'S THE MATTER? DON'T CRY, EVE.

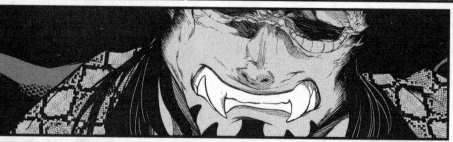

IS IT PARADISE IN YOUR BRAINS TOO?!

YOU!

HSSSSS!

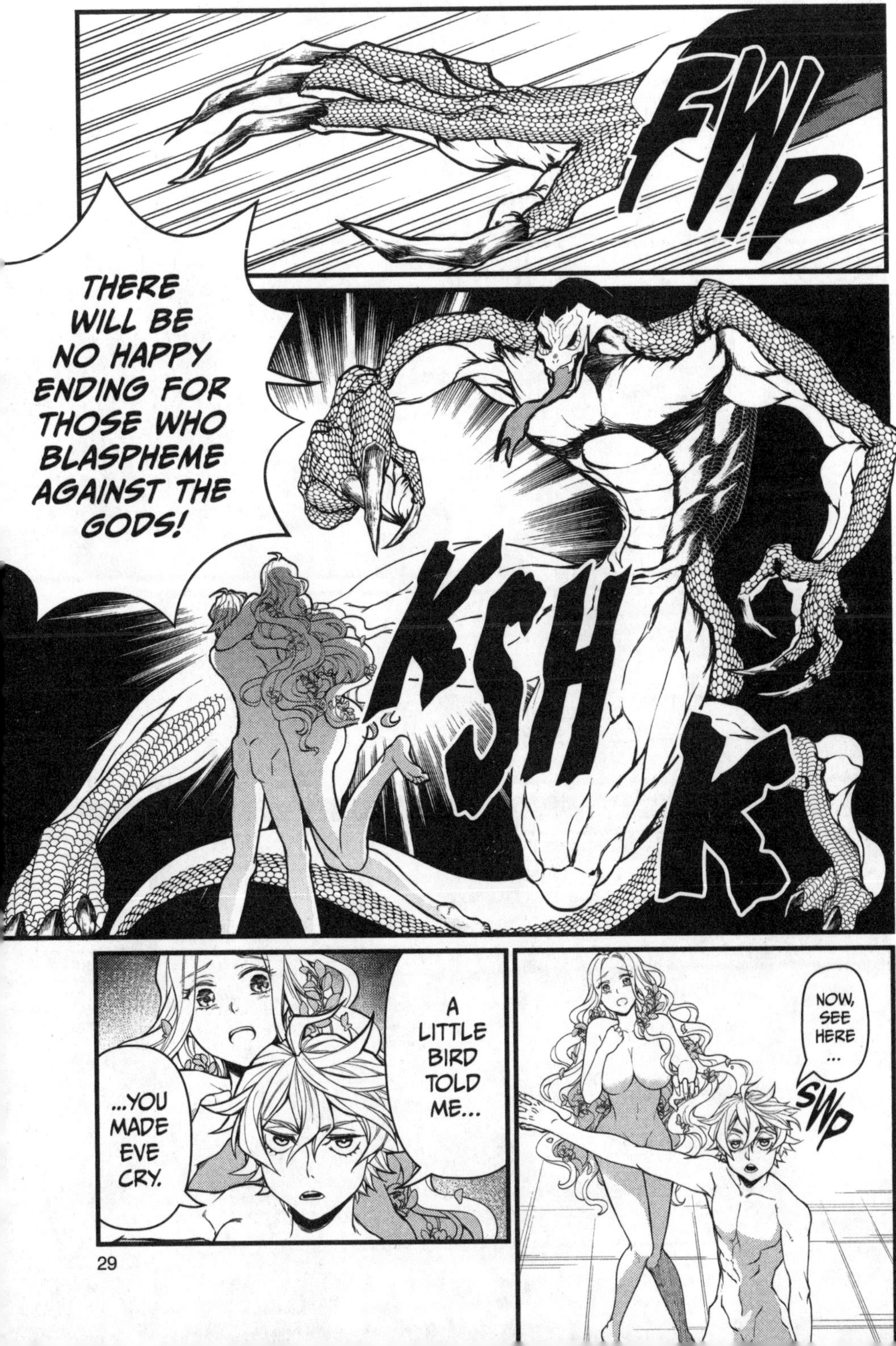
FWD
THERE WILL BE NO HAPPY ENDING FOR THOSE WHO BLASPHEME AGAINST THE GODS!
KSHK
NOW, SEE HERE ...
SWP
A LITTLE BIRD TOLD ME...
...YOU MADE EVE CRY.

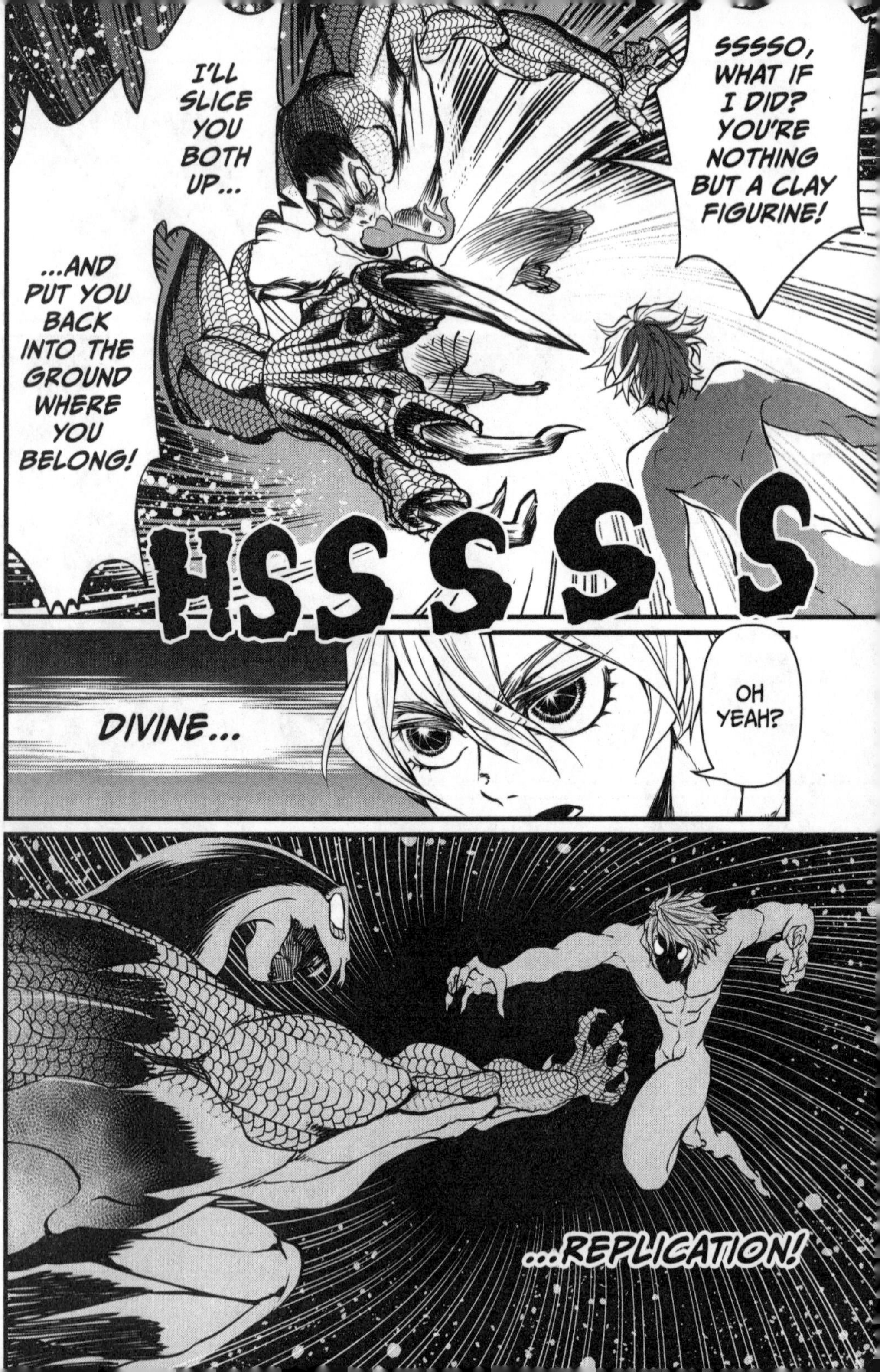
SSSSO, WHAT IF I DID? YOU'RE NOTHING BUT A CLAY FIGURINE!
I'LL SLICE YOU BOTH UP...
...AND PUT YOU BACK INTO THE GROUND WHERE YOU BELONG!
HSSSSS
OH YEAH?
DIVINE...
...REPLICATION!

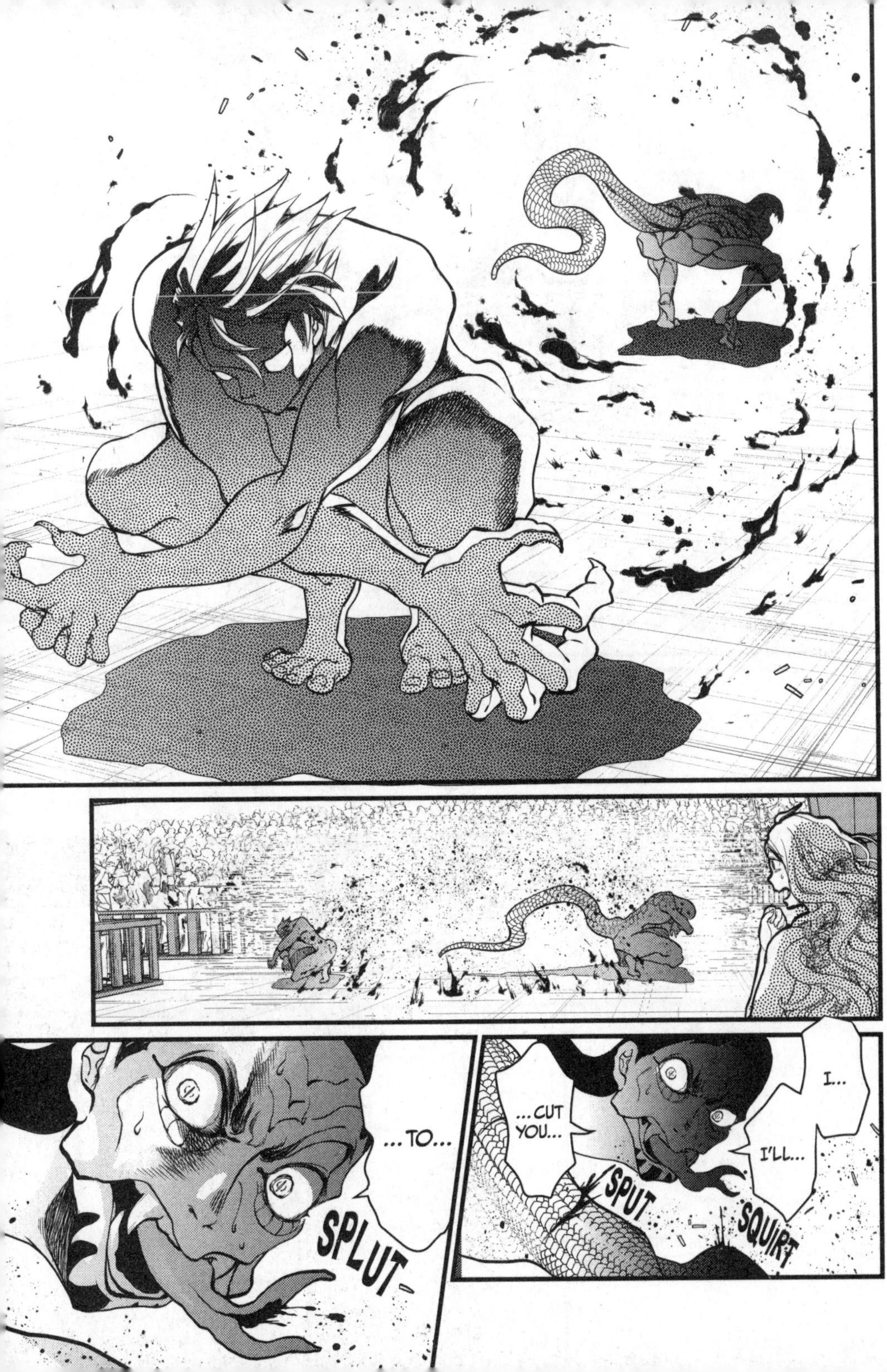
I...
I'LL...
...CUT YOU...
SQUIRT
SPUT
...TO...
SPLUT

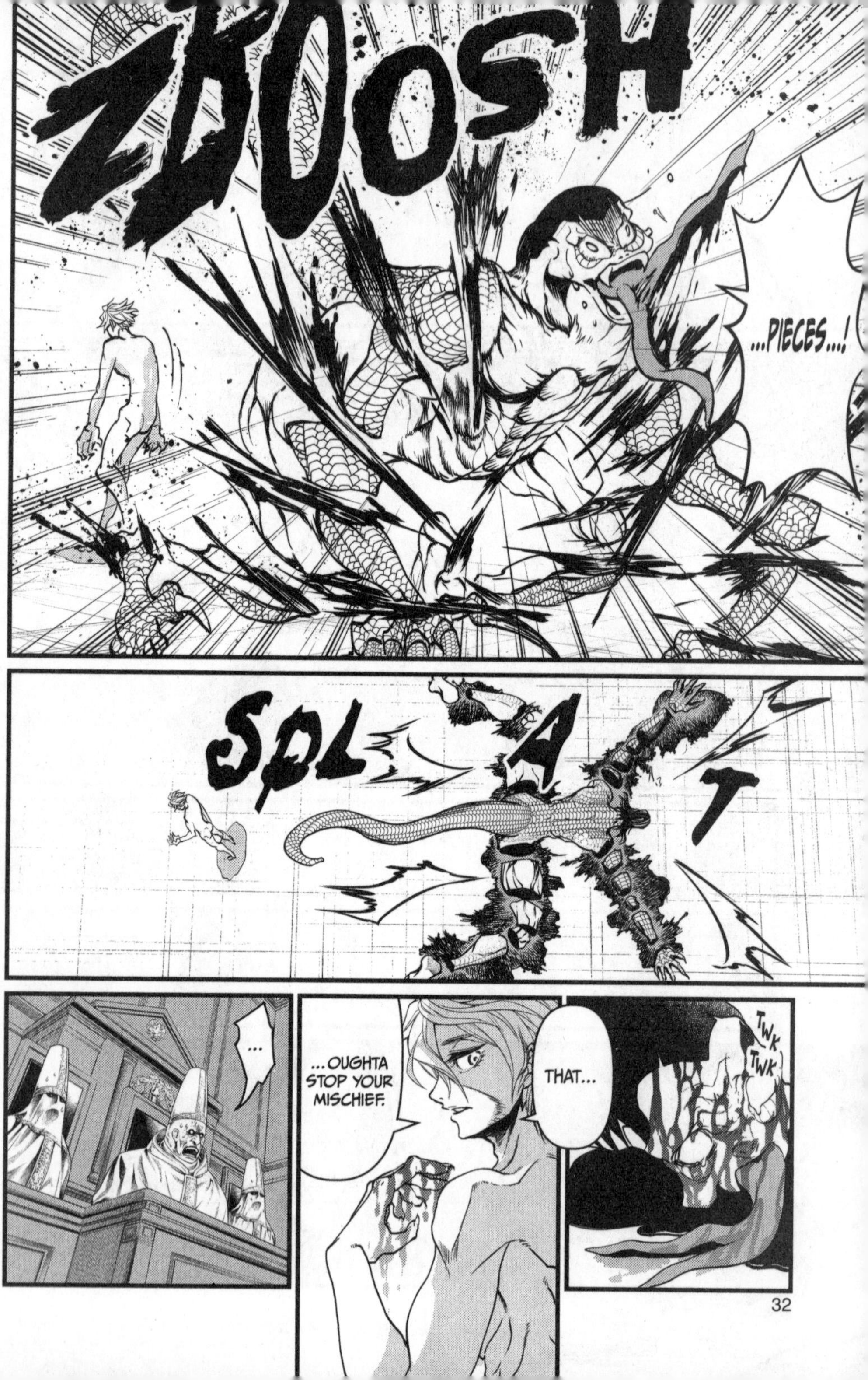
ZDOOSH
...PIECES...!
SPLAT
TWK TWK
THAT...
...OUGHTA STOP YOUR MISCHIEF.
...

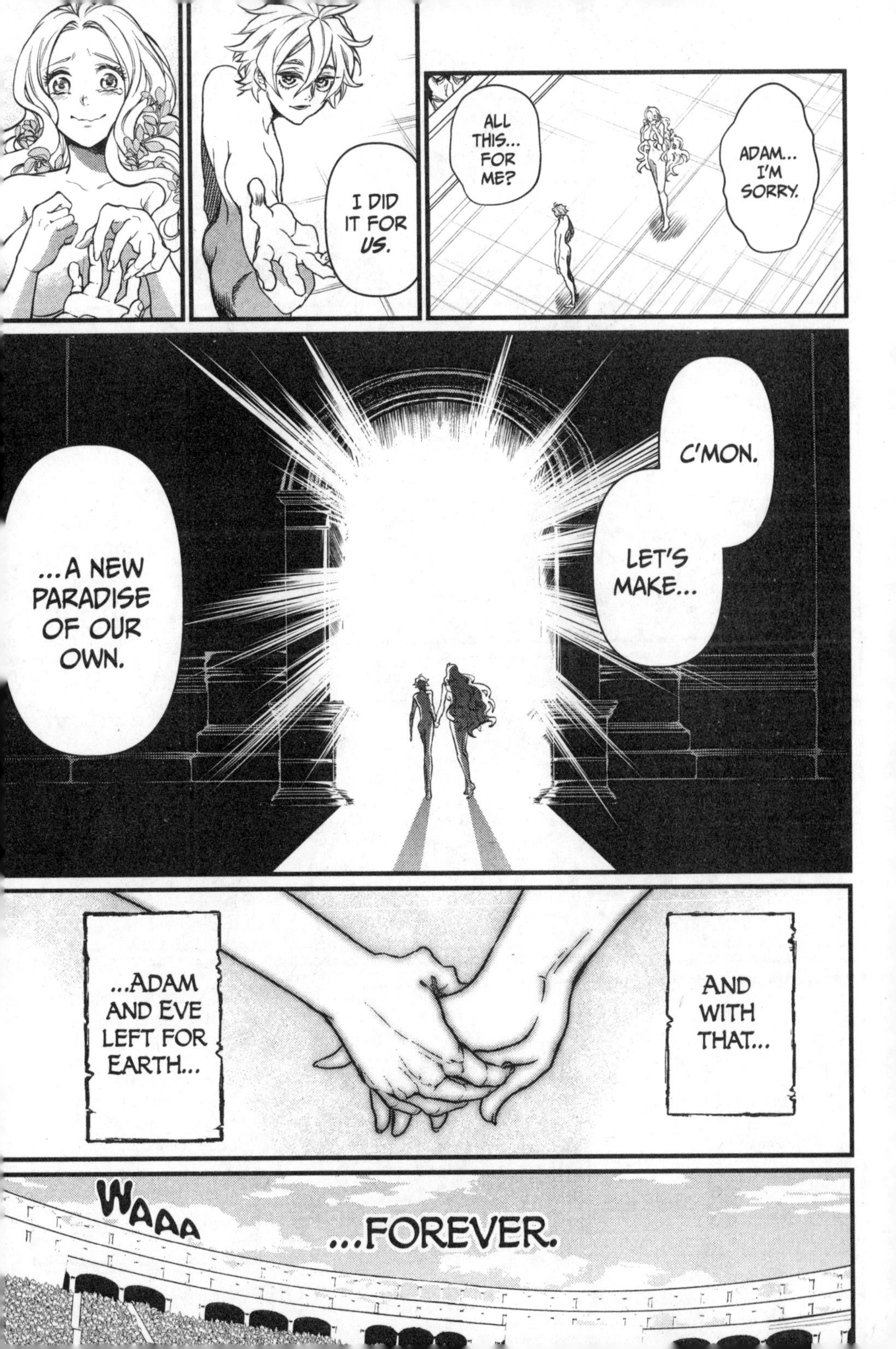
ADAM... I'M SORRY.
ALL THIS... FOR ME?
I DID IT FOR *US*.
C'MON.
LET'S MAKE...
...A NEW PARADISE OF OUR OWN.
AND WITH THAT...
...ADAM AND EVE LEFT FOR EARTH...
...FOREVER.
WAAA

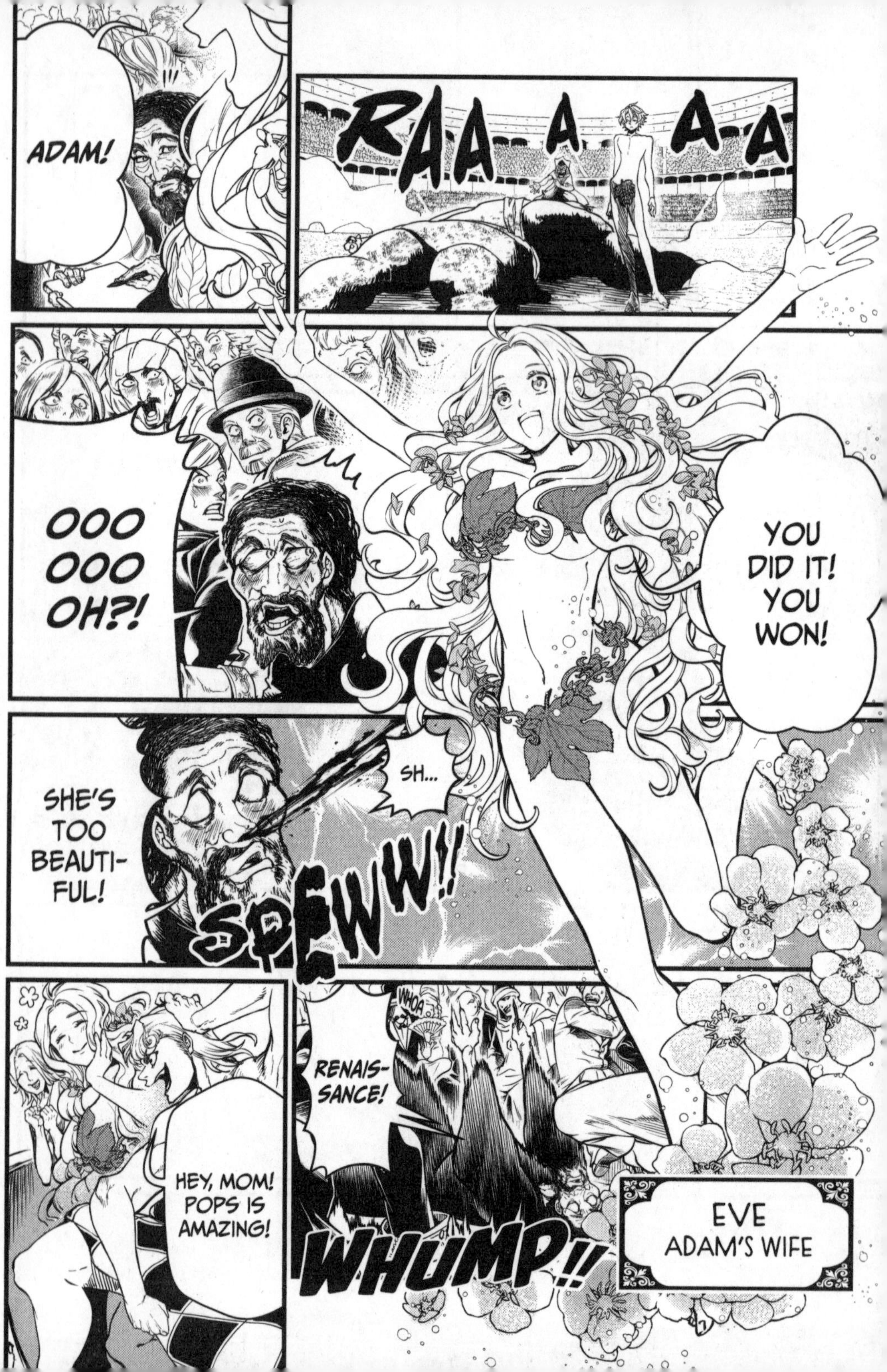
RAA A A A
ADAM!
YOU DID IT! YOU WON!
OOO OOO OH?!
SH...
SPEWW!!
SHE'S TOO BEAUTI-FUL!
EVE
ADAM'S WIFE
WHOA
RENAIS-SANCE!
WHUMP!!
HEY, MOM! POPS IS AMAZING!

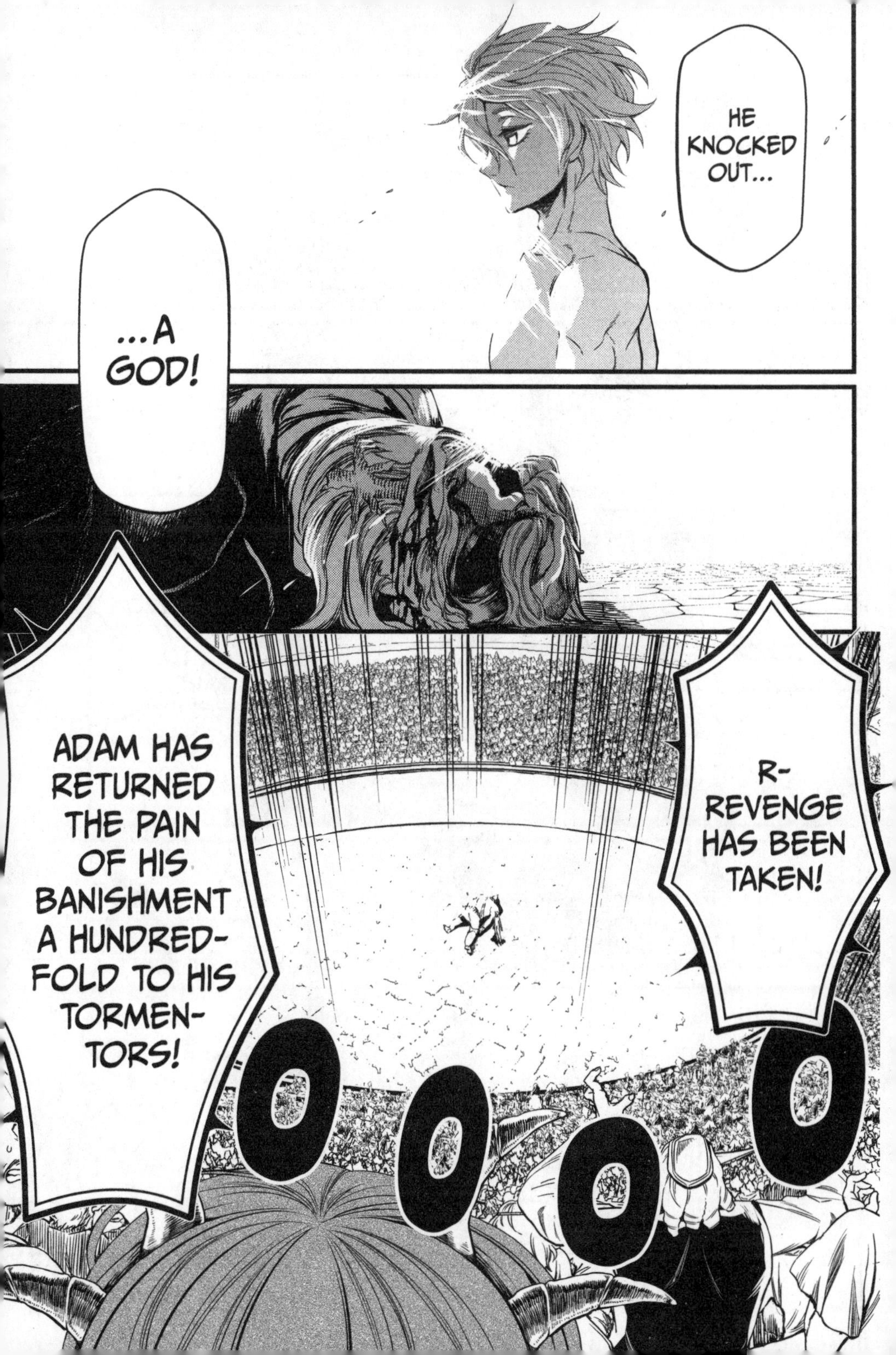
HE KNOCKED OUT...
...A GOD!
R-REVENGE HAS BEEN TAKEN!
ADAM HAS RETURNED THE PAIN OF HIS BANISHMENT A HUNDRED-FOLD TO HIS TORMEN-TORS!

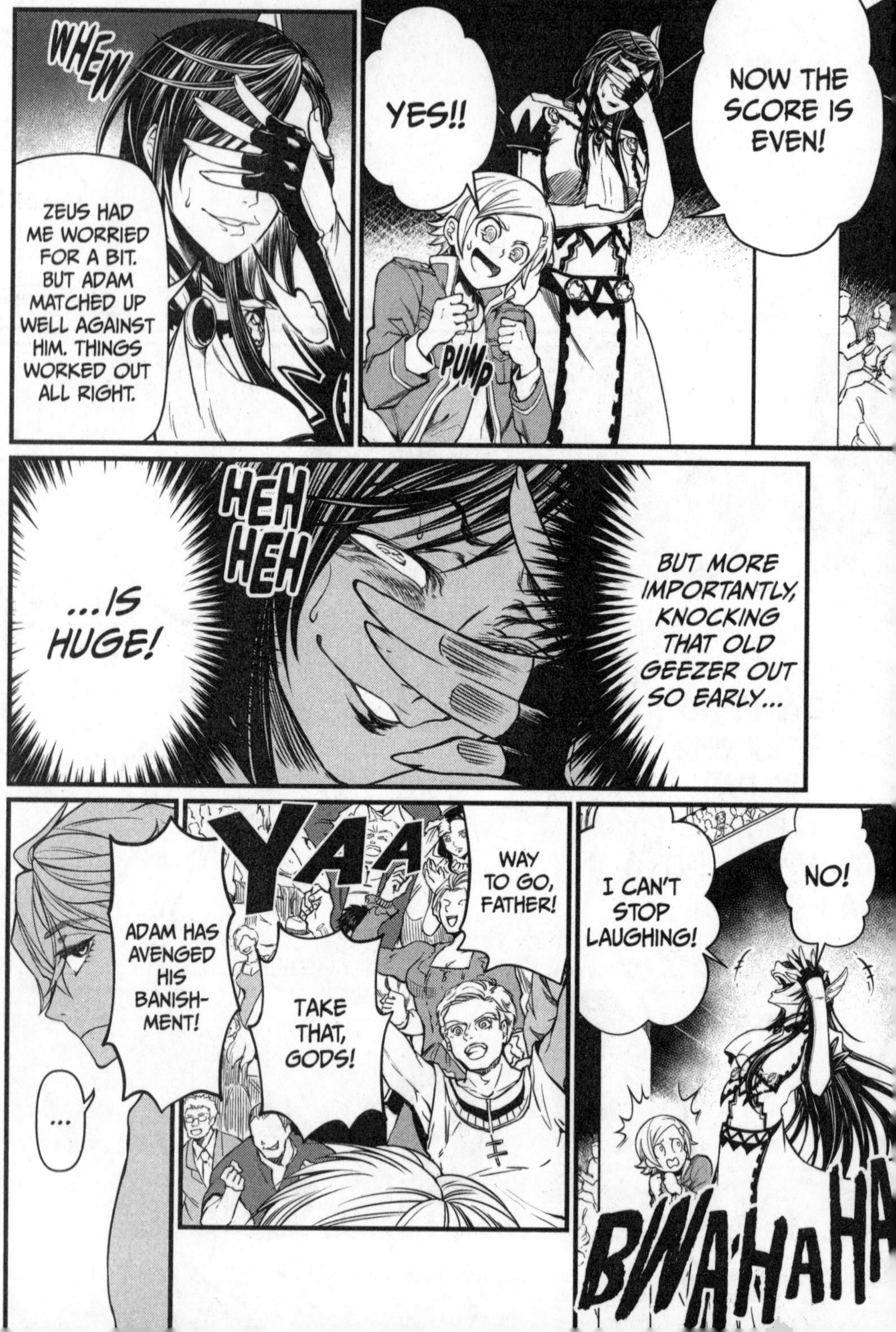
NOW THE SCORE IS EVEN!
YES!!
PUMP
WHEW
ZEUS HAD ME WORRIED FOR A BIT. BUT ADAM MATCHED UP WELL AGAINST HIM. THINGS WORKED OUT ALL RIGHT.
BUT MORE IMPORTANTLY, KNOCKING THAT OLD GEEZER OUT SO EARLY...
HEH HEH
...IS HUGE!
NO!
I CAN'T STOP LAUGHING!
BWAHAHA
YAA
WAY TO GO, FATHER!
TAKE THAT, GODS!
ADAM HAS AVENGED HIS BANISHMENT!
...

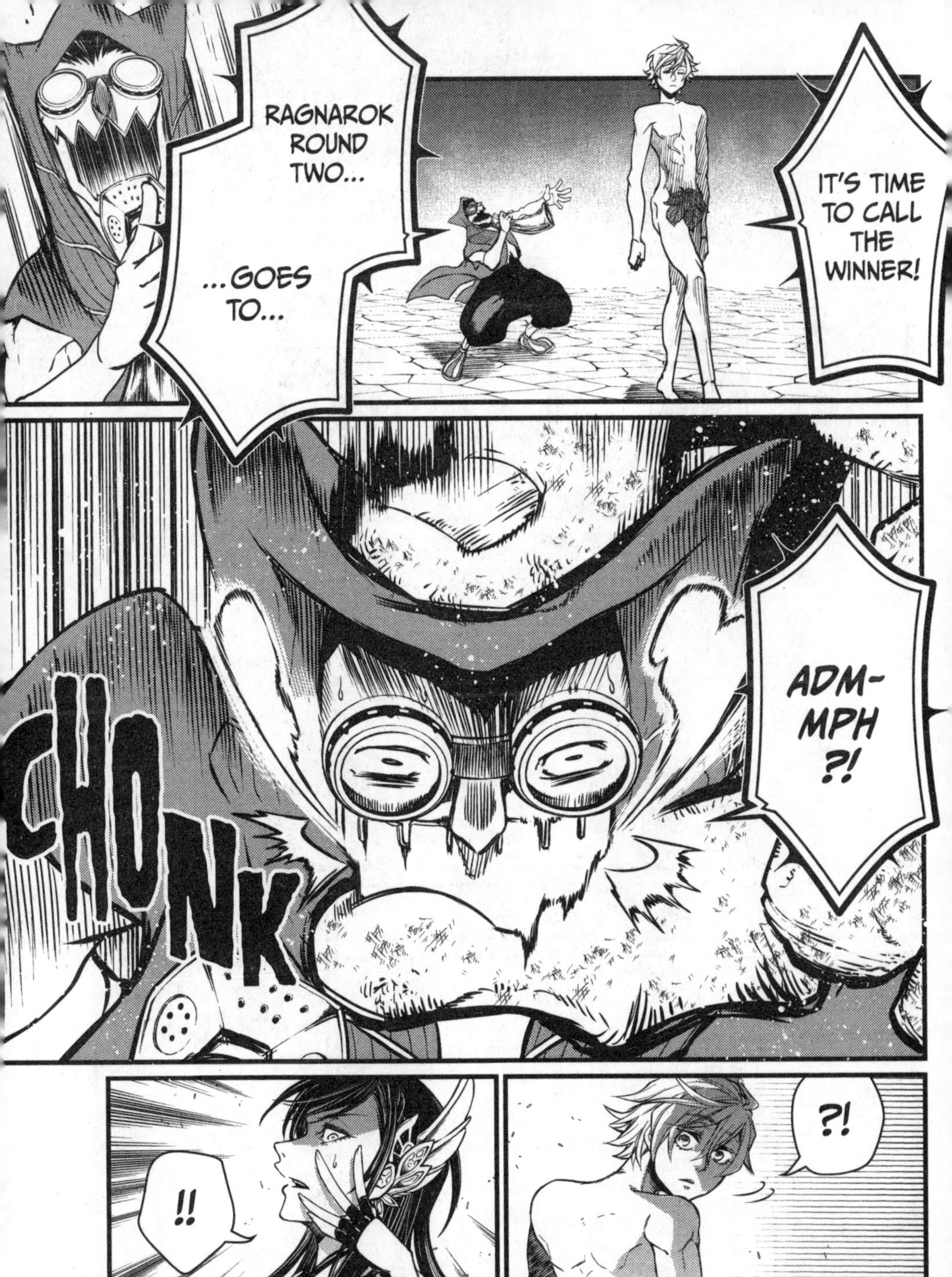
IT'S TIME TO CALL THE WINNER!
RAGNAROK ROUND TWO...
...GOES TO...
ADM-MPH ?!
CHONK
?!
!!

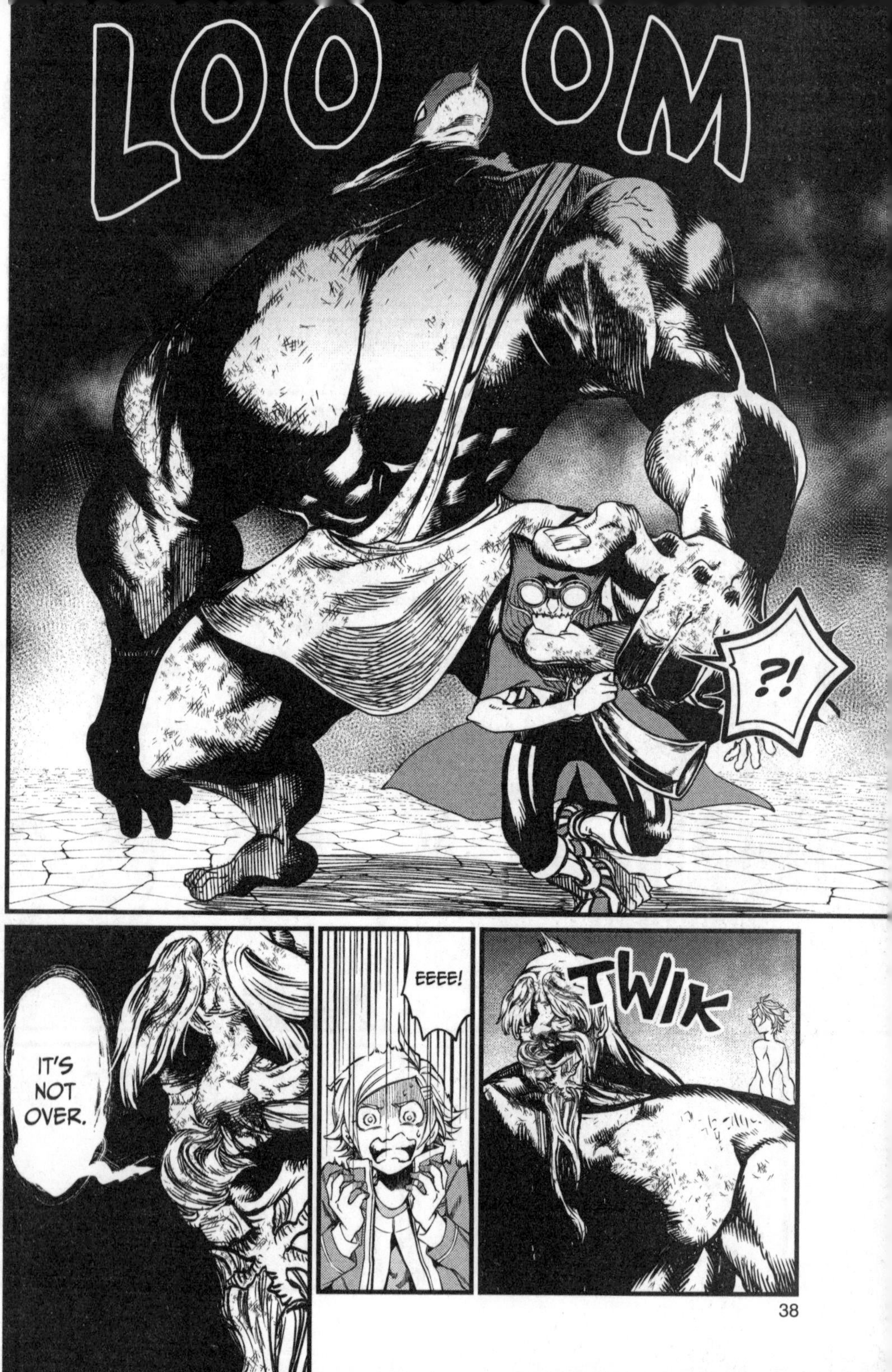
LOO OM
?!
TWIK
EEEE!
IT'S NOT OVER.

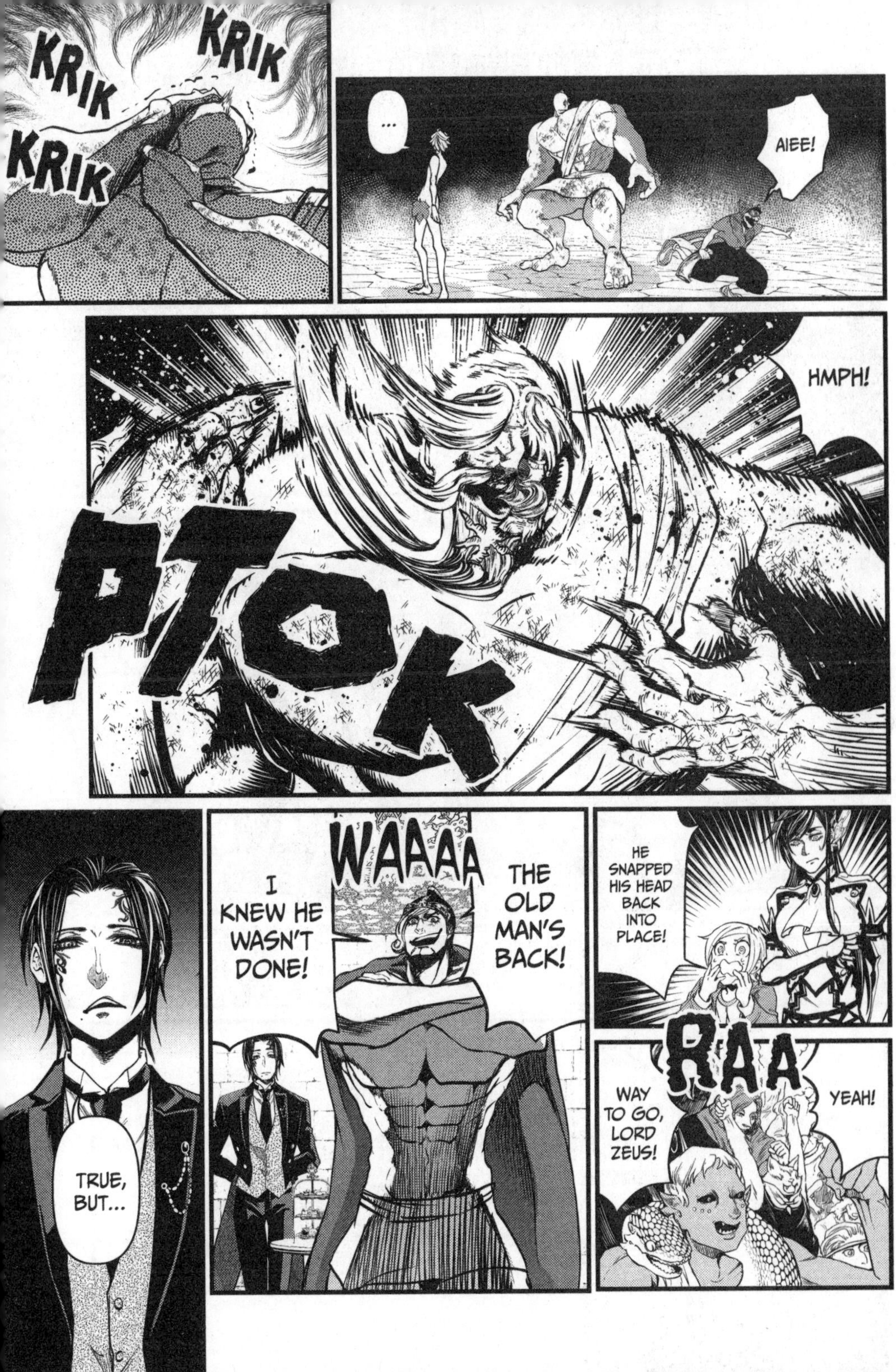
AIEE!
...
KRIK
KRIK
KRIK
KRIK
HMPH!
PTOK
HE SNAPPED HIS HEAD BACK INTO PLACE!
RAA
YEAH!
WAY TO GO, LORD ZEUS!
WAAAA
THE OLD MAN'S BACK!
I KNEW HE WASN'T DONE!
TRUE, BUT...

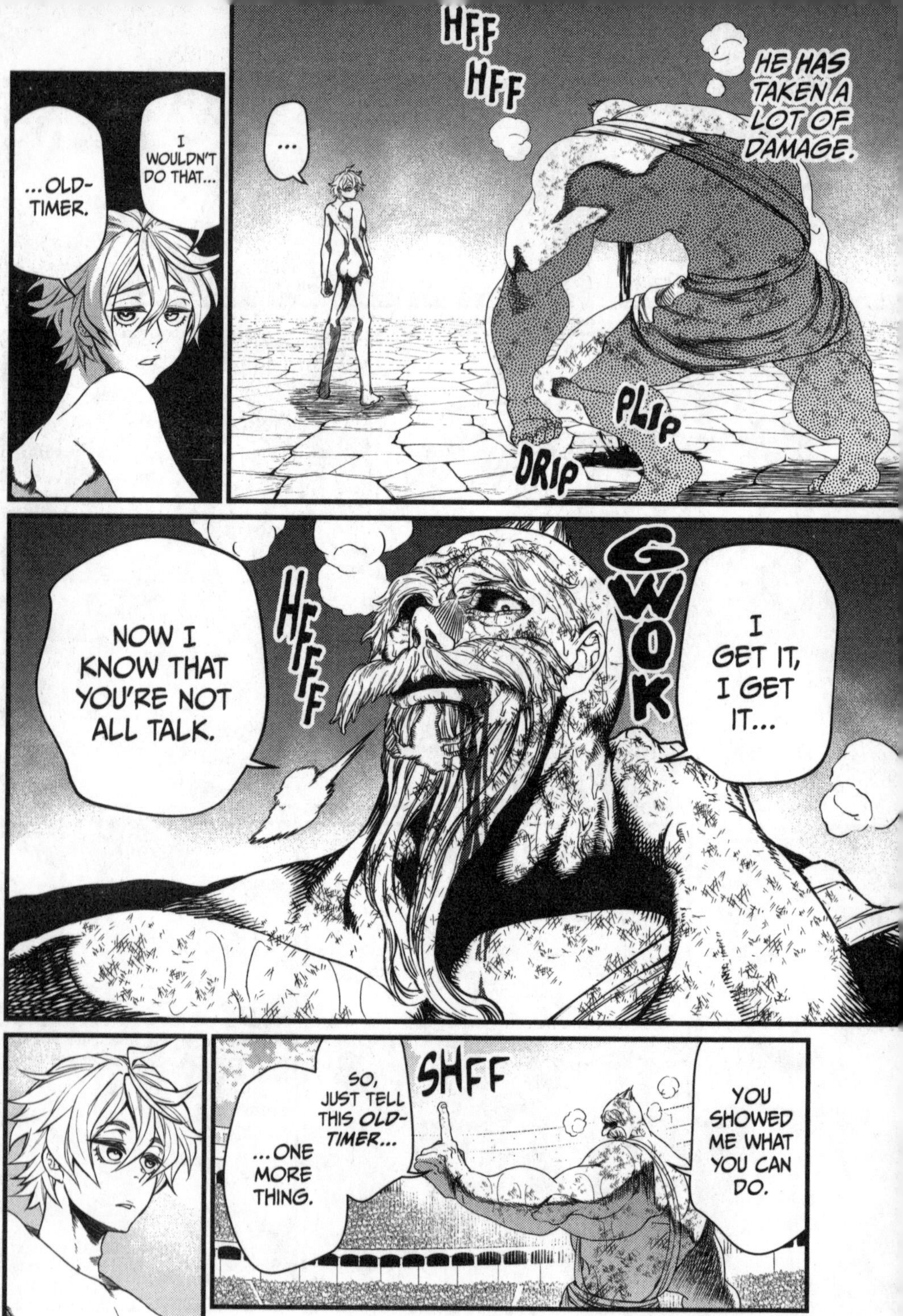
HFF HFF
HE HAS TAKEN A LOT OF DAMAGE.
...
PLIP
DRIP
I WOULDN'T DO THAT...
...OLD-TIMER.
GWOK
I GET IT, I GET IT...
HFFF
NOW I KNOW THAT YOU'RE NOT ALL TALK.
YOU SHOWED ME WHAT YOU CAN DO.
SHFF
SO, JUST TELL THIS *OLD-TIMER*...
...ONE MORE THING.

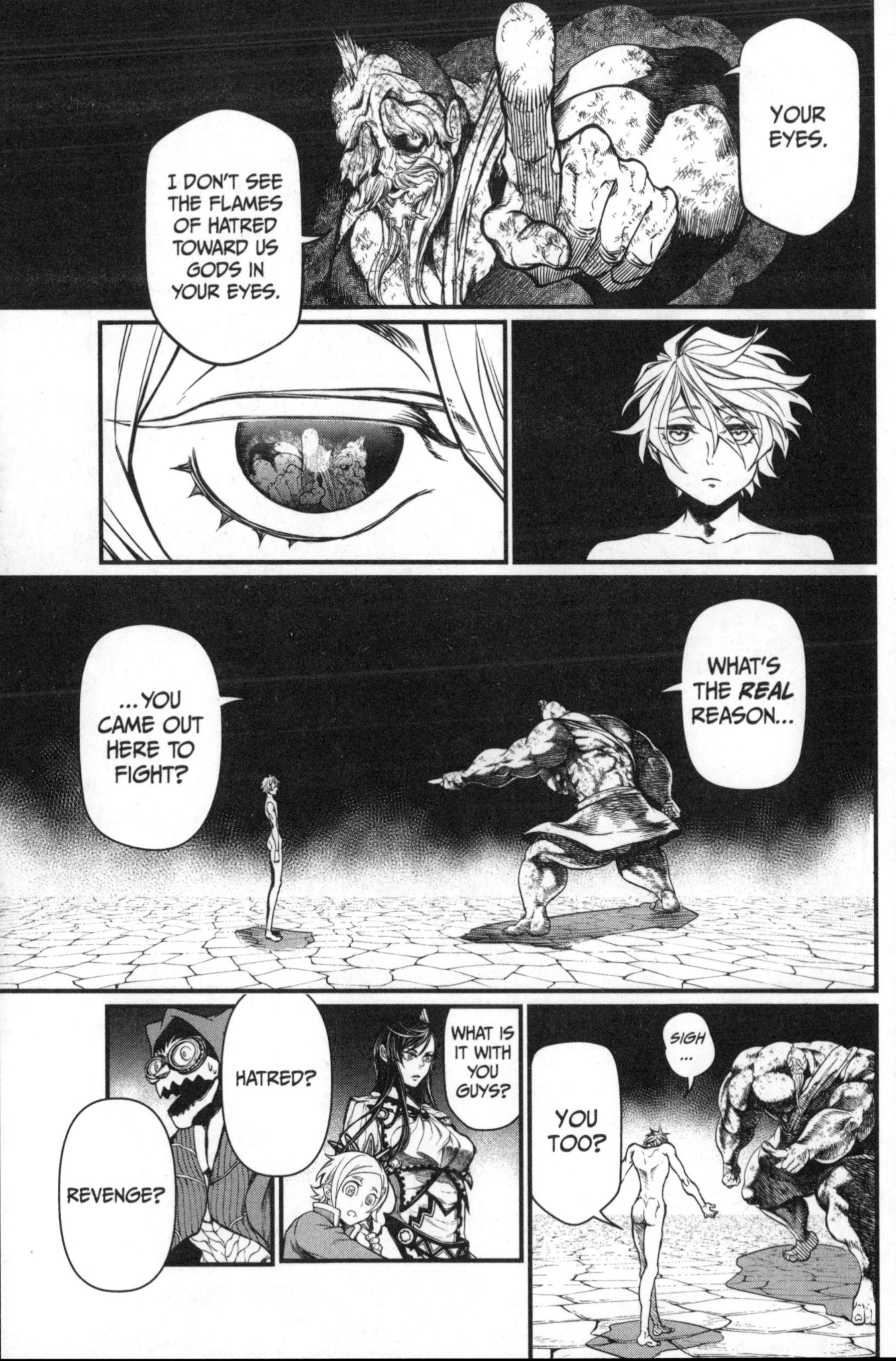
YOUR EYES.
I DON'T SEE THE FLAMES OF HATRED TOWARD US GODS IN YOUR EYES.
WHAT'S THE *REAL* REASON...
...YOU CAME OUT HERE TO FIGHT?
SIGH ...
YOU TOO?
WHAT IS IT WITH YOU GUYS?
HATRED?
REVENGE?

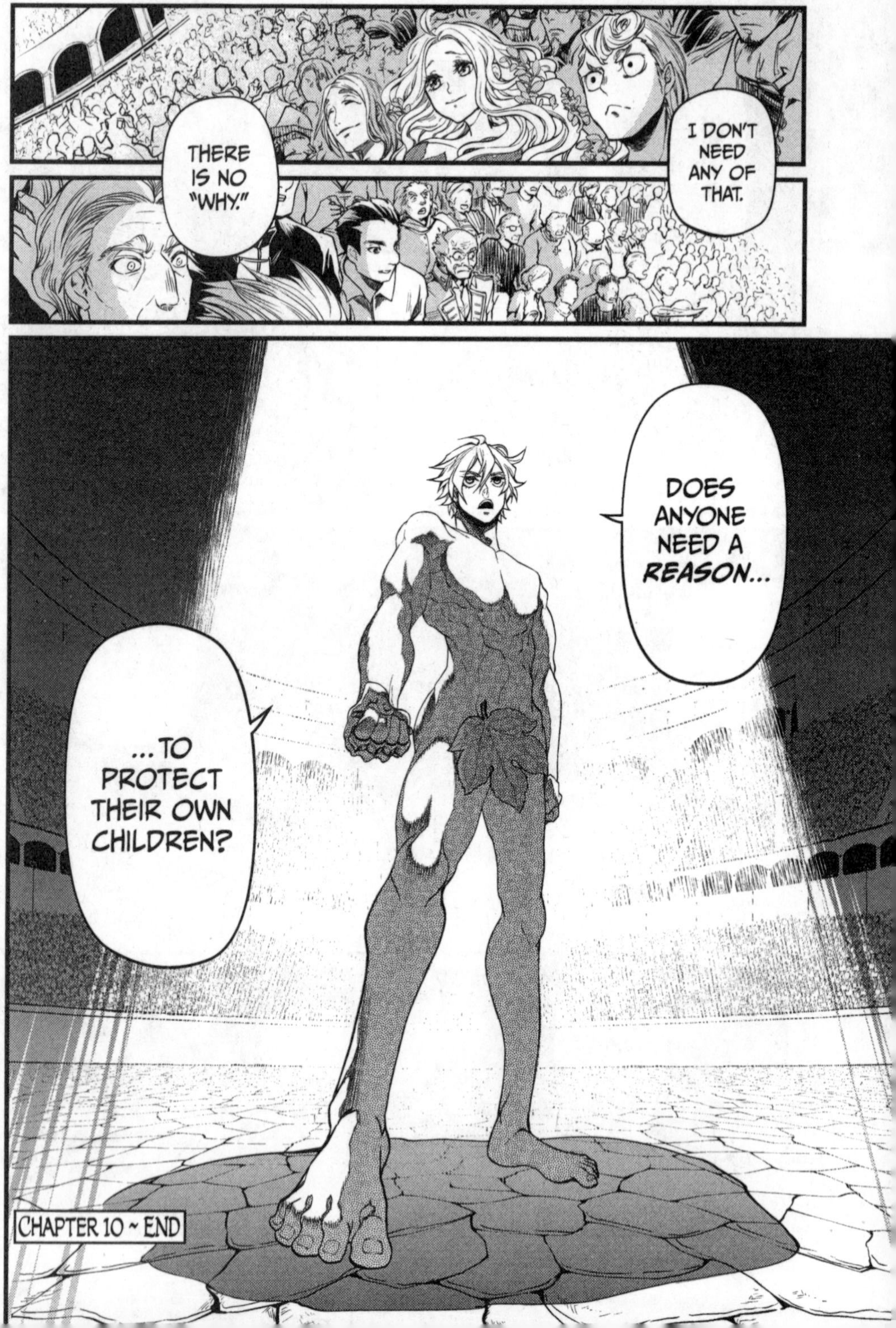
I DON'T NEED ANY OF THAT.
THERE IS NO "WHY."
DOES ANYONE NEED A REASON...
...TO PROTECT THEIR OWN CHILDREN?
CHAPTER 10 ~ END

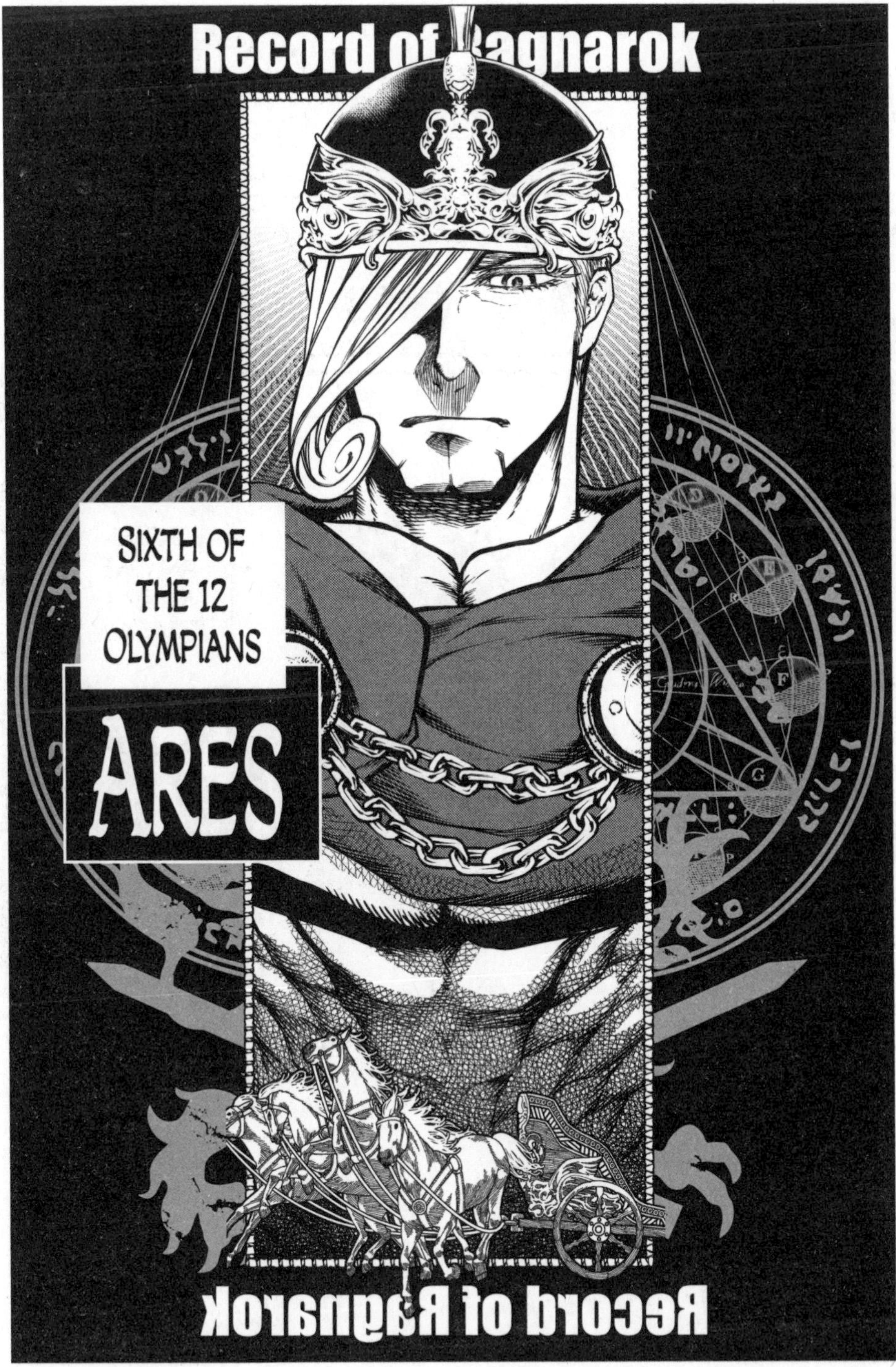
Record of Ragnarok
SIXTH OF THE 12 OLYMPIANS
ARES
Record of Ragnarok

RECORD OF RAGNAROK

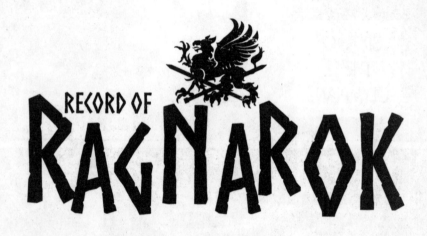

WHY RISK ONE'S LIFE TO FIGHT?

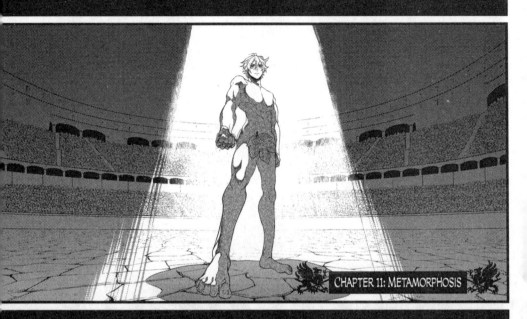

CHAPTER 11: METAMORPHOSIS

ONE DOES NOT *NEED* A REASON.

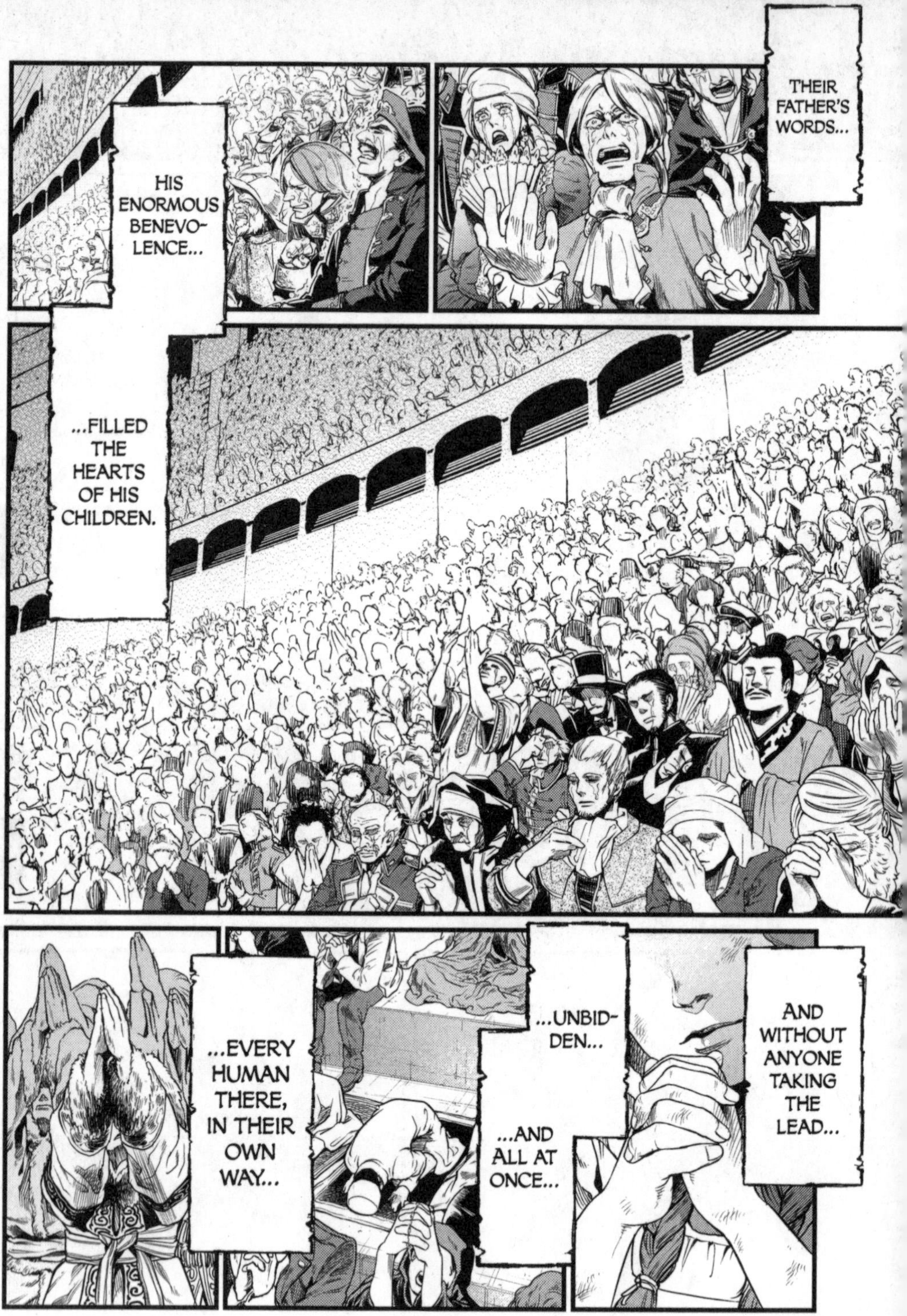
THEIR FATHER'S WORDS...
HIS ENORMOUS BENEVO-LENCE...
...FILLED THE HEARTS OF HIS CHILDREN.
AND WITHOUT ANYONE TAKING THE LEAD...
...UNBID-DEN...
...AND ALL AT ONCE...
...EVERY HUMAN THERE, IN THEIR OWN WAY...

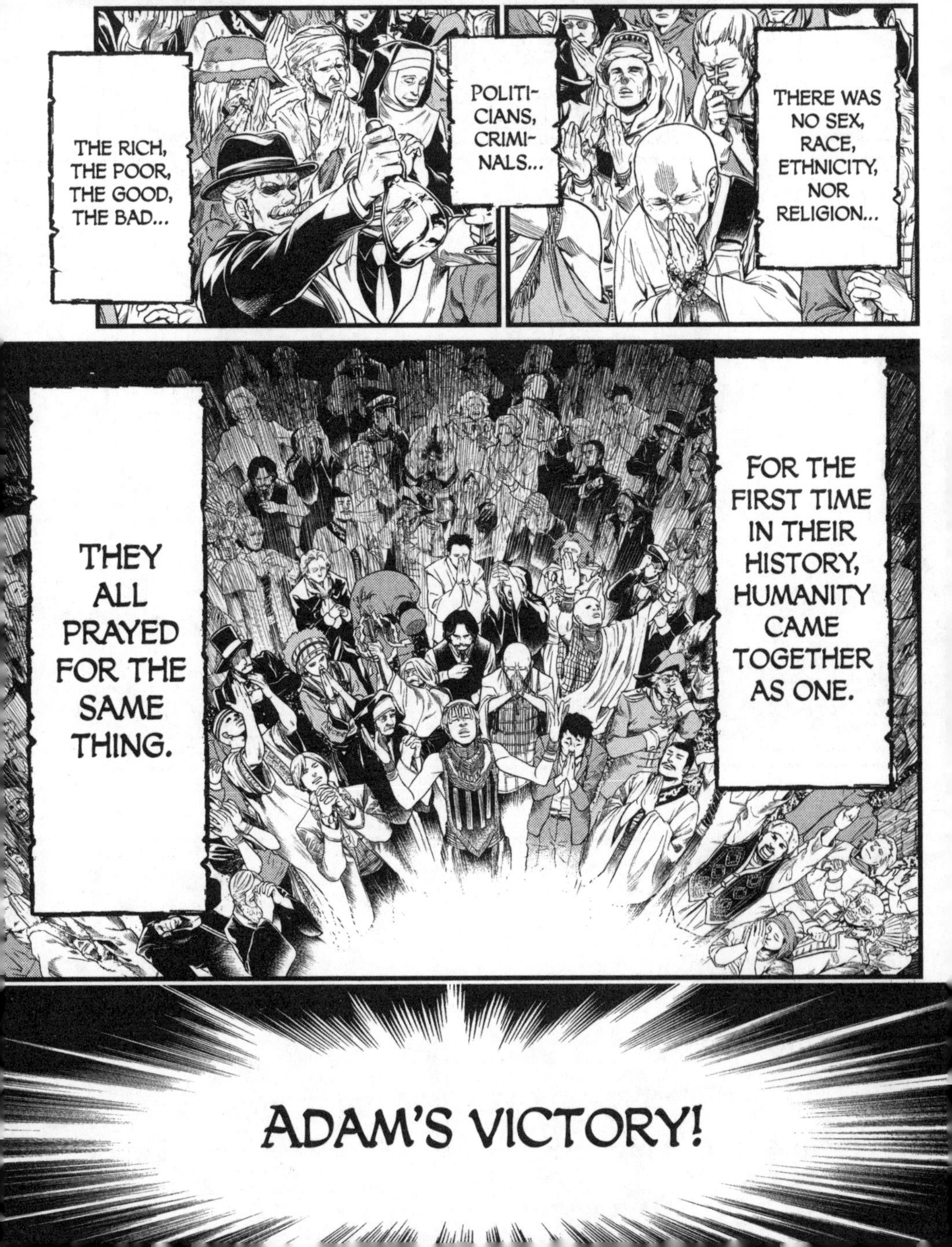
THERE WAS NO SEX, RACE, ETHNICITY, NOR RELIGION...
POLITI-CIANS, CRIMI-NALS...
THE RICH, THE POOR, THE GOOD, THE BAD...
FOR THE FIRST TIME IN THEIR HISTORY, HUMANITY CAME TOGETHER AS ONE.
THEY ALL PRAYED FOR THE SAME THING.
ADAM'S VICTORY!

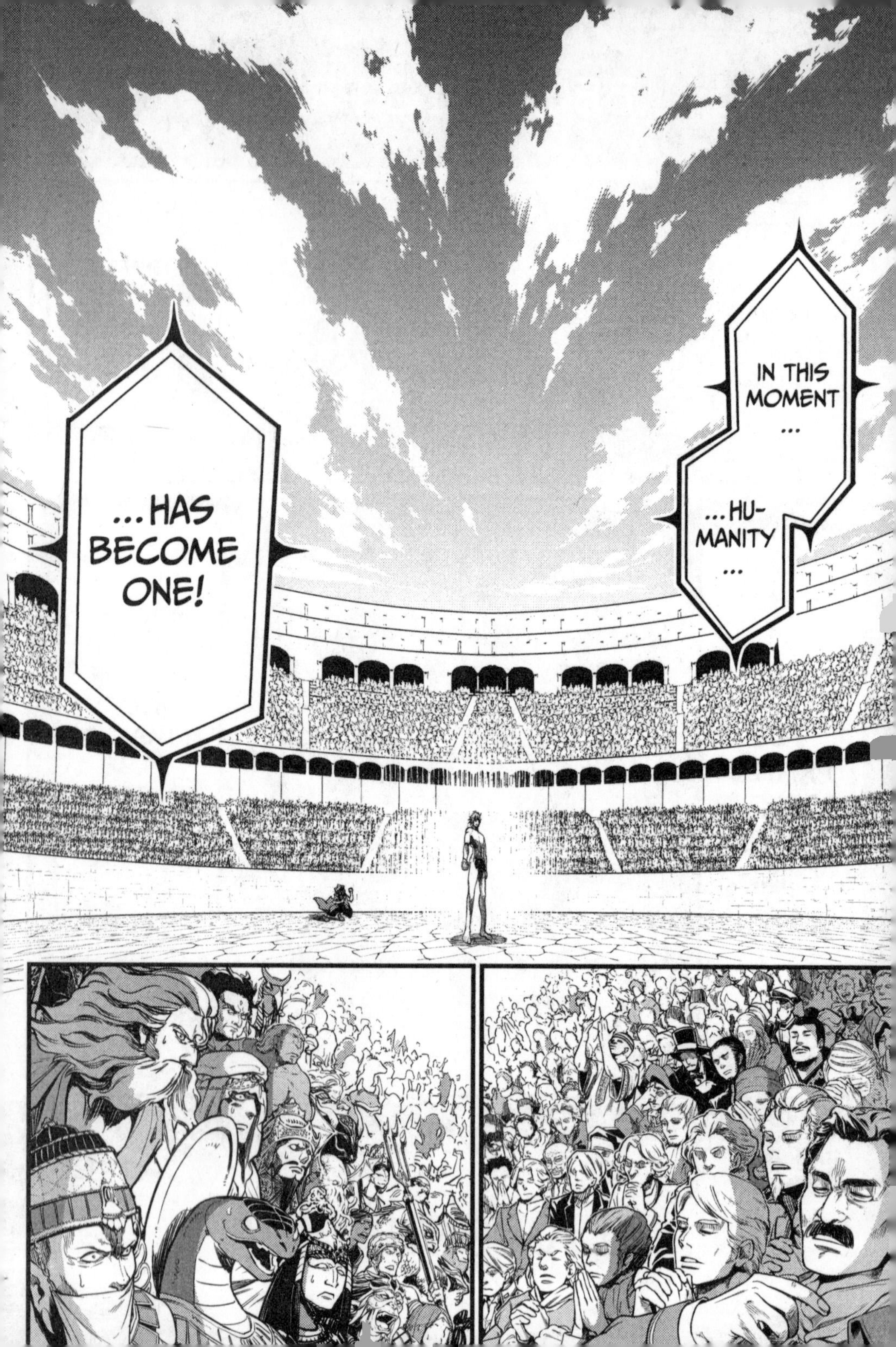
IN THIS MOMENT ...
...HU-MANITY ...
...HAS BECOME ONE!

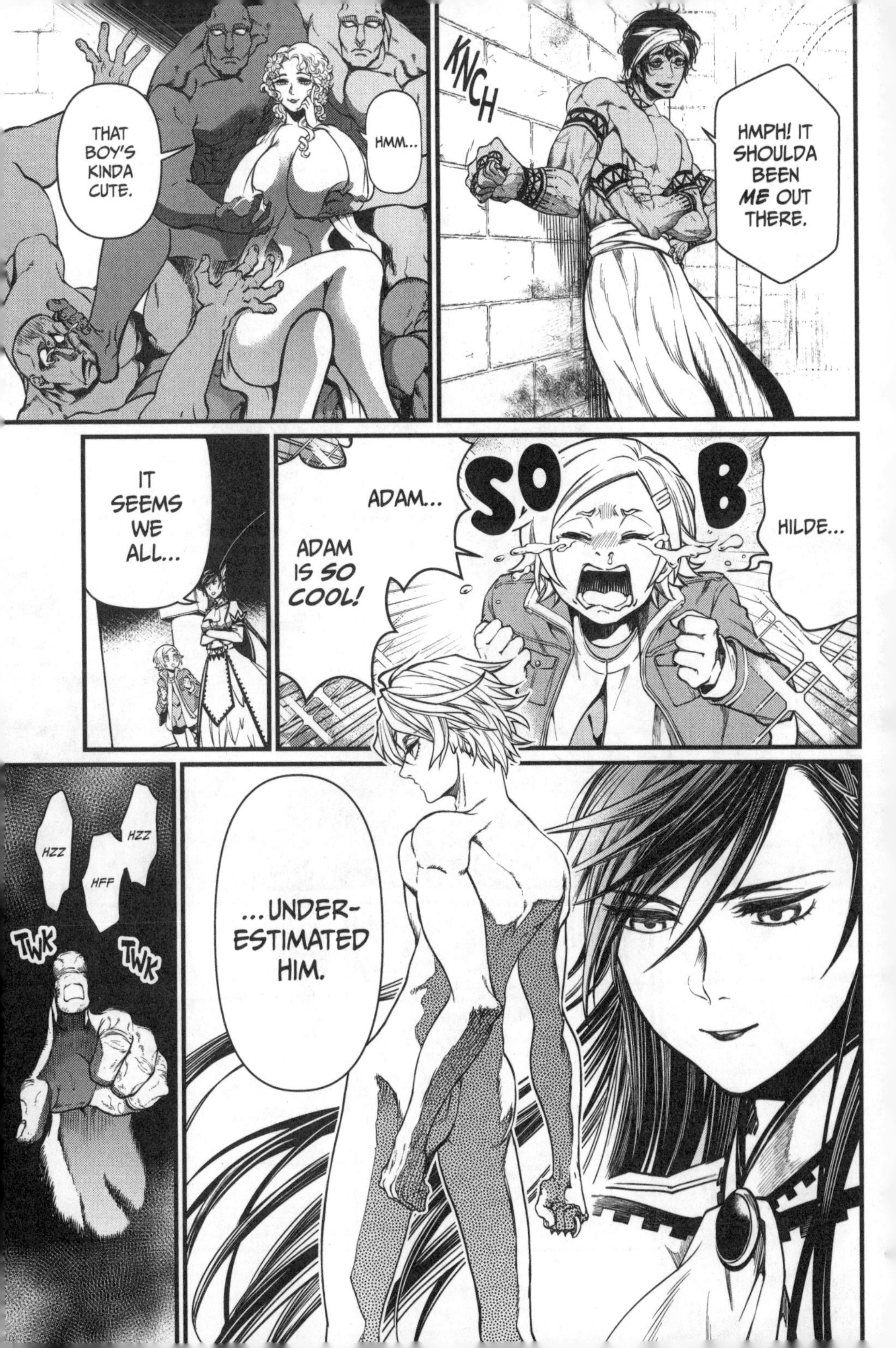
KNCH
HMPH! IT SHOULDA BEEN ME OUT THERE.
HMM...
THAT BOY'S KINDA CUTE.
HILDE...
SOB
ADAM...
ADAM IS SO COOL!
IT SEEMS WE ALL...
...UNDER-ESTIMATED HIM.
HZZ
HFF
HZZ
TWK
TWK

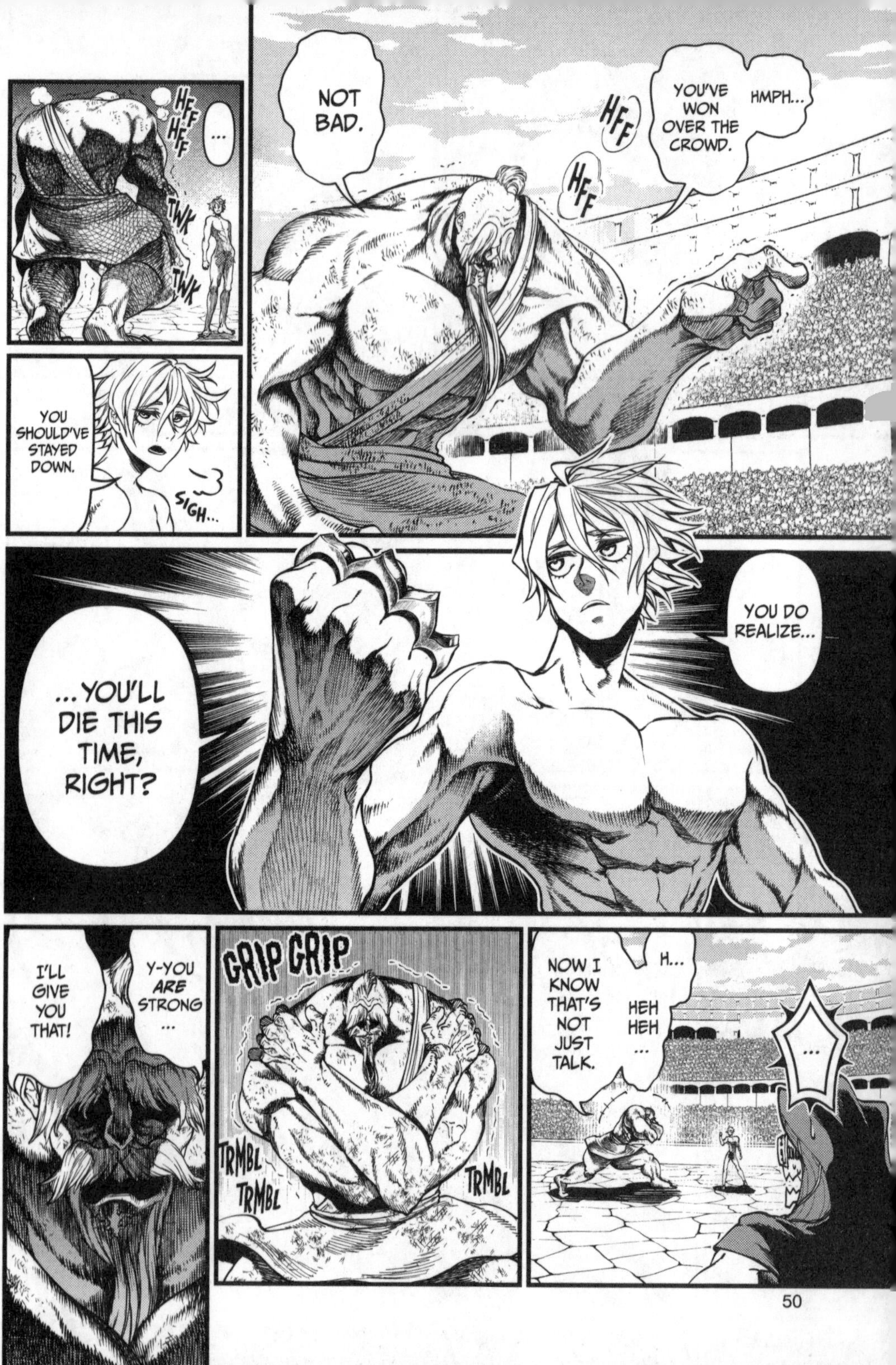
HMPH...
YOU'VE WON OVER THE CROWD.
HFF
HFF
NOT BAD.
HFF HFF
...
TWK
TWK
YOU SHOULD'VE STAYED DOWN.
SIGH...
YOU DO REALIZE...
...YOU'LL DIE THIS TIME, RIGHT?
...
H...
HEH HEH ...
NOW I KNOW THAT'S NOT JUST TALK.
GRIP GRIP
TRMBL
TRMBL TRMBL
Y-YOU *ARE* STRONG ...
I'LL GIVE YOU THAT!

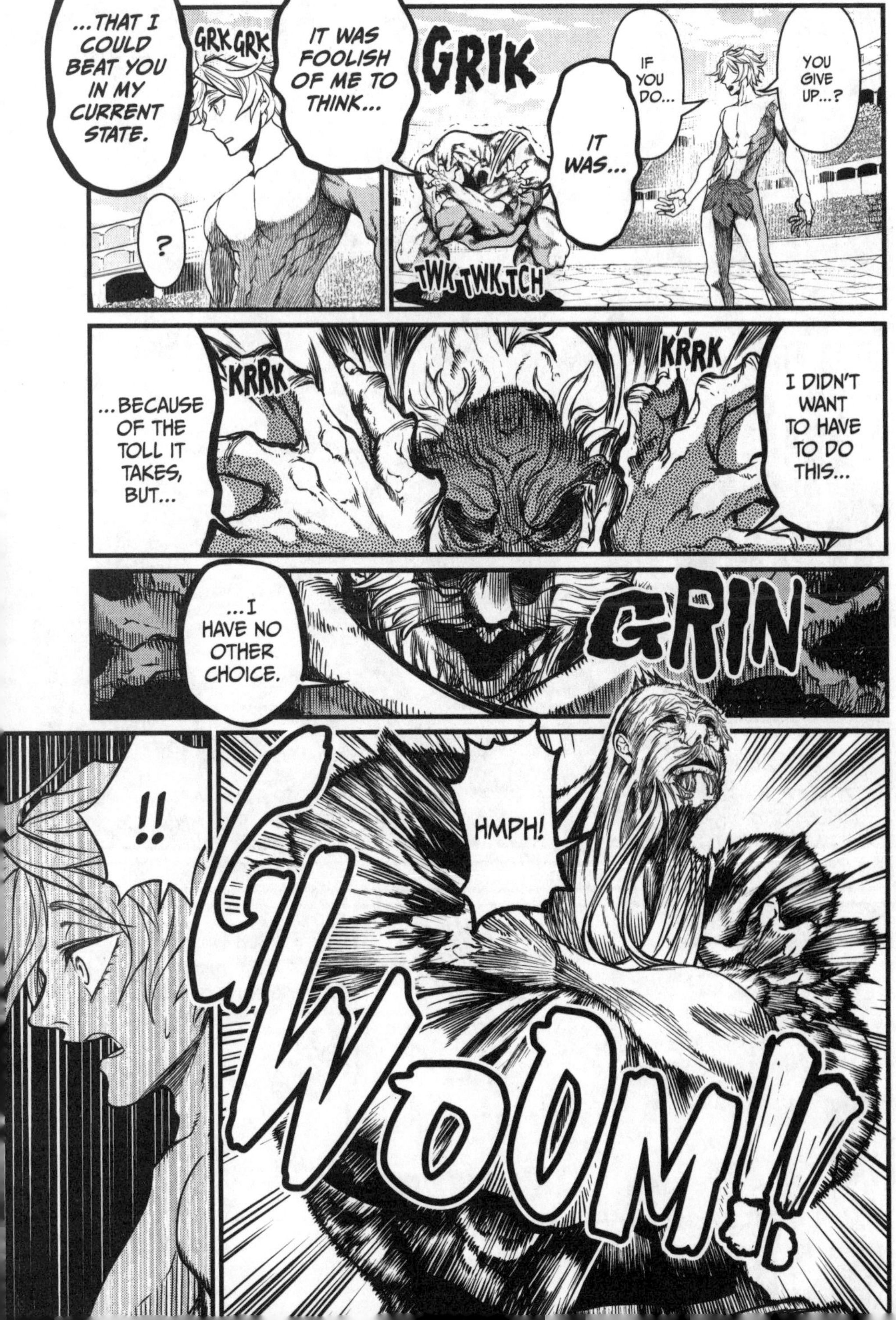
YOU GIVE UP...?
IF YOU DO...
IT WAS...
GRIK
TWK TWK TCH
IT WAS FOOLISH OF ME TO THINK...
GRK GRK
...THAT I COULD BEAT YOU IN MY CURRENT STATE.
?
KRRK
I DIDN'T WANT TO HAVE TO DO THIS...
KRRK
...BECAUSE OF THE TOLL IT TAKES, BUT...
GRIN
...I HAVE NO OTHER CHOICE.
HMPH!
WOOM!!
!!

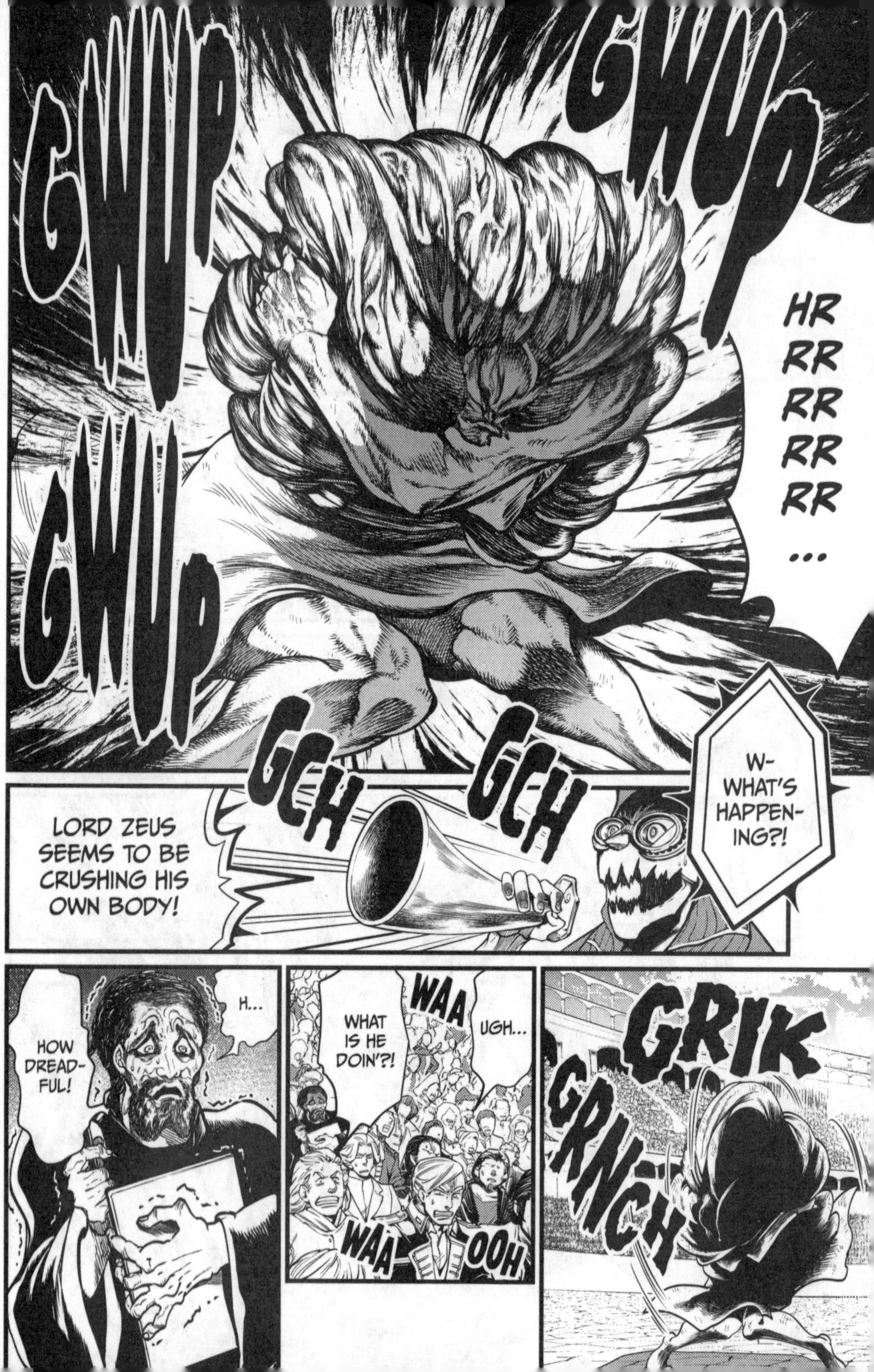

GWUP
HRRRRRRRRR...
GWUP
GWUP
W-WHAT'S HAPPENING?!
GCH
GCH
LORD ZEUS SEEMS TO BE CRUSHING HIS OWN BODY!
GRIK
GRNCH
UGH...
WAA
WHAT IS HE DOIN'?!
OOH
WAA
H...
HOW DREADFUL!

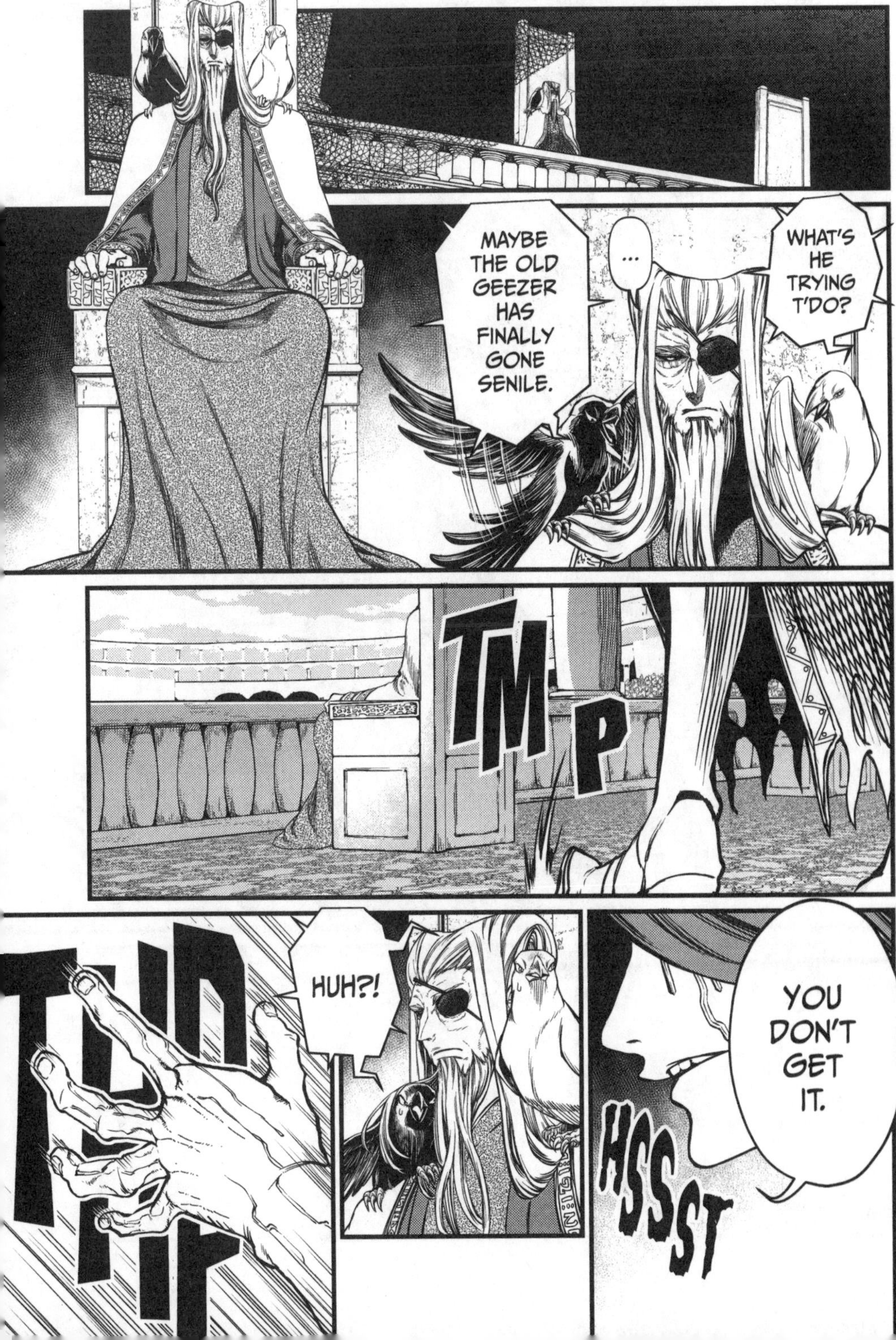
WHAT'S HE TRYING T'DO?
...
MAYBE THE OLD GEEZER HAS FINALLY GONE SENILE.
TMP
YOU DON'T GET IT.
HSSST
HUH?!

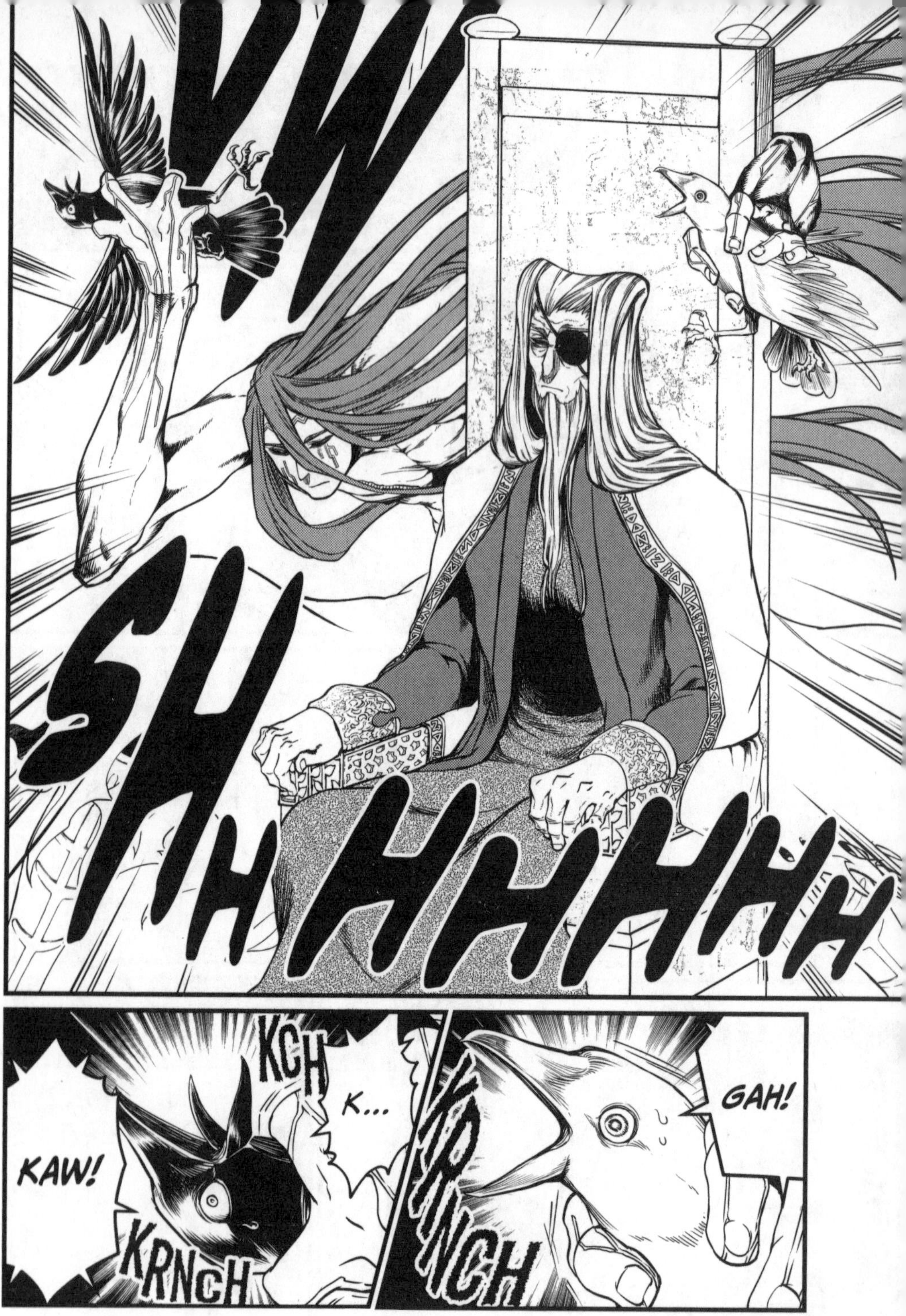
VWSHHHHHHH
GAH!
KRRUNCH
KCH
K...
KAW!
KRNCH

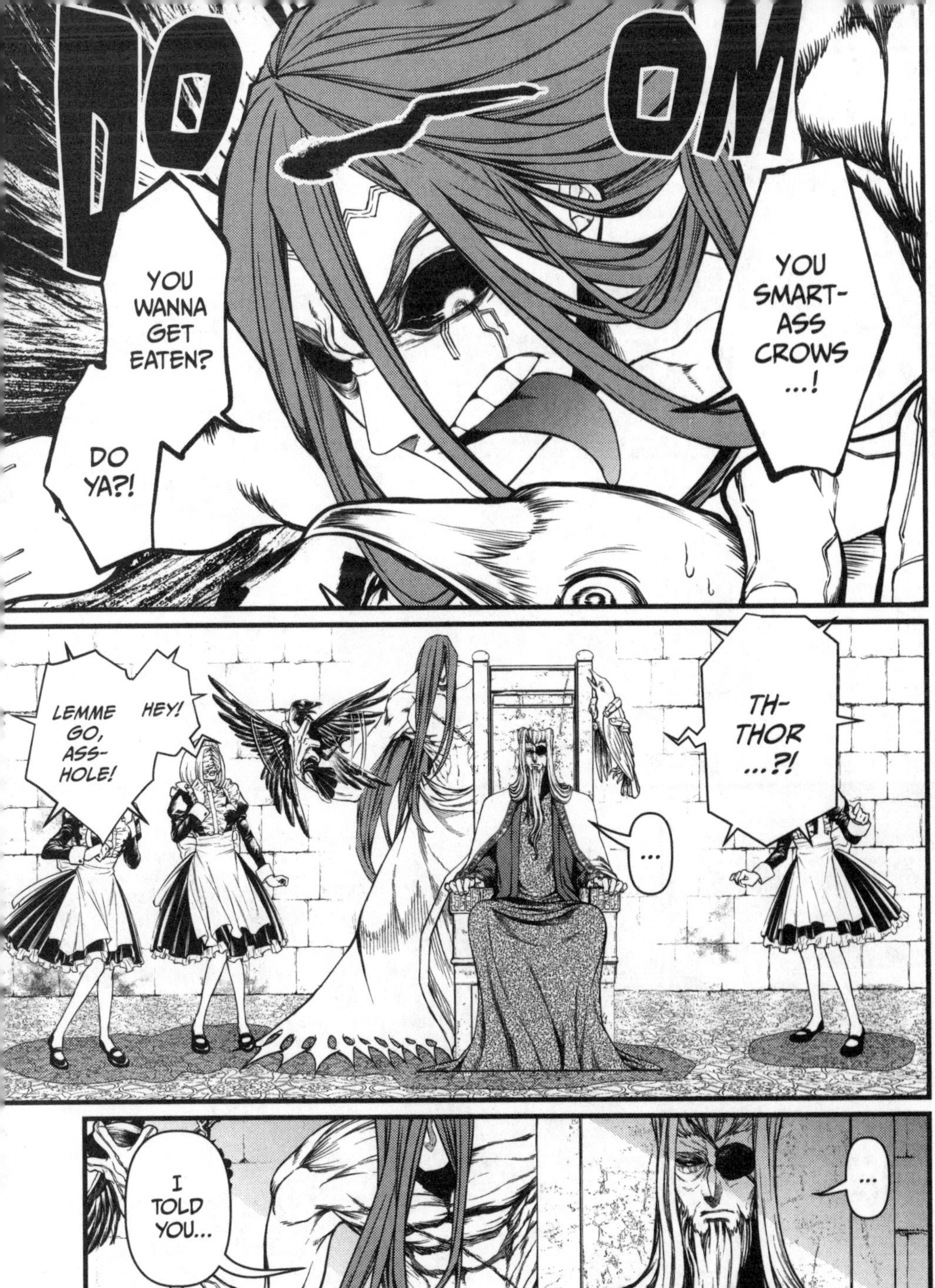
DO—OM
YOU SMART-ASS CROWS...!
YOU WANNA GET EATEN?
DO YA?!
TH-THOR...?!
...
HEY!
LEMME GO, ASS-HOLE!
...
I TOLD YOU...

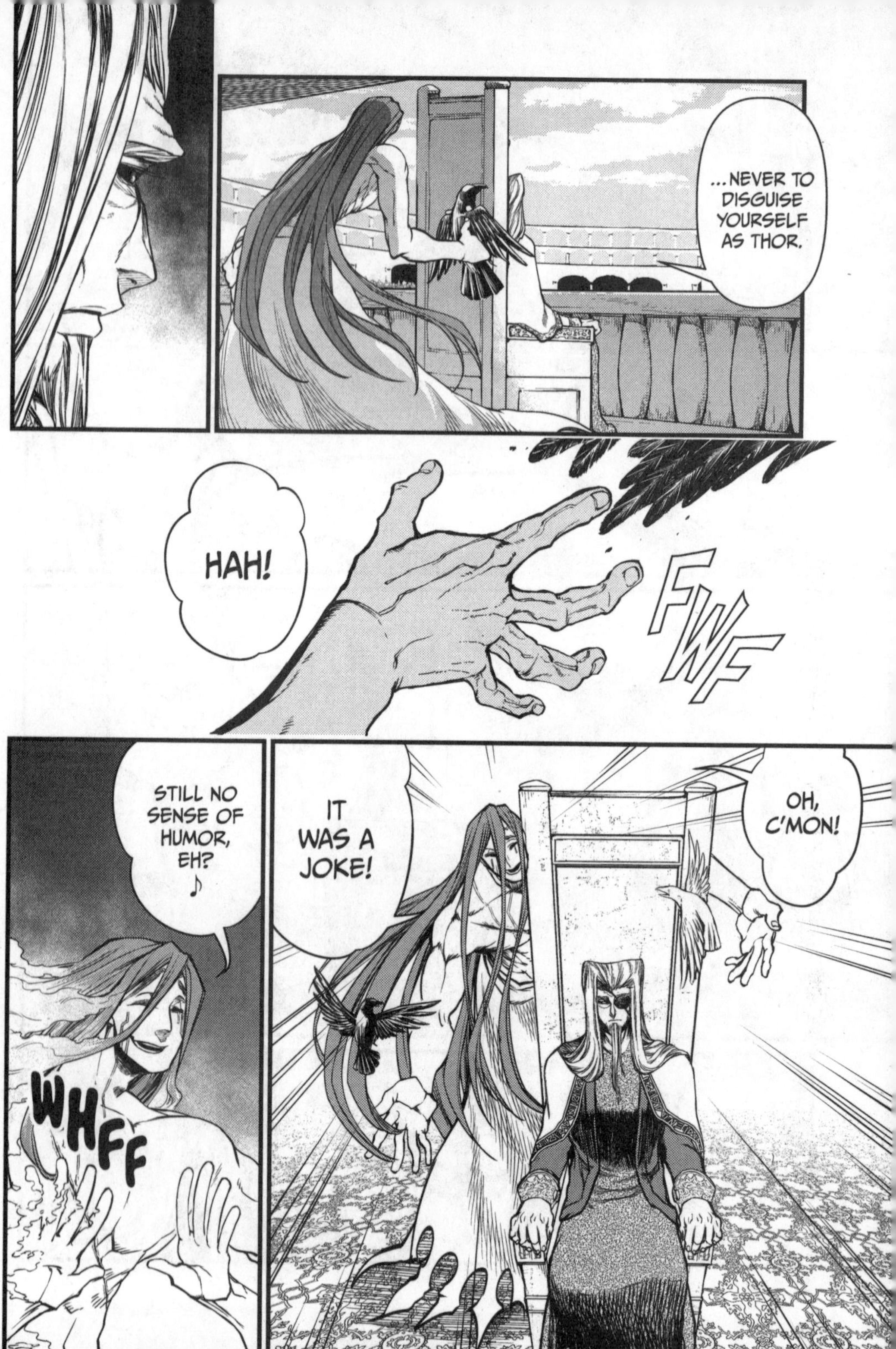
...NEVER TO DISGUISE YOURSELF AS THOR.
HAH!
FWF
OH, C'MON!
IT WAS A JOKE!
STILL NO SENSE OF HUMOR, EH? ♪
WHFF

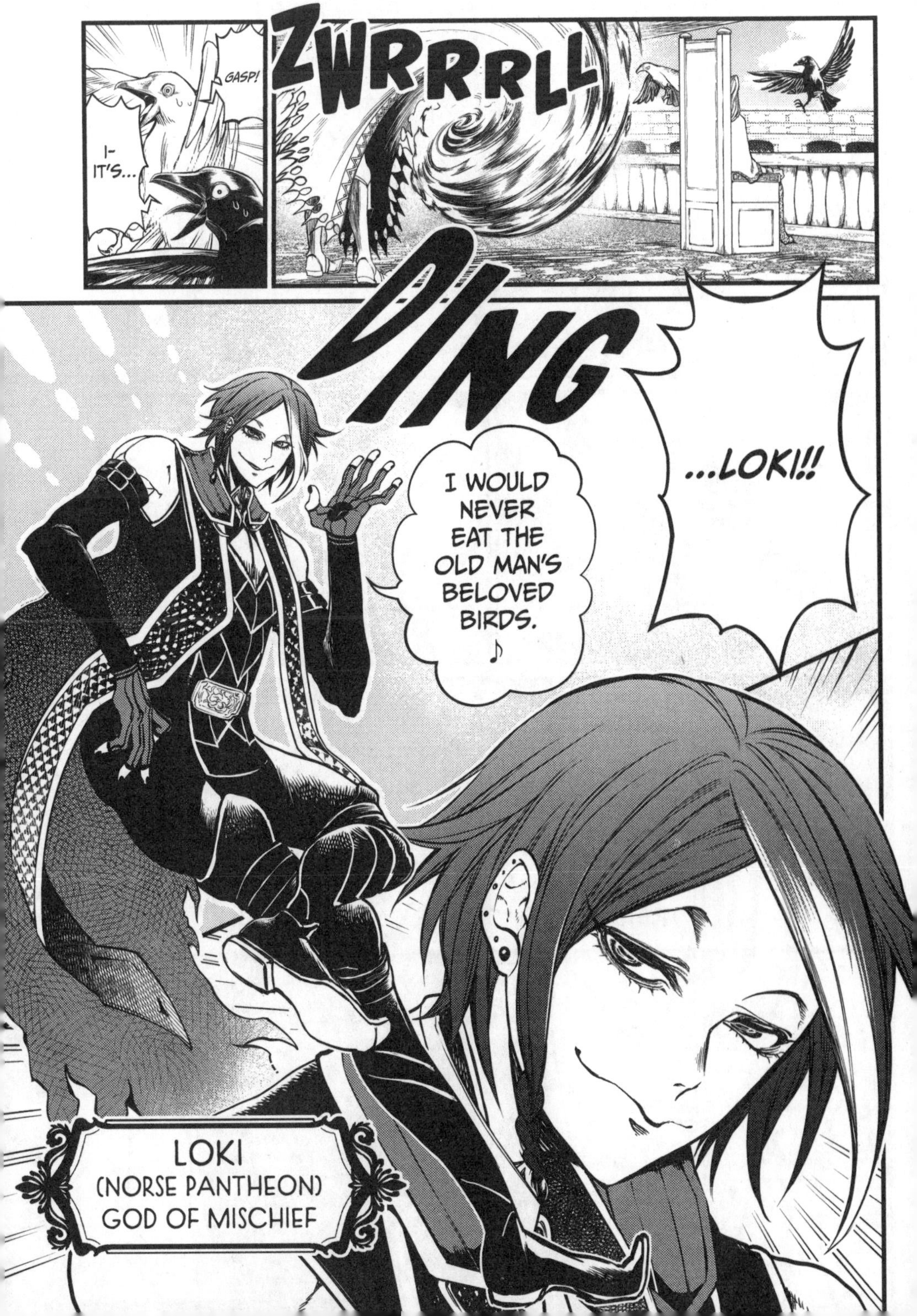
ZWRRRLL
GASP!
I- IT'S...
DING
...LOKI!!
I WOULD NEVER EAT THE OLD MAN'S BELOVED BIRDS. ♪
LOKI (NORSE PANTHEON) GOD OF MISCHIEF

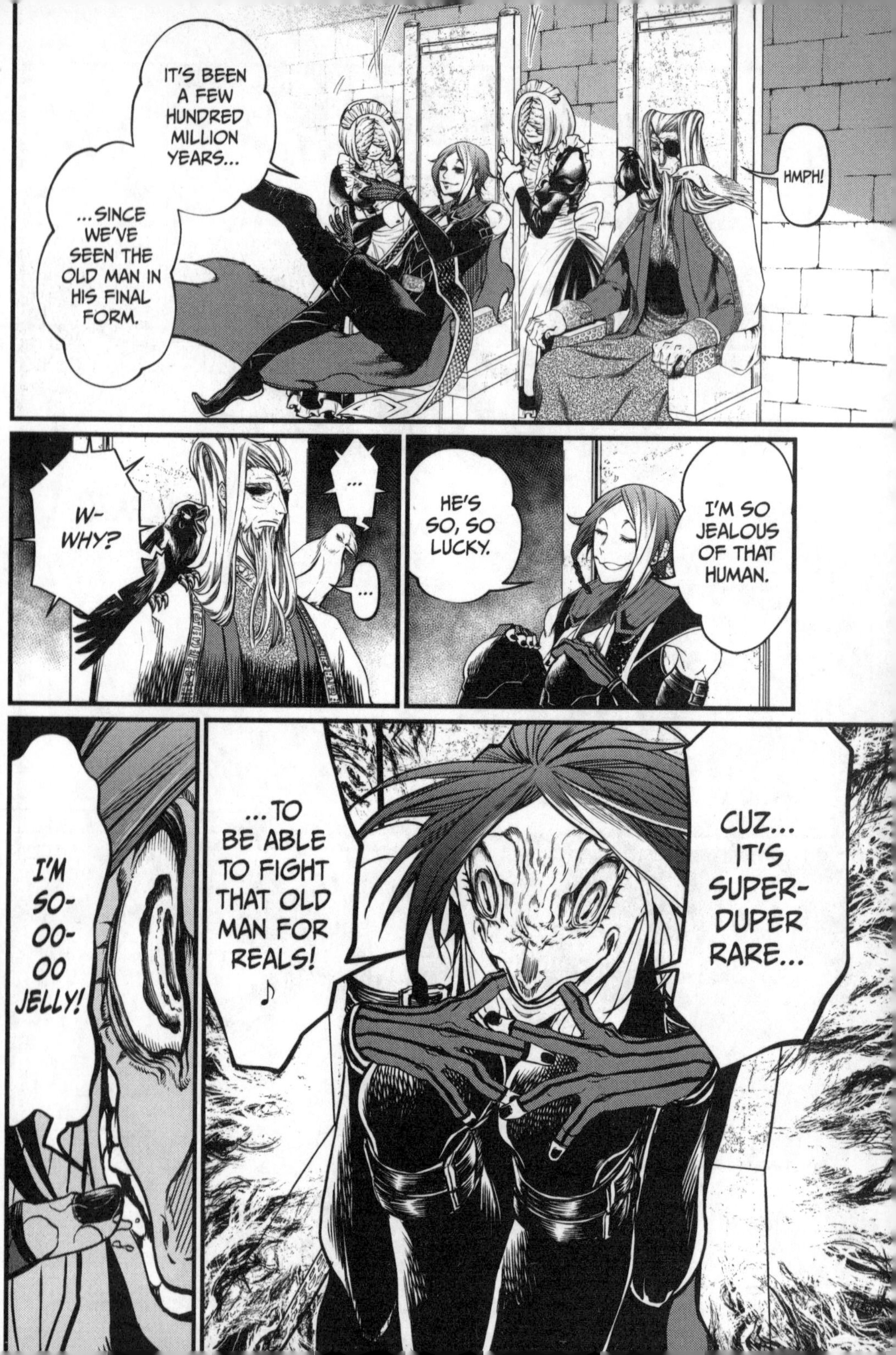
IT'S BEEN A FEW HUNDRED MILLION YEARS...
...SINCE WE'VE SEEN THE OLD MAN IN HIS FINAL FORM.
HMPH!
I'M SO JEALOUS OF THAT HUMAN.
HE'S SO, SO LUCKY.
...
...
W-WHY?
CUZ... IT'S SUPER-DUPER RARE...
...TO BE ABLE TO FIGHT THAT OLD MAN FOR REALS! ♪
I'M SO-OO-OO JELLY!

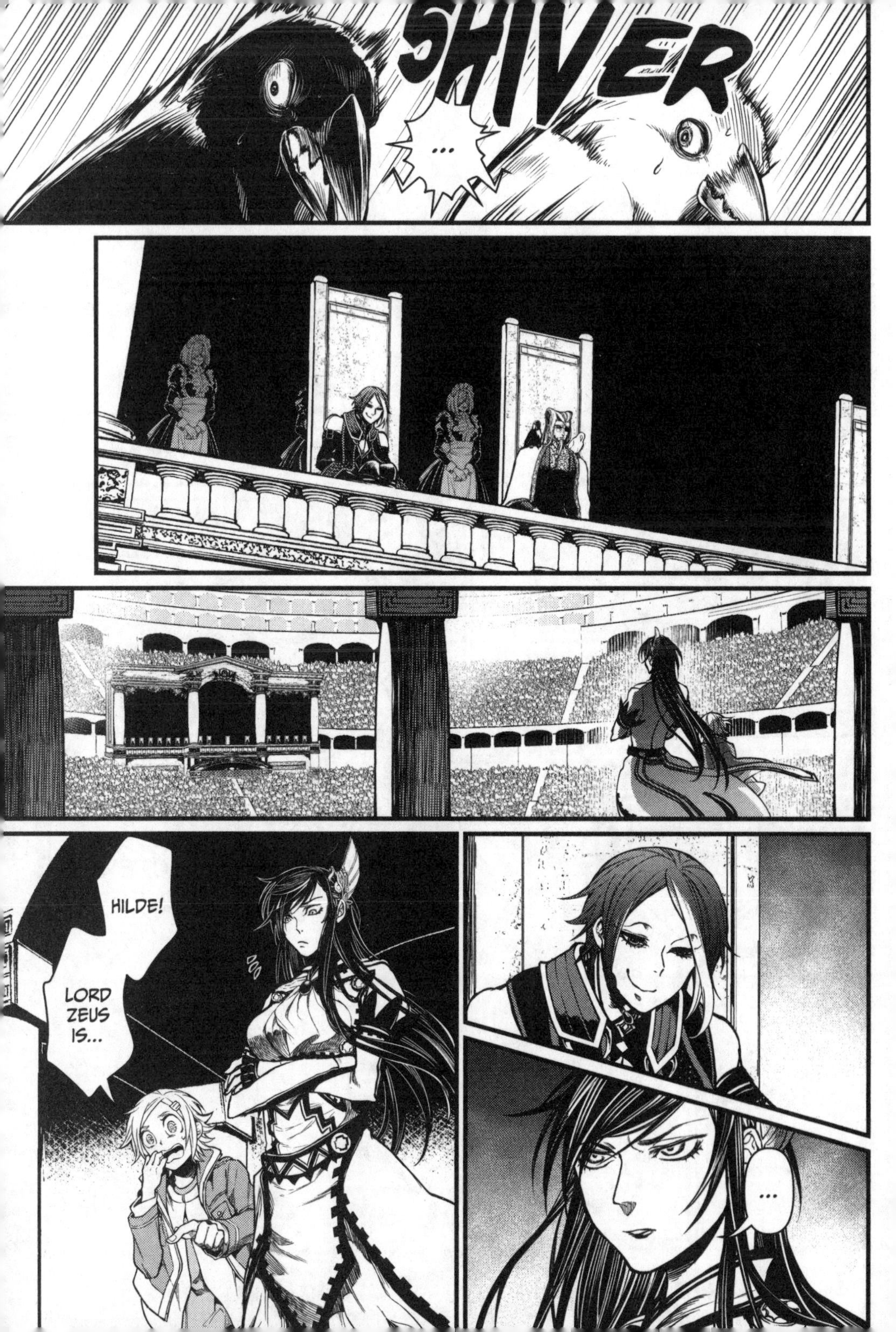
SHIVER
...
...
HILDE!
LORD ZEUS IS...

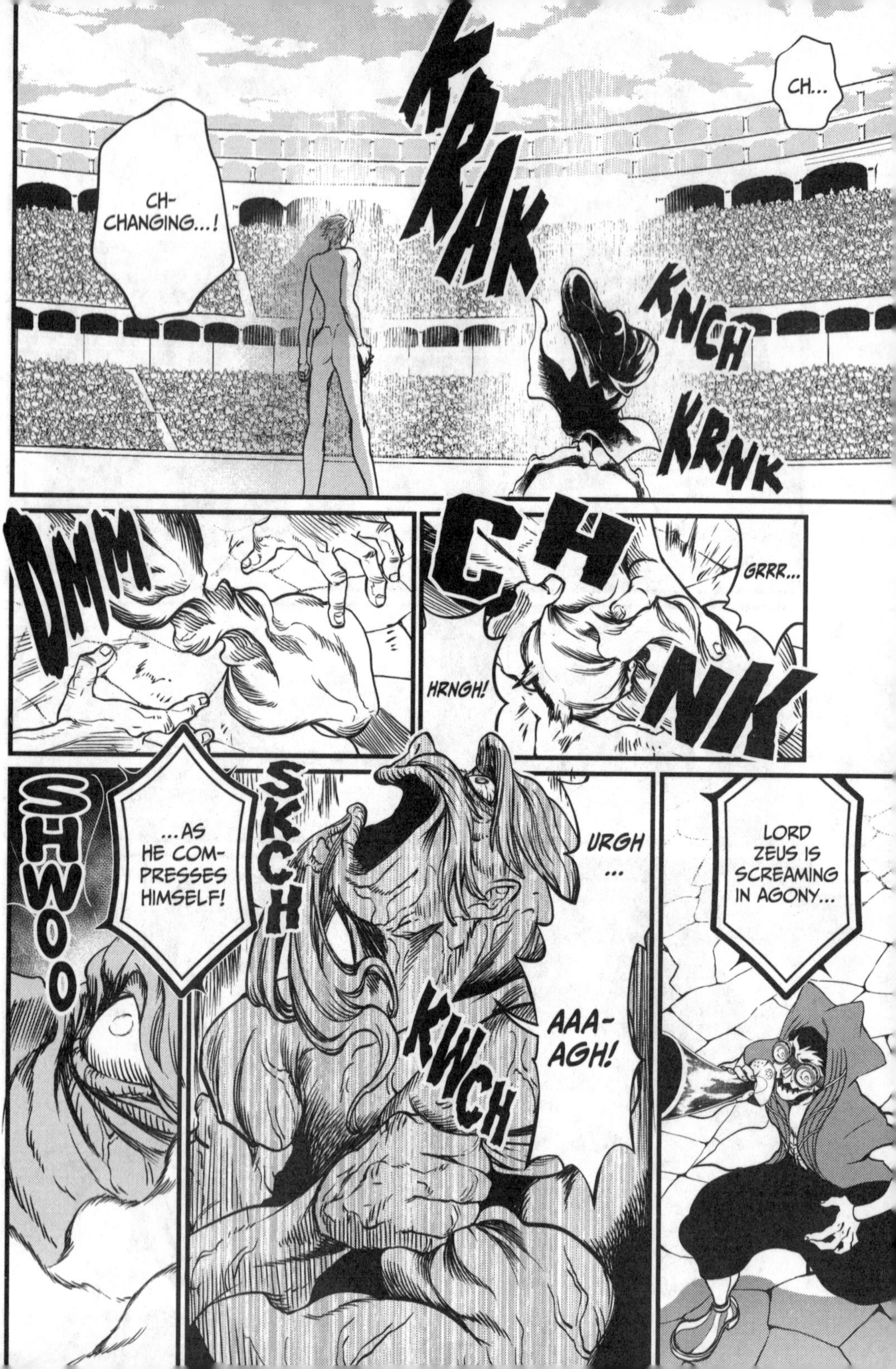
CH...
KRAK
KNCH
KRNK
CH-CHANGING...!
CHNK
GRRR...
HRNGH!
DMM
LORD ZEUS IS SCREAMING IN AGONY...
URGH...
AAA-AGH!
KWCH
SKCH
...AS HE COM-PRESSES HIMSELF!
SHWOO

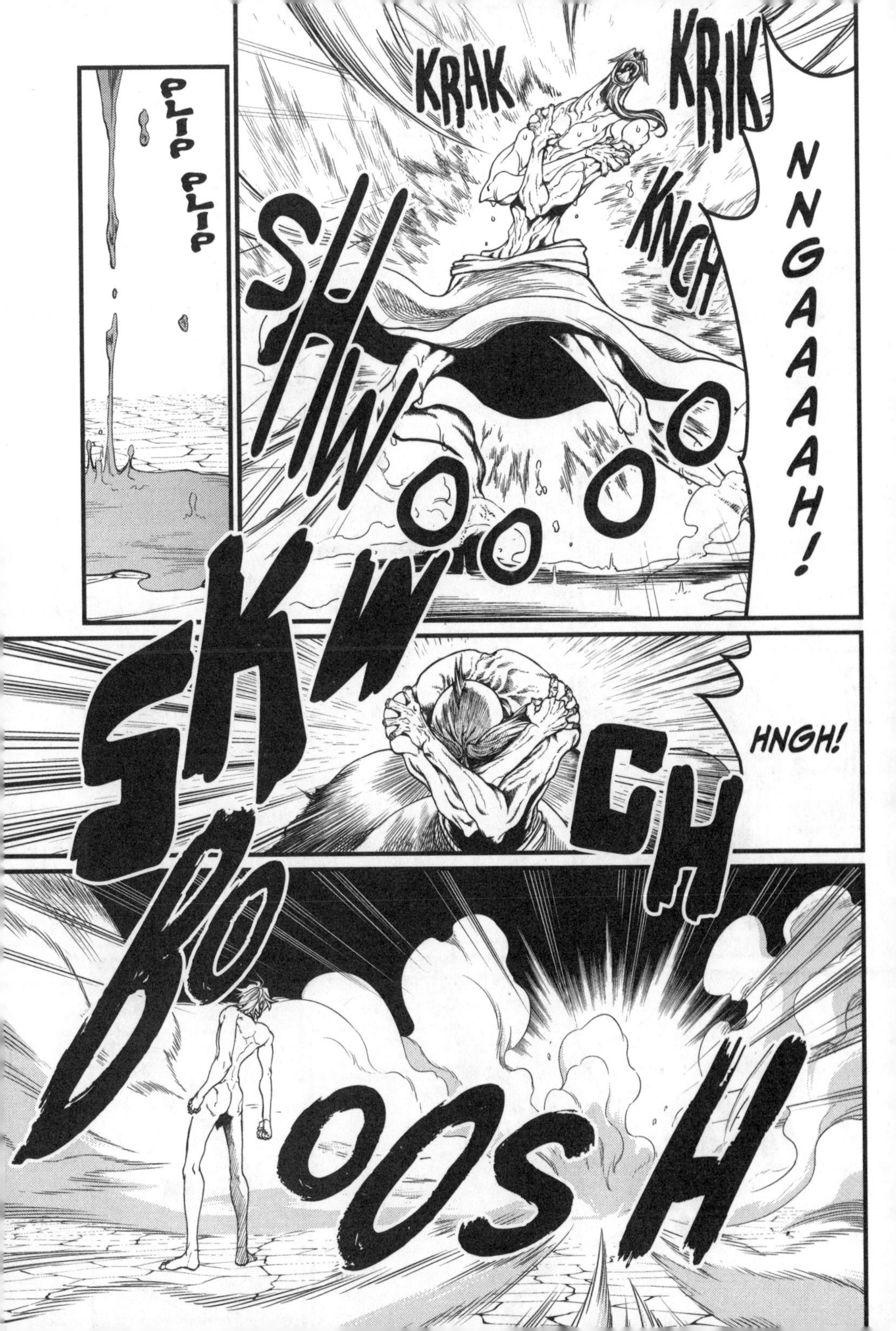
KRAK
KRIK
KNCH
NNGAAAAAH!
SHWOOOO
PLIP PLIP PLIP
HNGH!
SKWCH
BOOOOSH

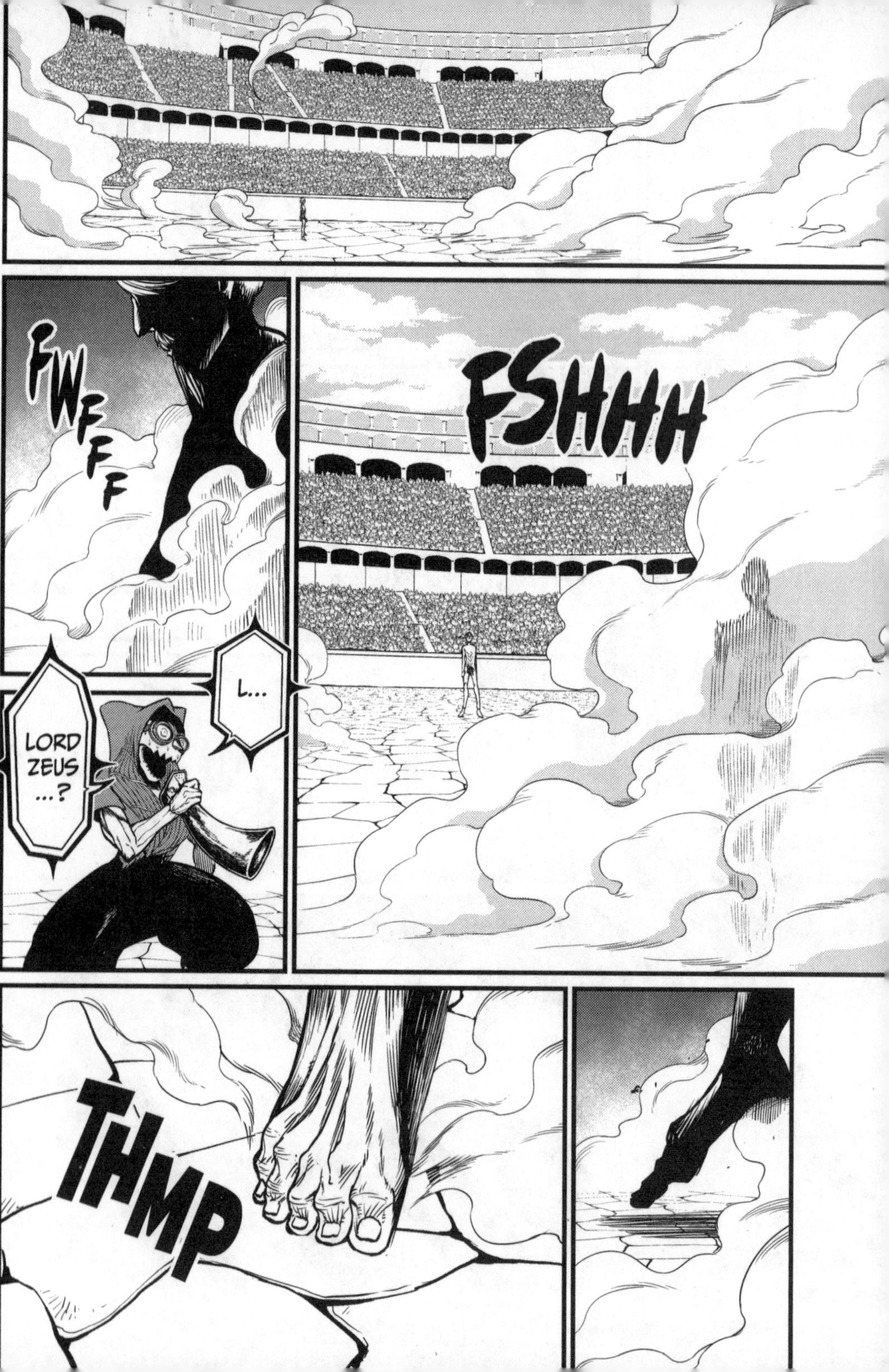
FSHHH
FWFFF
L...
LORD ZEUS ...?
THMP

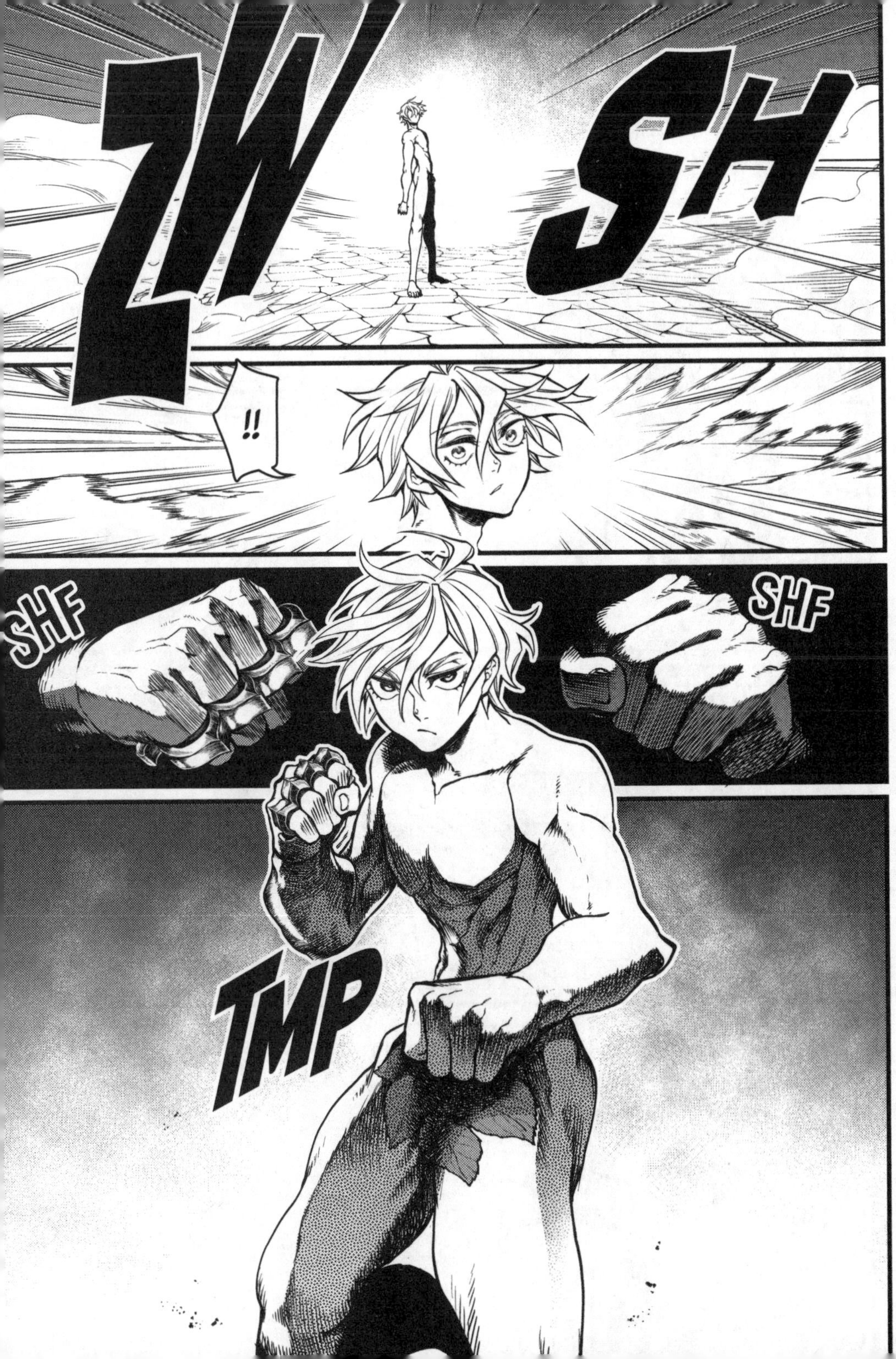
ZW SH
!!
SHF
SHF
TMP

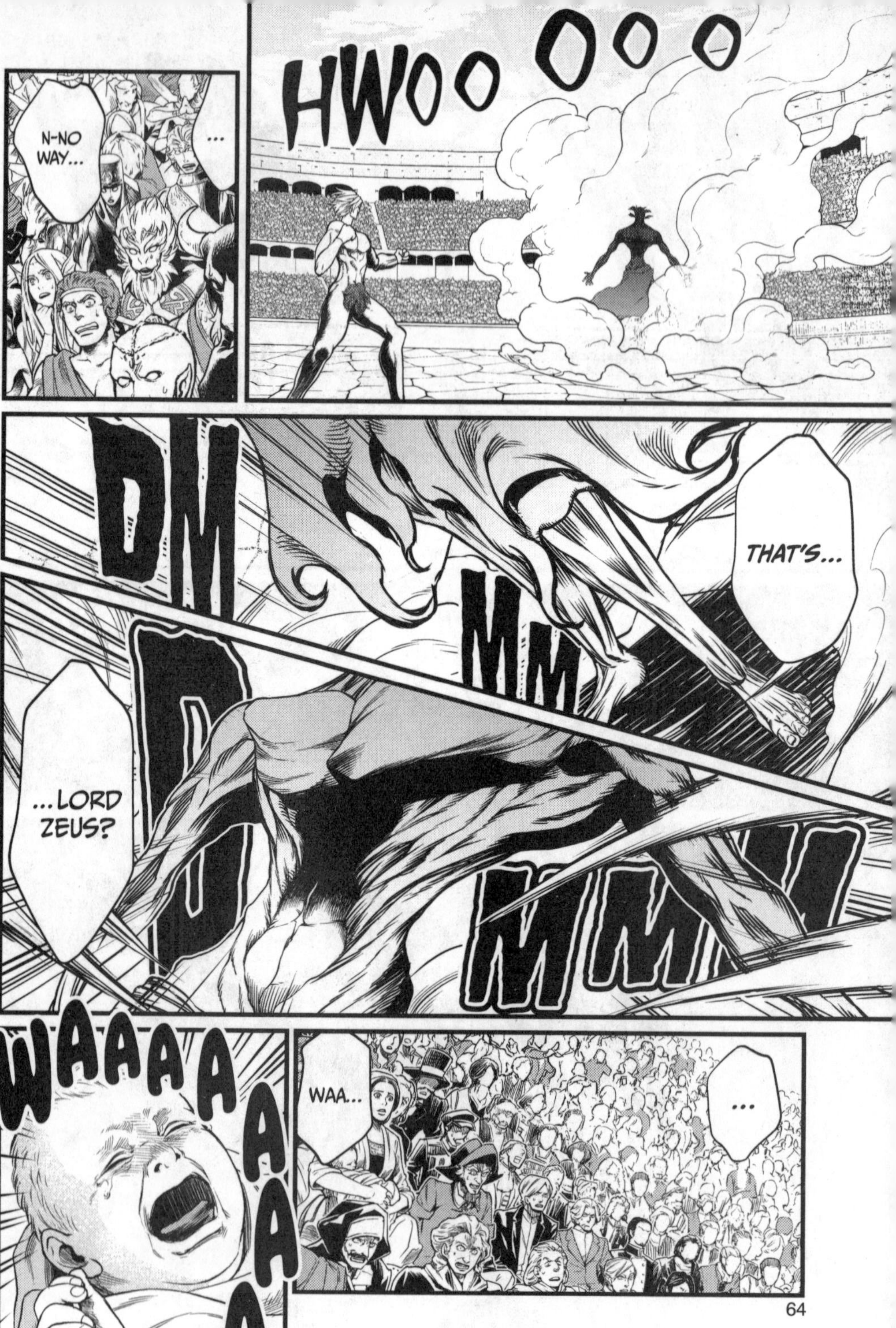
HWOO OOO
...
N-NO WAY...
THAT'S...
DM MM
...LORD ZEUS?
D MMMM
...
WAA...
WAAAAAAAA

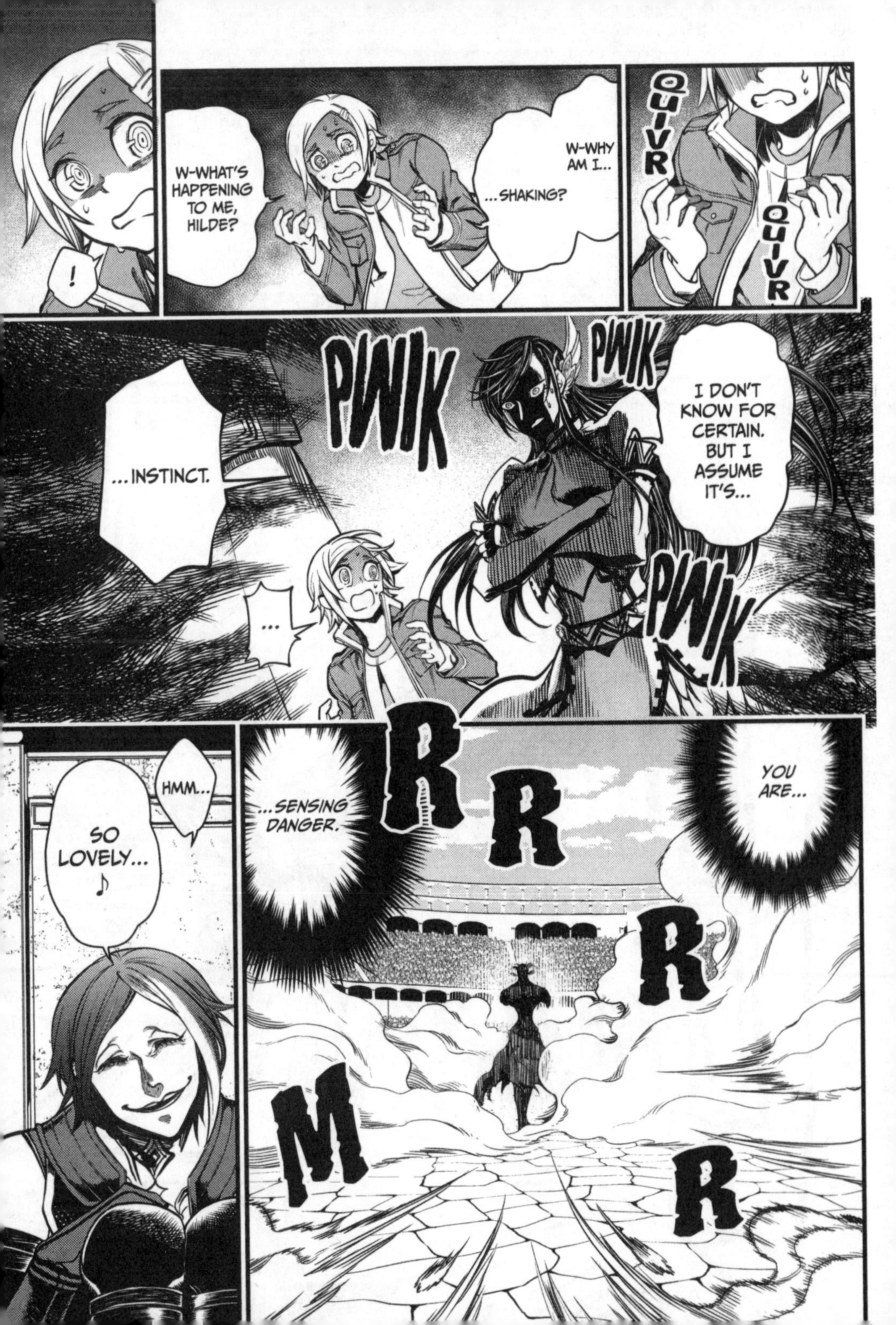
QUIVR
QUIVR
W-WHAT'S HAPPENING TO ME, HILDE?
W-WHY AM I...
...SHAKING?
!
PWIK
PWIK
I DON'T KNOW FOR CERTAIN. BUT I ASSUME IT'S...
...INSTINCT.
...
PWIK
YOU ARE...
...SENSING DANGER.
RRRRMR
HMM...
SO LOVELY... ♪

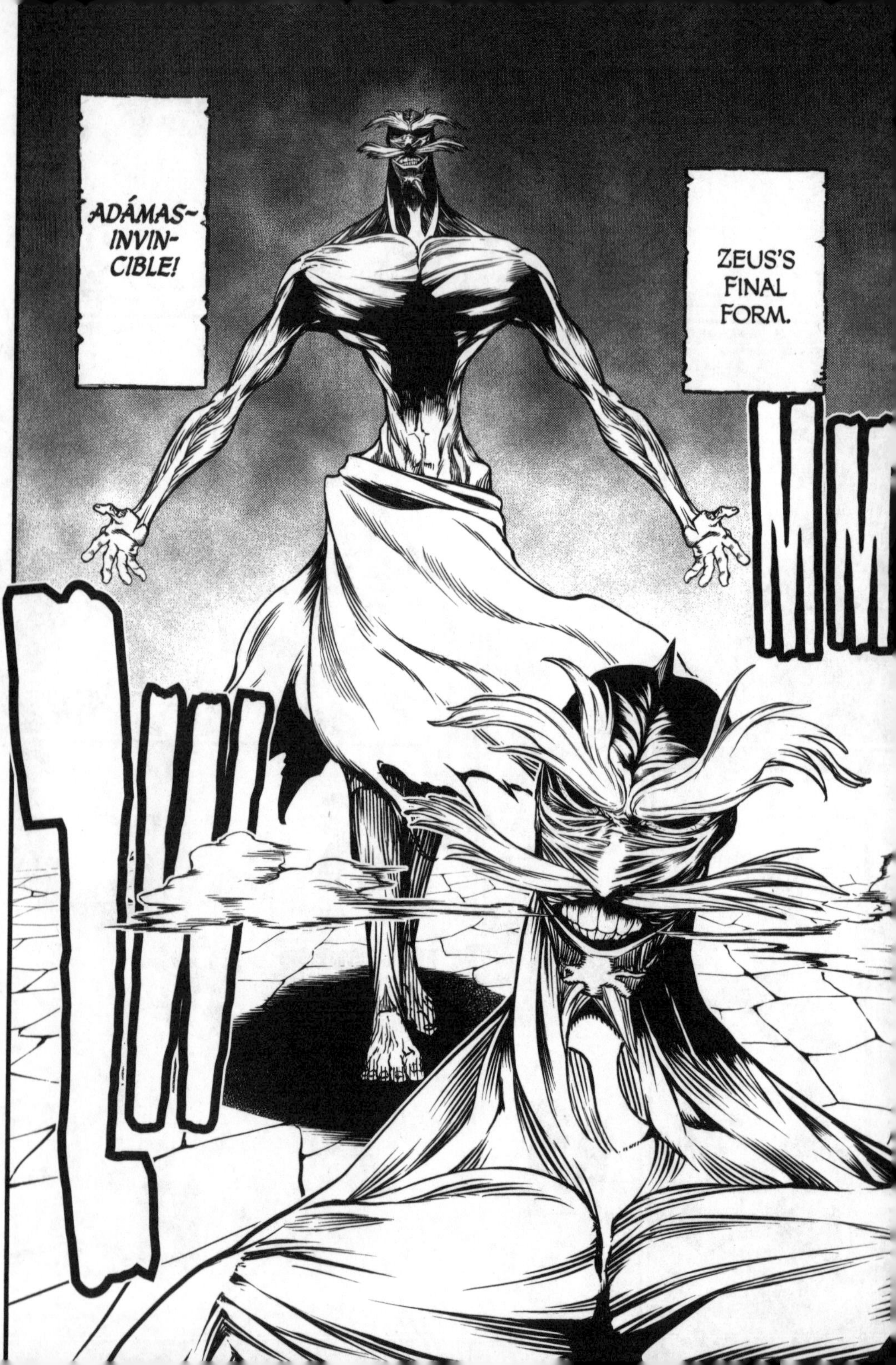
ZEUS'S FINAL FORM.
ADÁMAS-INVINCIBLE!

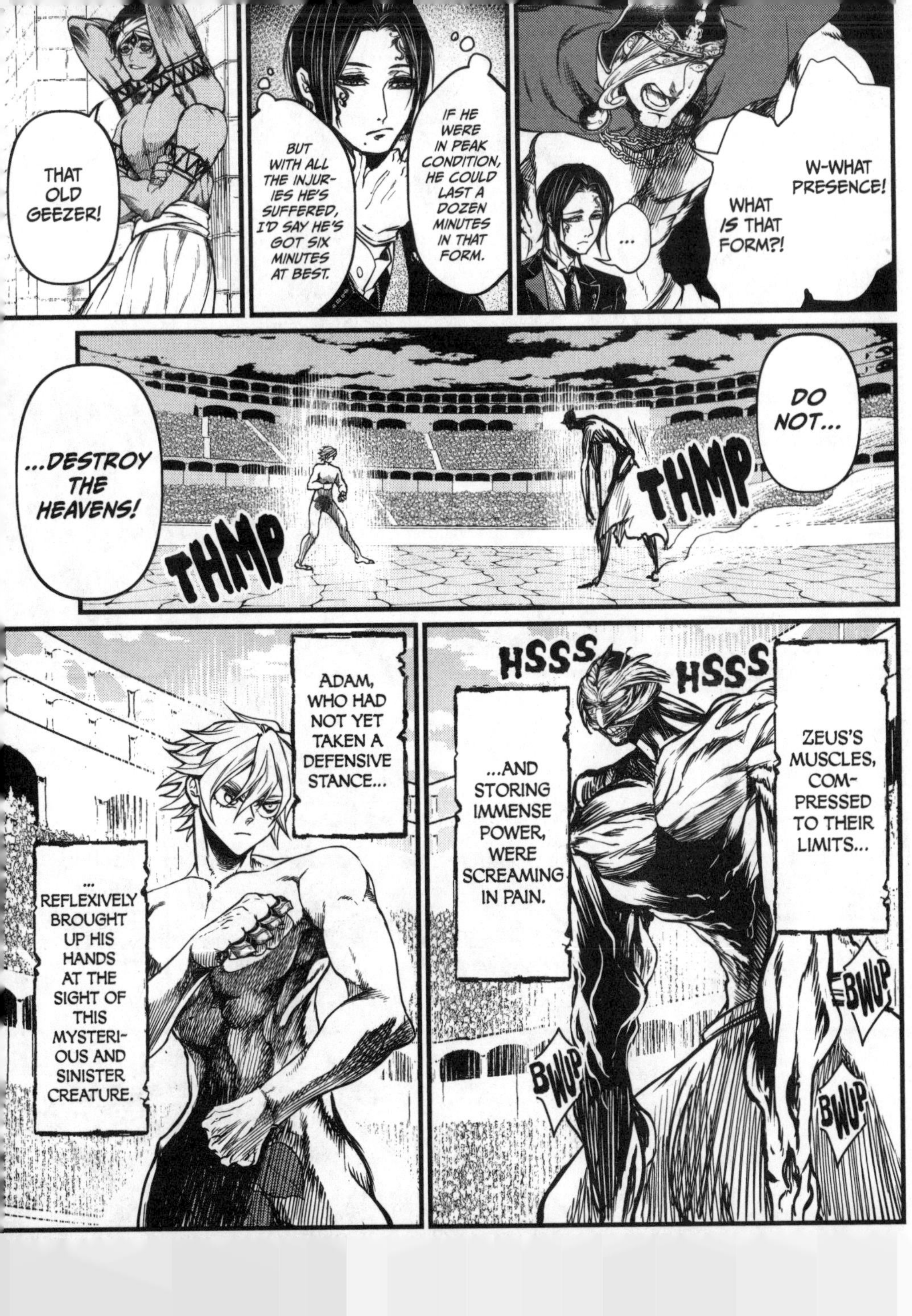
W-WHAT PRESENCE!
WHAT IS THAT FORM?!
...
IF HE WERE IN PEAK CONDITION, HE COULD LAST A DOZEN MINUTES IN THAT FORM.
BUT WITH ALL THE INJURIES HE'S SUFFERED, I'D SAY HE'S GOT SIX MINUTES AT BEST.
THAT OLD GEEZER!
DO NOT...
THMP
...DESTROY THE HEAVENS!
THMP
ZEUS'S MUSCLES, COMPRESSED TO THEIR LIMITS...
HSSS
HSSS
...AND STORING IMMENSE POWER, WERE SCREAMING IN PAIN.
BWUP
BWUP
BWUP
ADAM, WHO HAD NOT YET TAKEN A DEFENSIVE STANCE...
...REFLEXIVELY BROUGHT UP HIS HANDS AT THE SIGHT OF THIS MYSTERIOUS AND SINISTER CREATURE.

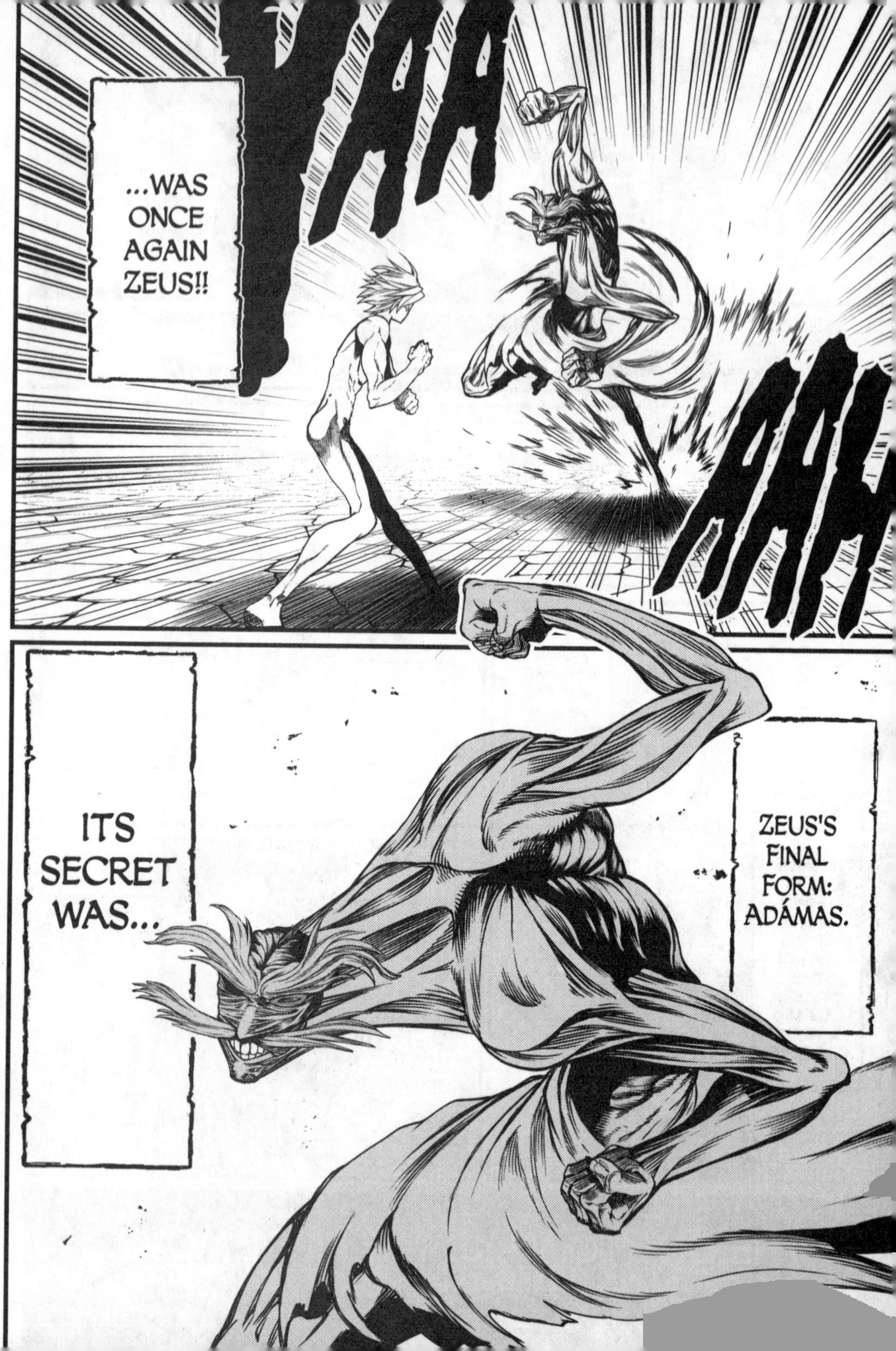
...WAS ONCE AGAIN ZEUS!!
ZEUS'S FINAL FORM: ADÁMAS.
ITS SECRET WAS...

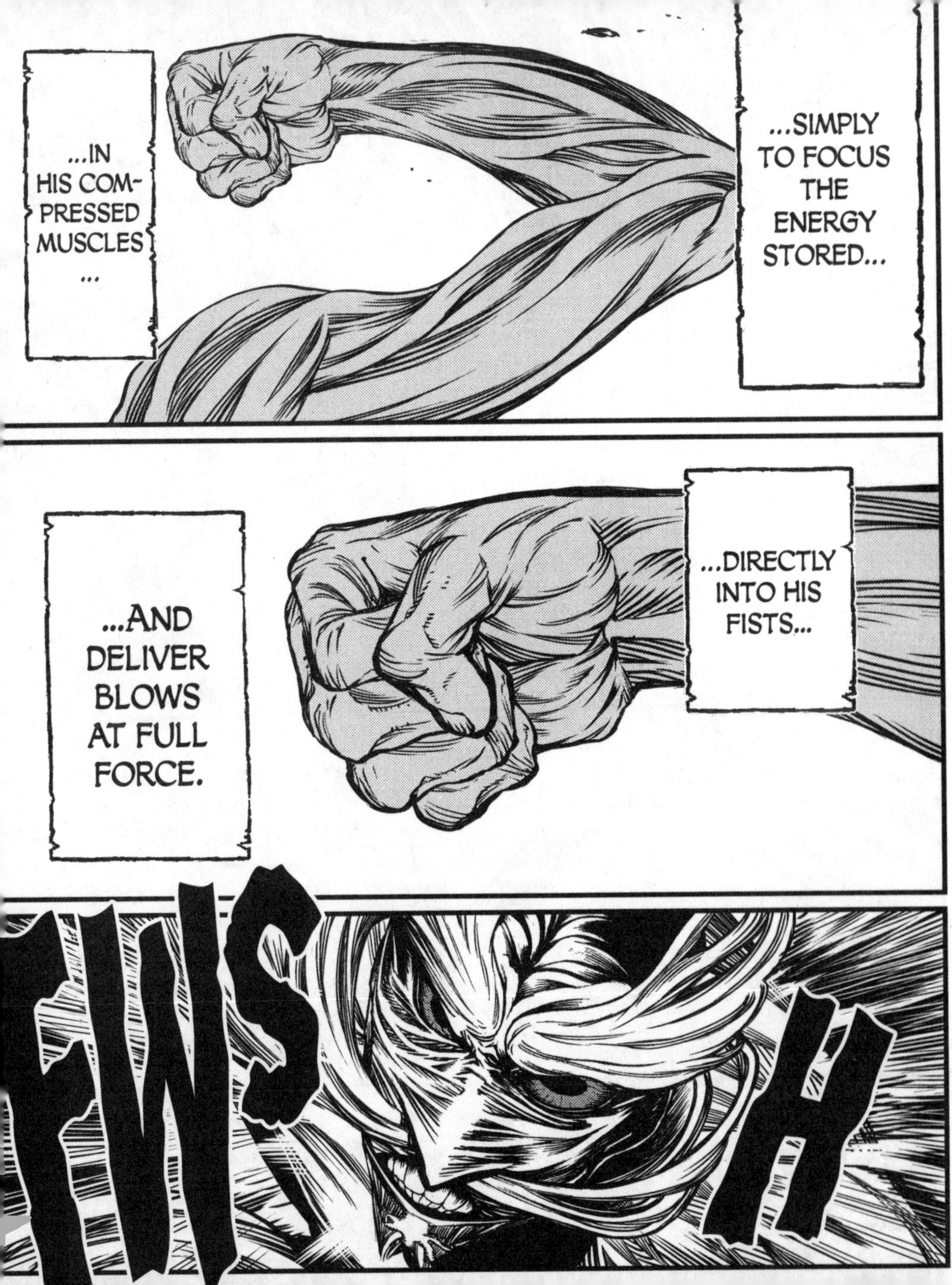
...SIMPLY TO FOCUS THE ENERGY STORED...
...IN HIS COMPRESSED MUSCLES...
...DIRECTLY INTO HIS FISTS...
...AND DELIVER BLOWS AT FULL FORCE.
FWSH

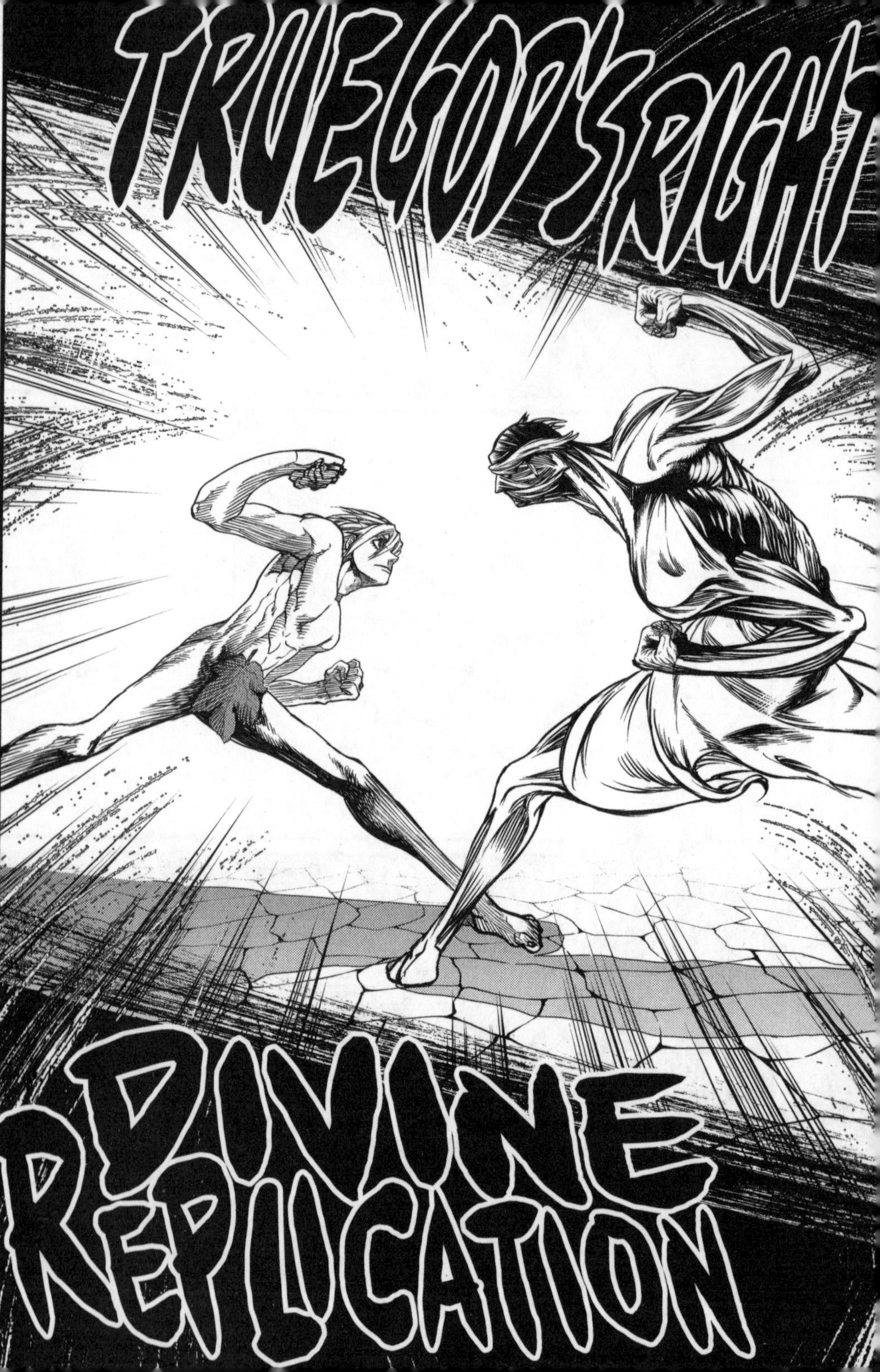
TRUE GOD'S RIGHT
DIVINE REPLICATION

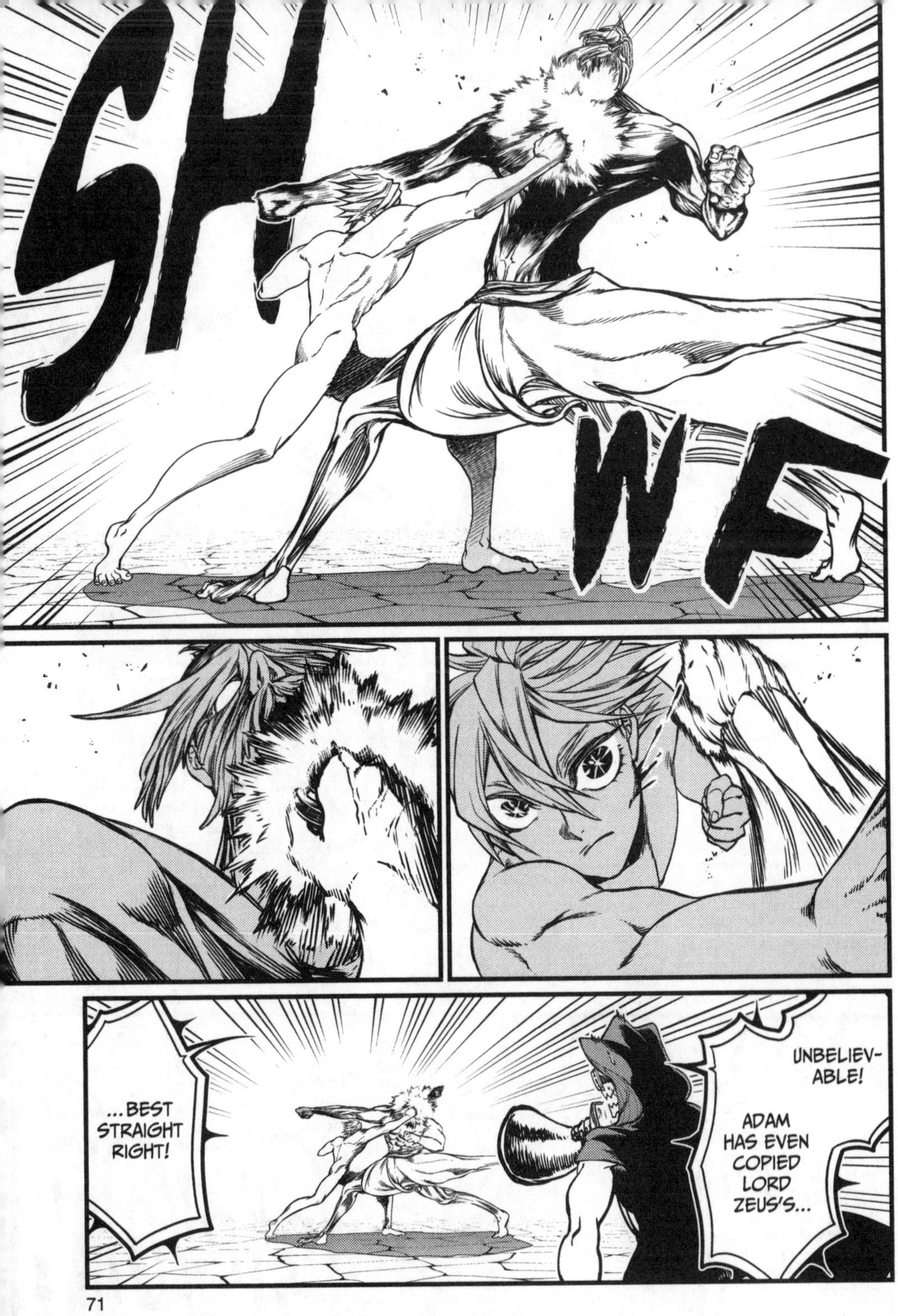
SHWF
UNBELIEVABLE!
ADAM HAS EVEN COPIED LORD ZEUS'S...
...BEST STRAIGHT RIGHT!

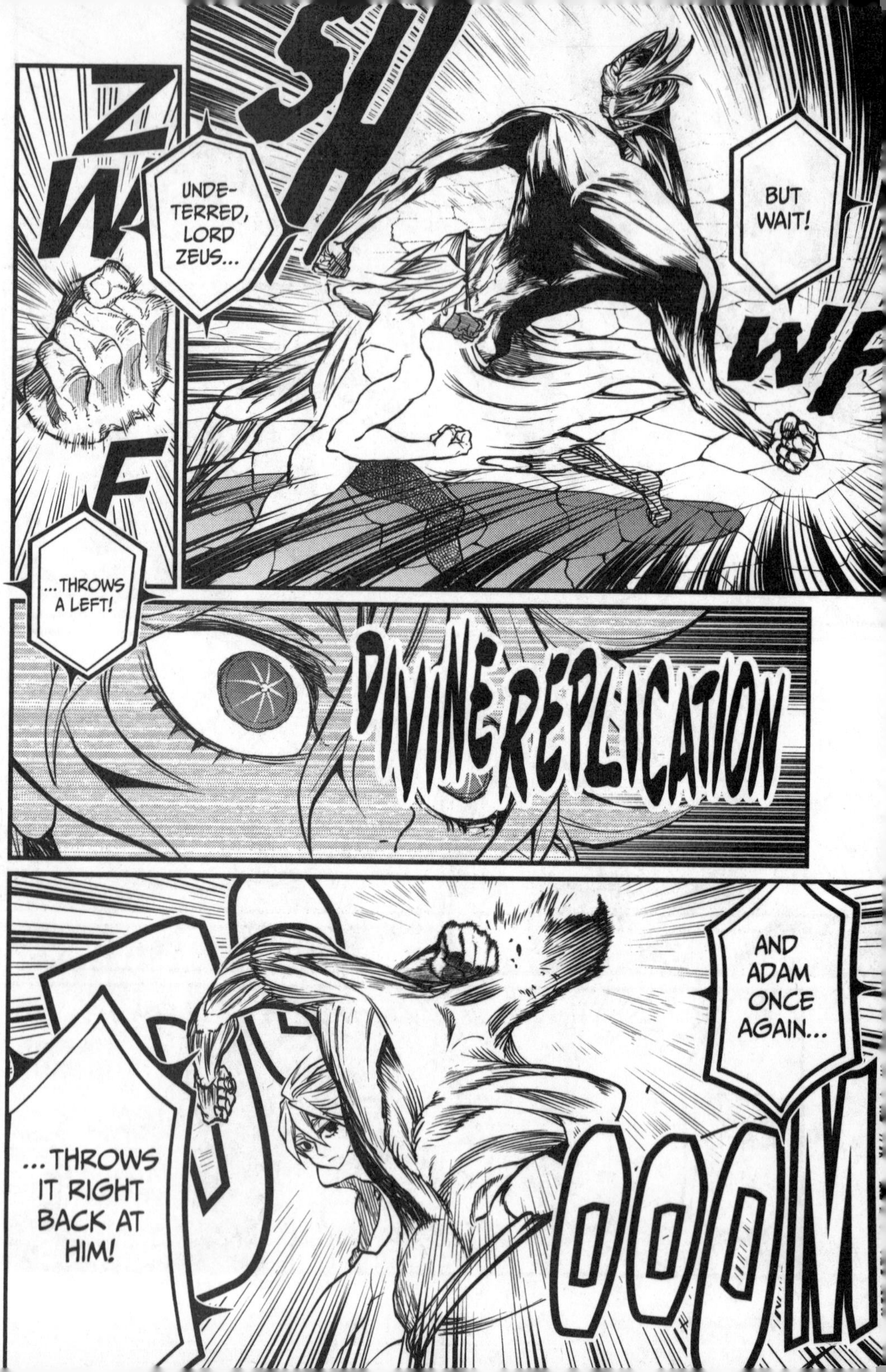
BUT WAIT!
SH
WF
UNDE-TERRED, LORD ZEUS...
ZW
F
...THROWS A LEFT!
DIVINE REPLICATION
AND ADAM ONCE AGAIN...
OOOM
...THROWS IT RIGHT BACK AT HIM!

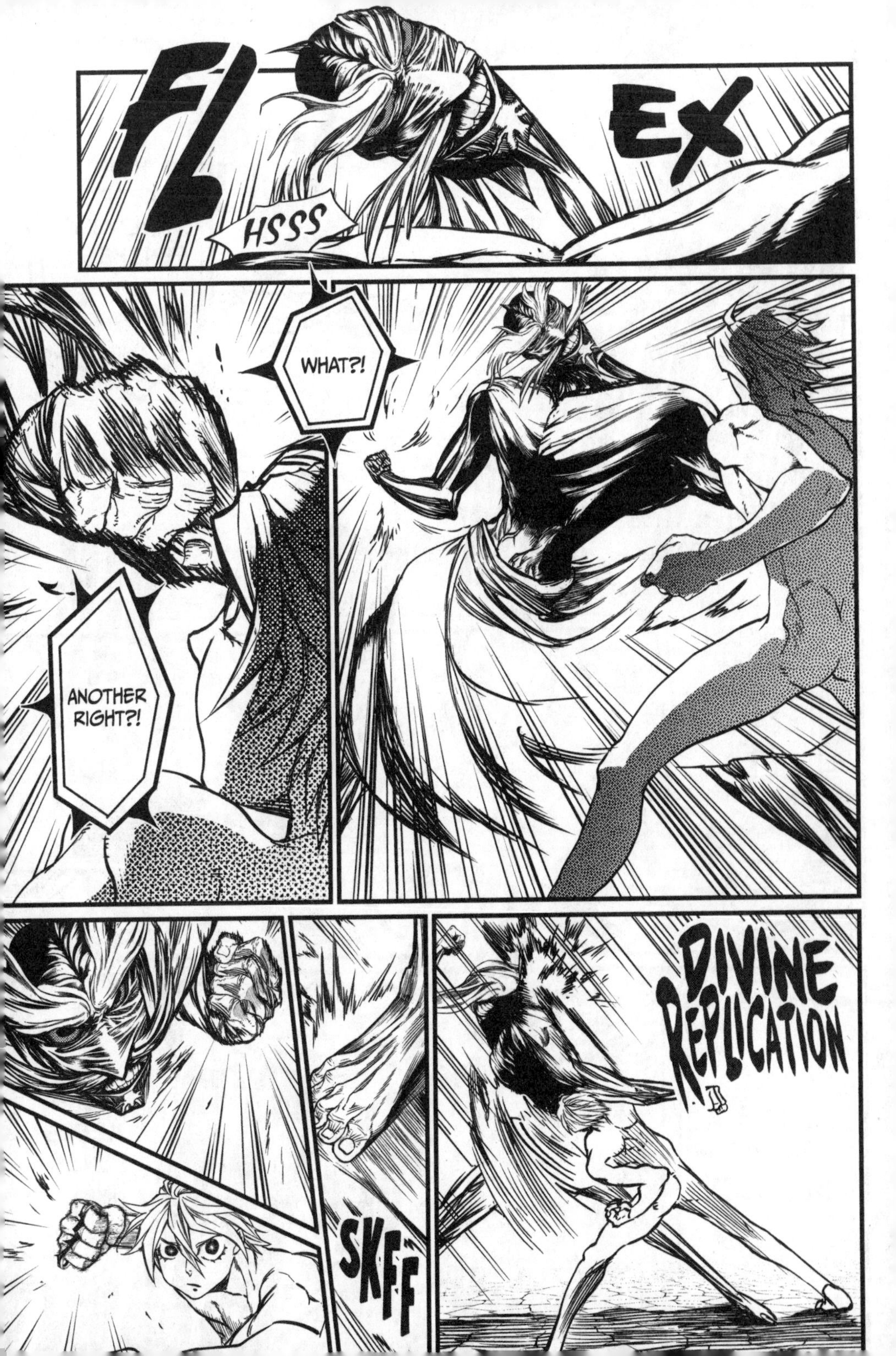
FLEX
HSSS
WHAT?!
ANOTHER RIGHT?!
DIVINE REPLICATION
SKFF

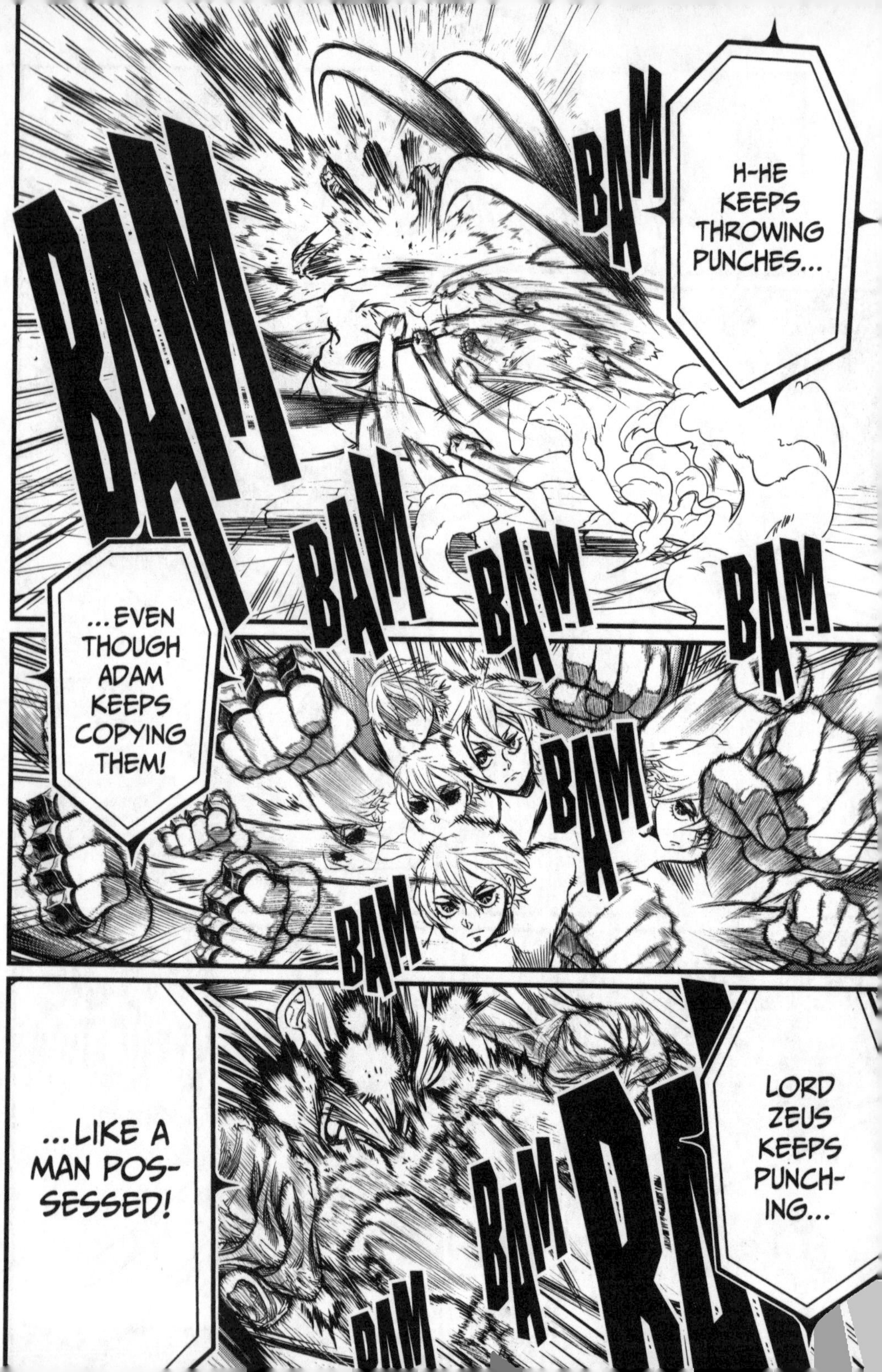
H-HE KEEPS THROWING PUNCHES...
BAM
BAM
BAM
BAM
BAM
...EVEN THOUGH ADAM KEEPS COPYING THEM!
BAM
BAM
BAM
LORD ZEUS KEEPS PUNCHING...
BAM
BAM
...LIKE A MAN POSSESSED!

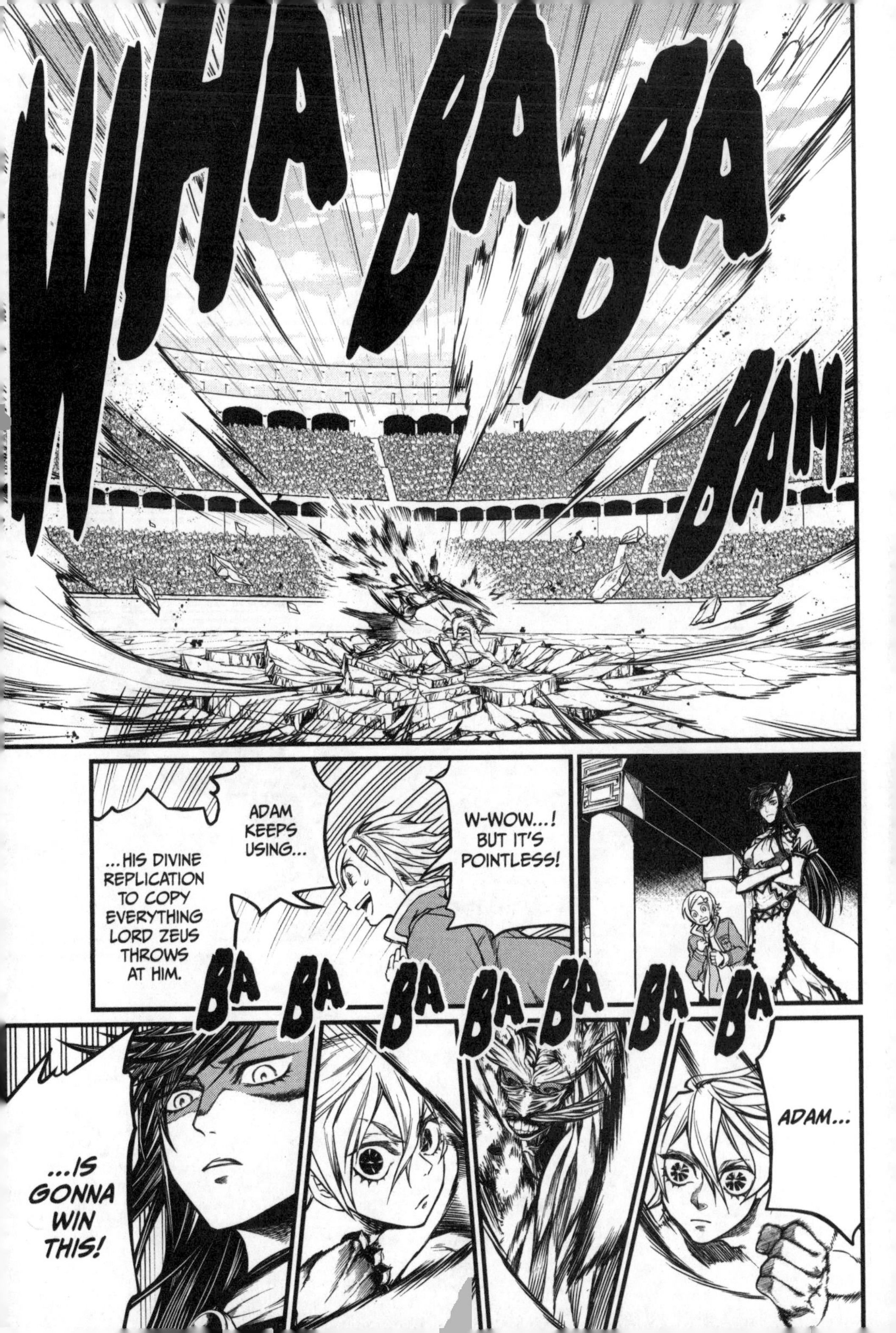
WHA BA BA BAM!
W-WOW...! BUT IT'S POINTLESS!
ADAM KEEPS USING...
...HIS DIVINE REPLICATION TO COPY EVERYTHING LORD ZEUS THROWS AT HIM.
BA BA BA BA BA BA BA
ADAM...
...IS GONNA WIN THIS!

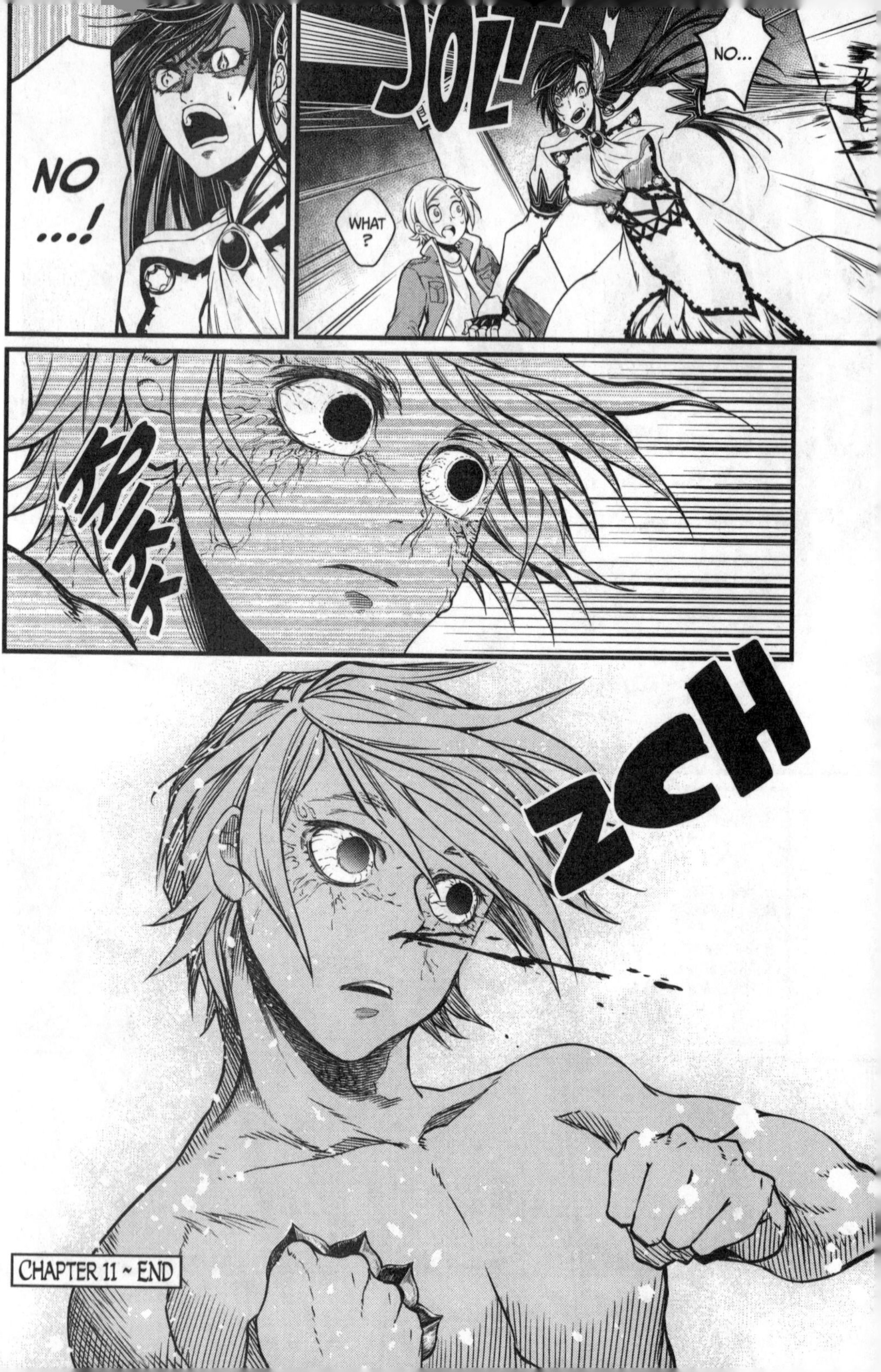
NO...
JOLT
WHAT ?
NO ...!
KRIKK
ZCH
CHAPTER 11 ~ END

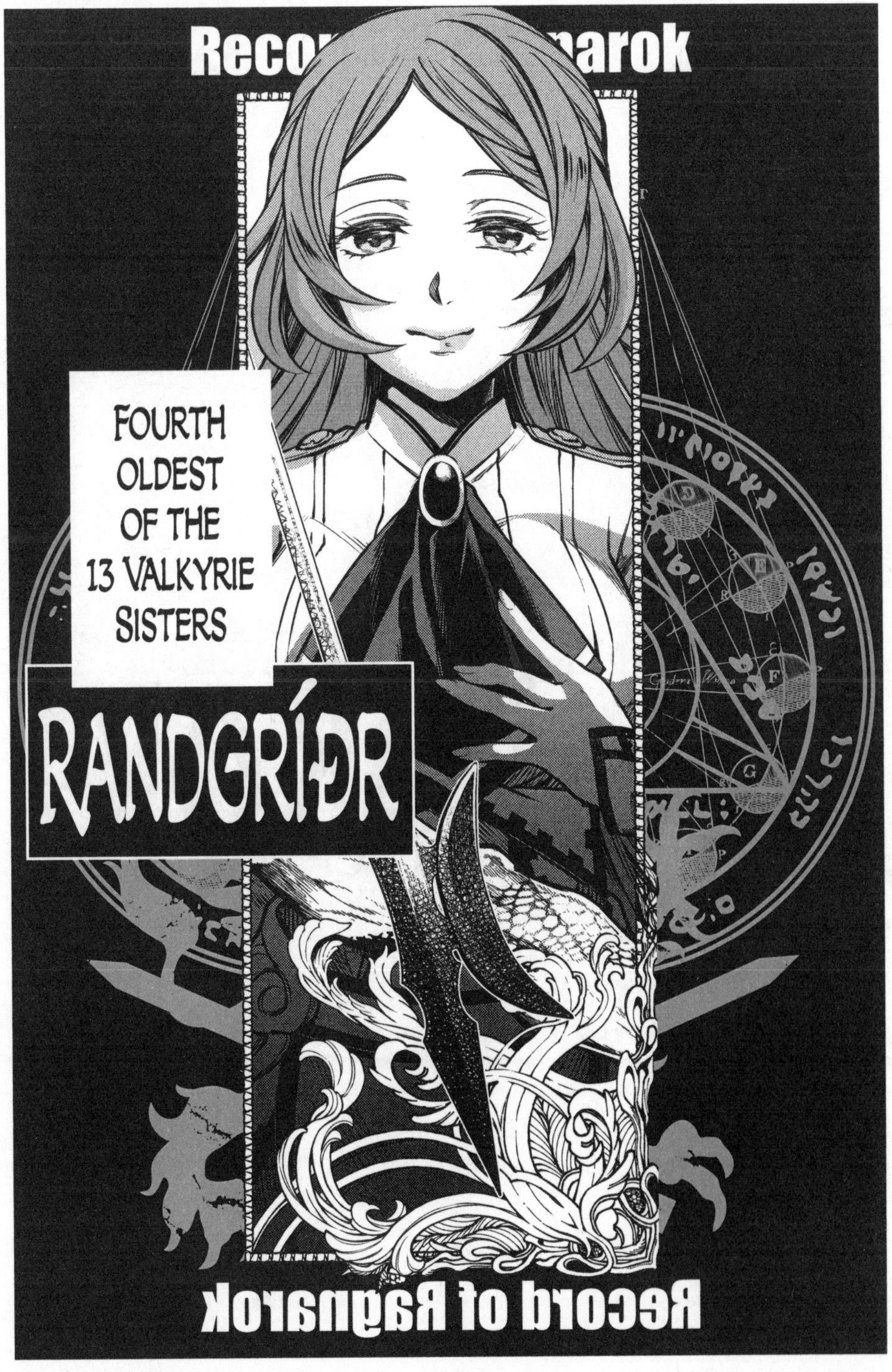
FOURTH OLDEST OF THE 13 VALKYRIE SISTERS
RANDGRÍÐR
Record of Ragnarok

RECORD OF RAGNAROK

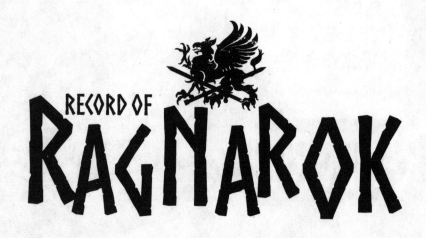

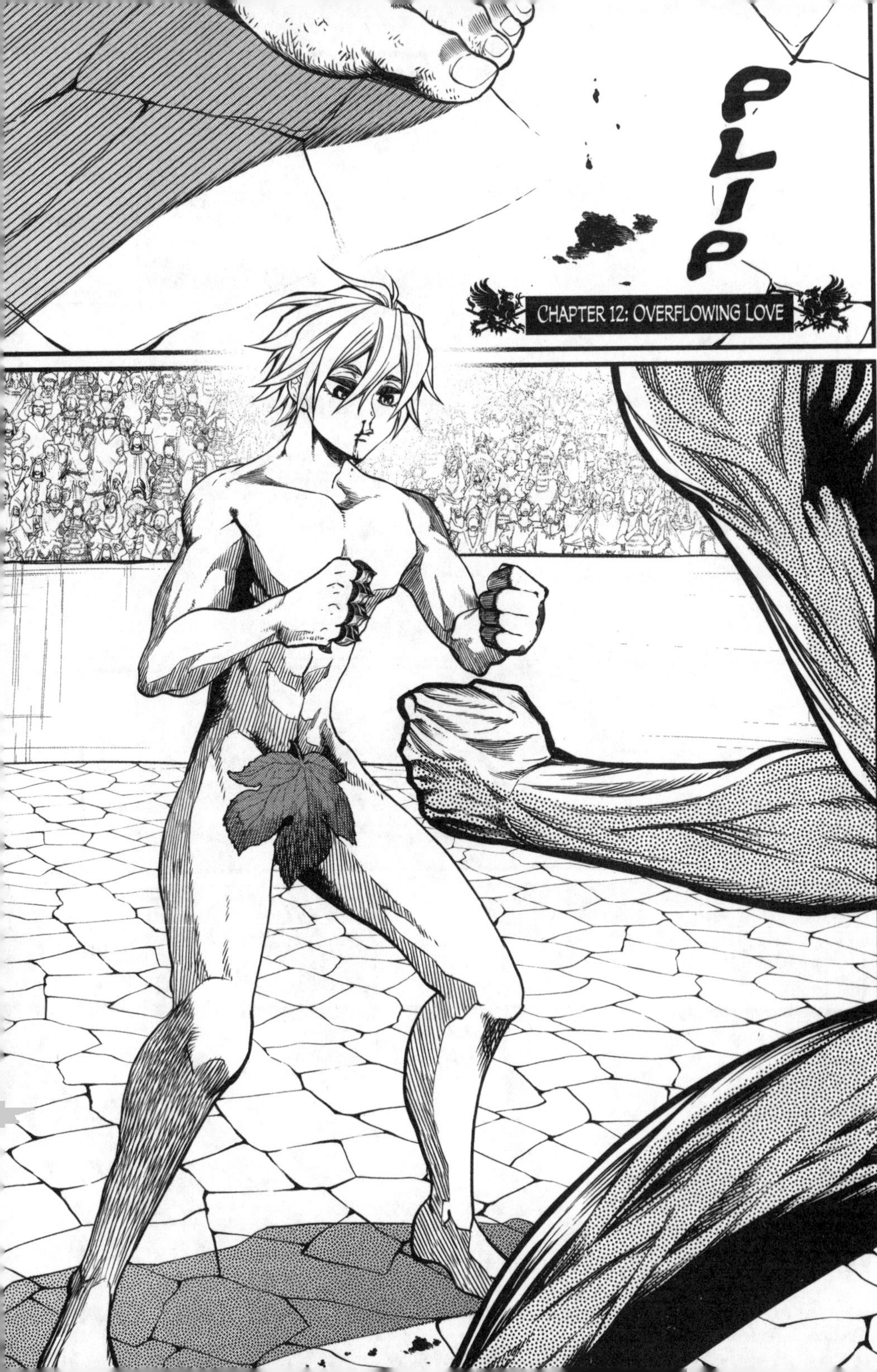
PLIP
CHAPTER 12: OVERFLOWING LOVE

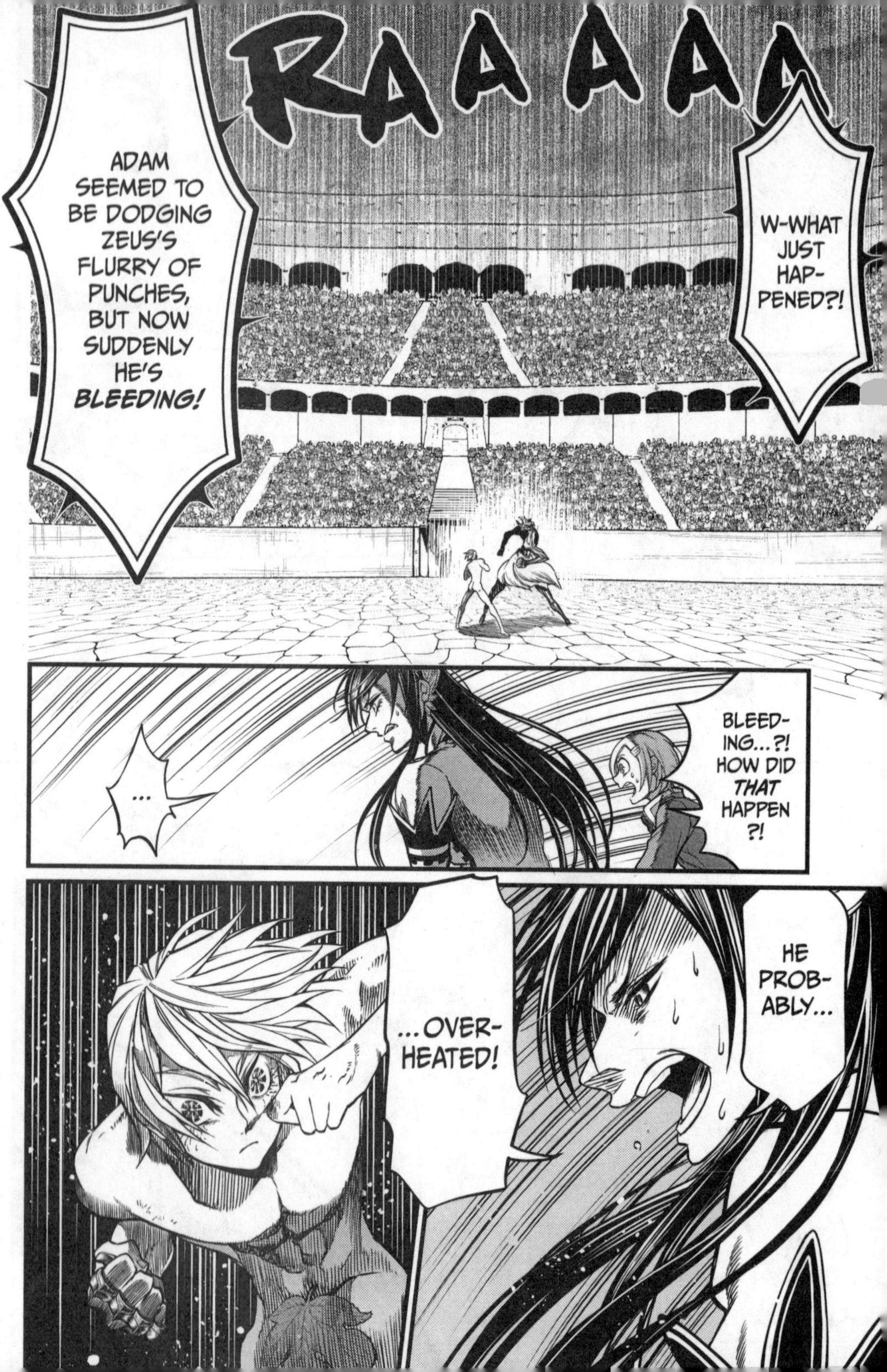
RAAAAA
W-WHAT JUST HAP-PENED?!
ADAM SEEMED TO BE DODGING ZEUS'S FLURRY OF PUNCHES, BUT NOW SUDDENLY HE'S *BLEEDING!*
BLEED-ING...?! HOW DID *THAT* HAPPEN?!
...
HE PROB-ABLY...
...OVER-HEATED!

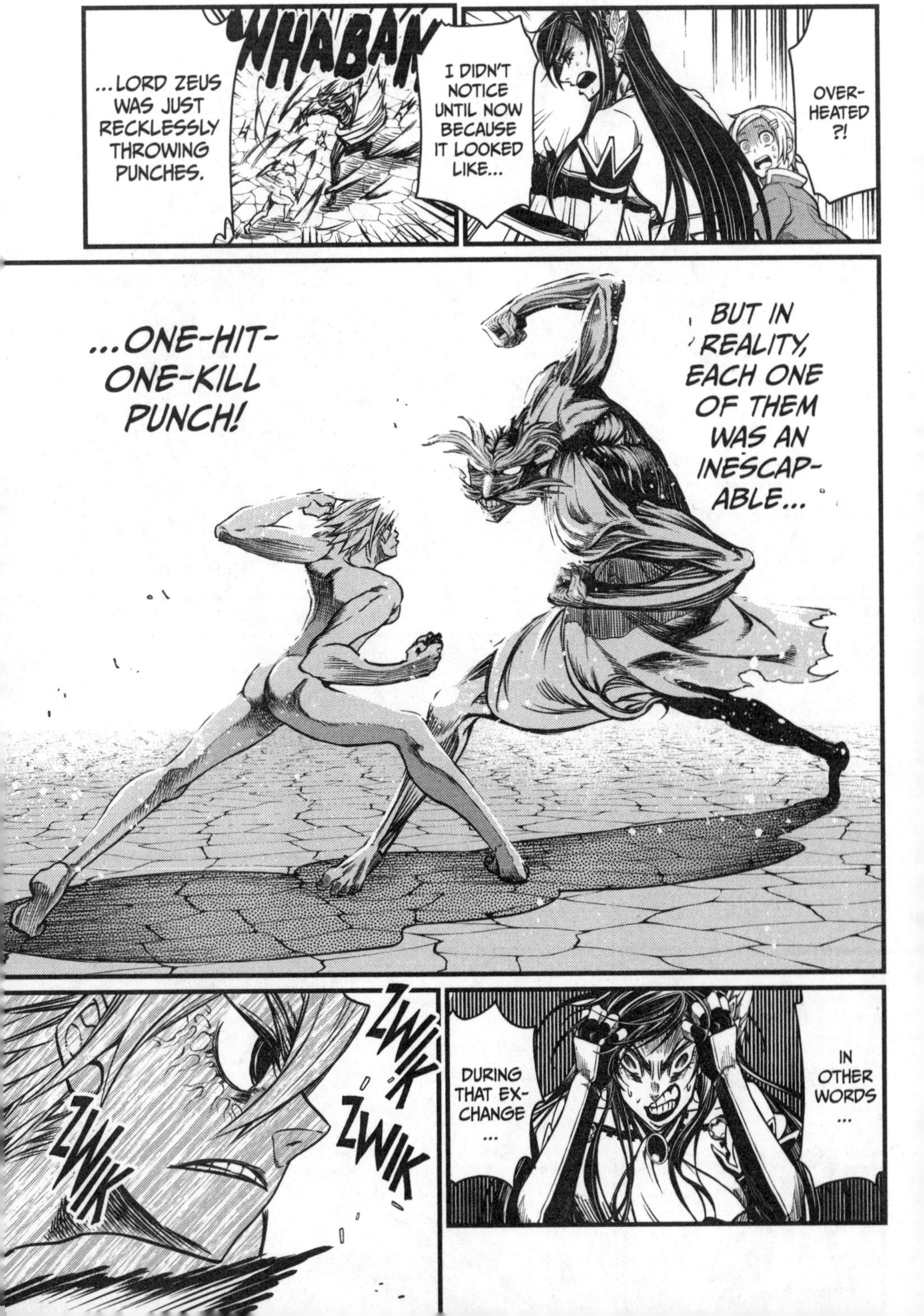
OVER-HEATED?!
I DIDN'T NOTICE UNTIL NOW BECAUSE IT LOOKED LIKE...
WHABAN
...LORD ZEUS WAS JUST RECKLESSLY THROWING PUNCHES.
BUT IN REALITY, EACH ONE OF THEM WAS AN INESCAP-ABLE...
...ONE-HIT-ONE-KILL PUNCH!
IN OTHER WORDS...
DURING THAT EX-CHANGE...
ZWIK
ZWIK
ZWIK

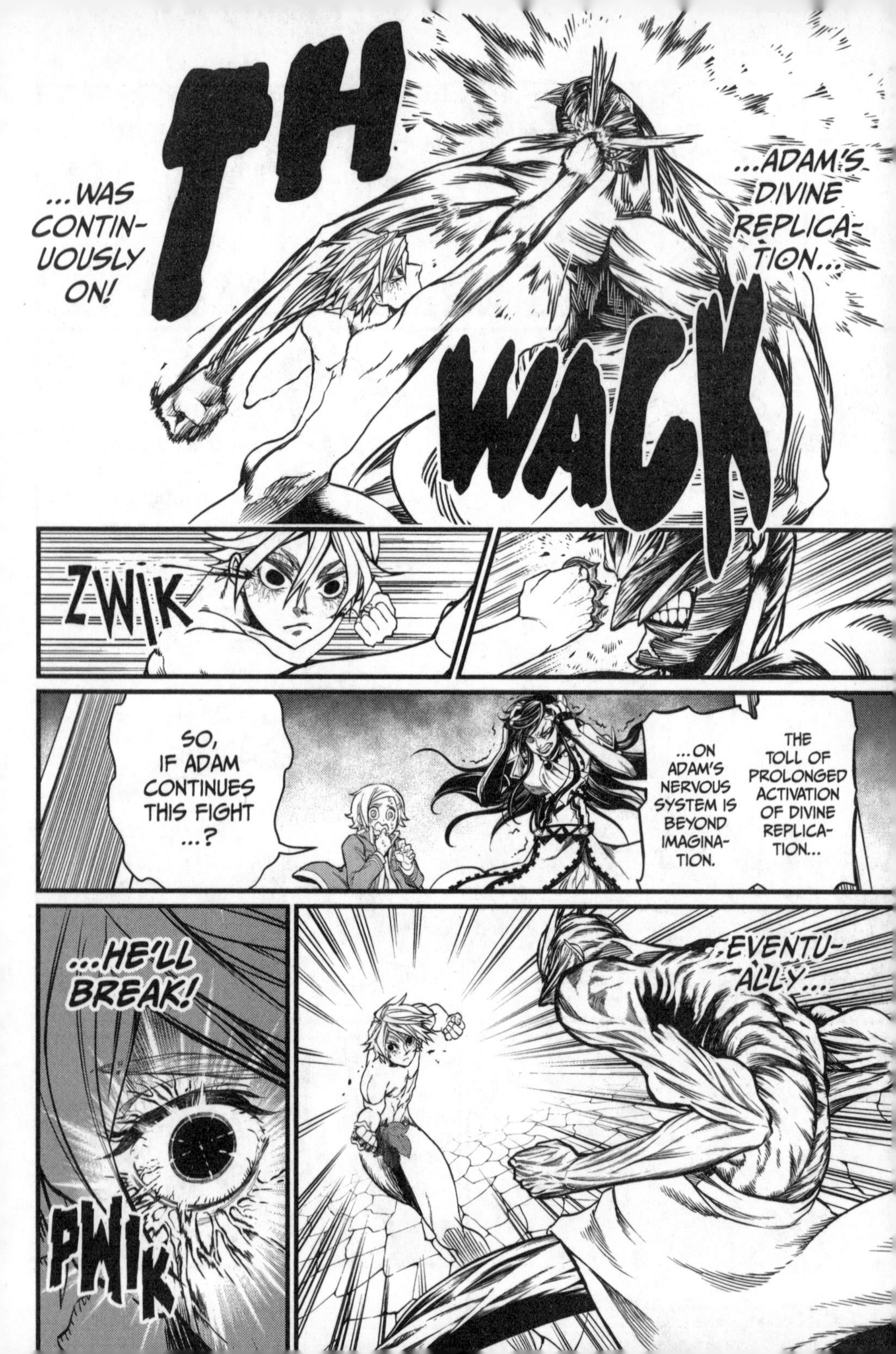

...ADAM'S DIVINE REPLICATION...
...WAS CONTINUOUSLY ON!
TH
WACK
ZWIK
THE TOLL OF PROLONGED ACTIVATION OF DIVINE REPLICATION...
...ON ADAM'S NERVOUS SYSTEM IS BEYOND IMAGINATION.
SO, IF ADAM CONTINUES THIS FIGHT ...?
EVENTUALLY...
...HE'LL BREAK!
PWIK

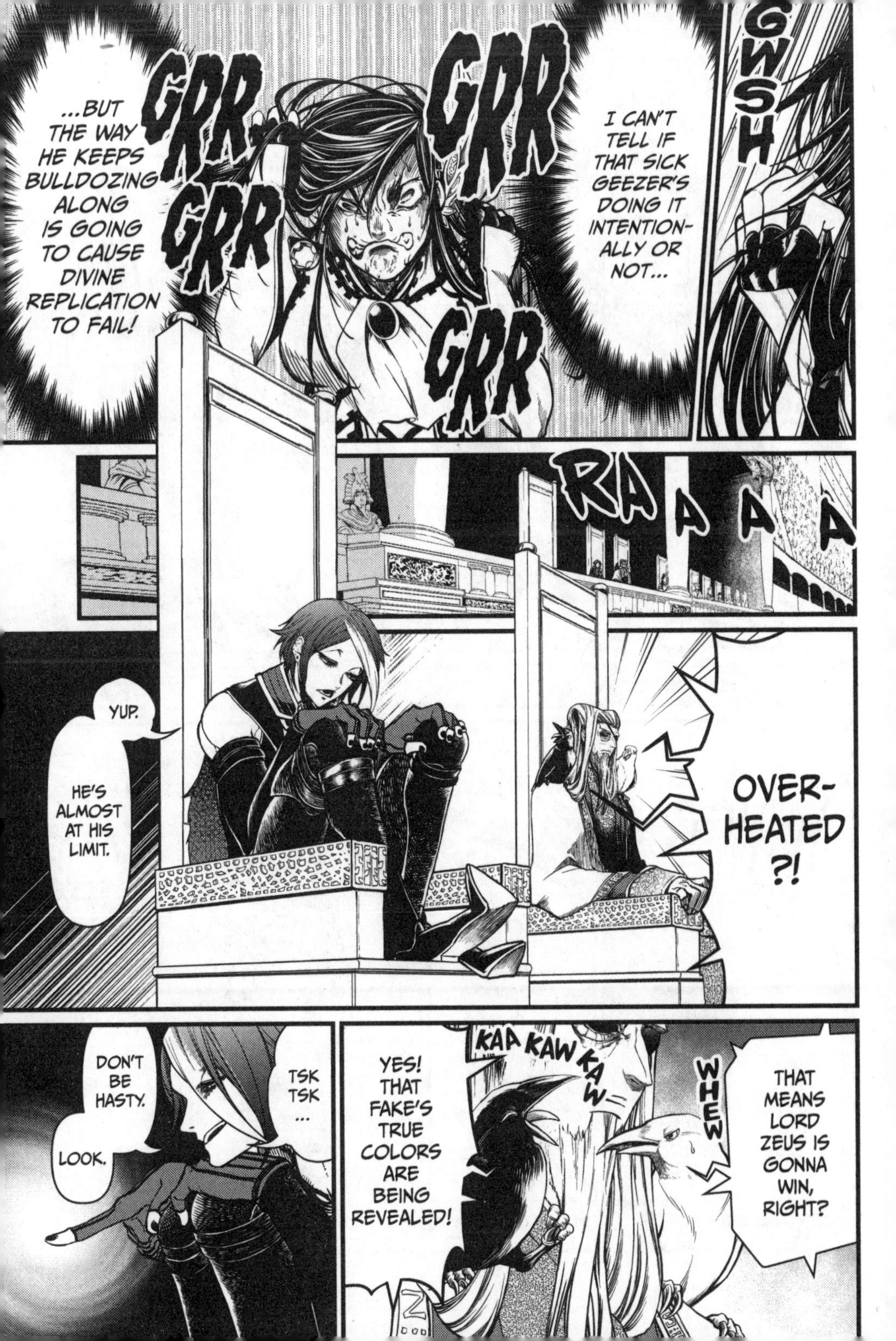
GWSH
I CAN'T TELL IF THAT SICK GEEZER'S DOING IT INTENTIONALLY OR NOT...
GRR GRR GRR GRR GRR
...BUT THE WAY HE KEEPS BULLDOZING ALONG IS GOING TO CAUSE DIVINE REPLICATION TO FAIL!
RAAAA
OVER-HEATED?!
YUP.
HE'S ALMOST AT HIS LIMIT.
THAT MEANS LORD ZEUS IS GONNA WIN, RIGHT?
WHEW
KAA KAW KAW
YES! THAT FAKE'S TRUE COLORS ARE BEING REVEALED!
TSK TSK...
DON'T BE HASTY.
LOOK.

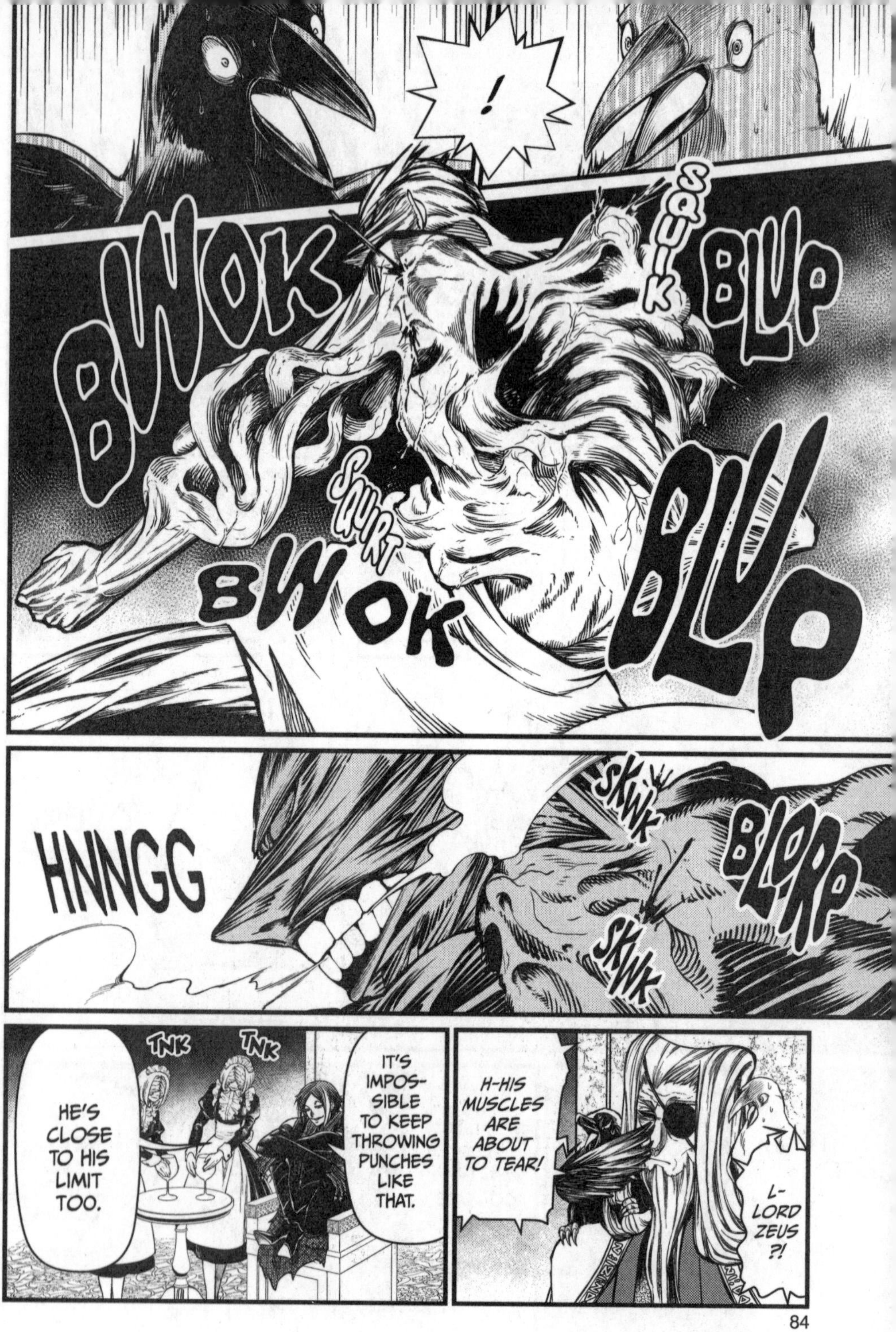
!
SQUIK
BLUP
BWOK
SQUIRT
BWOK
BLUP
BLORP
SKWK
SKWK
HNNGG
L-LORD ZEUS?!
H-HIS MUSCLES ARE ABOUT TO TEAR!
IT'S IMPOSSIBLE TO KEEP THROWING PUNCHES LIKE THAT.
TNK
TNK
HE'S CLOSE TO HIS LIMIT TOO.

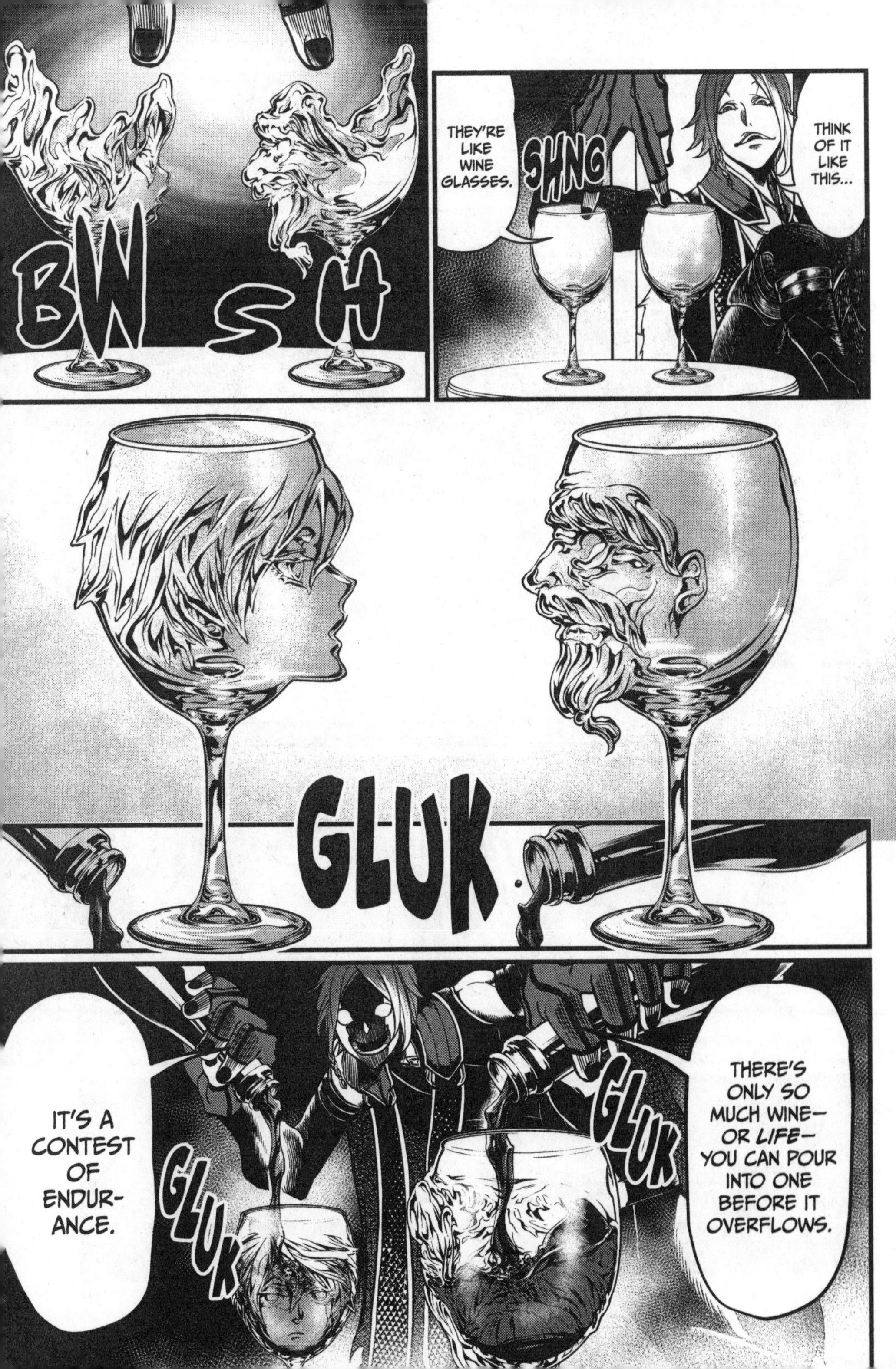
THINK OF IT LIKE THIS...
THEY'RE LIKE WINE GLASSES.
SHNG
BWSH
GLUK
THERE'S ONLY SO MUCH WINE—OR *LIFE*—YOU CAN POUR INTO ONE BEFORE IT OVERFLOWS.
GLUK
GLUK
IT'S A CONTEST OF ENDUR-ANCE.

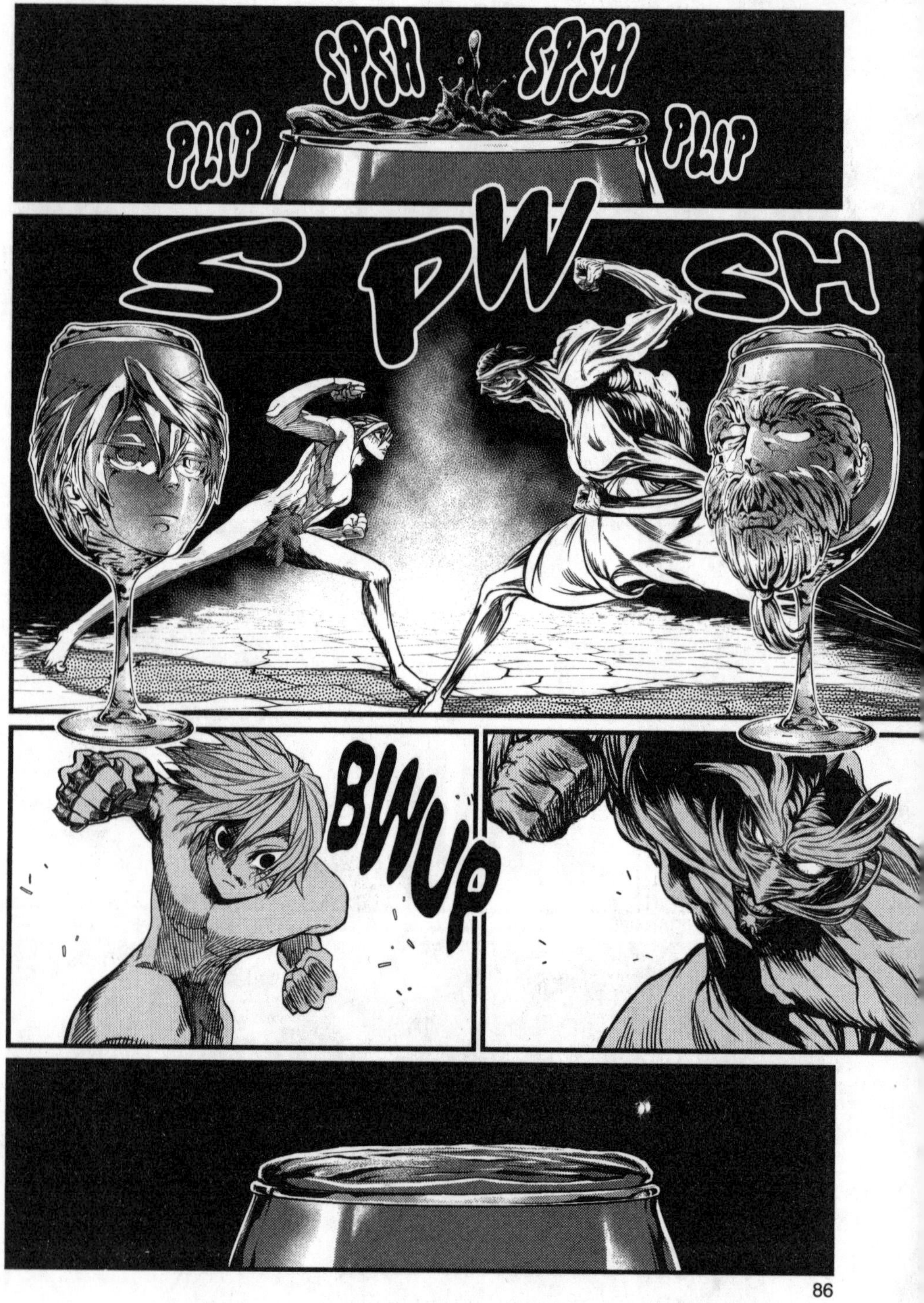
SPSH
PLIP
SPSH
PLIP
SPWSH
BWUP

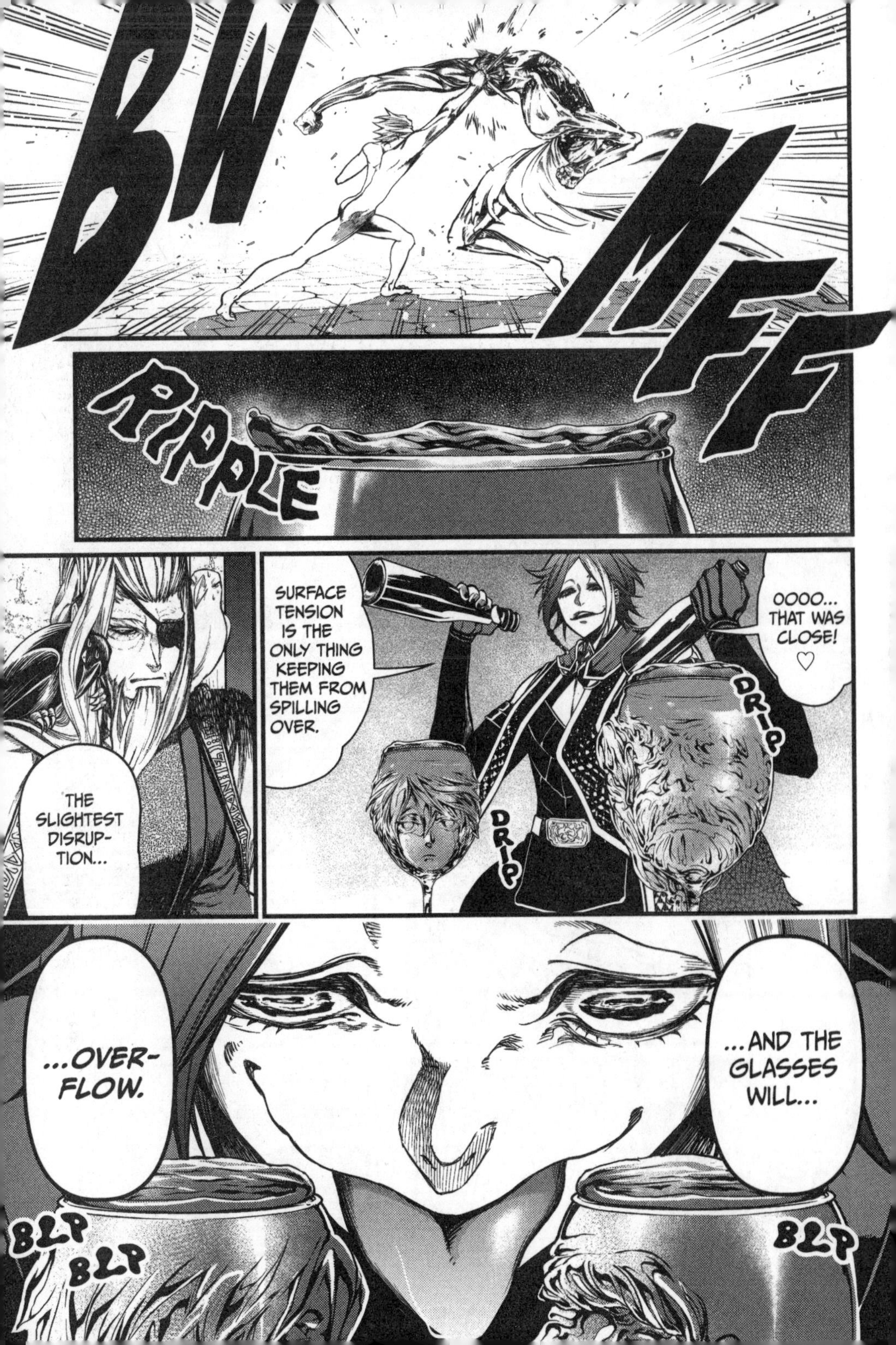
BWUFF
RIPPLE
OOOO... THAT WAS CLOSE! ♡
SURFACE TENSION IS THE ONLY THING KEEPING THEM FROM SPILLING OVER.
DRIP
DRIP
THE SLIGHTEST DISRUP-TION...
...AND THE GLASSES WILL...
...OVER-FLOW.
BLP
BLP
BLP

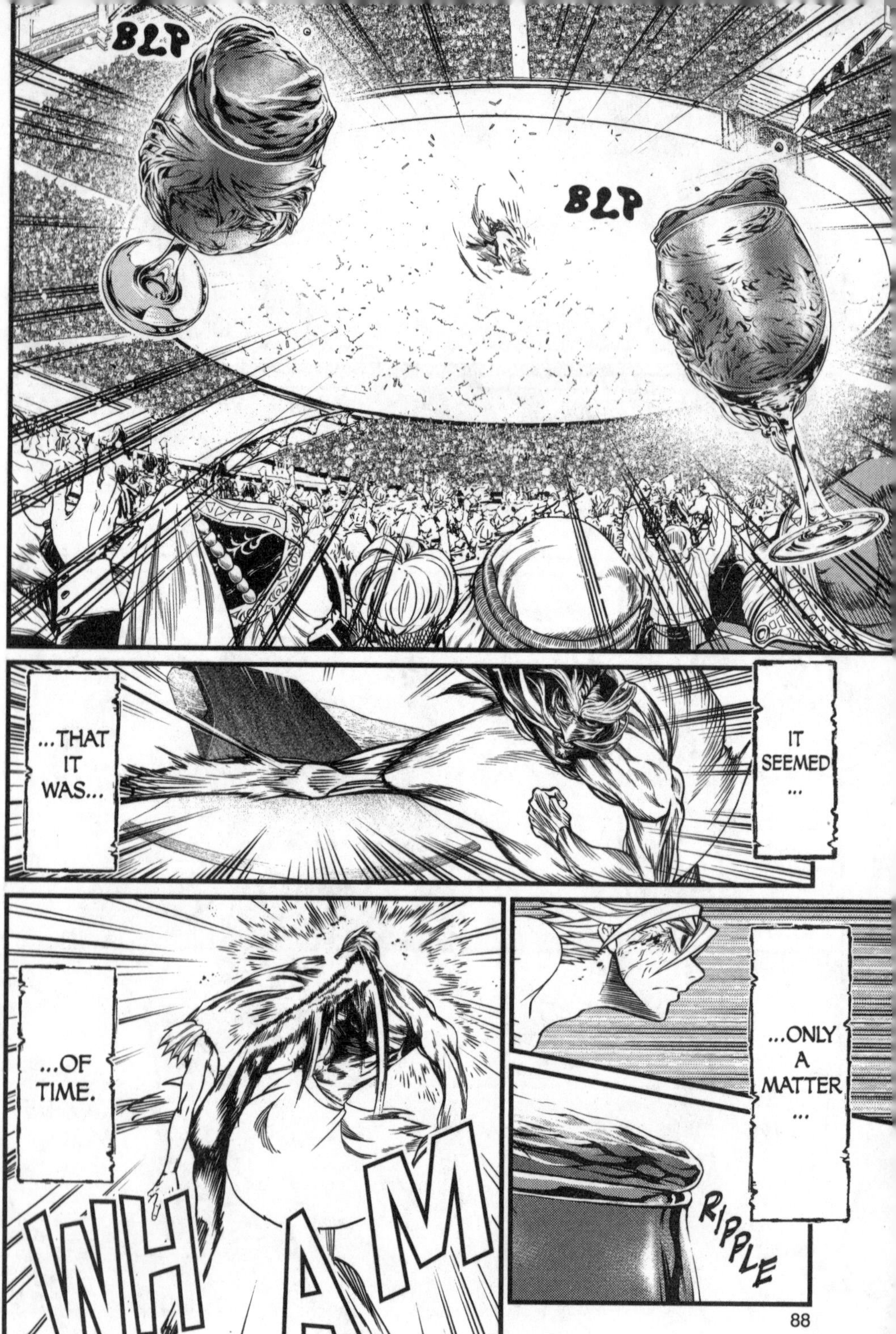
BLP
BLP
IT SEEMED ...
...THAT IT WAS...
...ONLY A MATTER ...
RIPPLE
...OF TIME.
WHAM

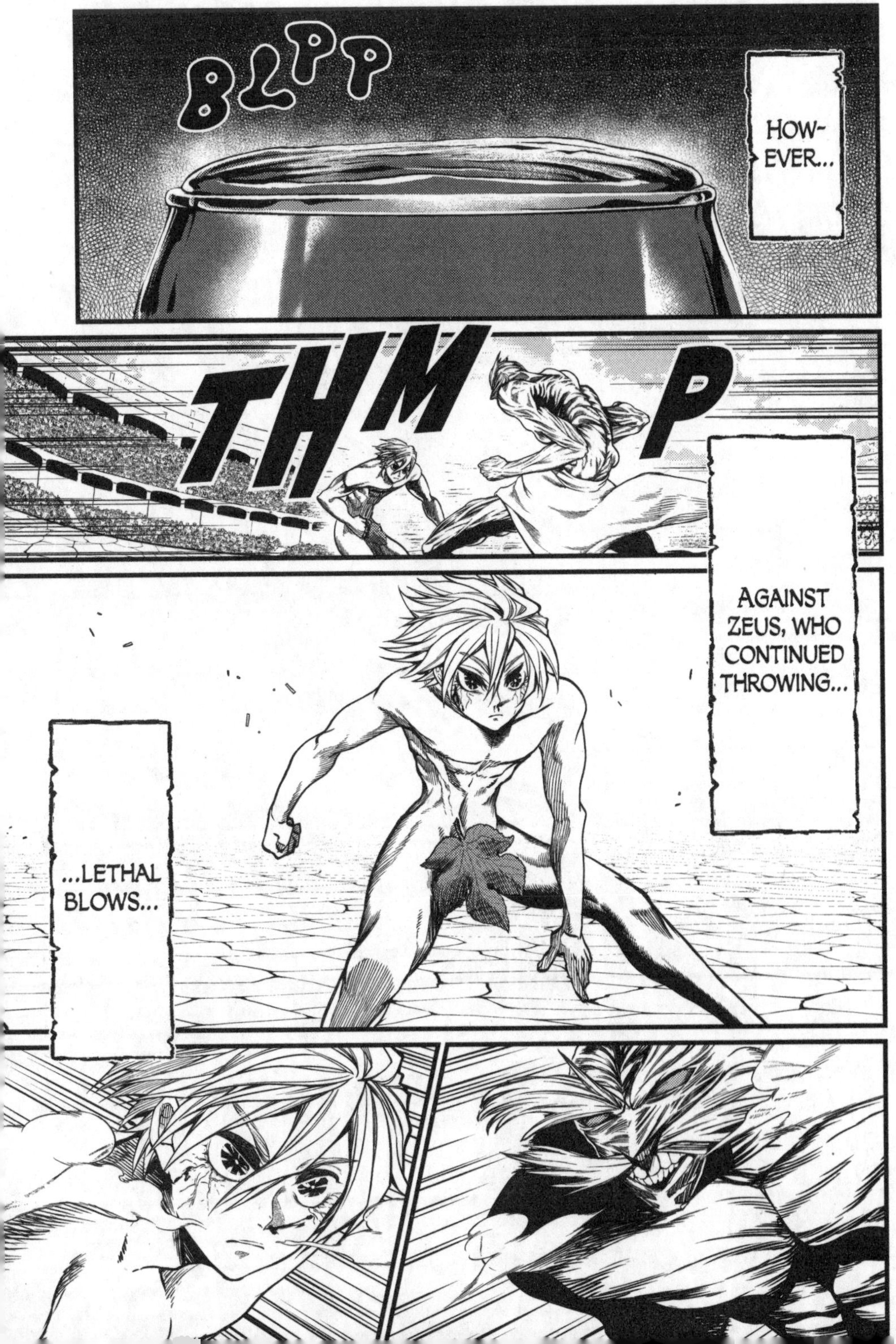
HOW-EVER...
BLPP
THMP
AGAINST ZEUS, WHO CONTINUED THROWING...
...LETHAL BLOWS...

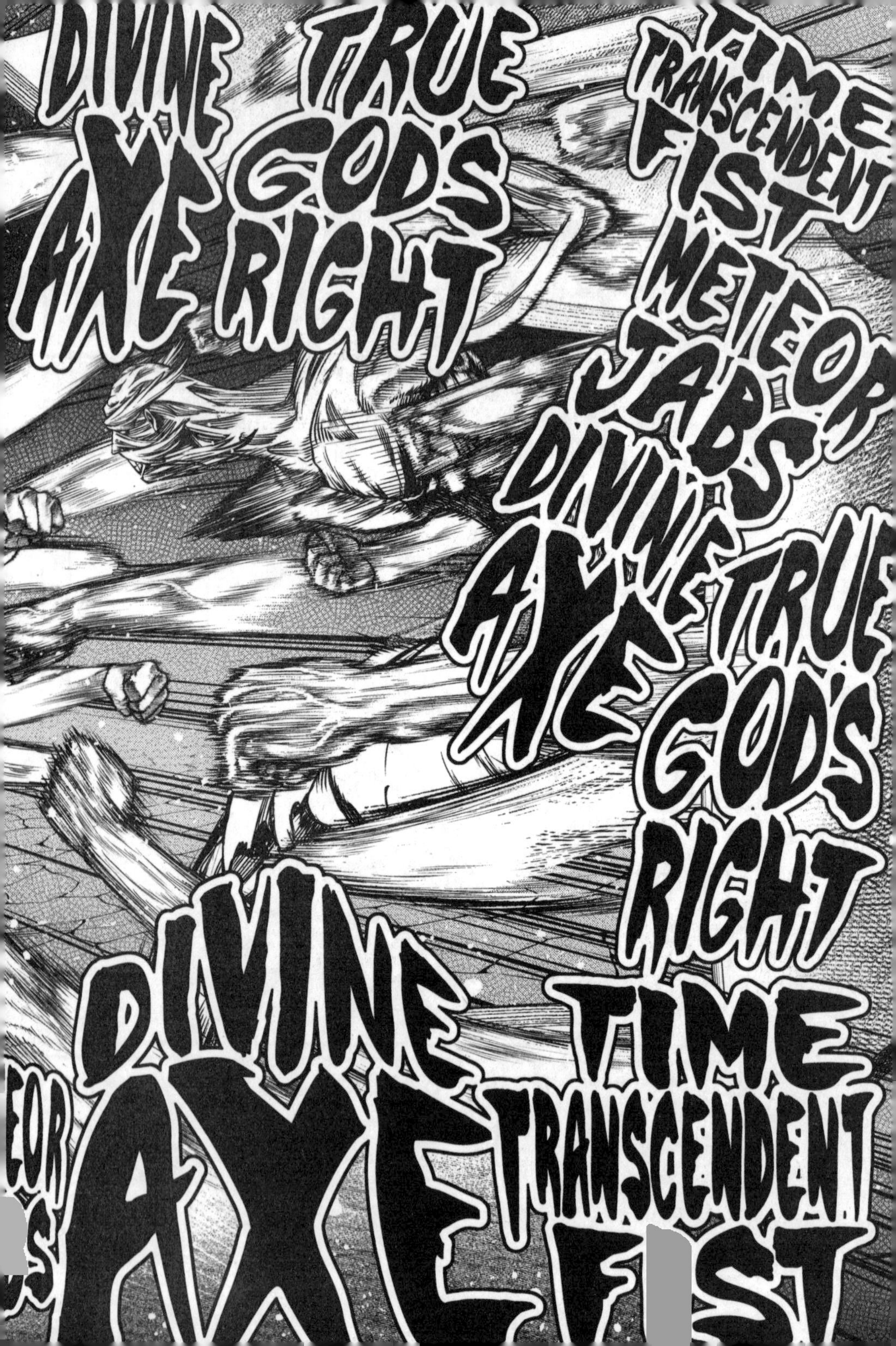
TIME TRANSCENDENT FIST
METEOR JABS
TRUE GOD'S RIGHT
DIVINE AXE
TRUE GOD'S RIGHT
DIVINE AXE
TIME TRANSCENDENT FIST
DIVINE AXE

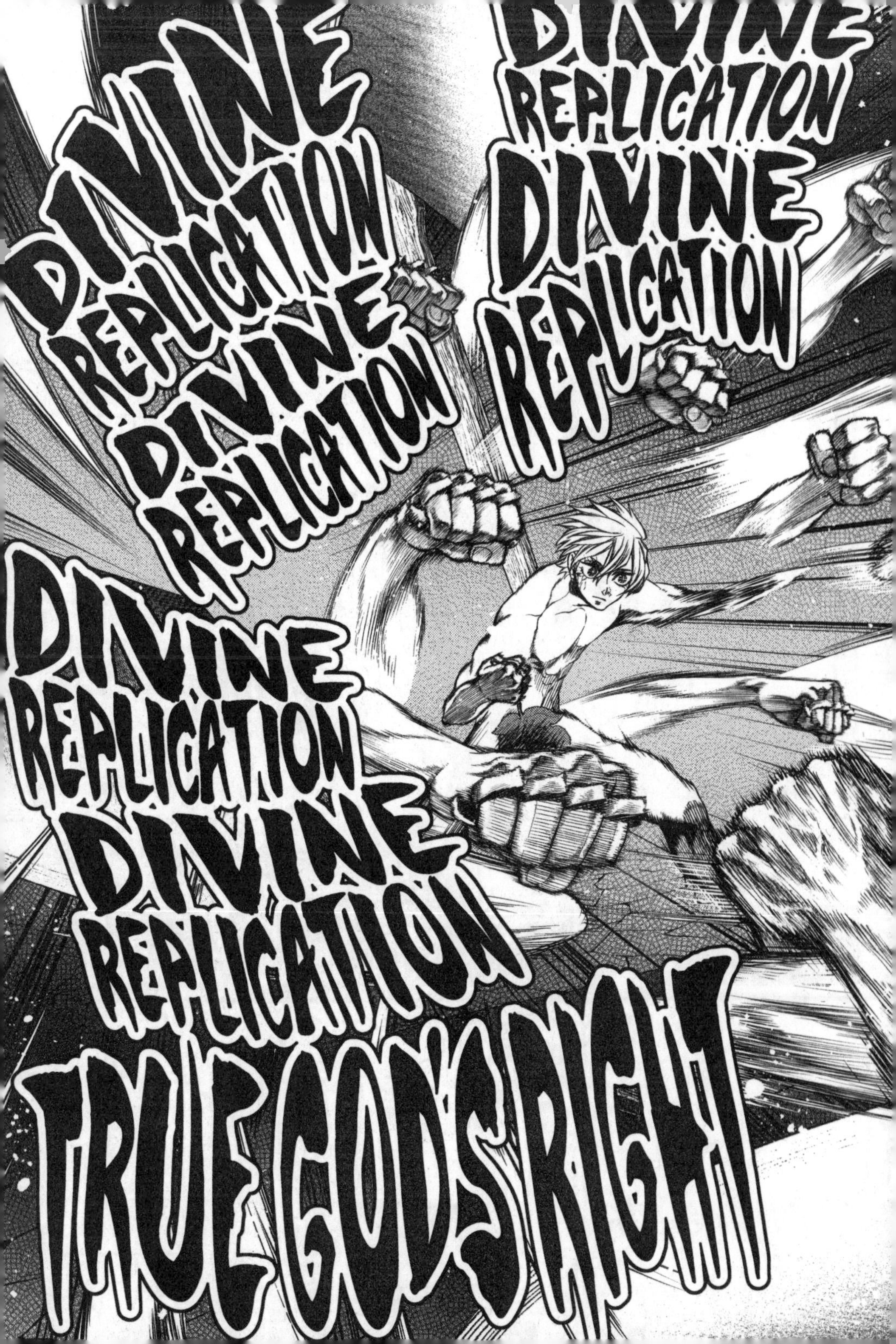
DIVINE REPLICATION
DIVINE REPLICATION
DIVINE REPLICATION
DIVINE REPLICATION
DIVINE REPLICATION
DIVINE REPLICATION
TRUE GOD'S RIGHT

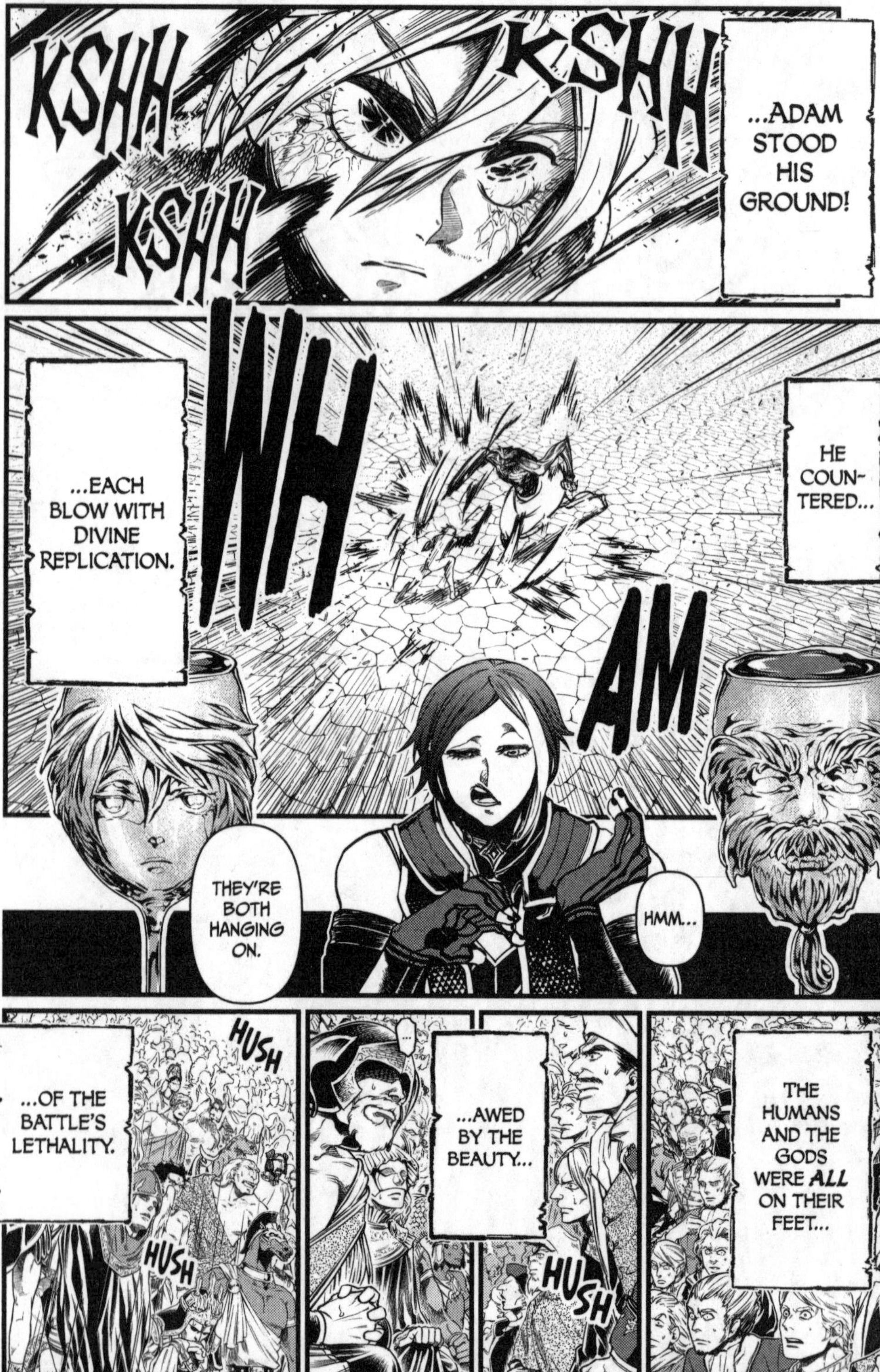
...ADAM STOOD HIS GROUND!
KSHH
KSHH
KSHH
HE COUNTERED...
...EACH BLOW WITH DIVINE REPLICATION.
WHAM
HMM...
THEY'RE BOTH HANGING ON.
THE HUMANS AND THE GODS WERE ALL ON THEIR FEET...
HUSH
...AWED BY THE BEAUTY...
...
...OF THE BATTLE'S LETHALITY.
HUSH
HUSH

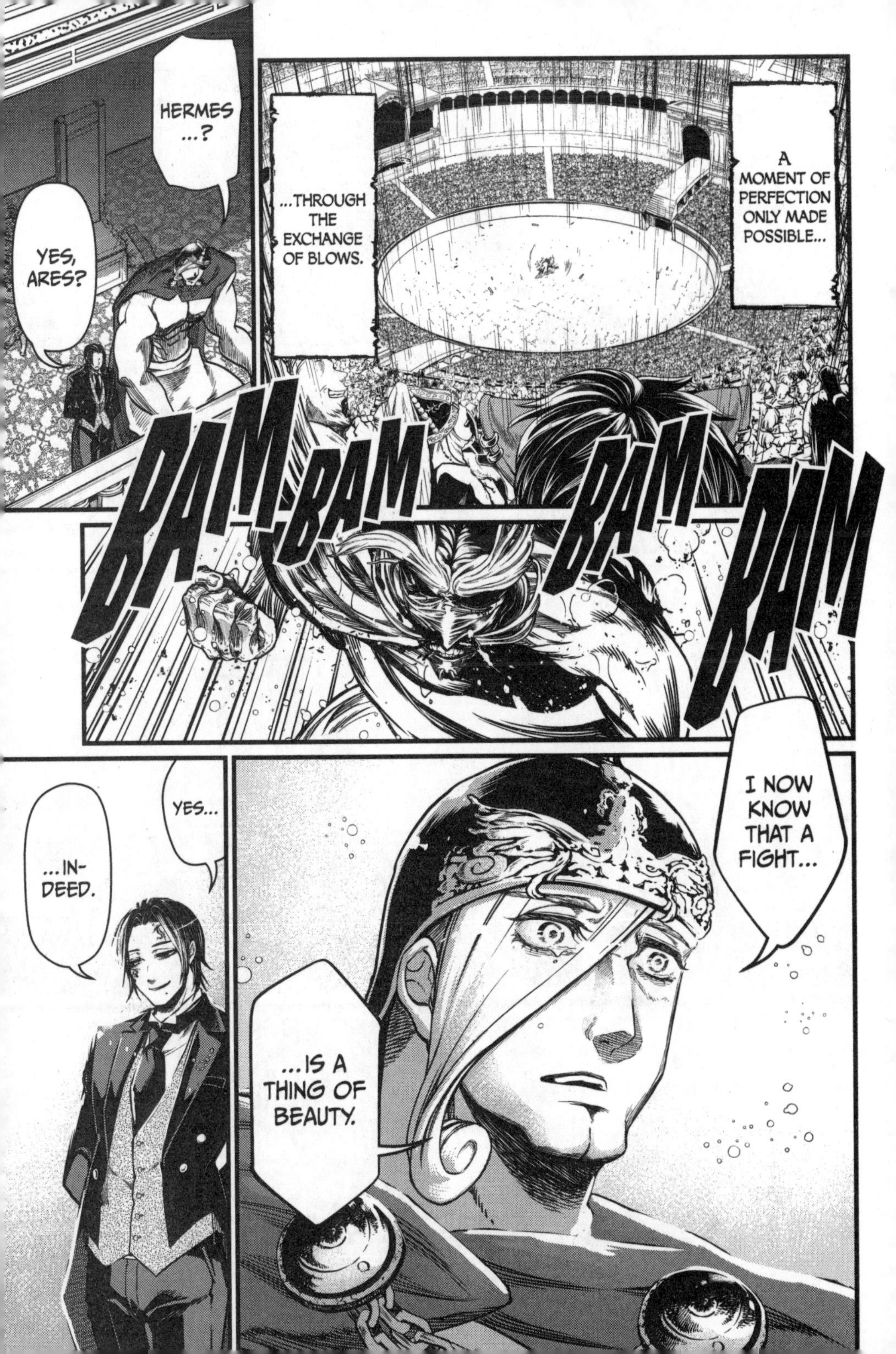
A MOMENT OF PERFECTION ONLY MADE POSSIBLE...
...THROUGH THE EXCHANGE OF BLOWS.
HERMES ...?
YES, ARES?
BAM BAM BAM BAM
I NOW KNOW THAT A FIGHT...
...IS A THING OF BEAUTY.
YES...
...IN-DEED.

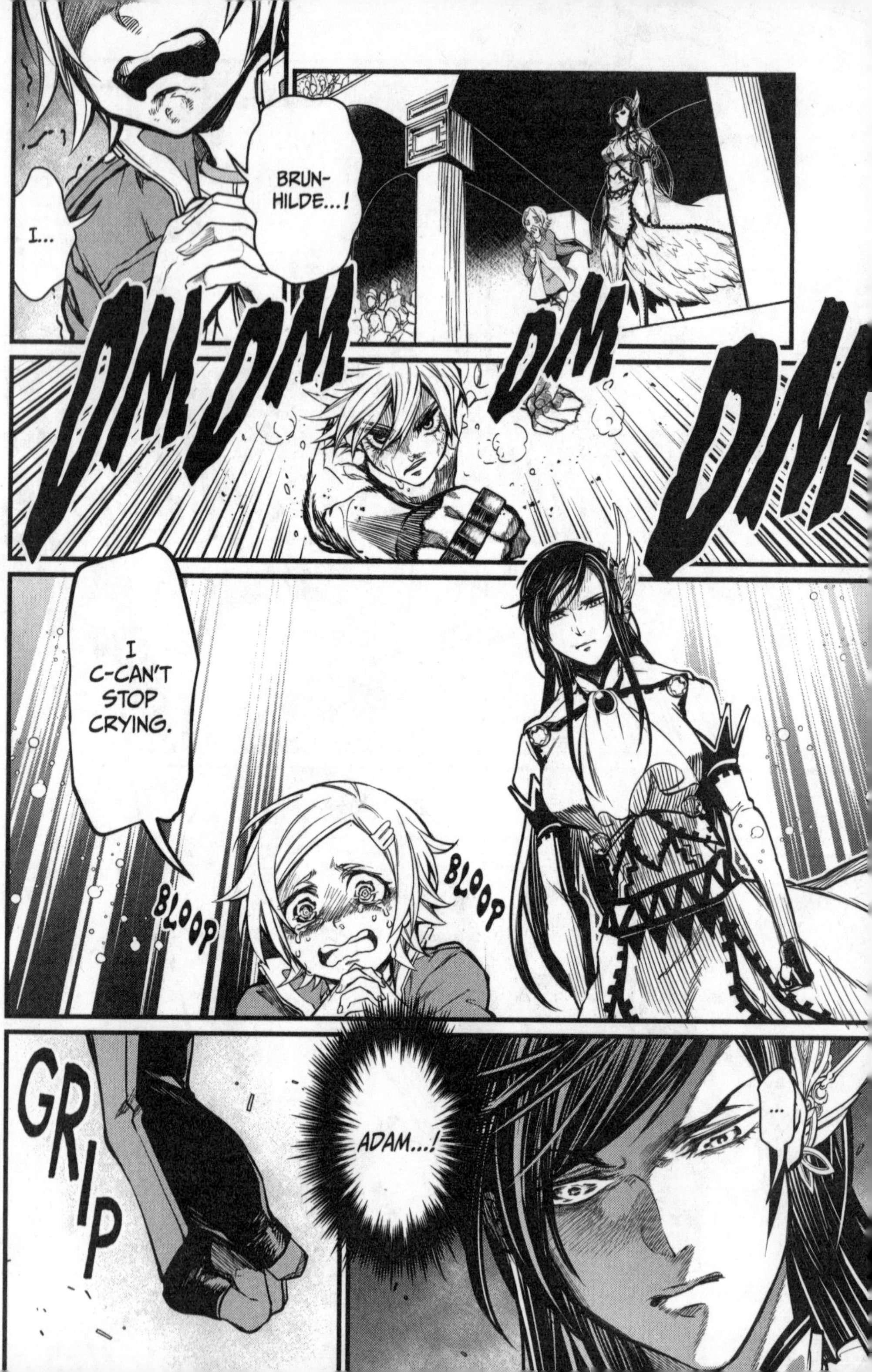
BRUN-HILDE...!
I...
DM
DM
DMDM
I C-CAN'T STOP CRYING.
BLOOP
BLOOP
...
ADAM...!
GRIP

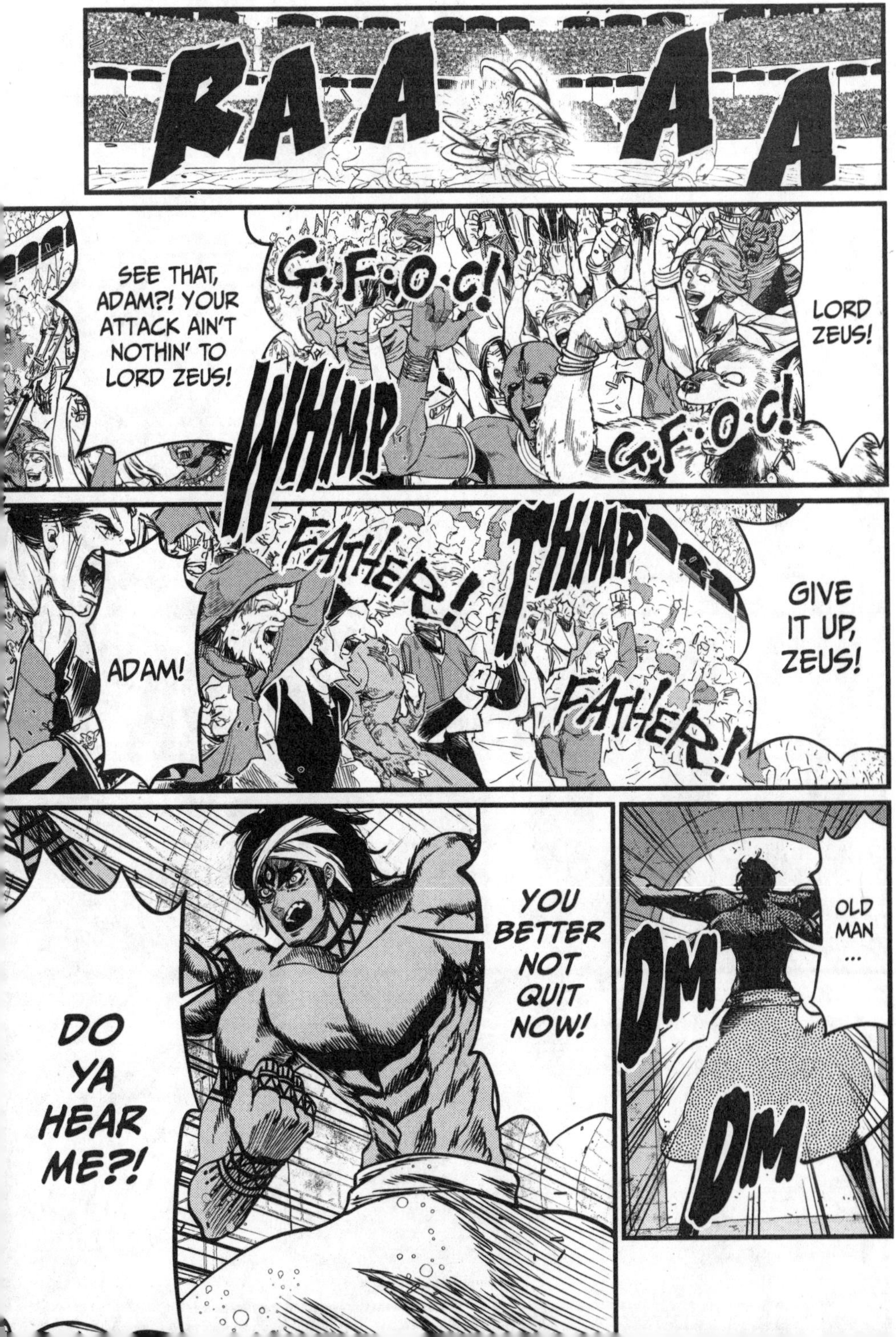
RAAAA
LORD ZEUS!
G.F.O.C!
G.F.O.C!
WHMP
SEE THAT, ADAM?! YOUR ATTACK AIN'T NOTHIN' TO LORD ZEUS!
GIVE IT UP, ZEUS!
FATHER!
THMP
FATHER!
ADAM!
OLD MAN ...
DM
DM
YOU BETTER NOT QUIT NOW!
DO YA HEAR ME?!

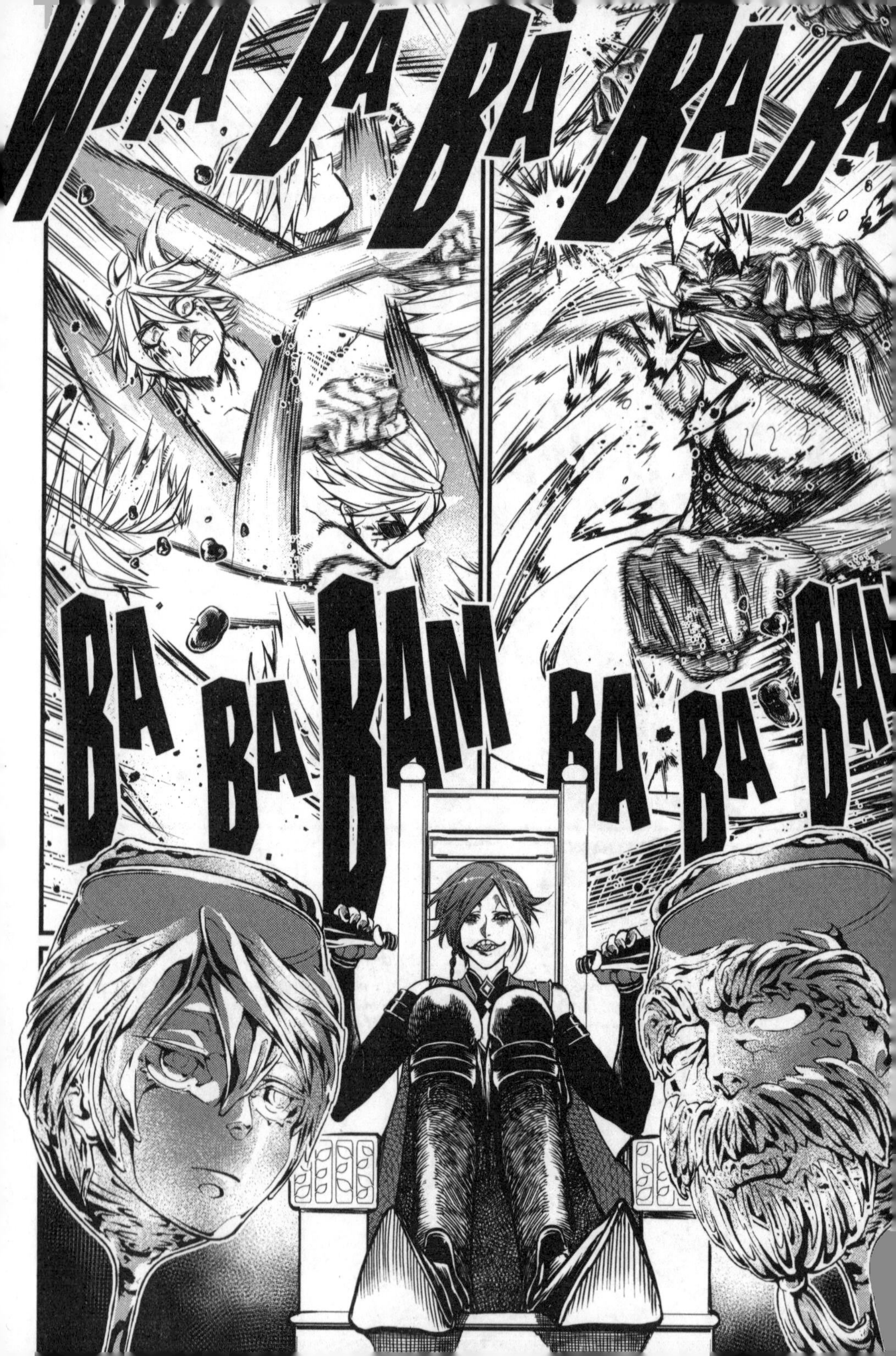
WHA BA BA BA BA BA
BA BA BAM
BA BA BA

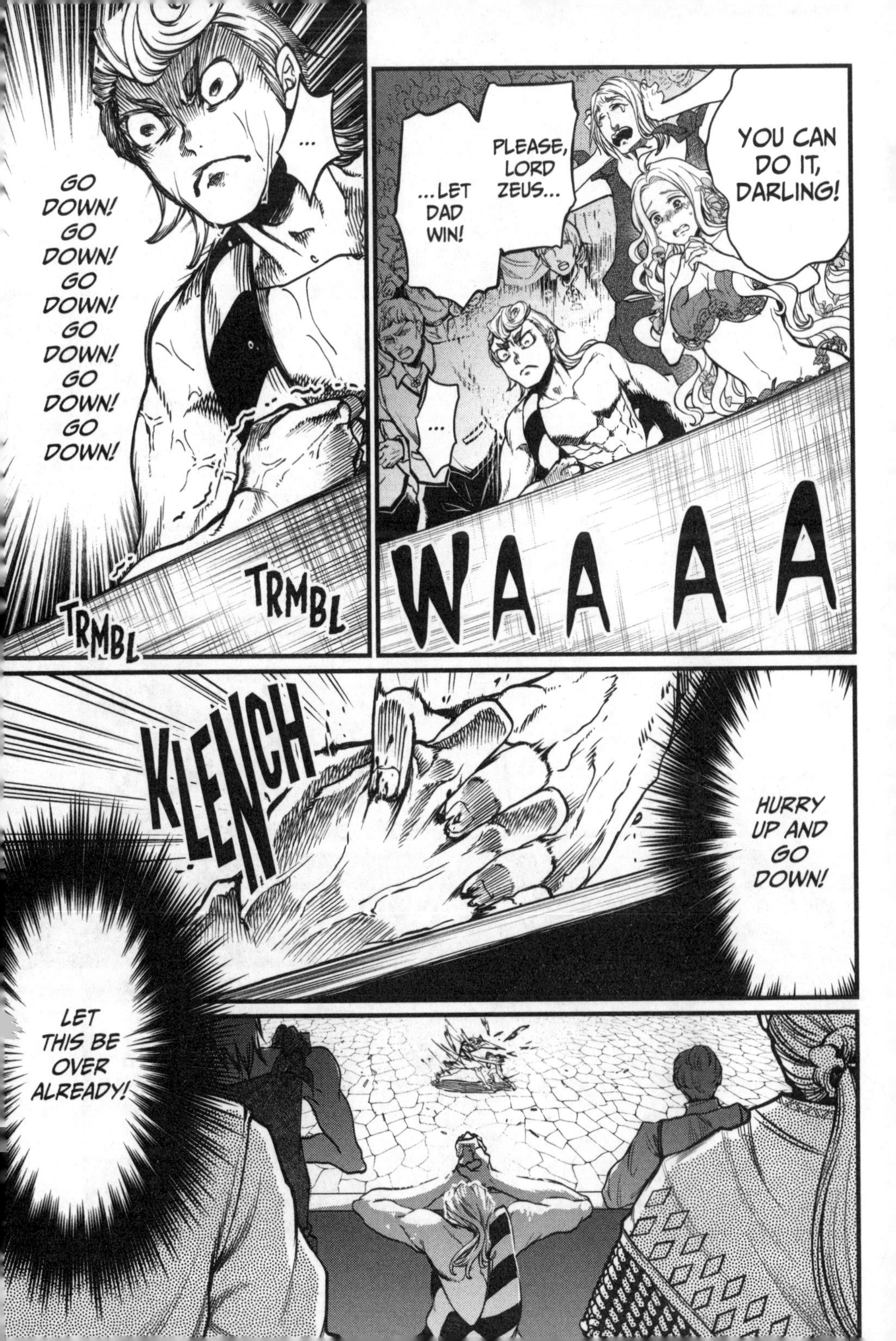
YOU CAN DO IT, DARLING!
PLEASE, LORD ZEUS...
...LET DAD WIN!
...
WAAAA
...
GO DOWN! GO DOWN! GO DOWN! GO DOWN! GO DOWN! GO DOWN!
TRMBL
TRMBL
HURRY UP AND GO DOWN!
KLENCH
LET THIS BE OVER ALREADY!

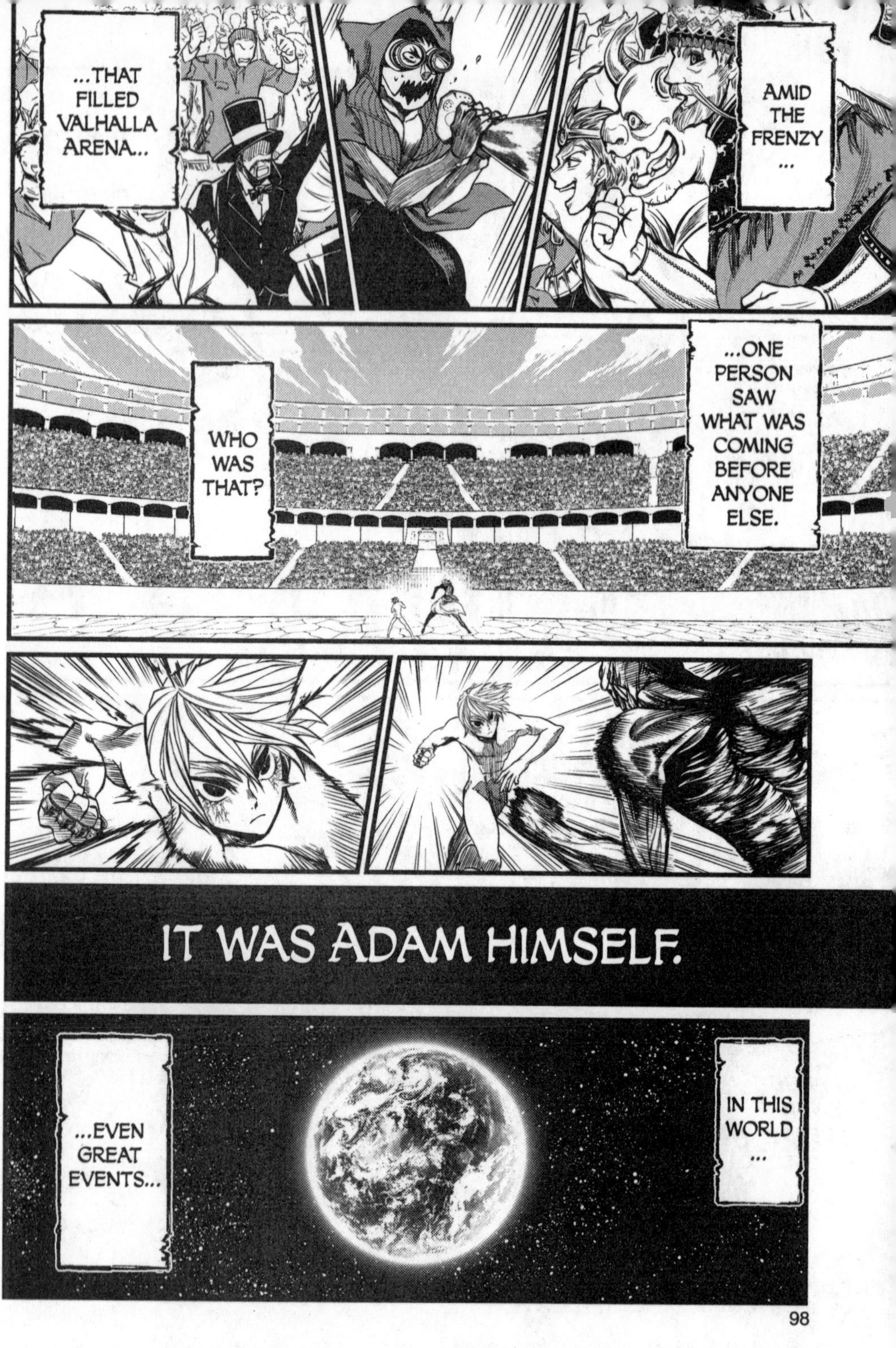
AMID THE FRENZY ...
...THAT FILLED VALHALLA ARENA...
...ONE PERSON SAW WHAT WAS COMING BEFORE ANYONE ELSE.
WHO WAS THAT?
IT WAS ADAM HIMSELF.
IN THIS WORLD ...
...EVEN GREAT EVENTS...

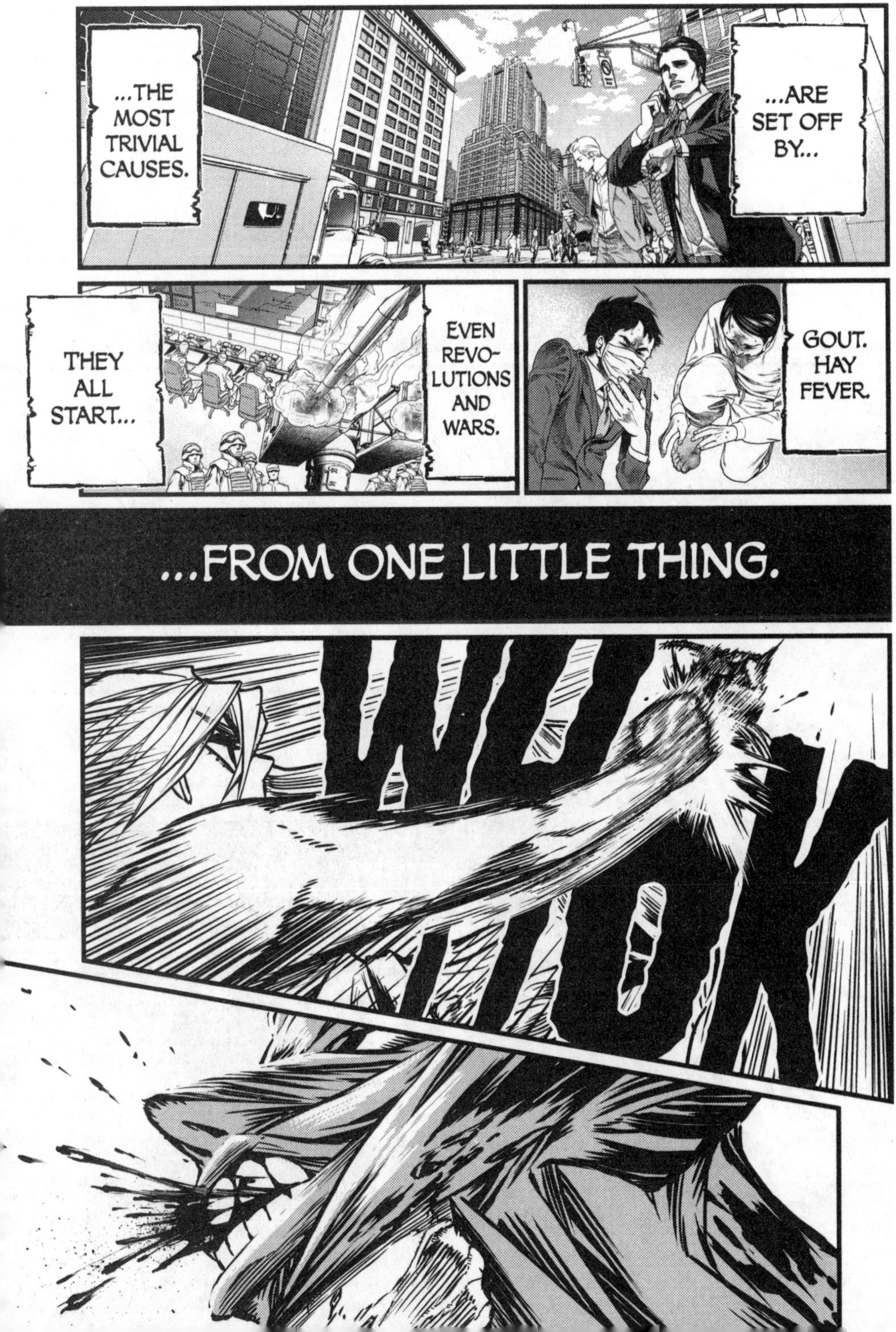
...ARE SET OFF BY...
...THE MOST TRIVIAL CAUSES.
GOUT. HAY FEVER.
EVEN REVOLUTIONS AND WARS.
THEY ALL START...
...FROM ONE LITTLE THING.
WHOK

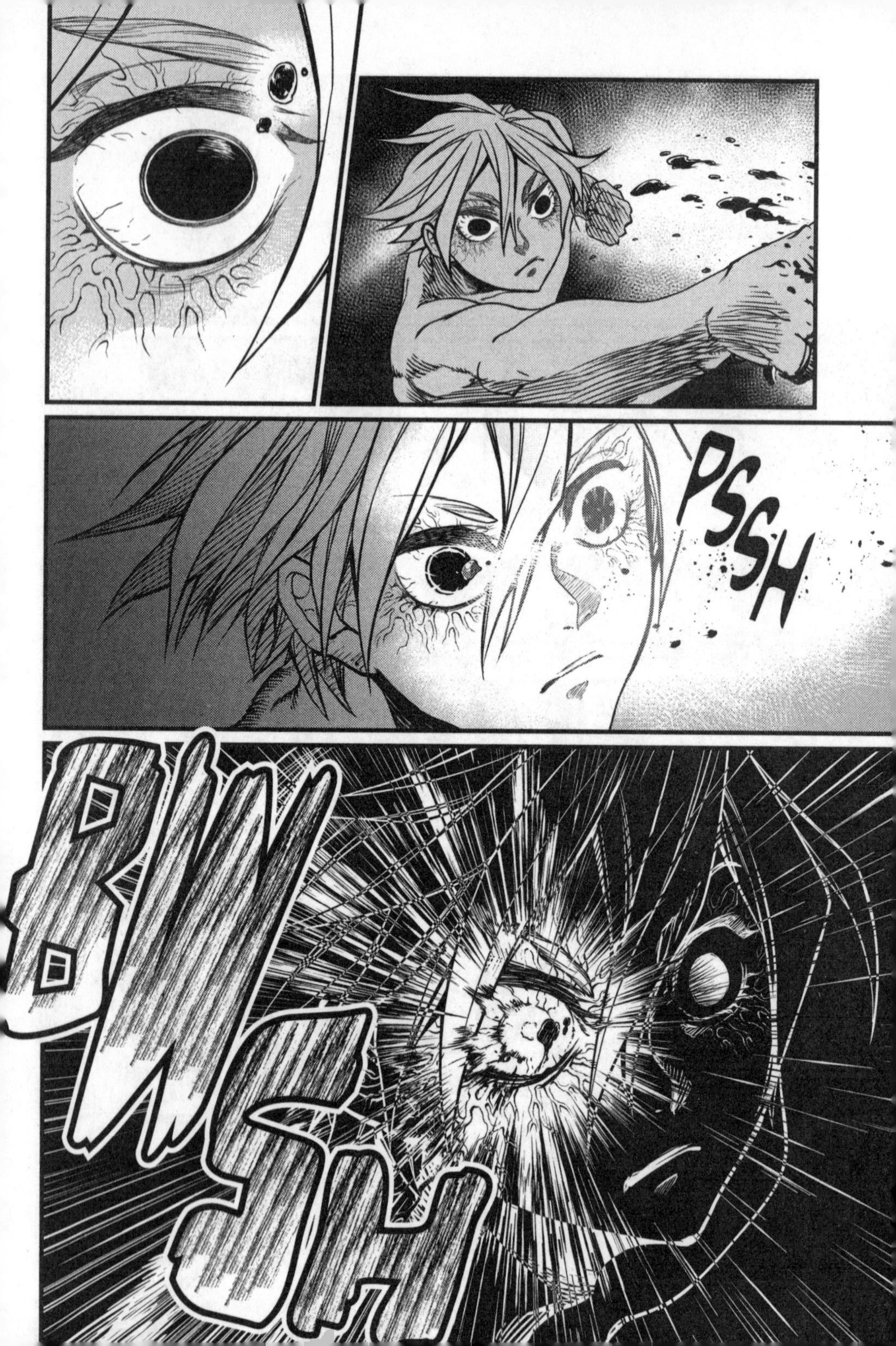
PSSH
BWSH

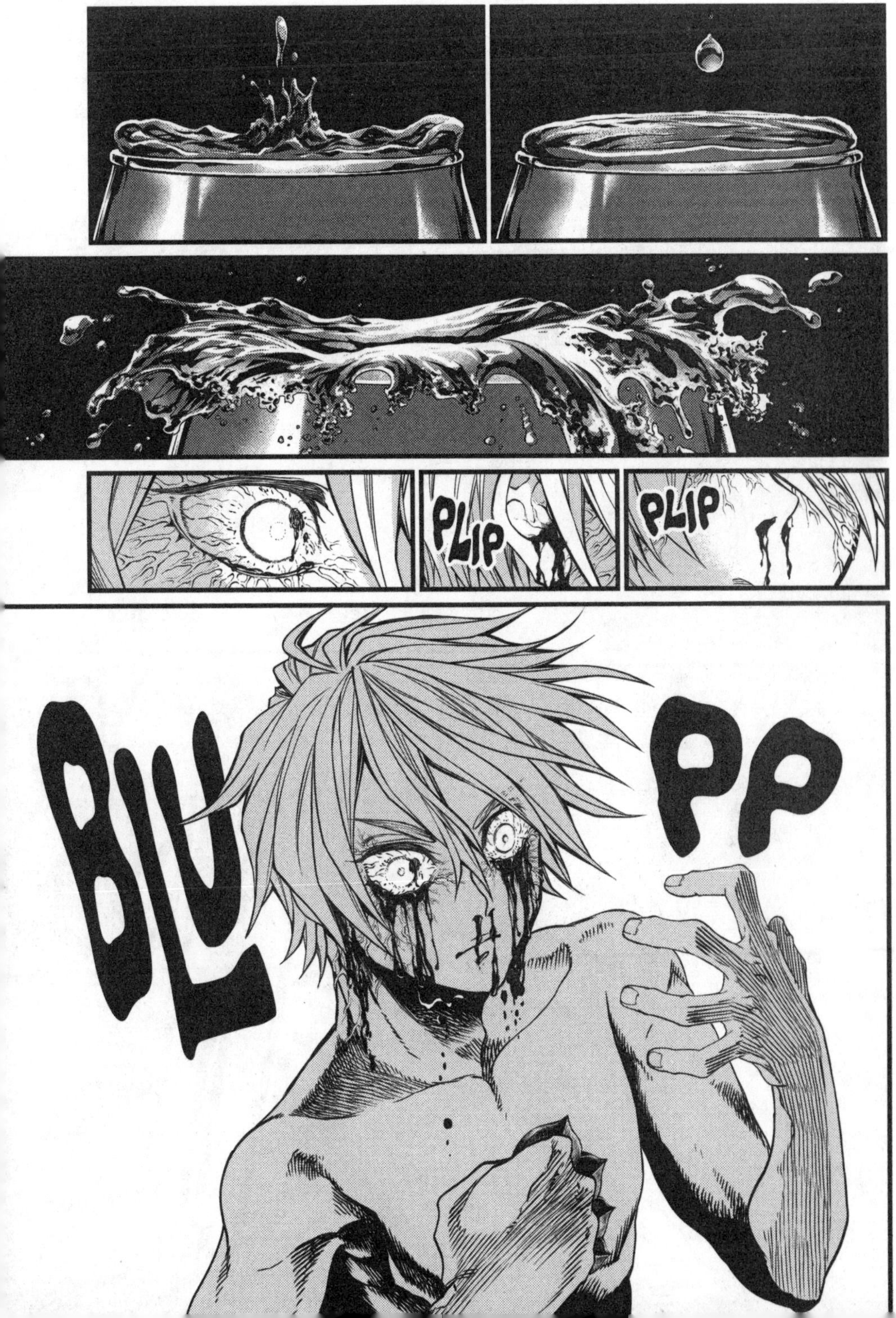
PLIP
PLIP
BLU
PP

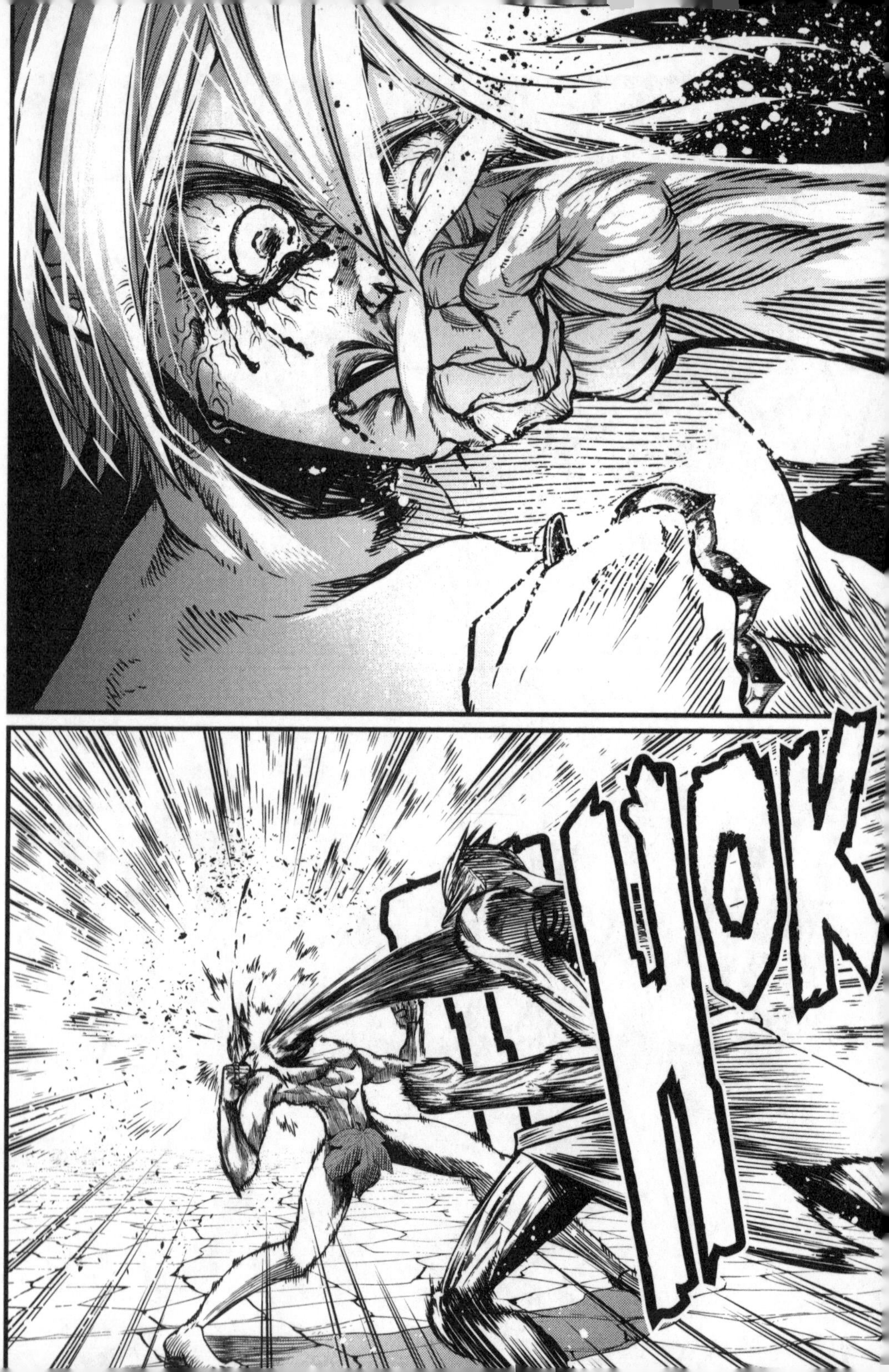
HOK

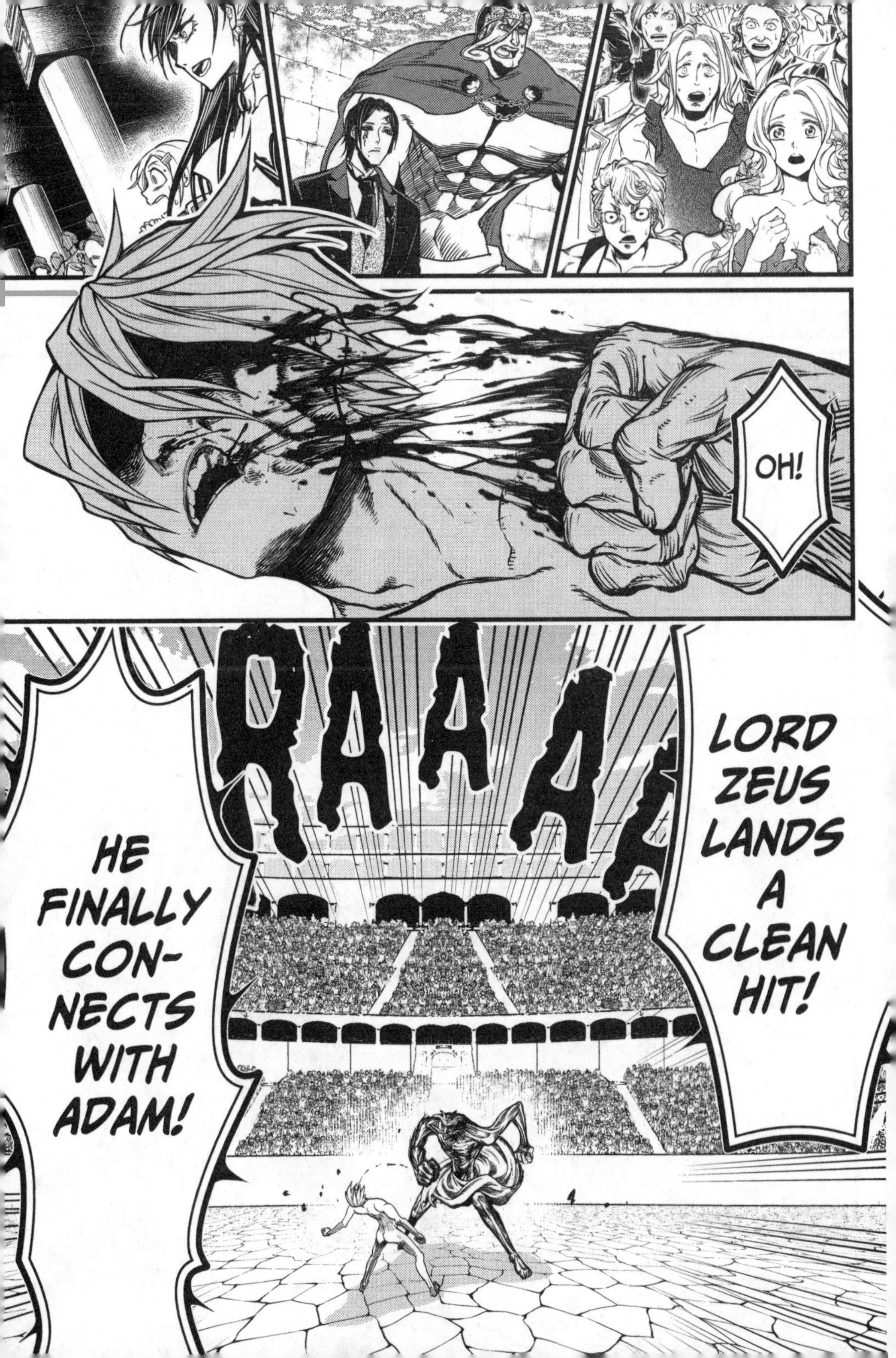
OH!
RAAA
LORD ZEUS LANDS A CLEAN HIT!
HE FINALLY CON-NECTS WITH ADAM!

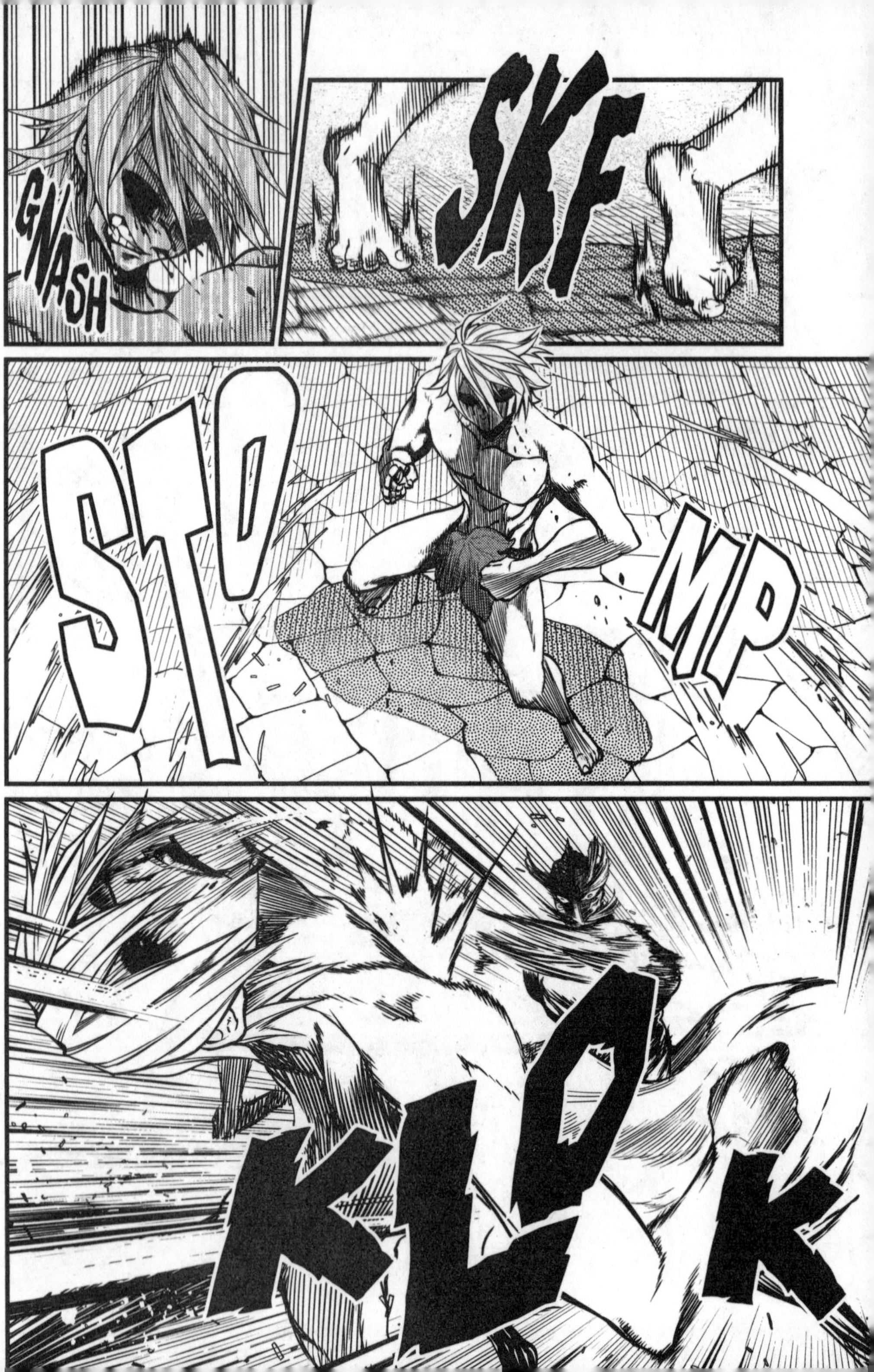
SKF
GNASH
STOMP
KLOK

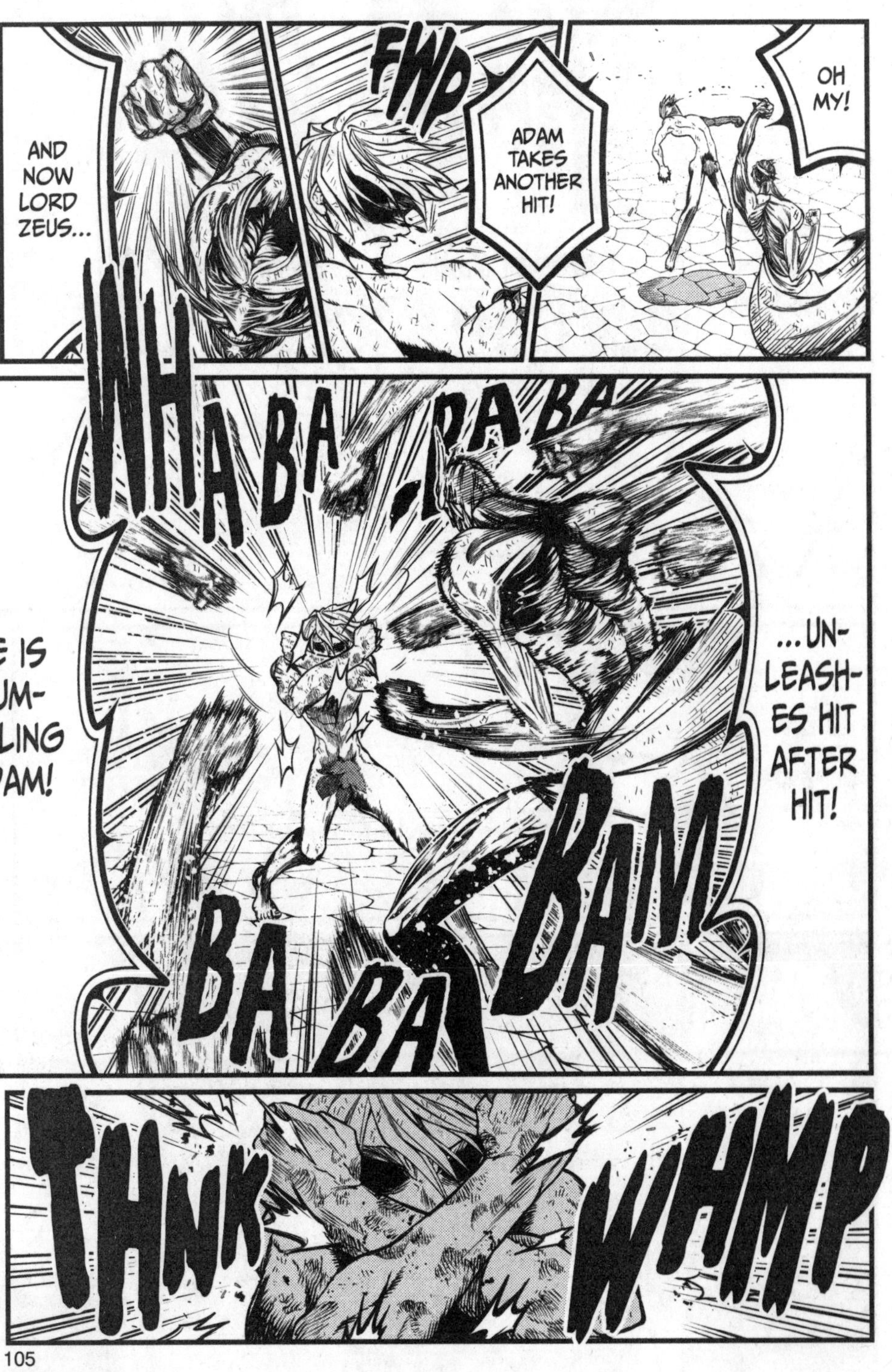
OH MY!
FWP
ADAM TAKES ANOTHER HIT!
AND NOW LORD ZEUS...
WHA BA BA BA
...UNLEASHES HIT AFTER HIT!
HE IS PUMMELING ADAM!
BA BA BA BAM
WHMP
THNK

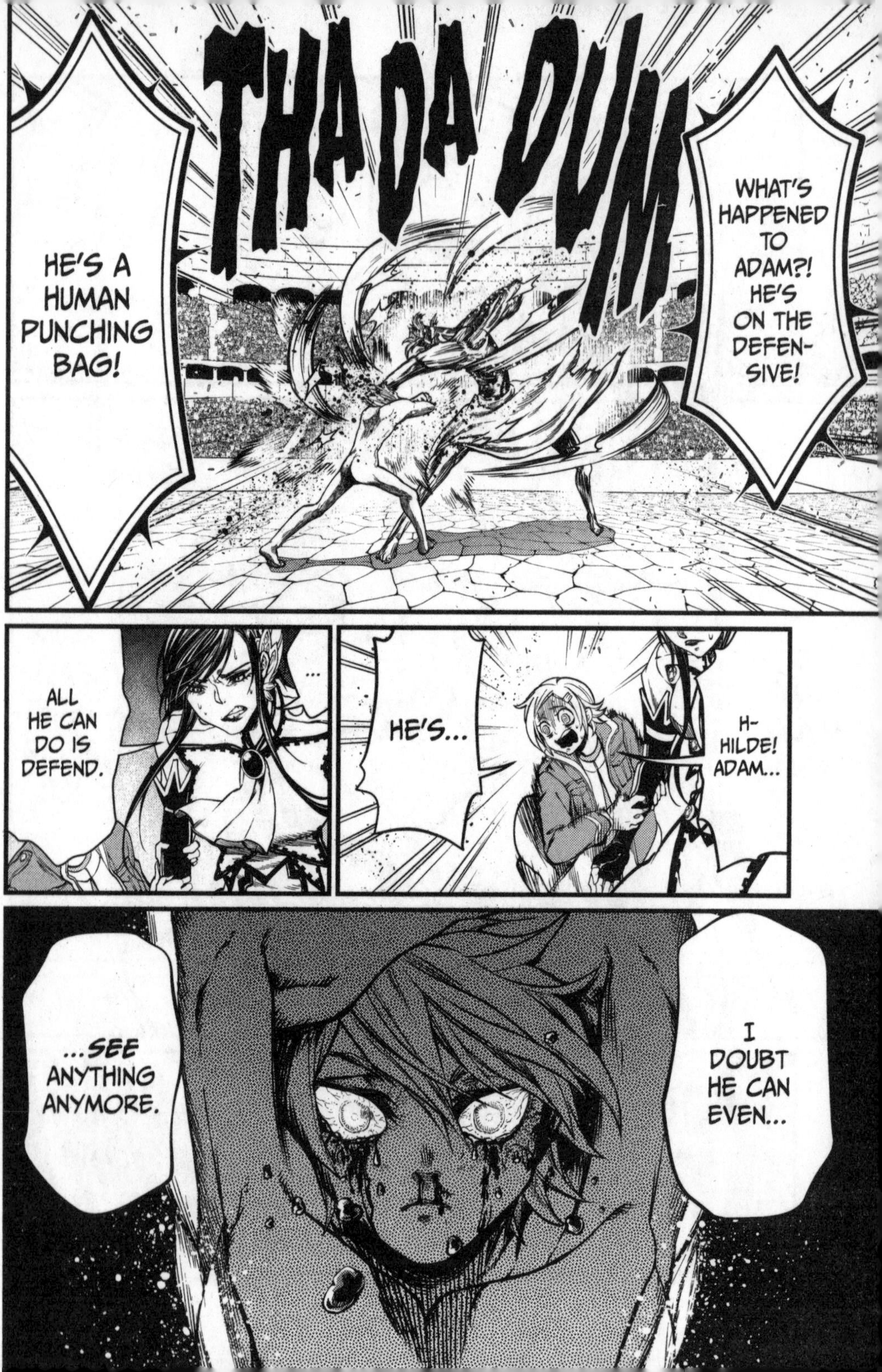
THADA DUM
WHAT'S HAPPENED TO ADAM?! HE'S ON THE DEFEN-SIVE!
HE'S A HUMAN PUNCHING BAG!
H-HILDE! ADAM...
HE'S...
...
ALL HE CAN DO IS DEFEND.
I DOUBT HE CAN EVEN...
...SEE ANYTHING ANYMORE.

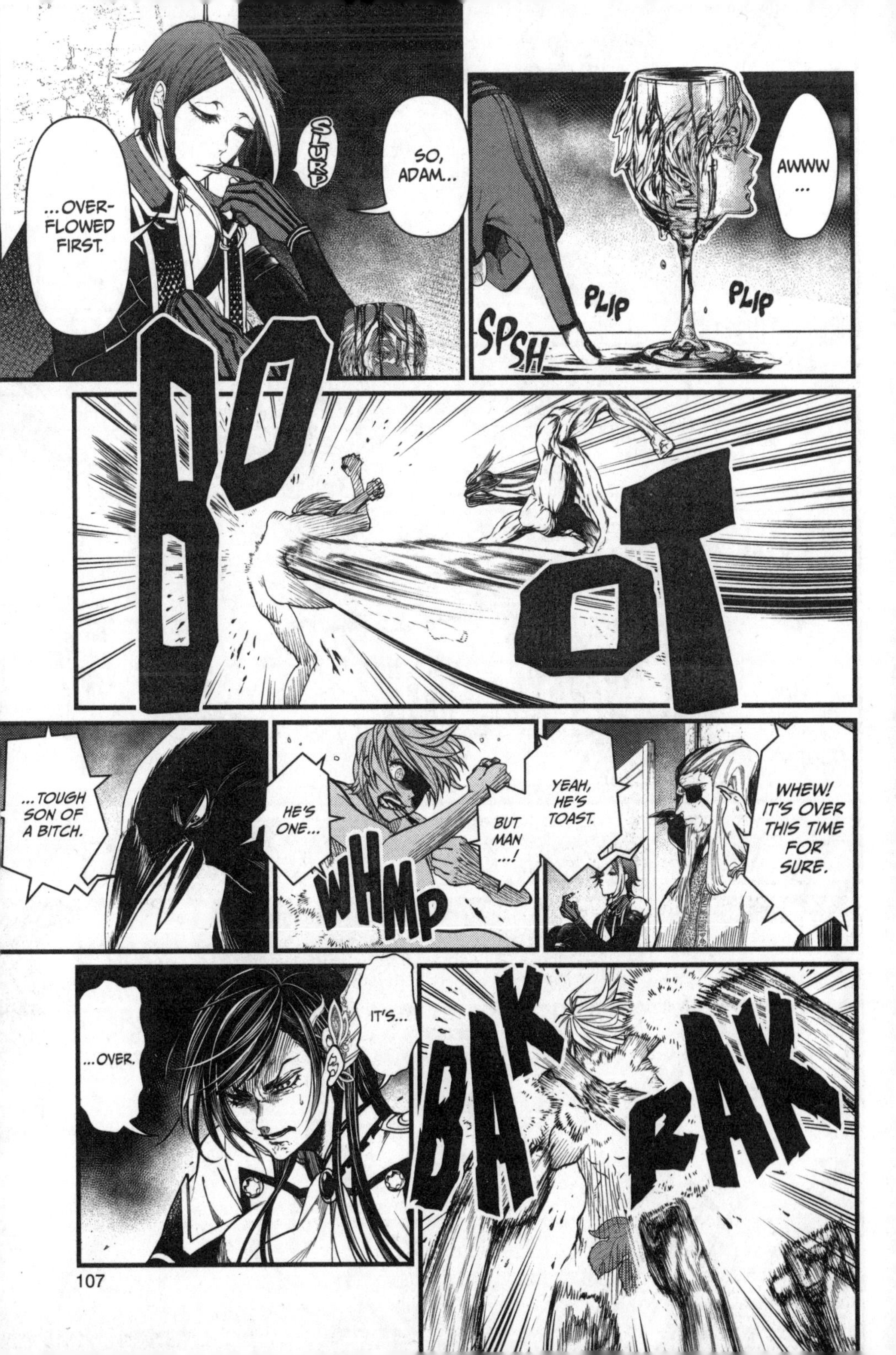
AWWW...
PLIP
PLIP
SPSH
SO, ADAM...
SLURP
...OVER-FLOWED FIRST.
BOOT
WHEW! IT'S OVER THIS TIME FOR SURE.
YEAH, HE'S TOAST.
BUT MAN...!
HE'S ONE...
WHMP
...TOUGH SON OF A BITCH.
BAK
BAK
IT'S...
...OVER.

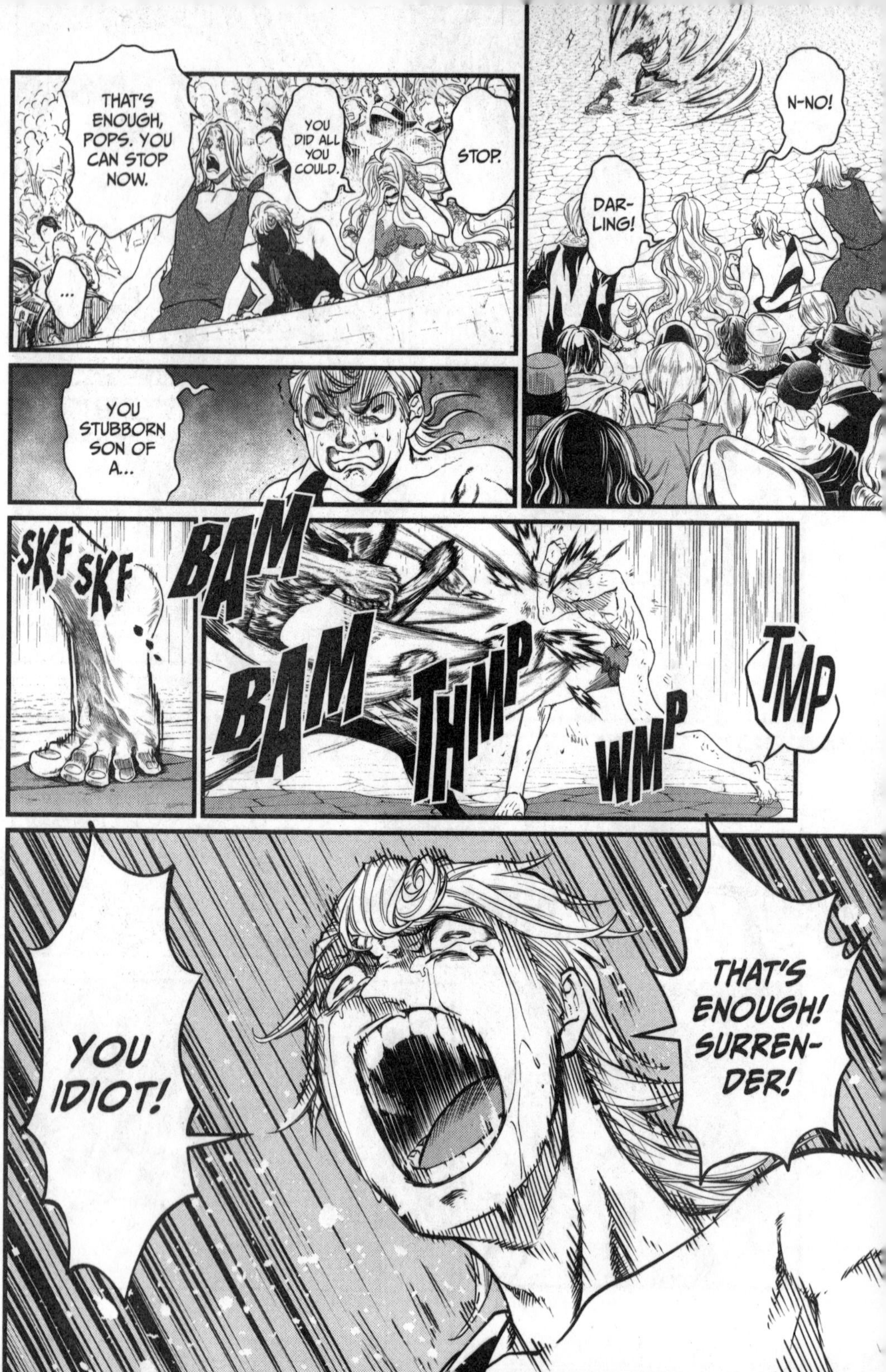
N-NO!
DAR-LING!
STOP.
YOU DID ALL YOU COULD.
THAT'S ENOUGH, POPS. YOU CAN STOP NOW.
...
YOU STUBBORN SON OF A...
TMP
WMP
THMP
BAM
BAM
SKF SKF
THAT'S ENOUGH! SURRENDER!
YOU IDIOT!

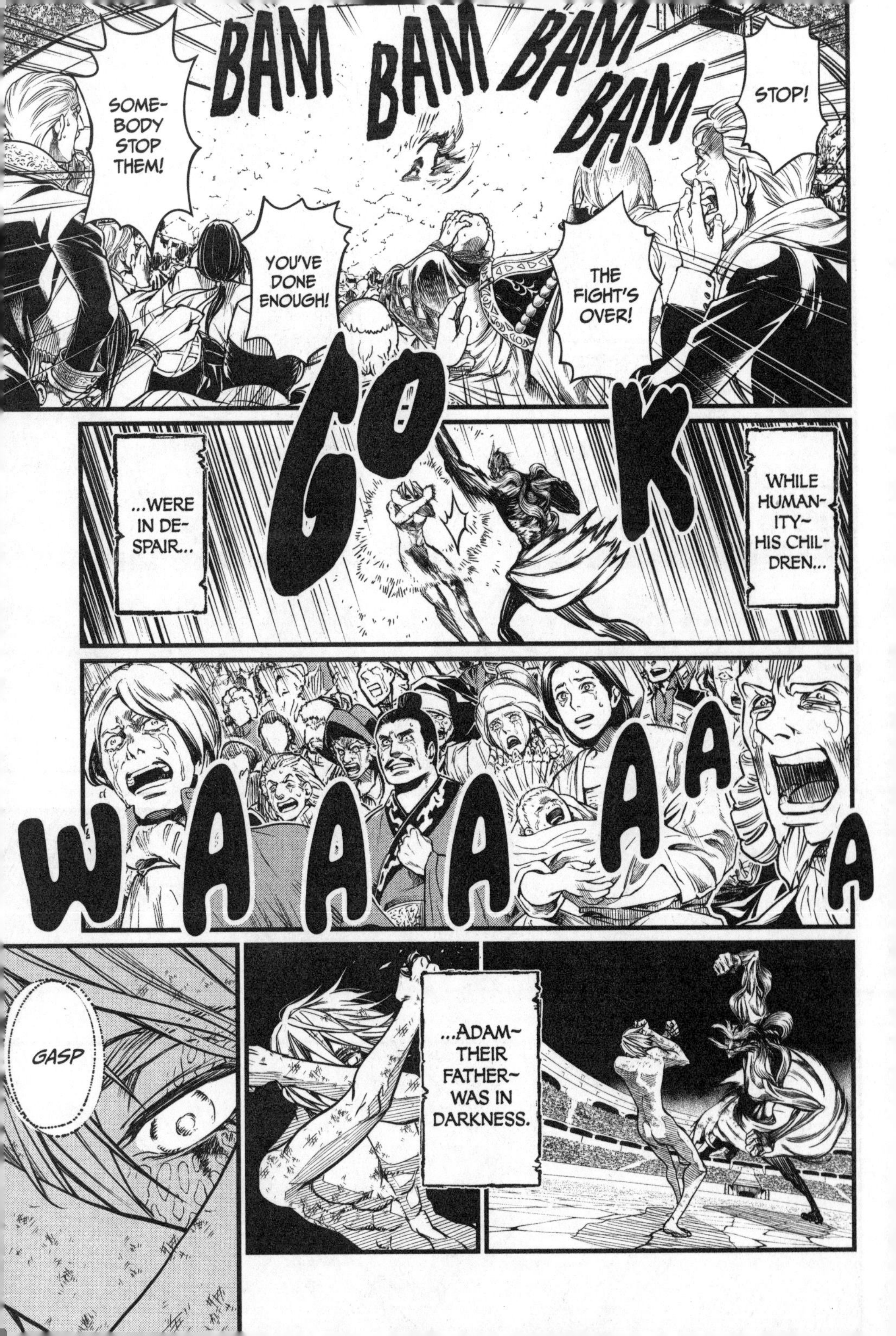
STOP!
BAM BAM BAM BAM
SOMEBODY STOP THEM!
THE FIGHT'S OVER!
YOU'VE DONE ENOUGH!
GOK
WHILE HUMANITY— HIS CHILDREN...
...WERE IN DESPAIR...
WAAAAAAA
...ADAM— THEIR FATHER— WAS IN DARKNESS.
GASP

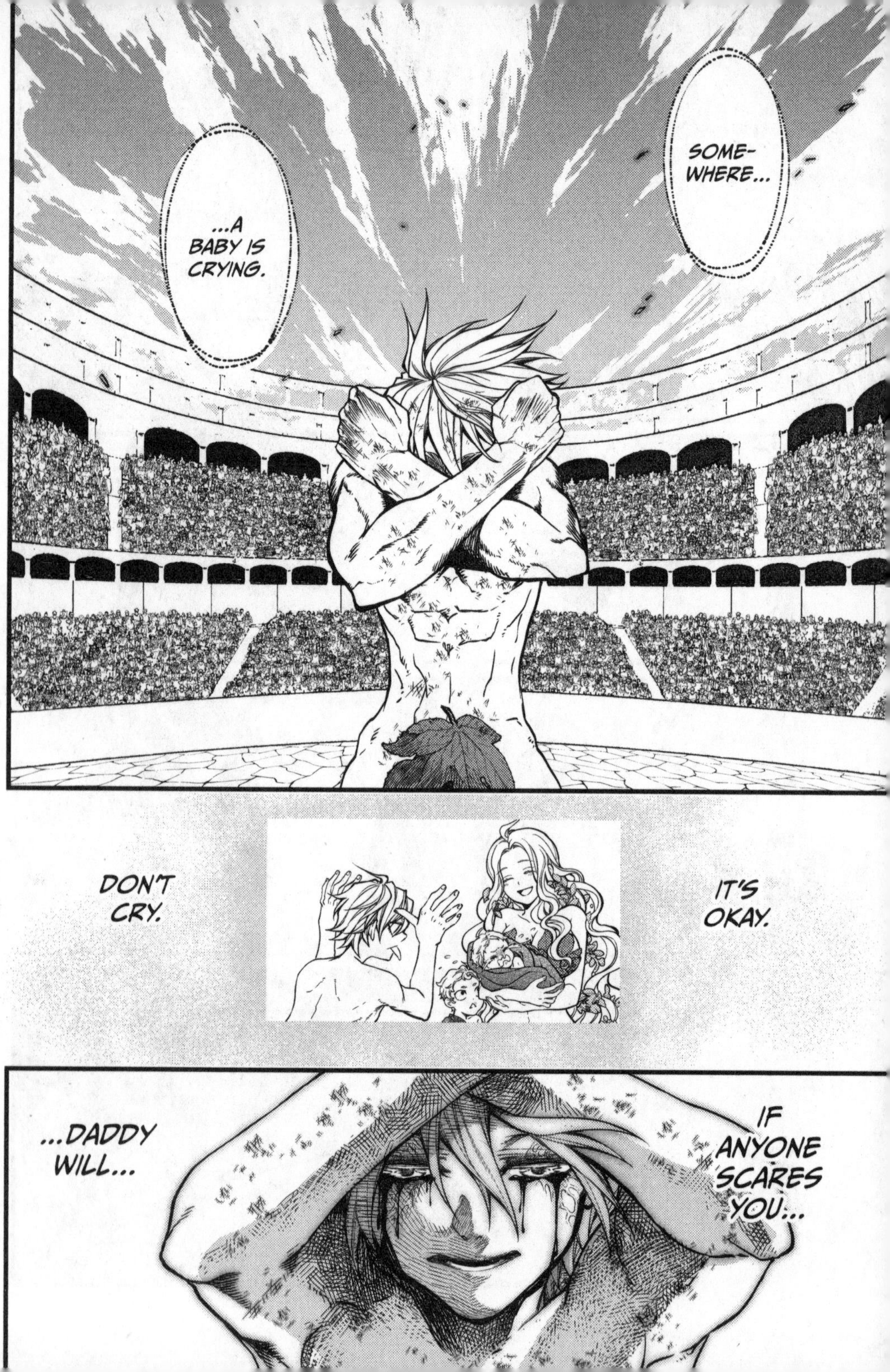
SOME-WHERE...
...A BABY IS CRYING.
IT'S OKAY.
DON'T CRY.
IF ANYONE SCARES YOU...
...DADDY WILL...

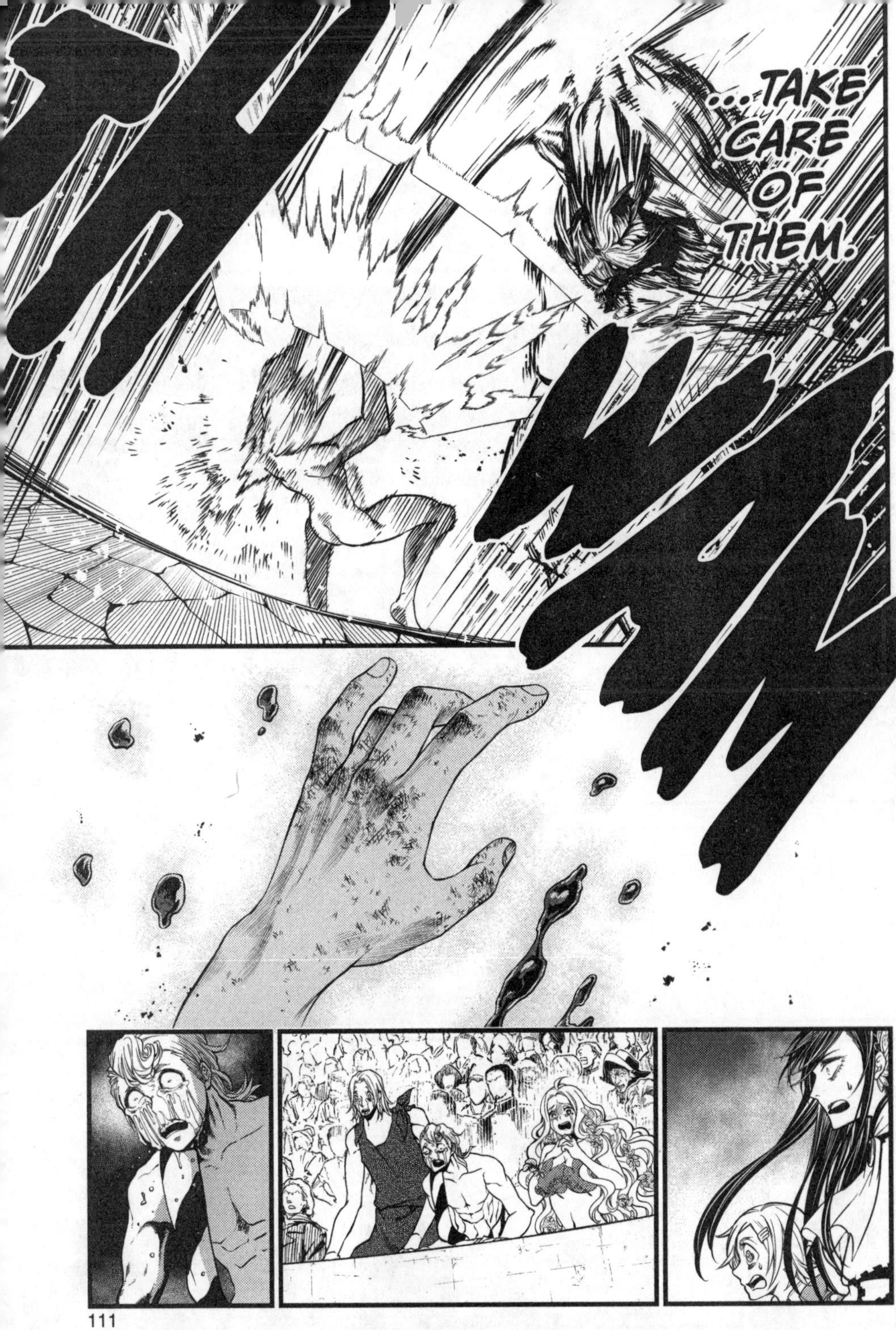
...TAKE CARE OF THEM.

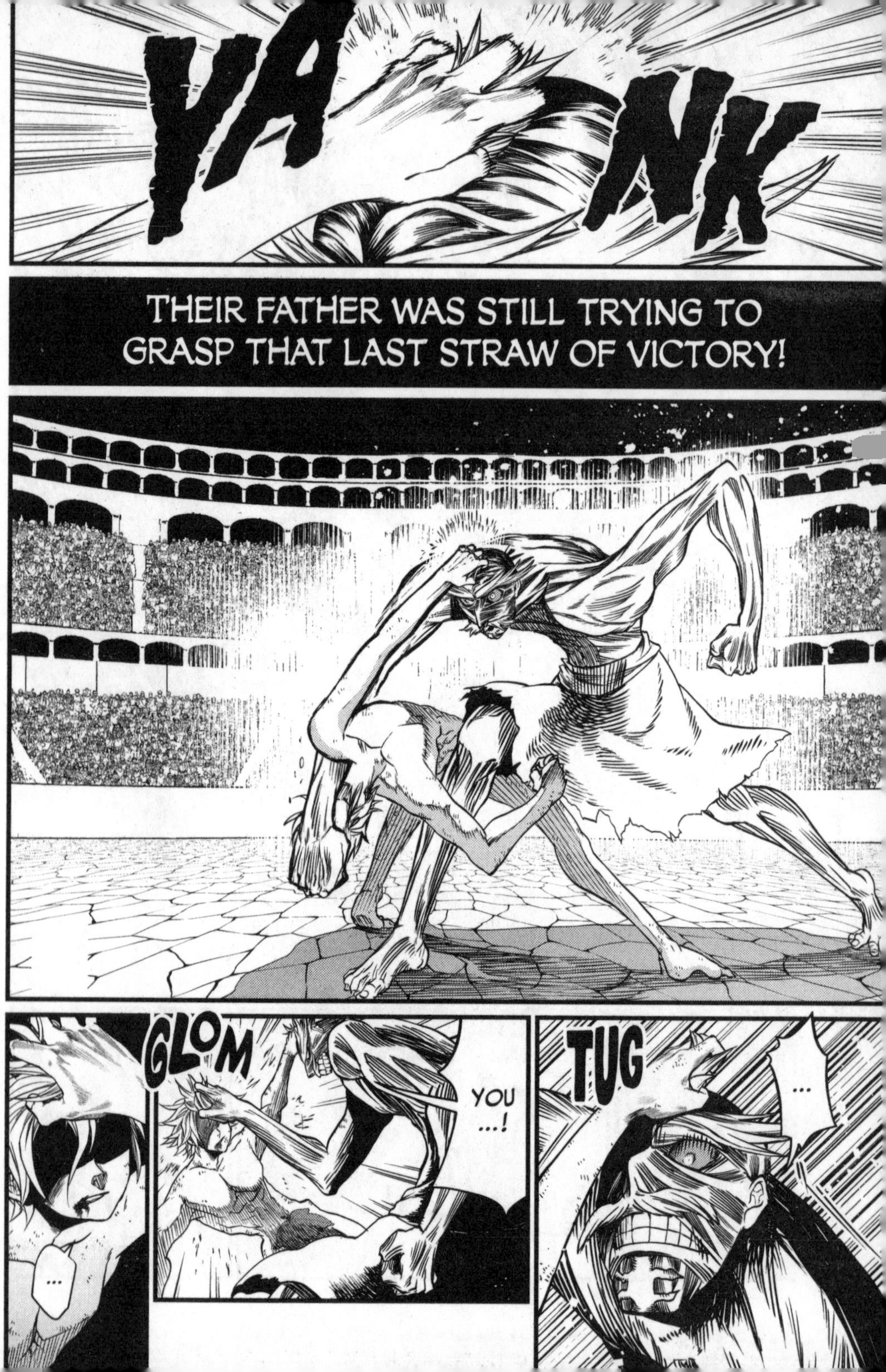
YANK
THEIR FATHER WAS STILL TRYING TO GRASP THAT LAST STRAW OF VICTORY!
TUG
...
GLOM
YOU ...!
...

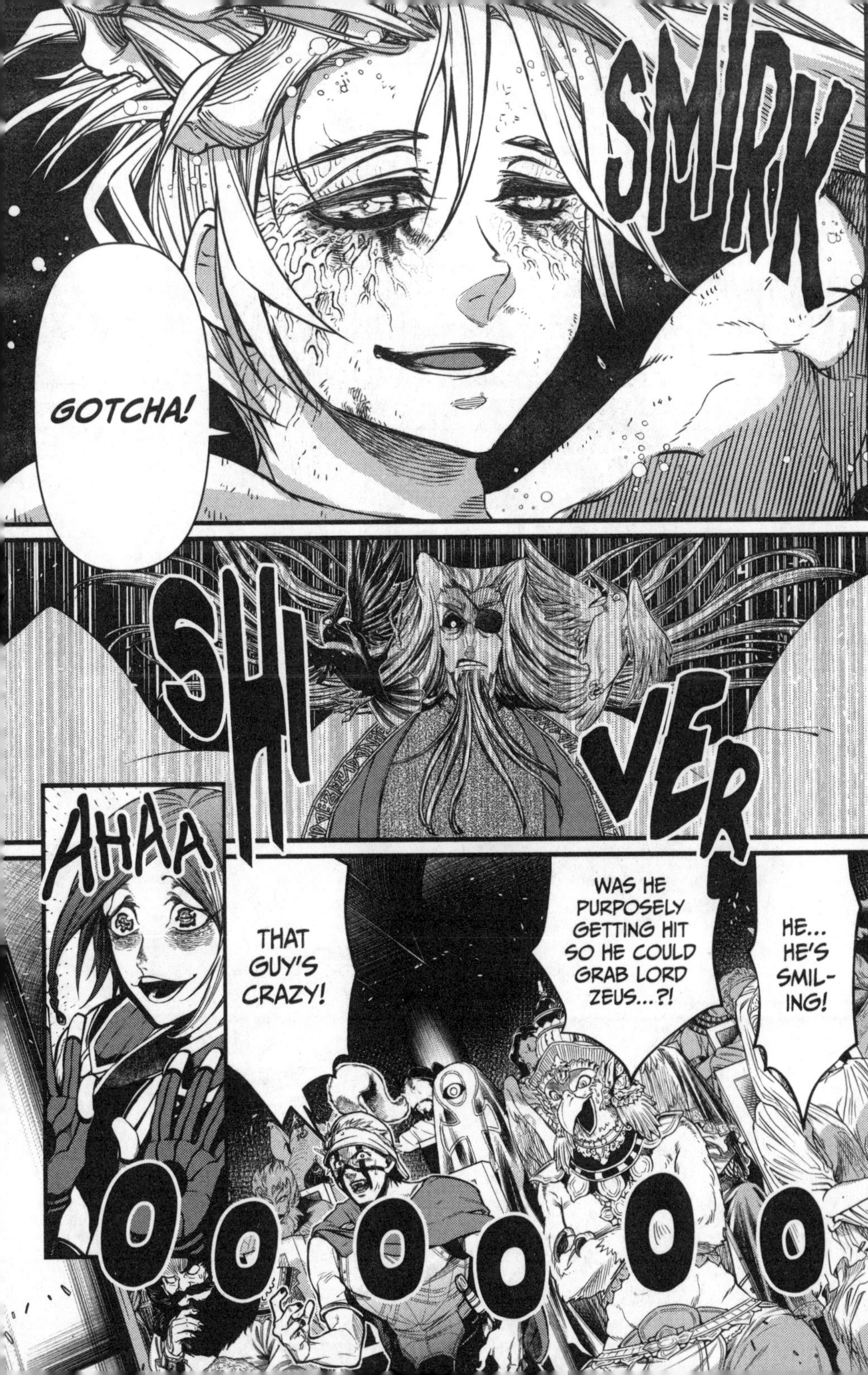
SMIRK
GOTCHA!
SHIVER
HE... HE'S SMIL- ING!
WAS HE PURPOSELY GETTING HIT SO HE COULD GRAB LORD ZEUS...?!
THAT GUY'S CRAZY!
AHAA
OOOOOOO

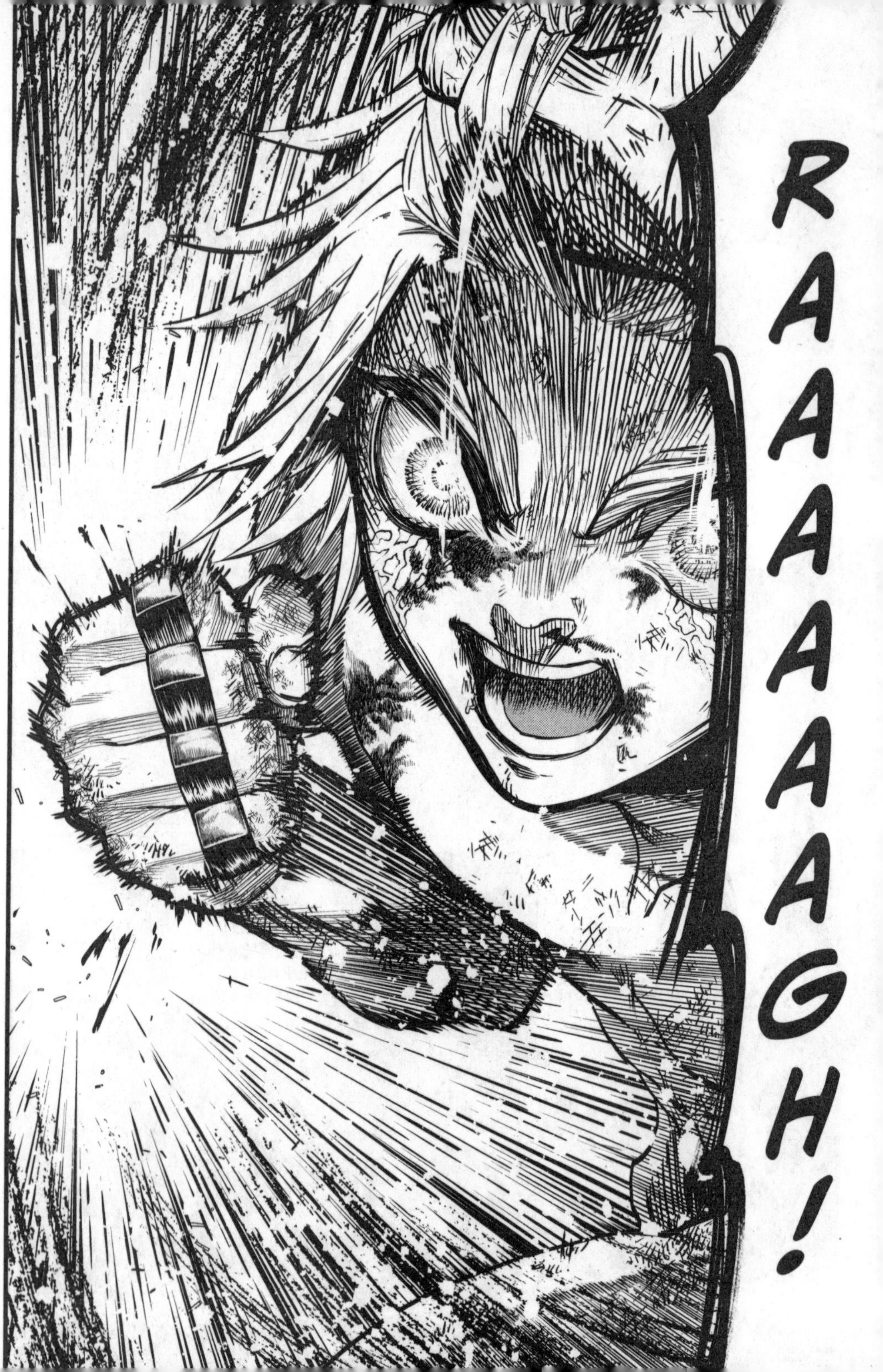
RAAAAAAGH!

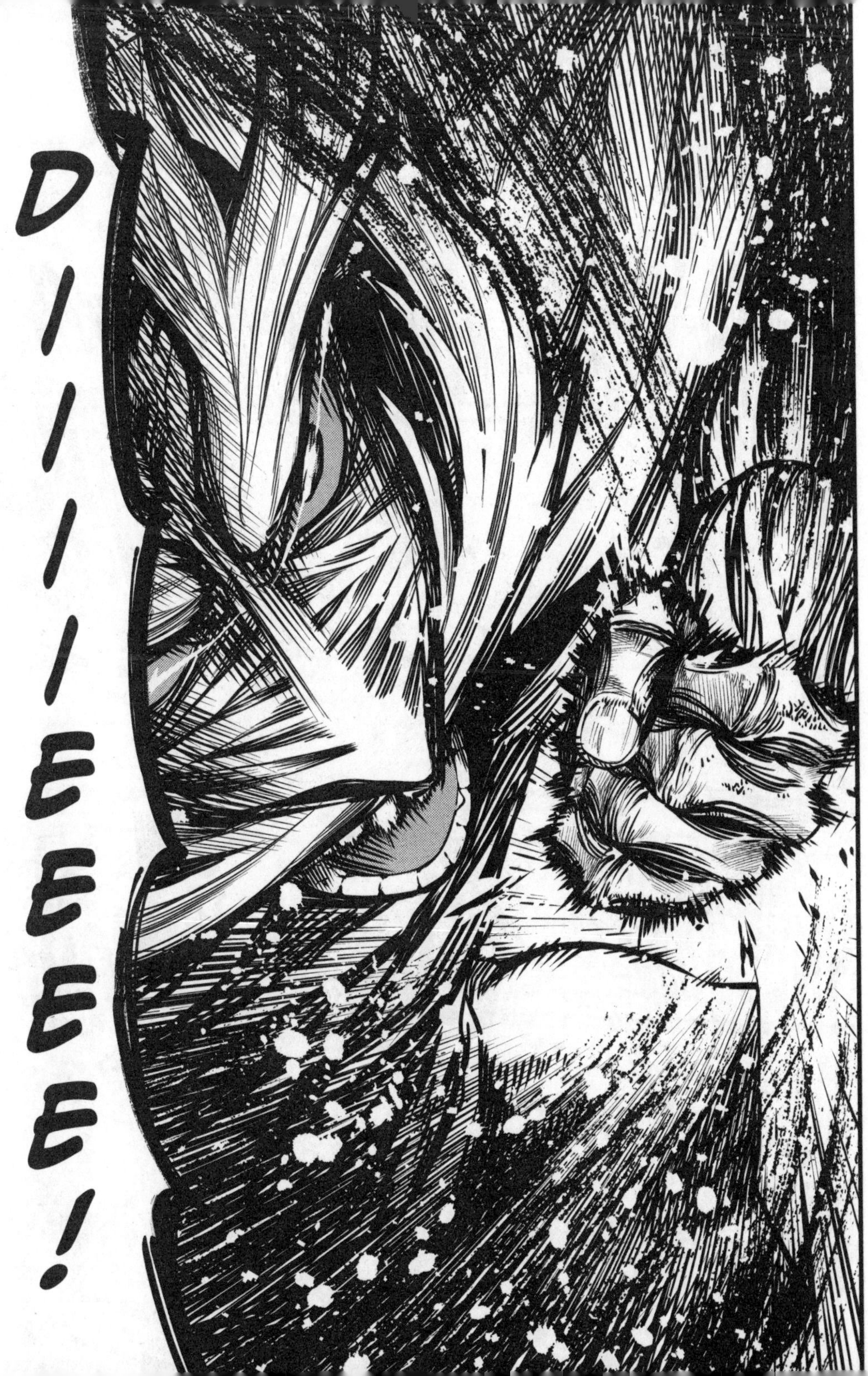
DIIIIEEEE!

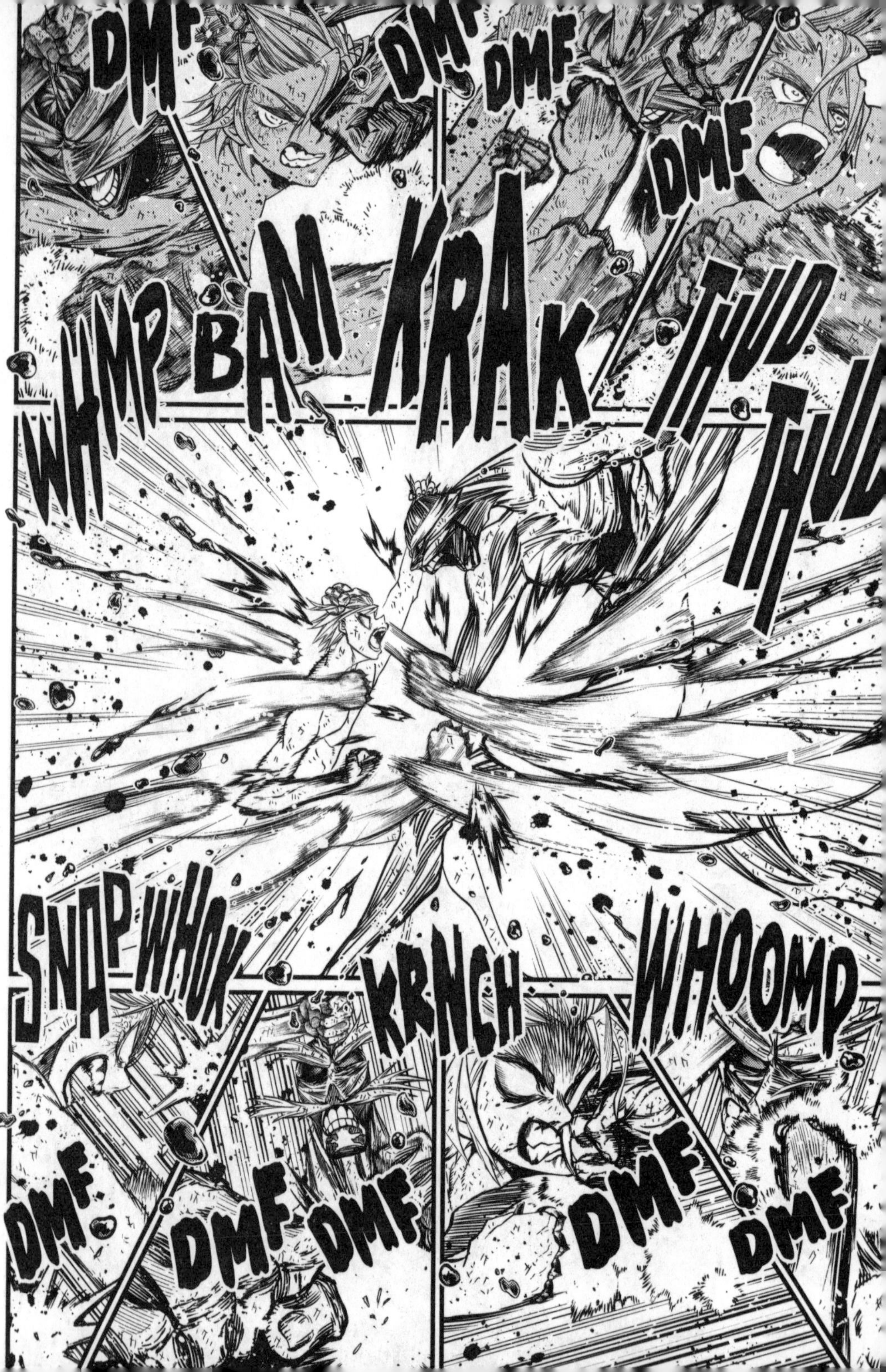
DMF
DMF
DMF
DMF
DMF
THUD
THUD
KRAK
BAM
WHMP
WHOOMP
KRNCH
WHOK
SNAP
DMF
DMF
DMF
DMF
DMF

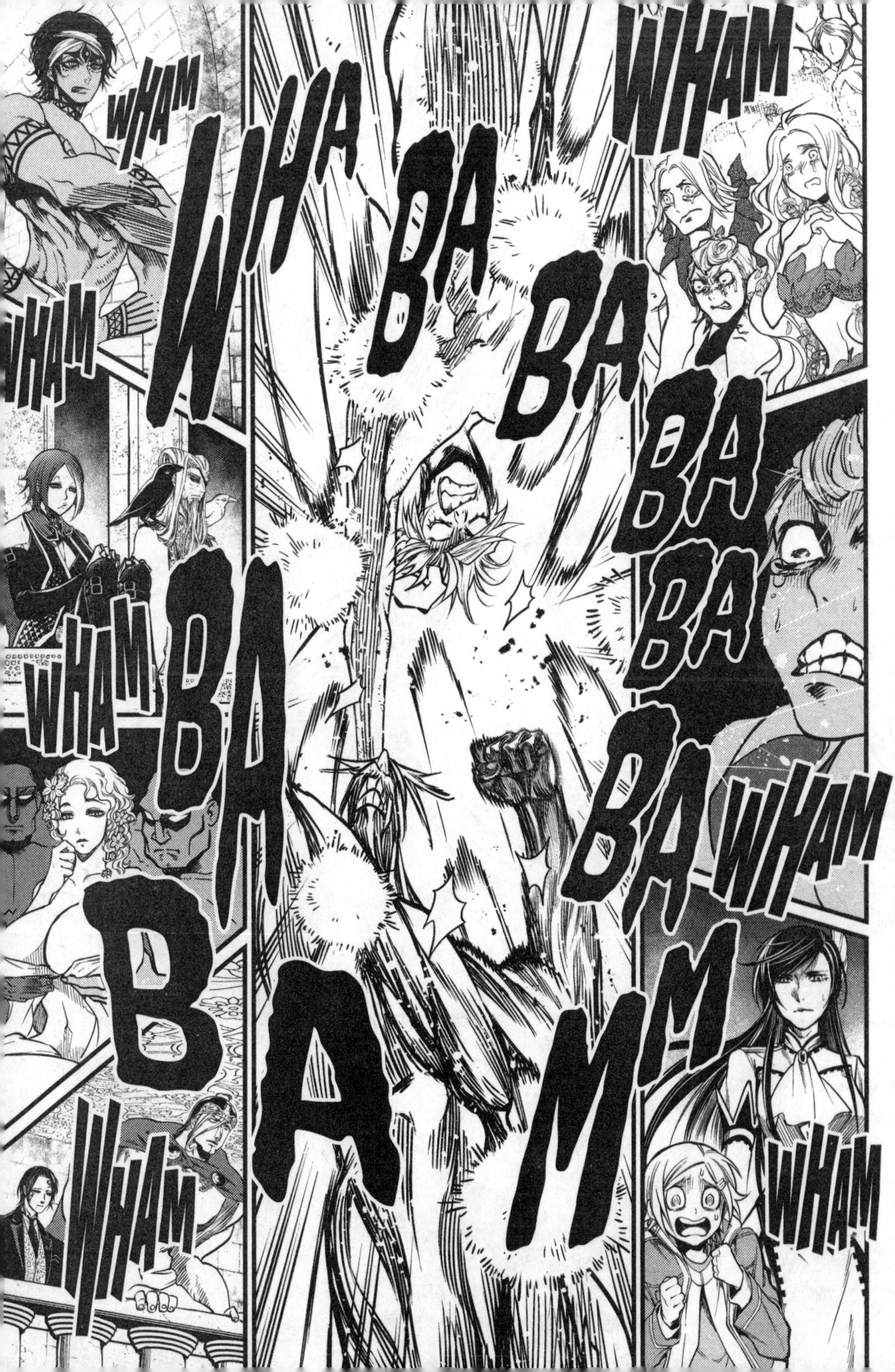
WHAM
WHAM
WHAM
WHA
BA
BA
BA
BA
BA
BA
BA
BAM
WHAM
WHAM
WHAM
WHAM

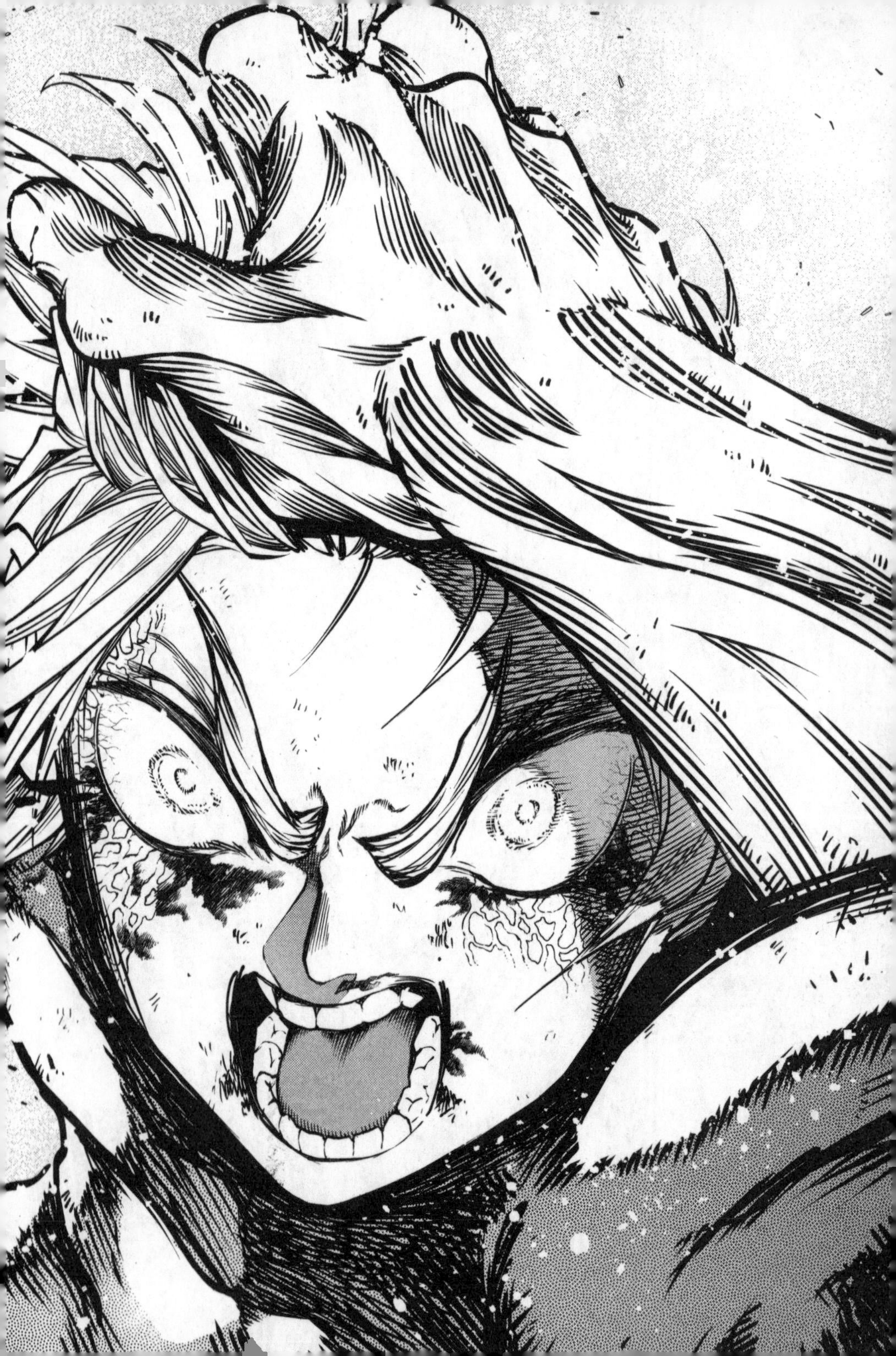

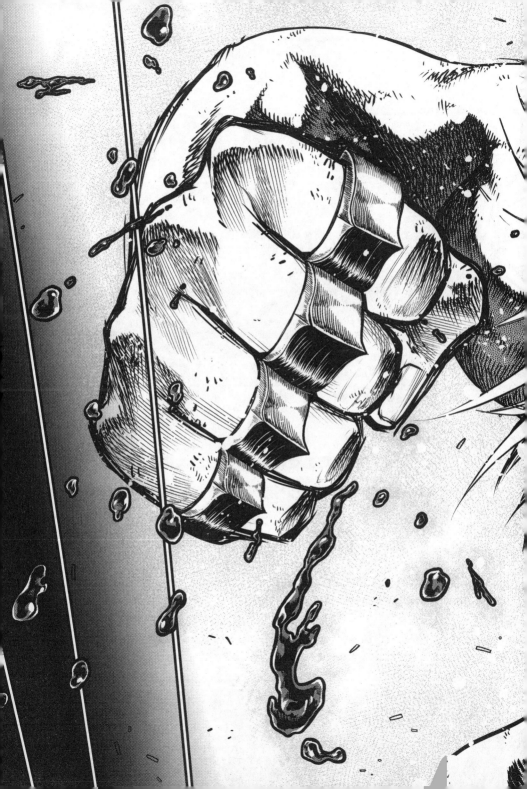

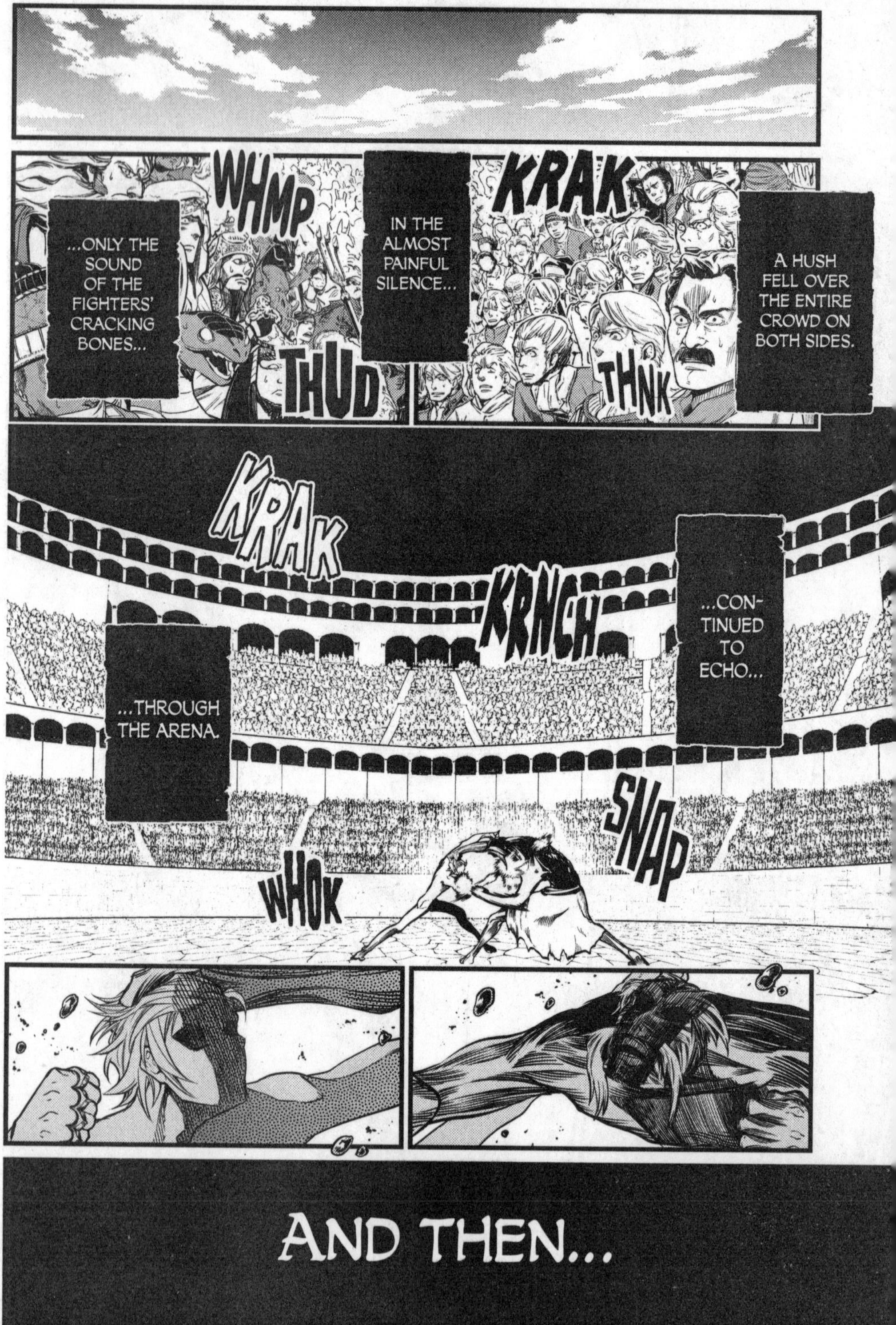
A HUSH FELL OVER THE ENTIRE CROWD ON BOTH SIDES.
KRAK
THNK
IN THE ALMOST PAINFUL SILENCE...
WHMP
...ONLY THE SOUND OF THE FIGHTERS' CRACKING BONES...
THUD
...CONTINUED TO ECHO...
KRAK
KRNCH
...THROUGH THE ARENA.
SNAP
WHOK
AND THEN...

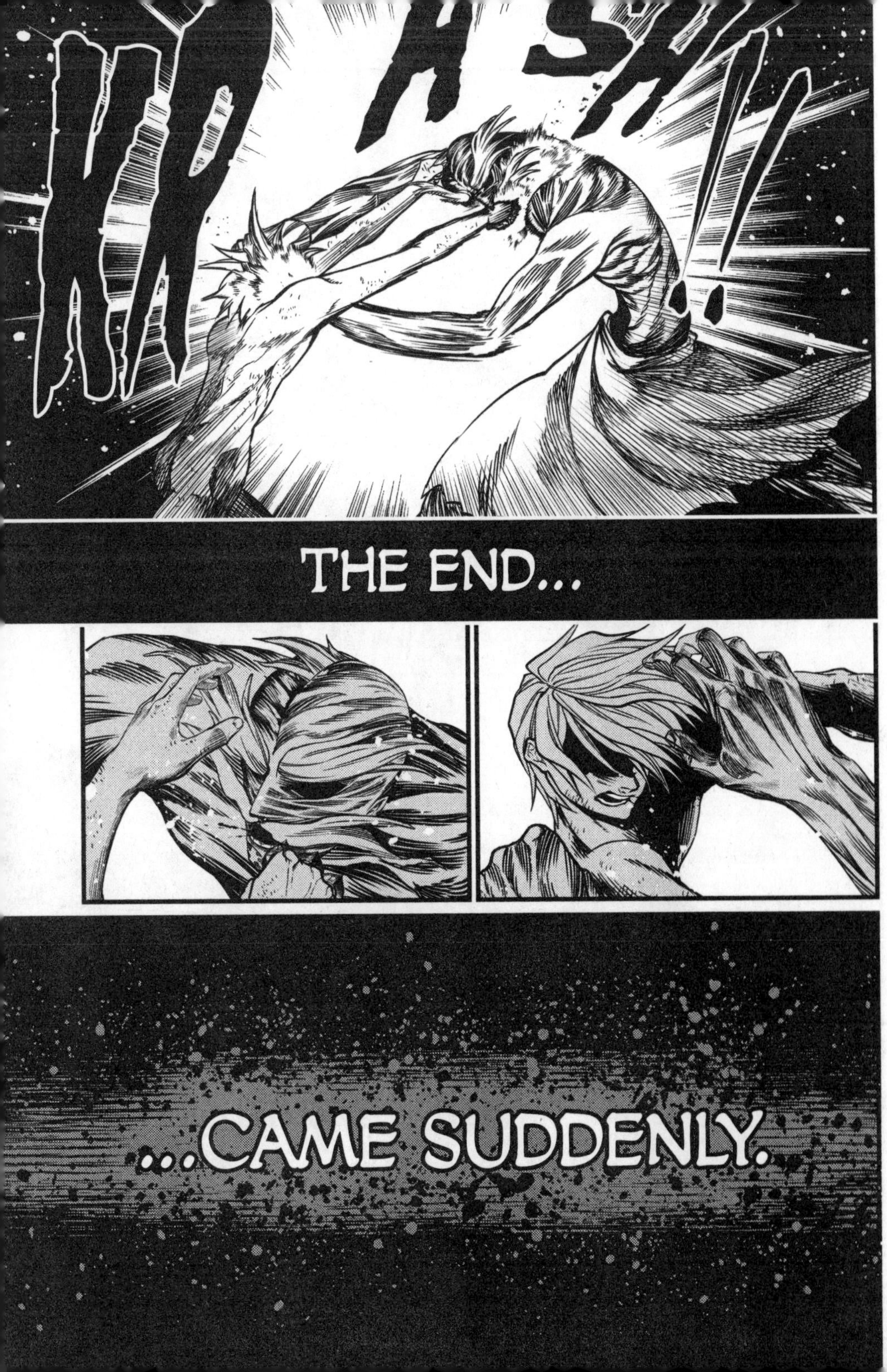
KRASH!!
THE END...
...CAME SUDDENLY.

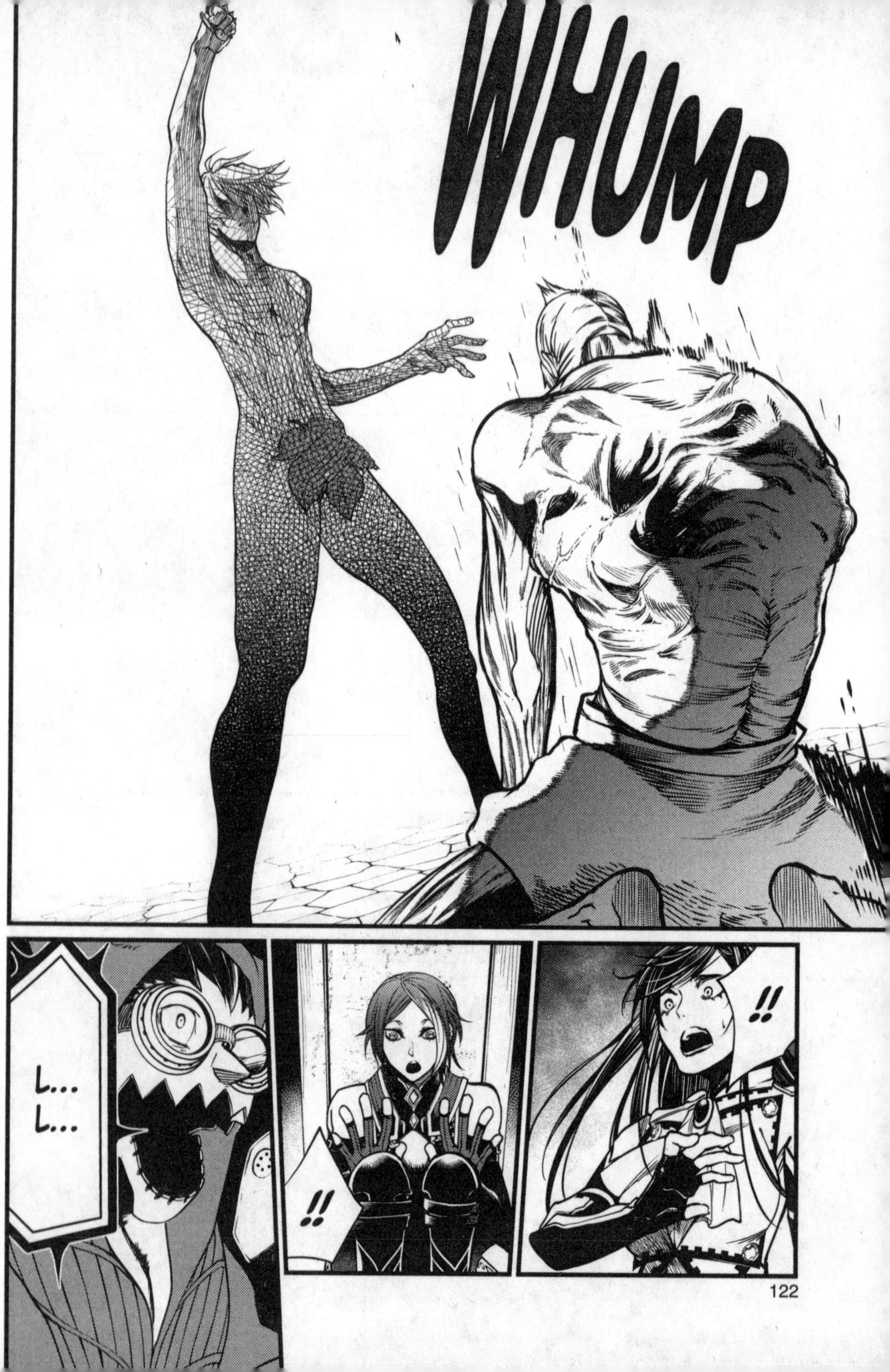
WHUMP
!!
!!
L...
L...

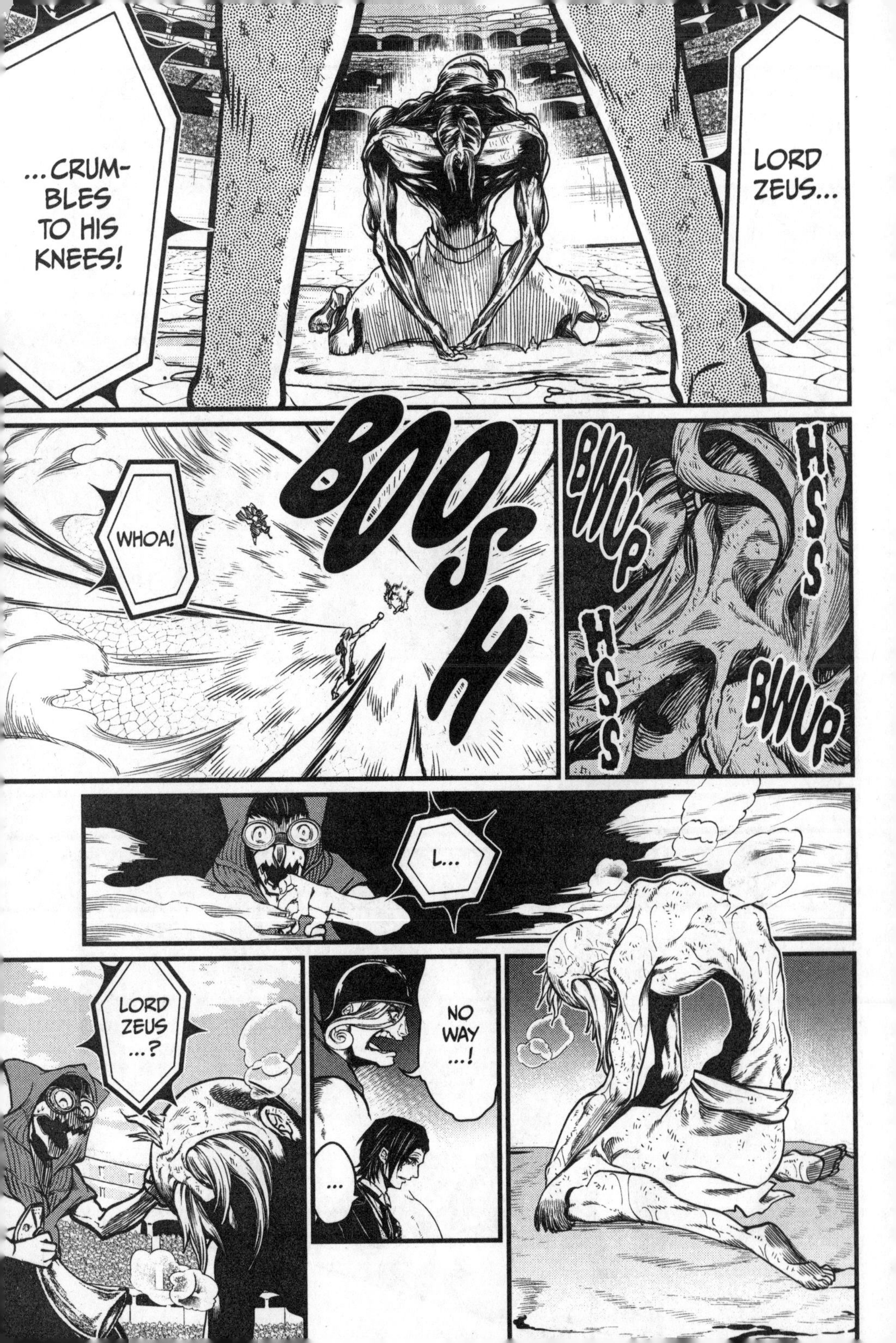
LORD ZEUS...
...CRUMBLES TO HIS KNEES!
HSS
BWUP
HSS
BWUP
BOOSH
WHOA!
L...
NO WAY ...!
...
LORD ZEUS ...?

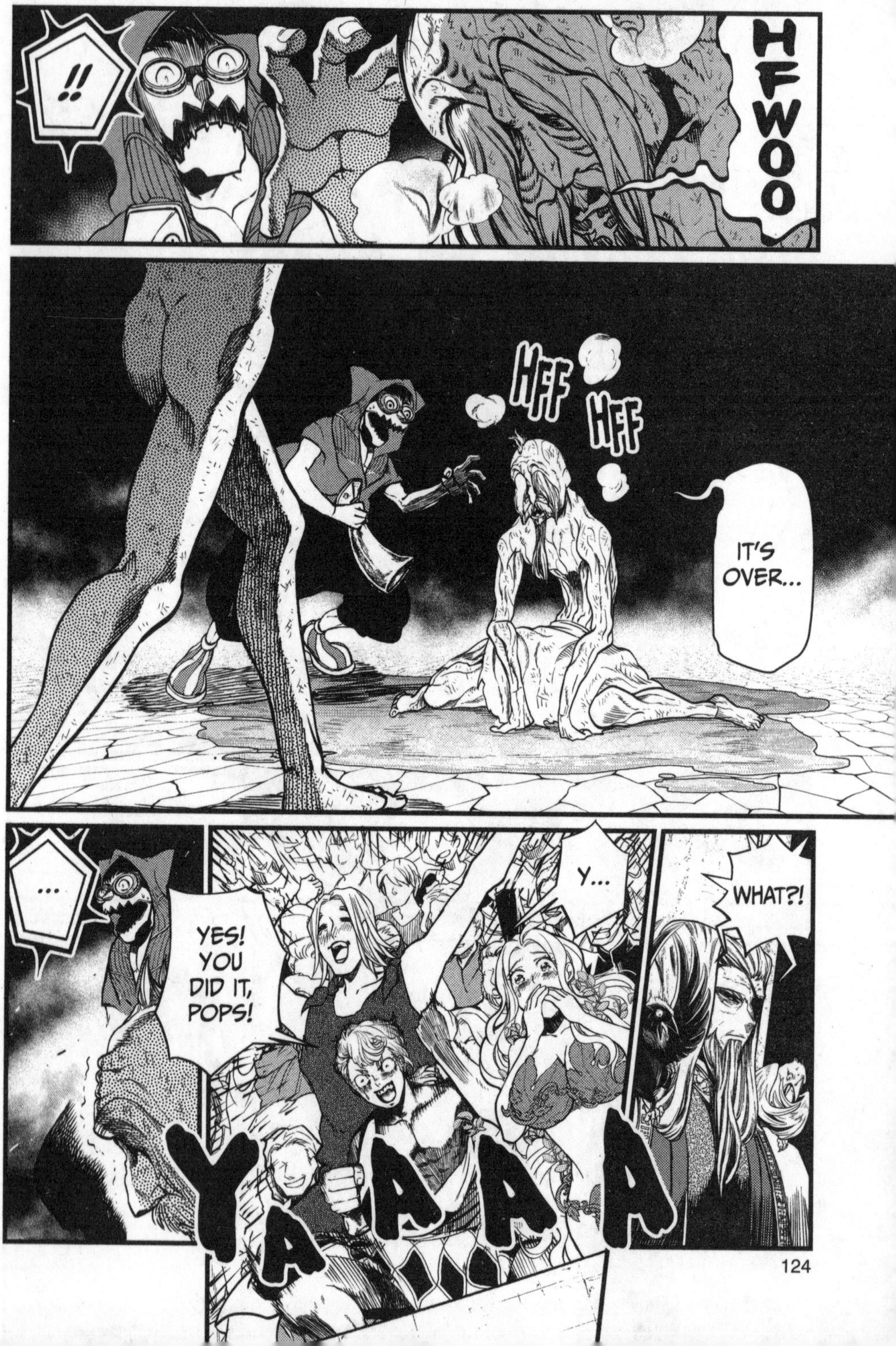
HFWOO
!!
HFF
HFF
IT'S OVER...
WHAT?!
Y...
YES! YOU DID IT, POPS!
YAAAA
...

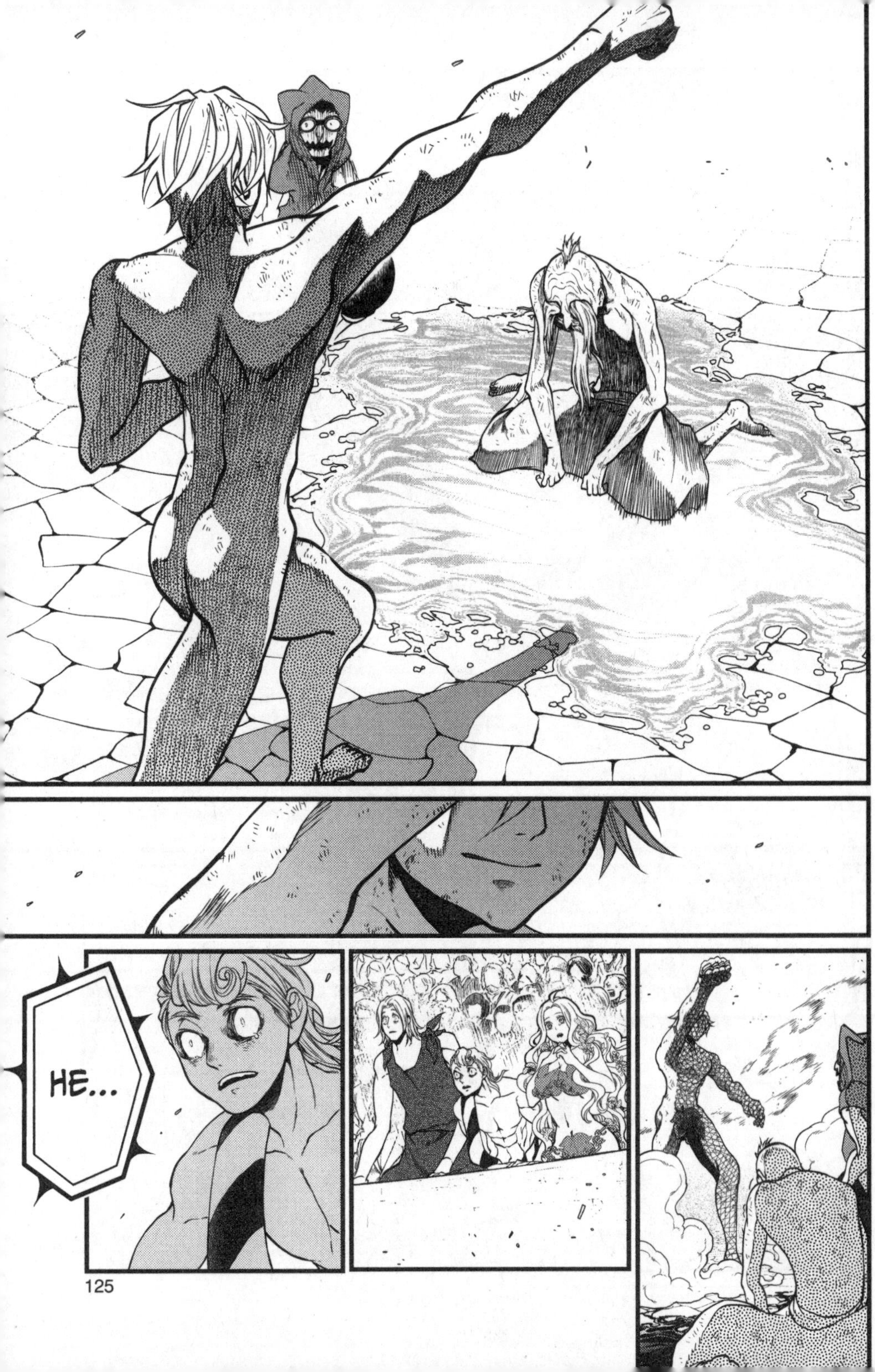
HE...

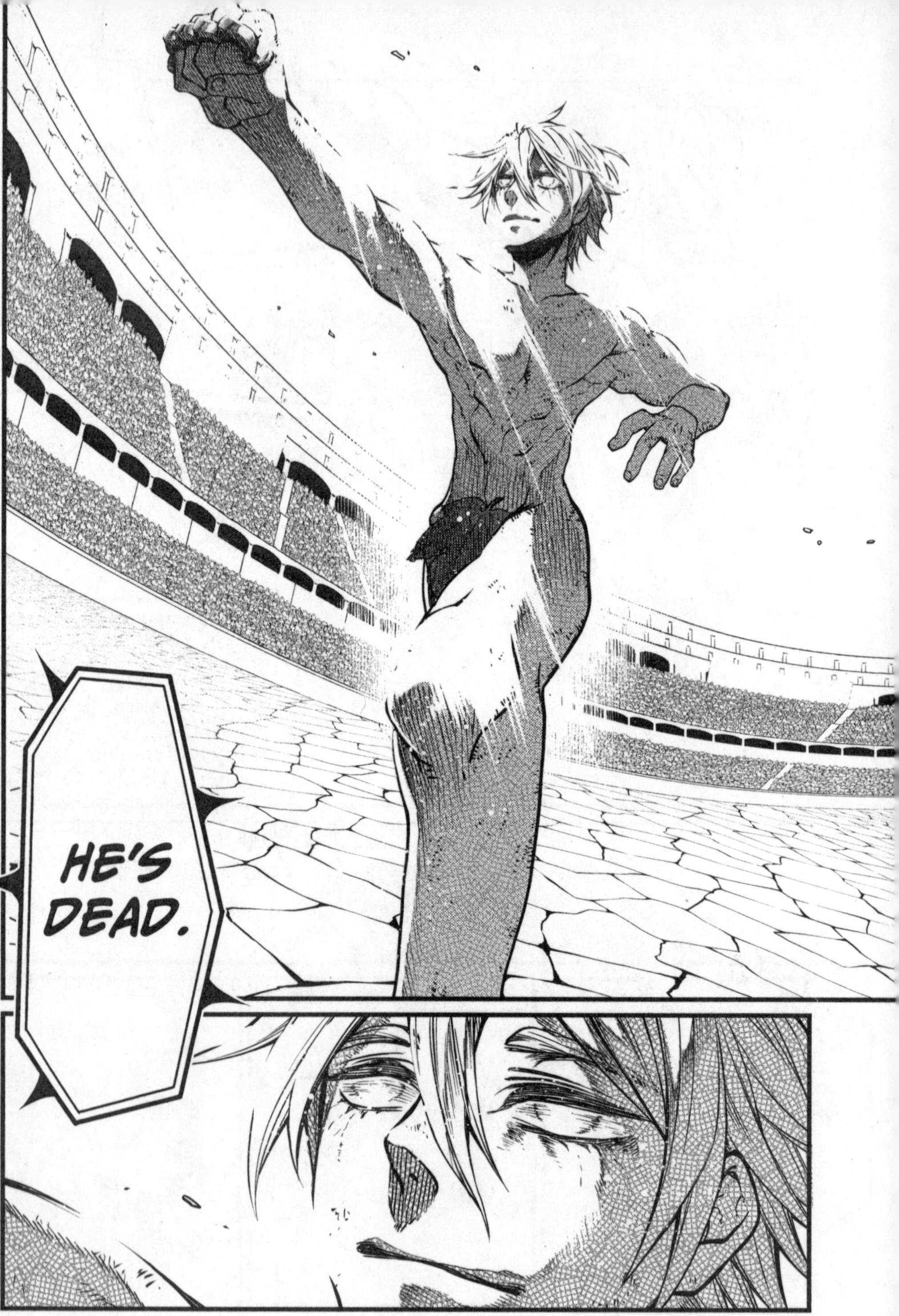
HE'S DEAD.

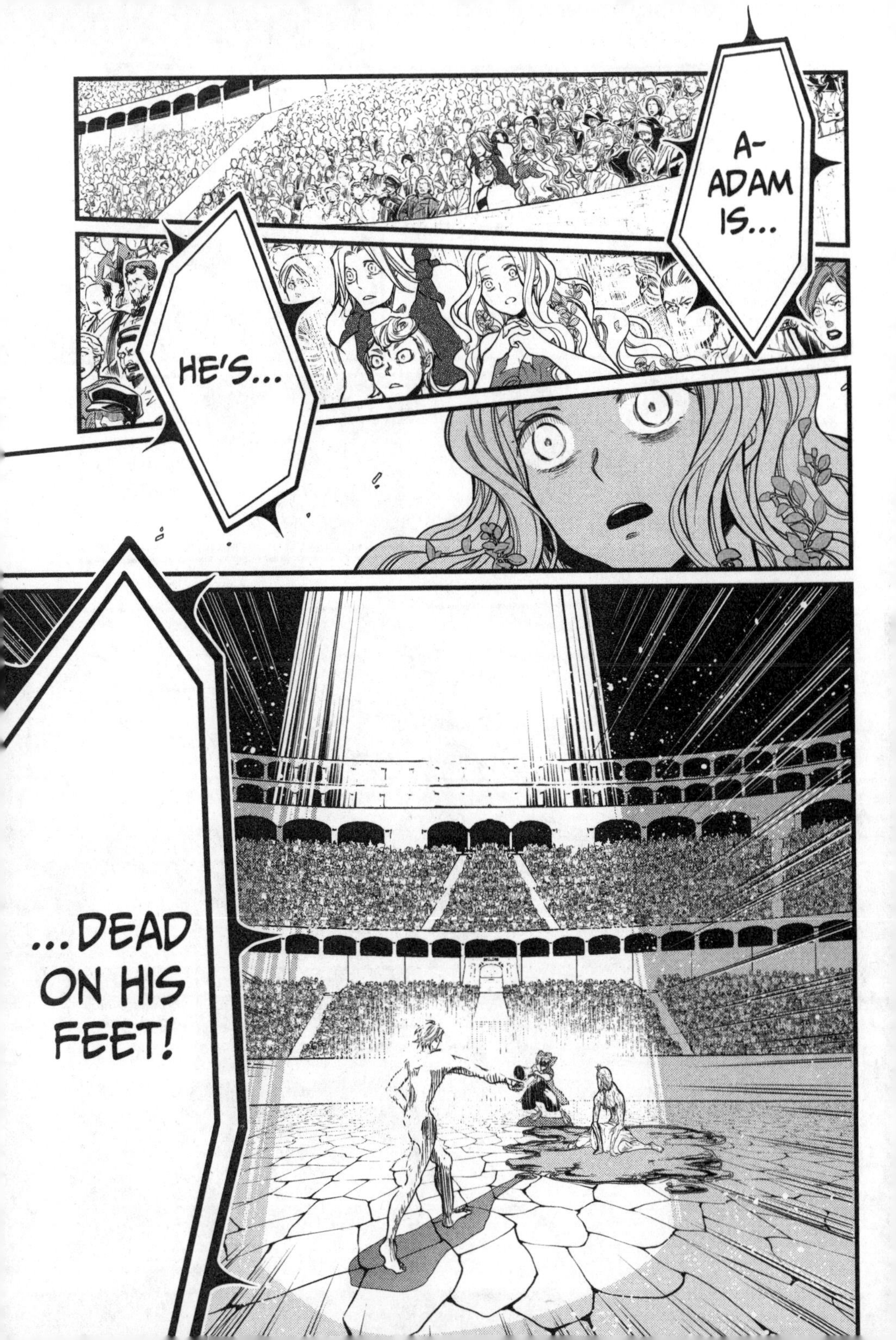
A-ADAM IS...
HE'S...
...DEAD ON HIS FEET!

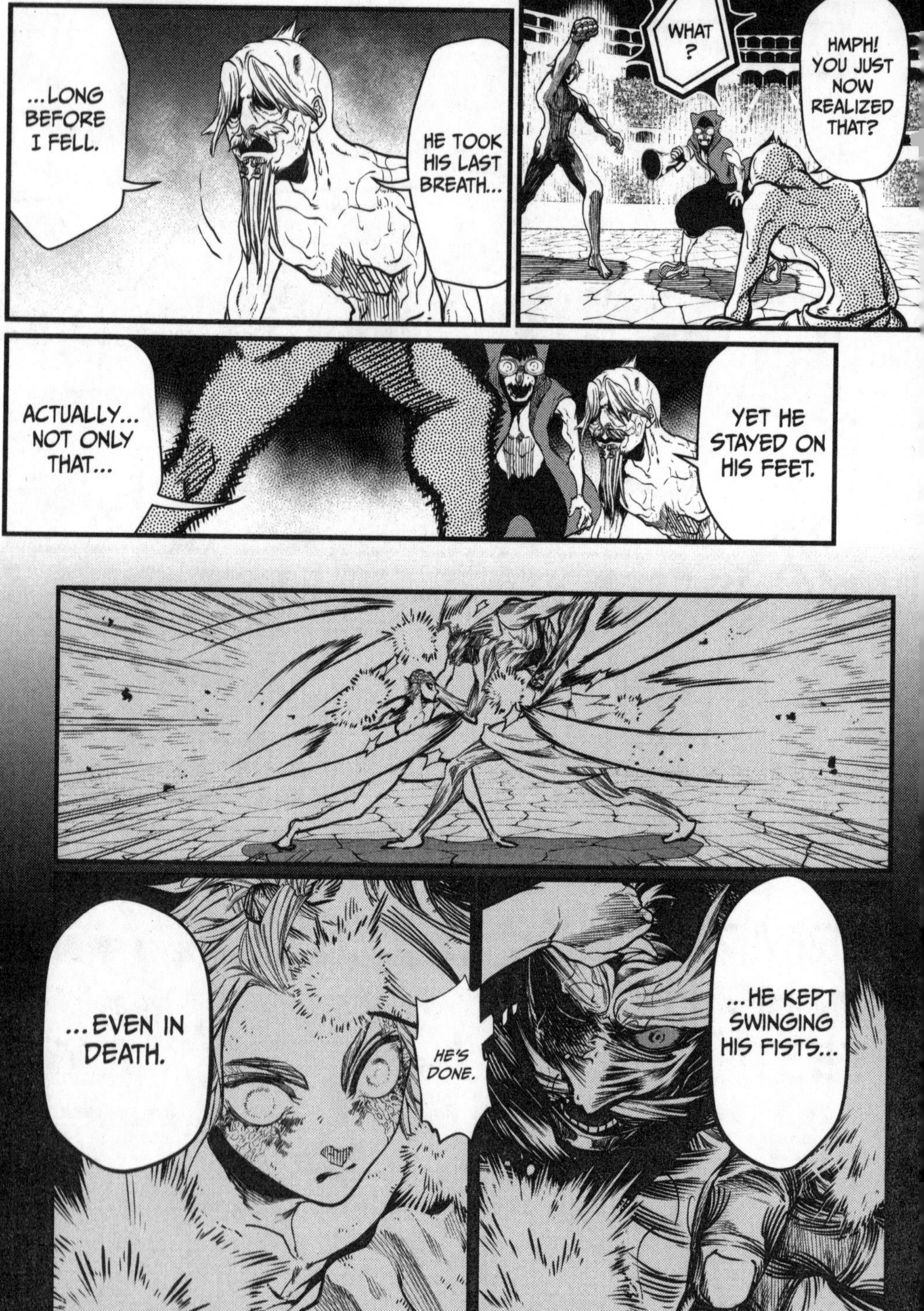
WHAT ?
HMPH! YOU JUST NOW REALIZED THAT?
HE TOOK HIS LAST BREATH...
...LONG BEFORE I FELL.
YET HE STAYED ON HIS FEET.
ACTUALLY... NOT ONLY THAT...
...HE KEPT SWINGING HIS FISTS...
...EVEN IN DEATH.
HE'S DONE.

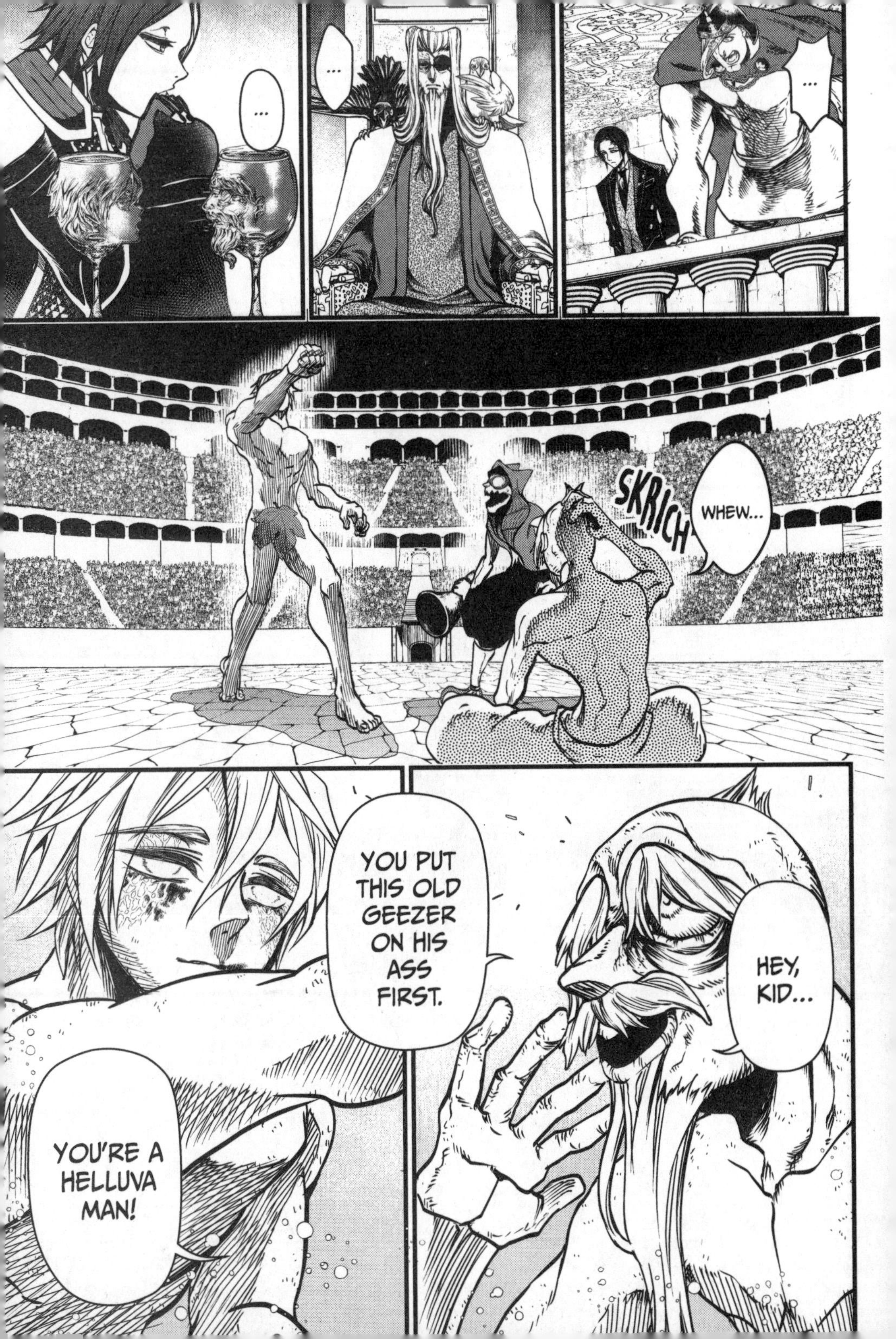
...
...
...
SKRICH
WHEW...
HEY, KID...
YOU PUT THIS OLD GEEZER ON HIS ASS FIRST.
YOU'RE A HELLUVA MAN!

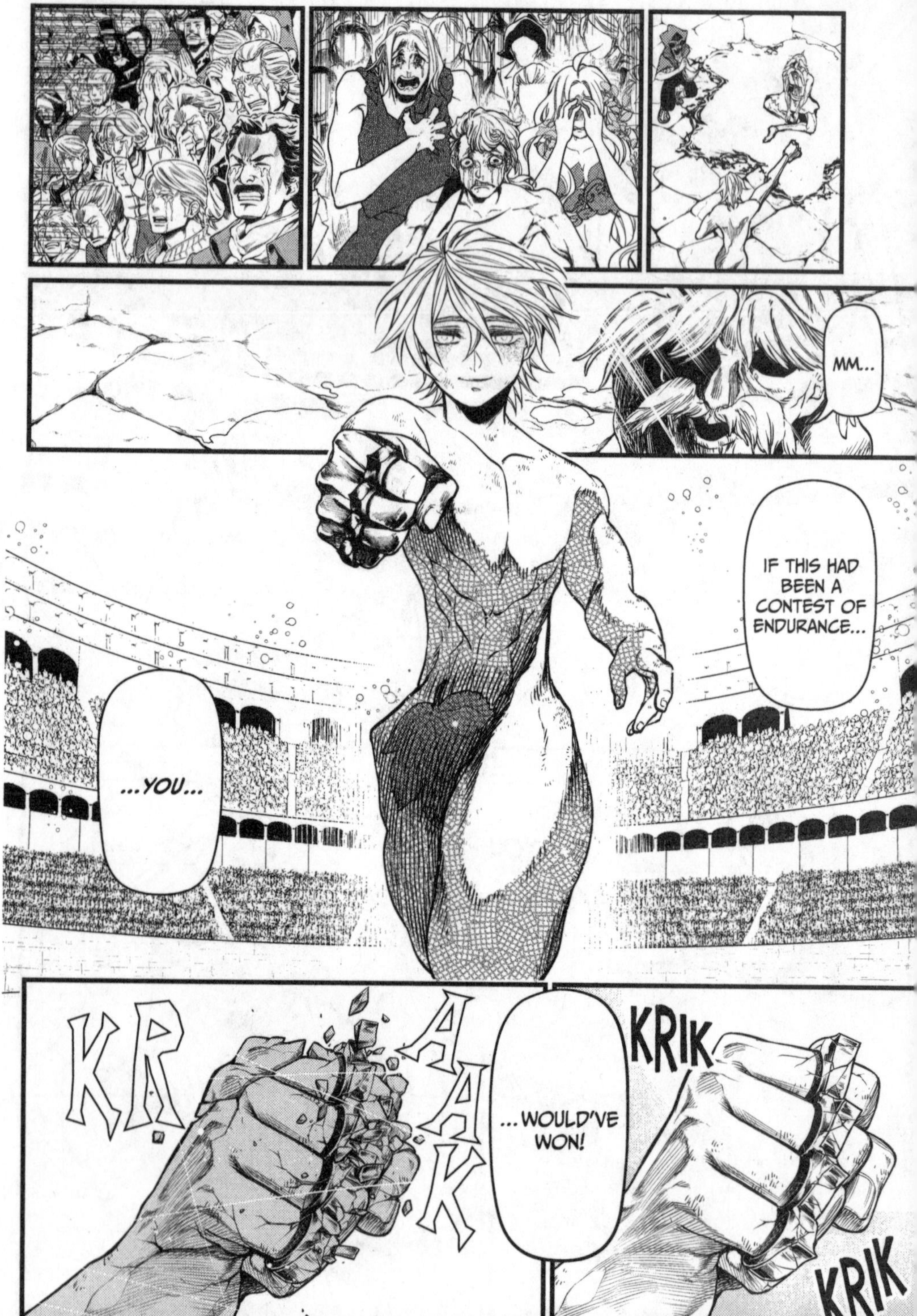
MM...
IF THIS HAD BEEN A CONTEST OF ENDURANCE...
...YOU...
KRIK
...WOULD'VE WON!
KRIK
KR
AAK

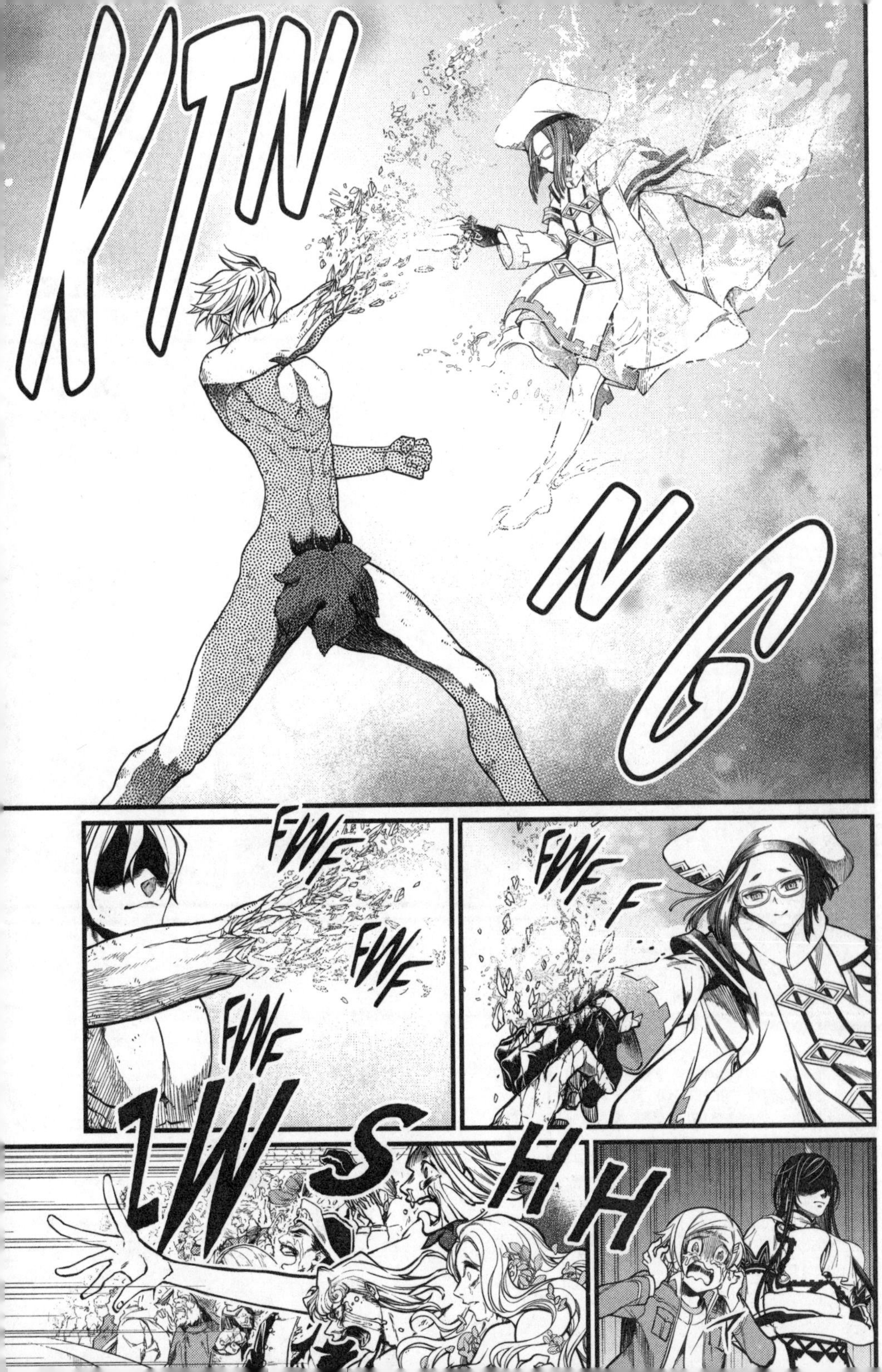
KTN
NG
FWF
F
FWF
FWF
FWF
ZWSHH

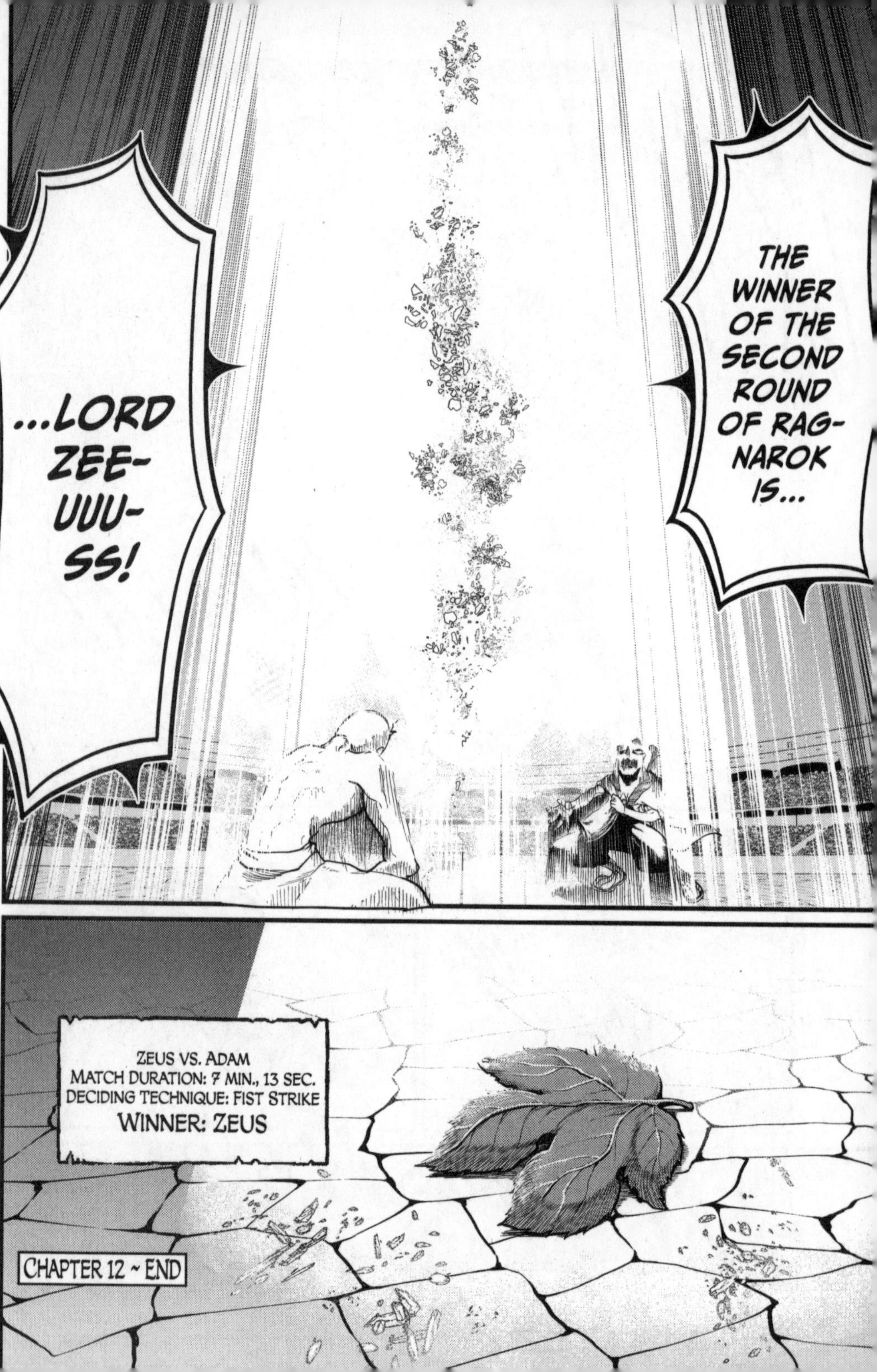
THE WINNER OF THE SECOND ROUND OF RAG-NAROK IS...
...LORD ZEE-UUU-SS!
ZEUS VS. ADAM
MATCH DURATION: 7 MIN., 13 SEC.
DECIDING TECHNIQUE: FIST STRIKE
WINNER: ZEUS
CHAPTER 12 ~ END

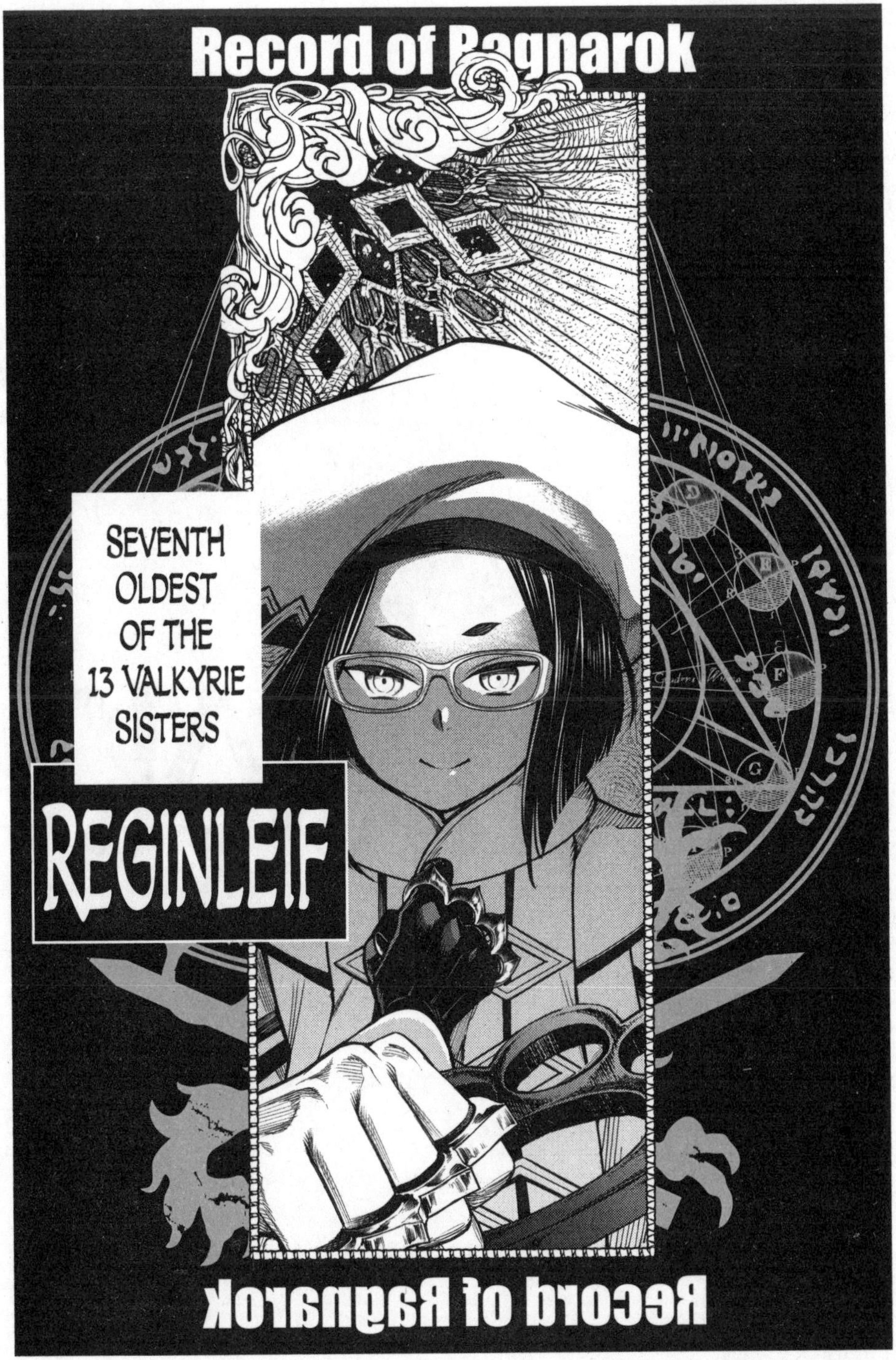
Record of Ragnarok
SEVENTH OLDEST OF THE 13 VALKYRIE SISTERS
REGINLEIF
Record of Ragnarok

RECORD OF

RAGNAROK

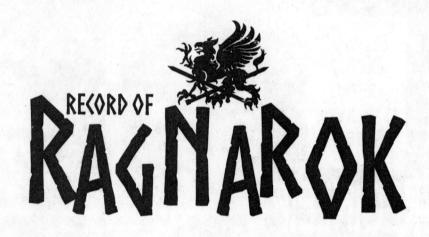

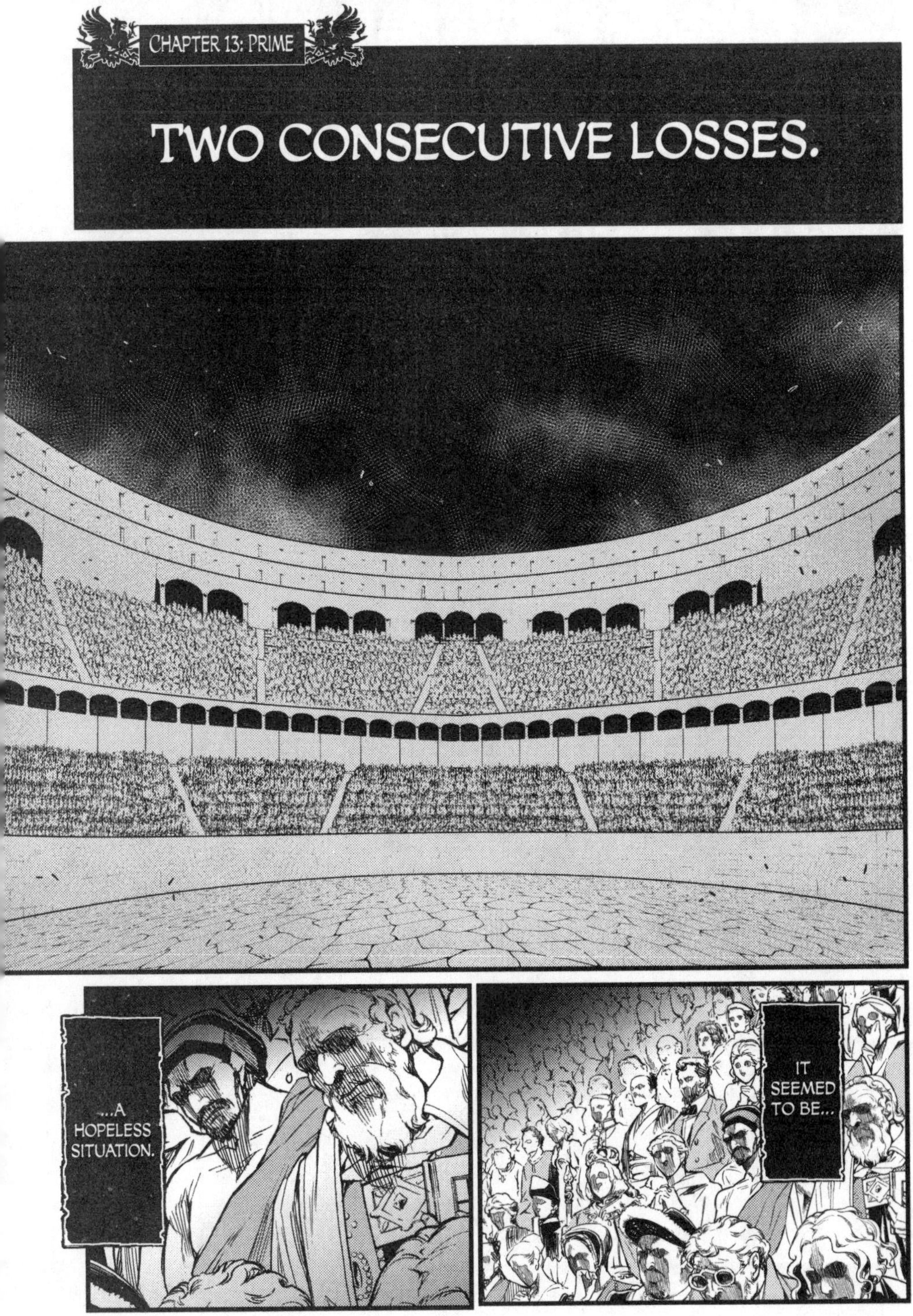
CHAPTER 13: PRIME
TWO CONSECUTIVE LOSSES.
IT SEEMED TO BE...
...A HOPELESS SITUATION.

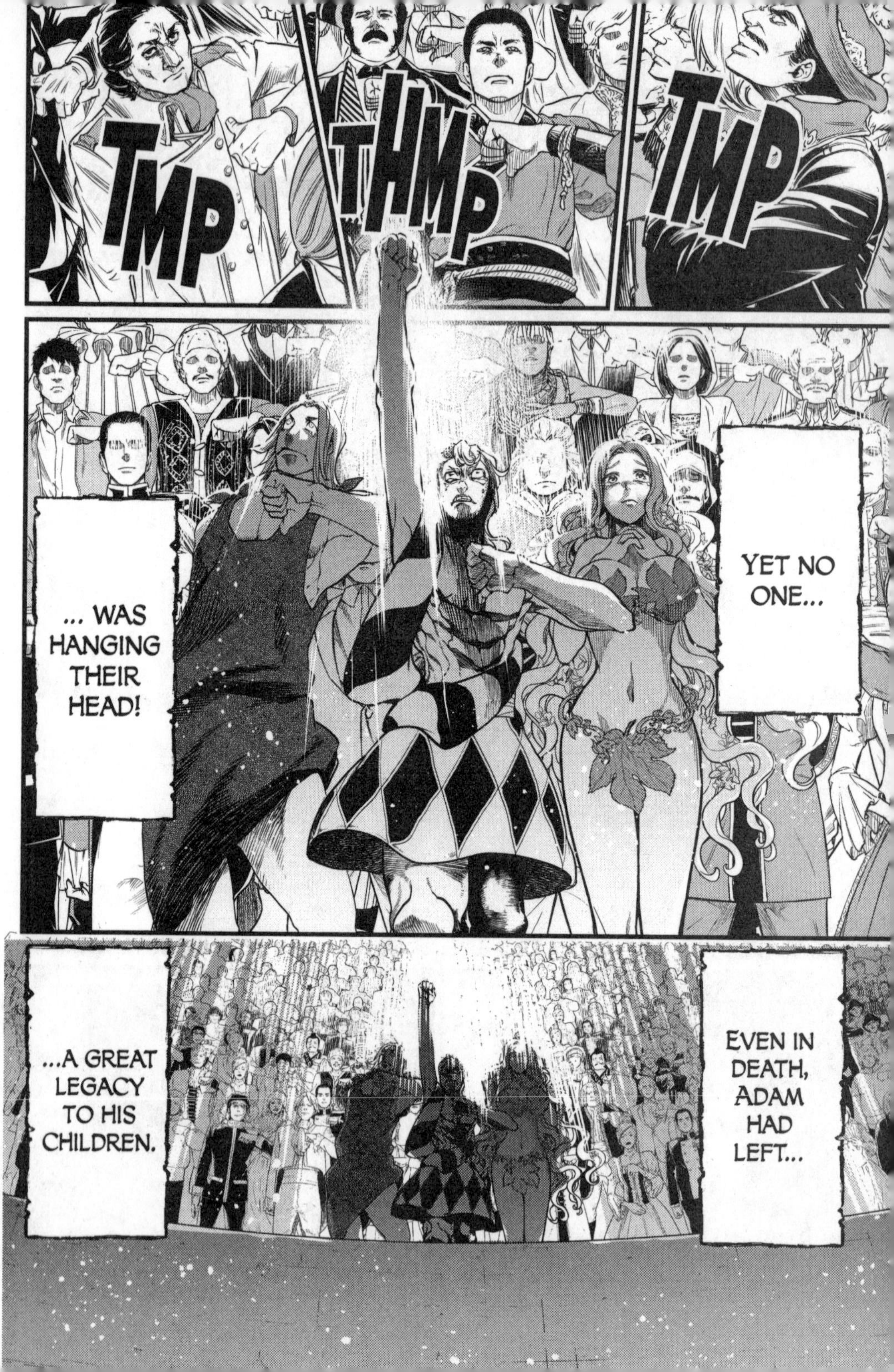
TMP
THMP
TMP
YET NO ONE...
... WAS HANGING THEIR HEAD!
EVEN IN DEATH, ADAM HAD LEFT...
...A GREAT LEGACY TO HIS CHILDREN.

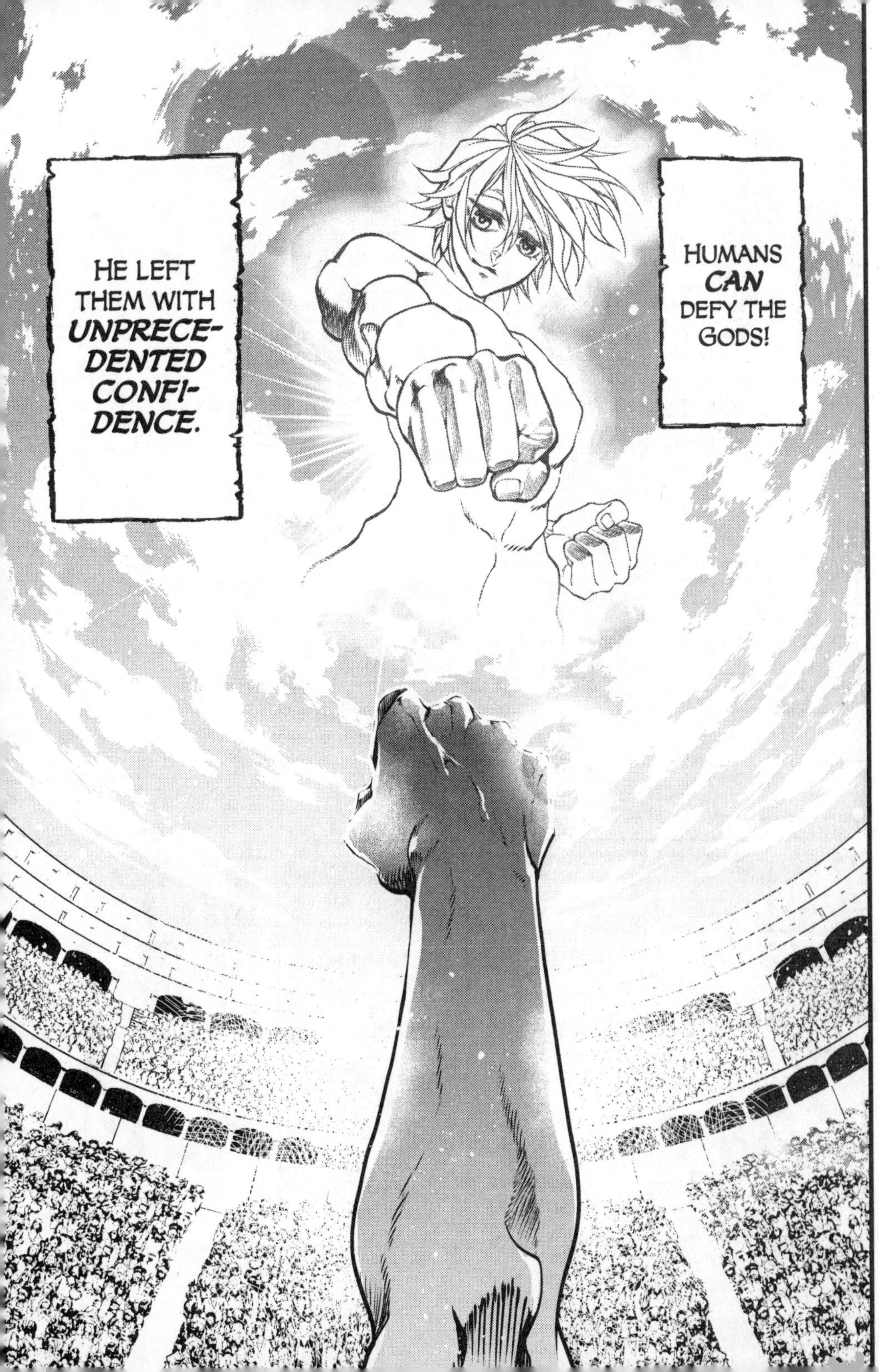
HUMANS CAN DEFY THE GODS!
HE LEFT THEM WITH UNPRECE-DENTED CONFI-DENCE.

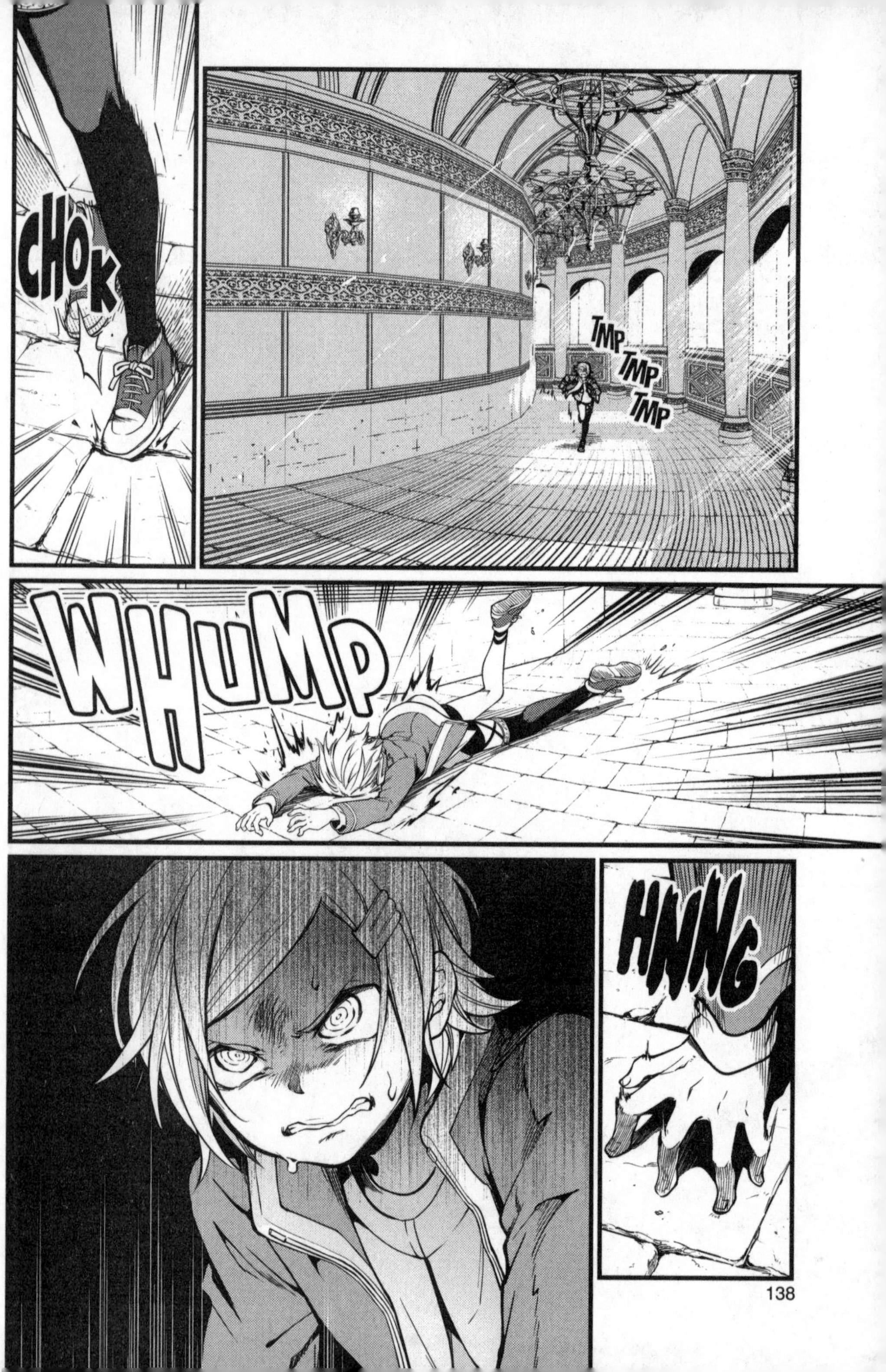
TMP
TMP
TMP
CHOK
WHUMP
HNNG

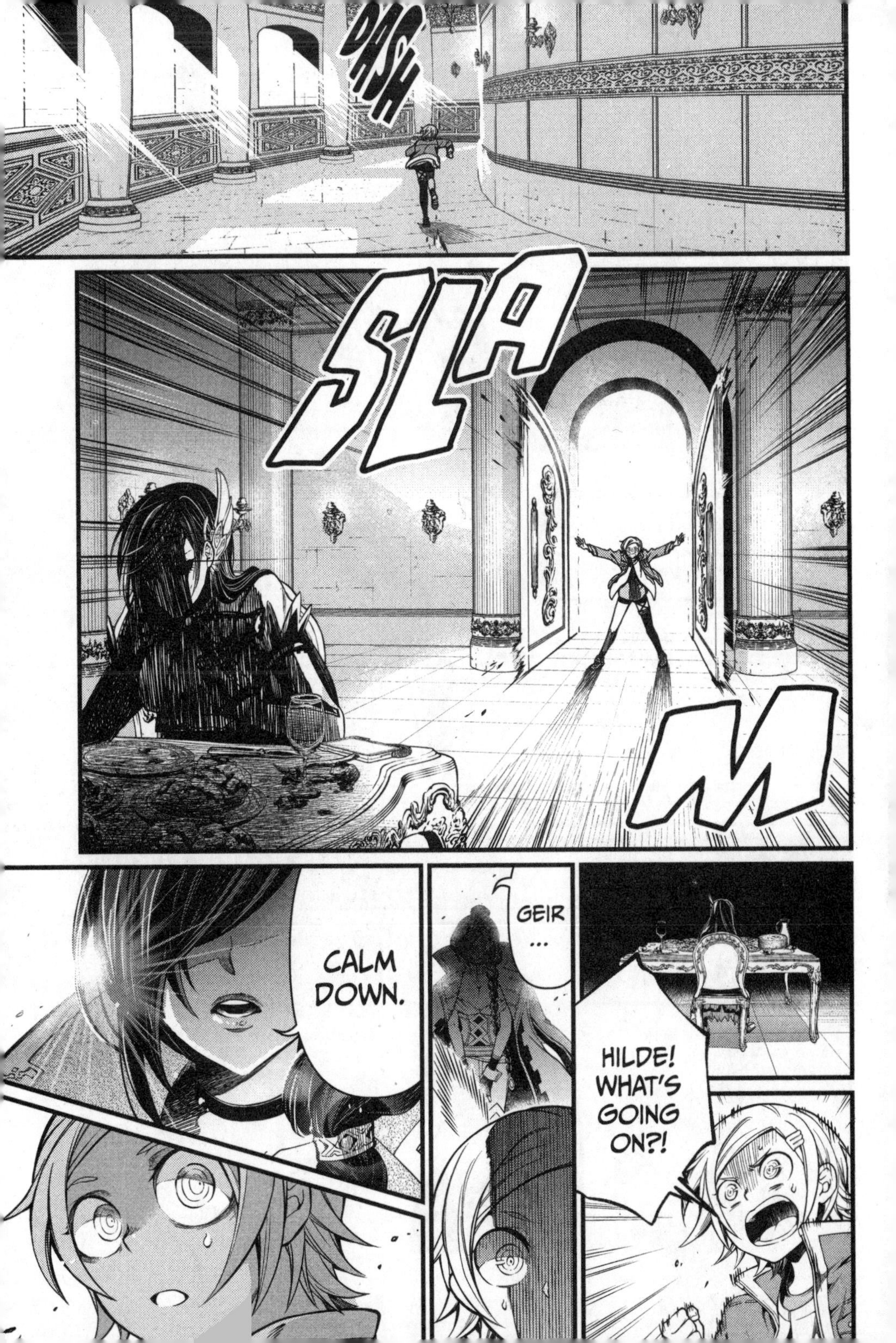
DASH
SLAM
HILDE! WHAT'S GOING ON?!
GEIR ...
CALM DOWN.

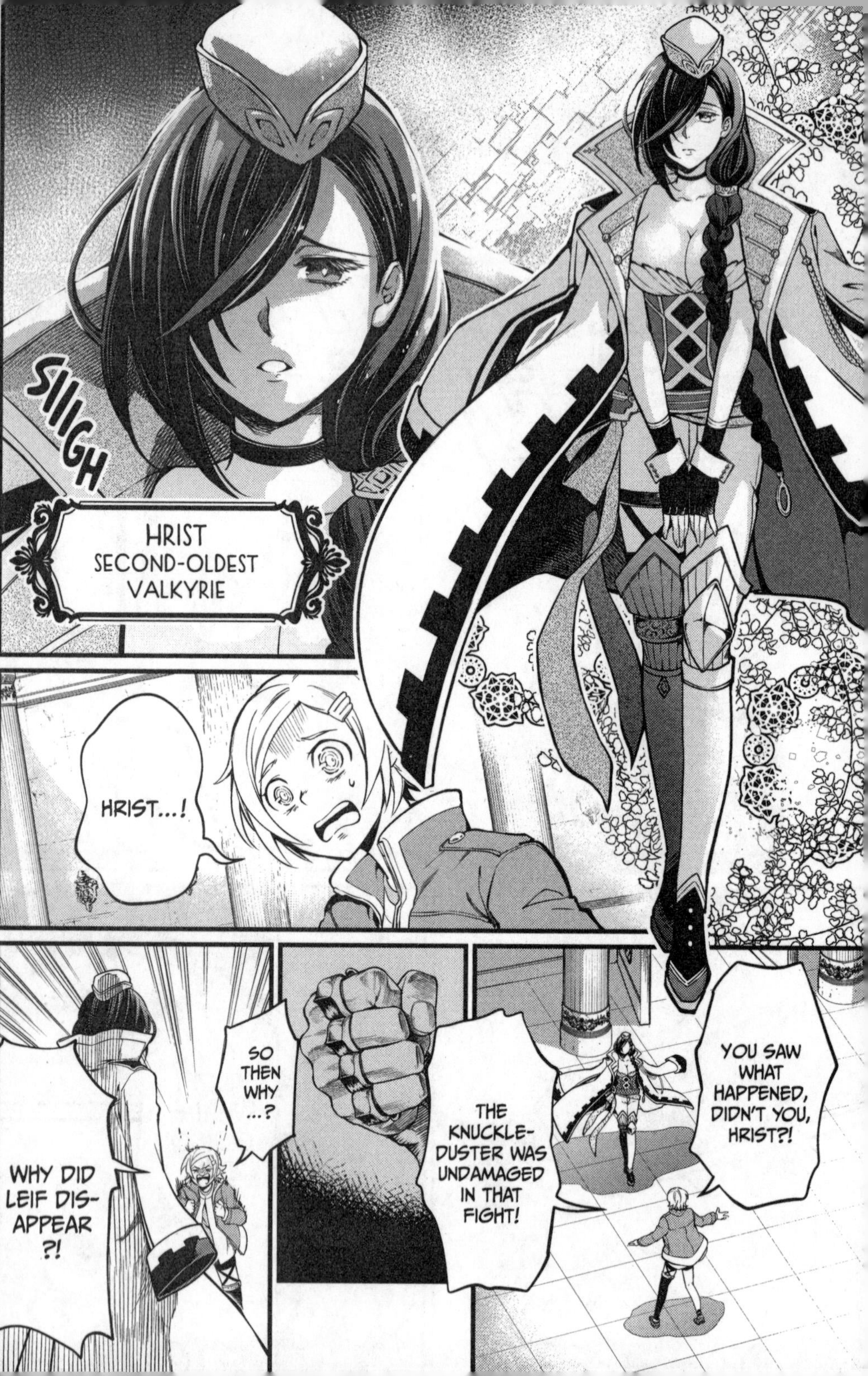
SIIIGH
HRIST SECOND-OLDEST VALKYRIE
HRIST...!
YOU SAW WHAT HAPPENED, DIDN'T YOU, HRIST?!
THE KNUCKLE-DUSTER WAS UNDAMAGED IN THAT FIGHT!
SO THEN WHY ...?
WHY DID LEIF DIS-APPEAR ?!

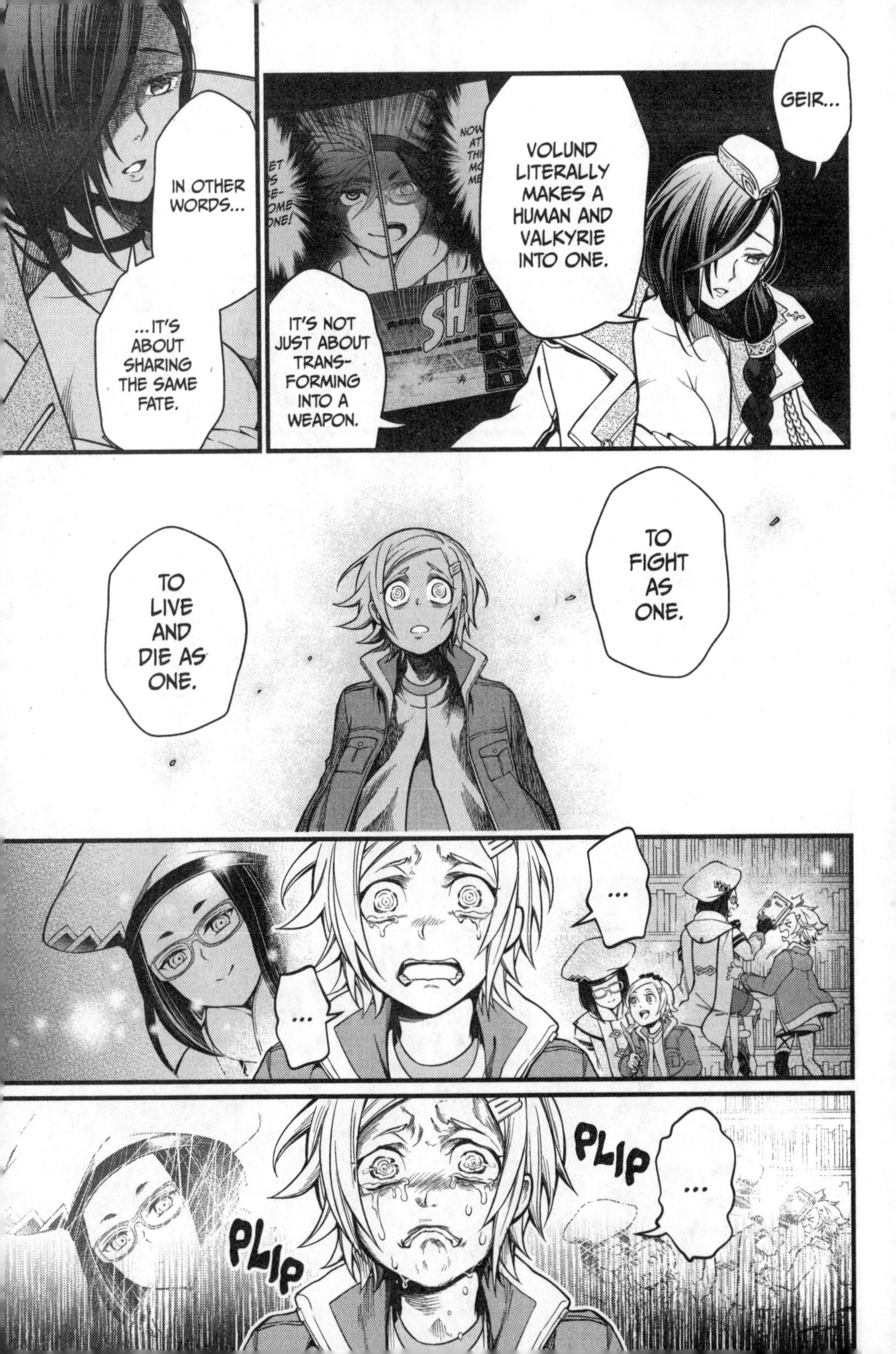

GEIR...
VOLUND LITERALLY MAKES A HUMAN AND VALKYRIE INTO ONE.
IT'S NOT JUST ABOUT TRANS-FORMING INTO A WEAPON.
IN OTHER WORDS...
...IT'S ABOUT SHARING THE SAME FATE.
TO FIGHT AS ONE.
TO LIVE AND DIE AS ONE.
...
...
PLIP
...
PLIP

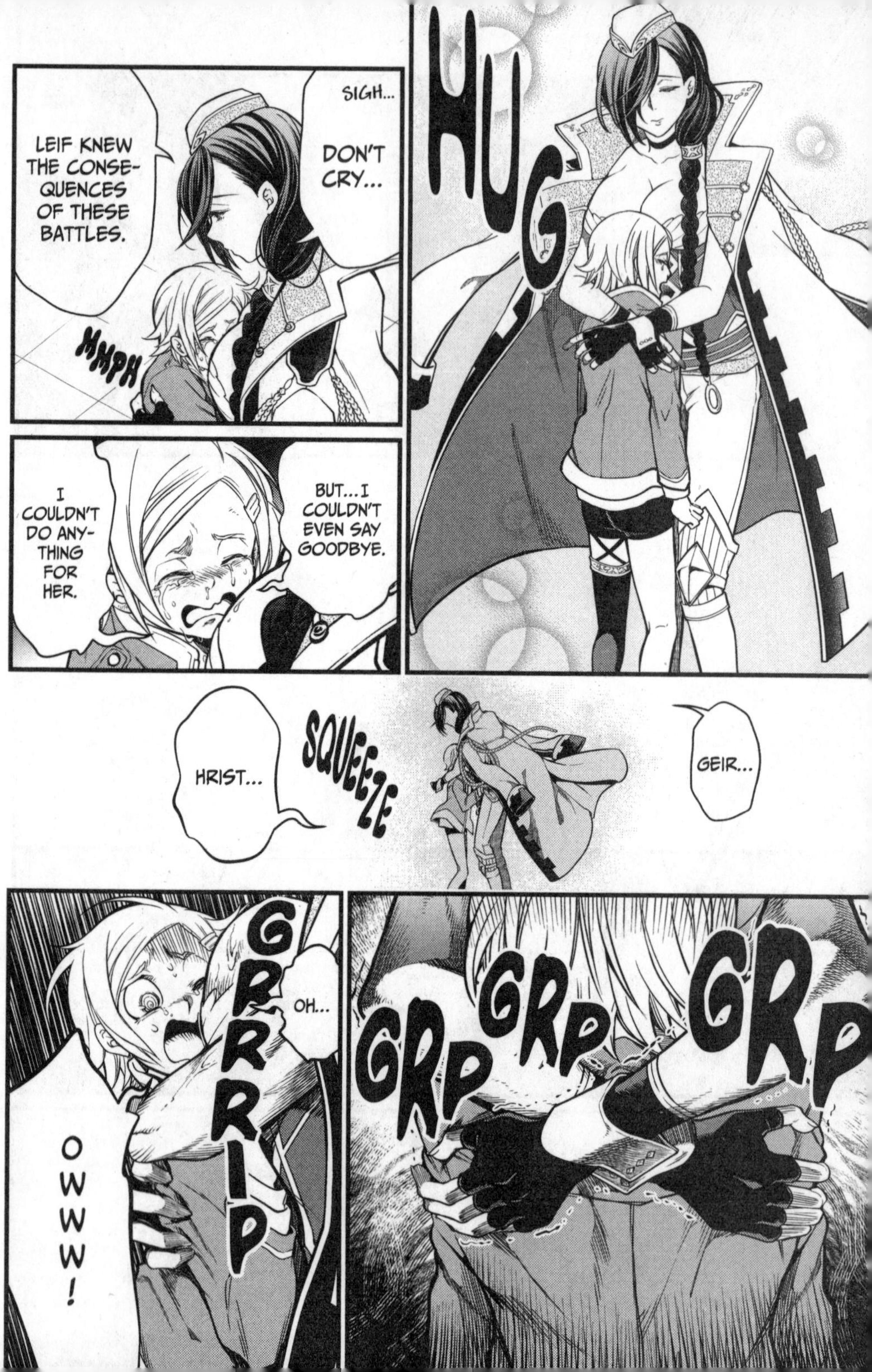
HUG
SIGH...
DON'T CRY...
LEIF KNEW THE CONSE-QUENCES OF THESE BATTLES.
HMMPH
BUT... I COULDN'T EVEN SAY GOODBYE.
I COULDN'T DO ANY-THING FOR HER.
GEIR...
SQUEEEZE
HRIST...
GRP GRP GRP GRP
OH...
GRRRRIP
OWWW!

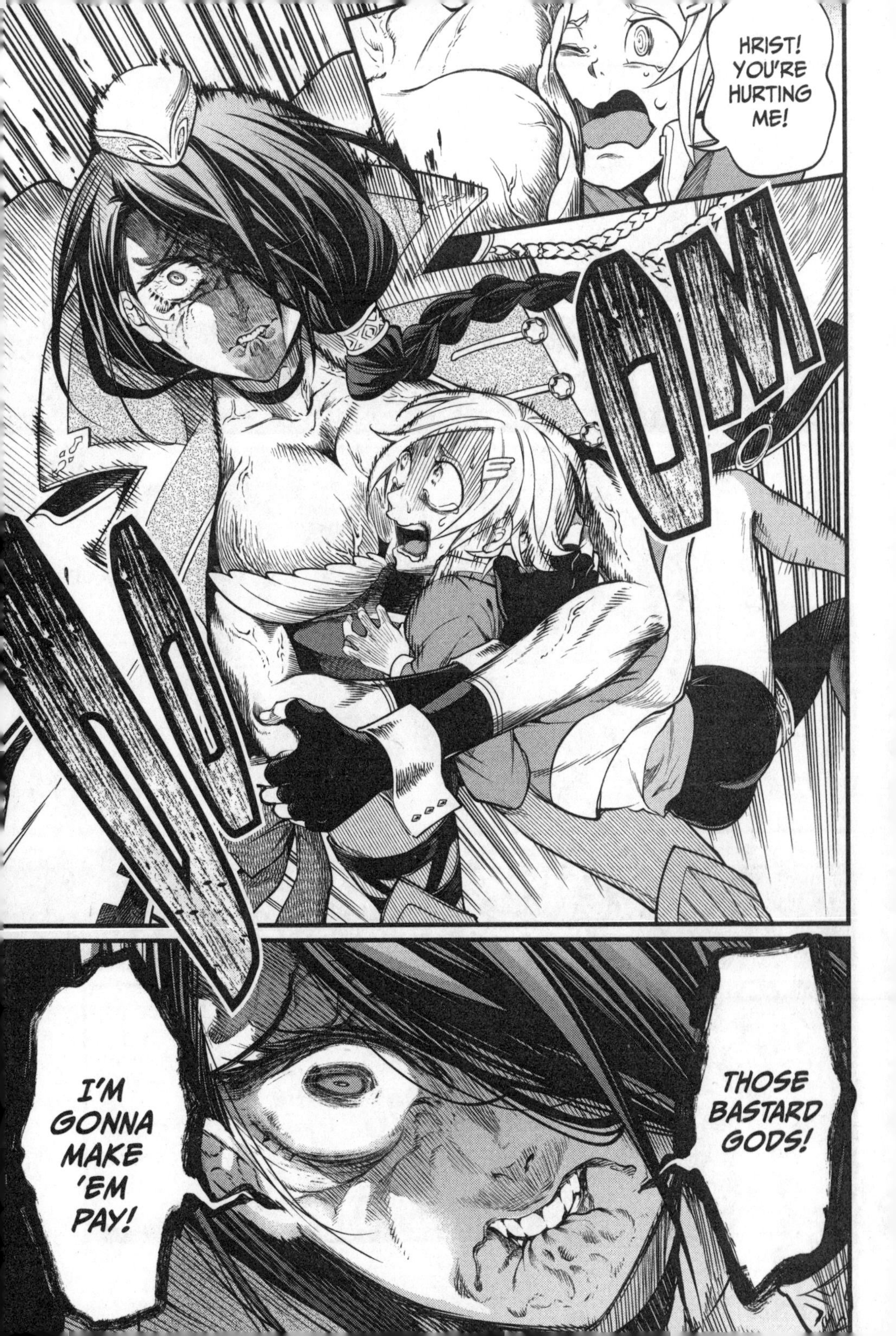
HRIST! YOU'RE HURTING ME!
THOSE BASTARD GODS!
I'M GONNA MAKE 'EM PAY!

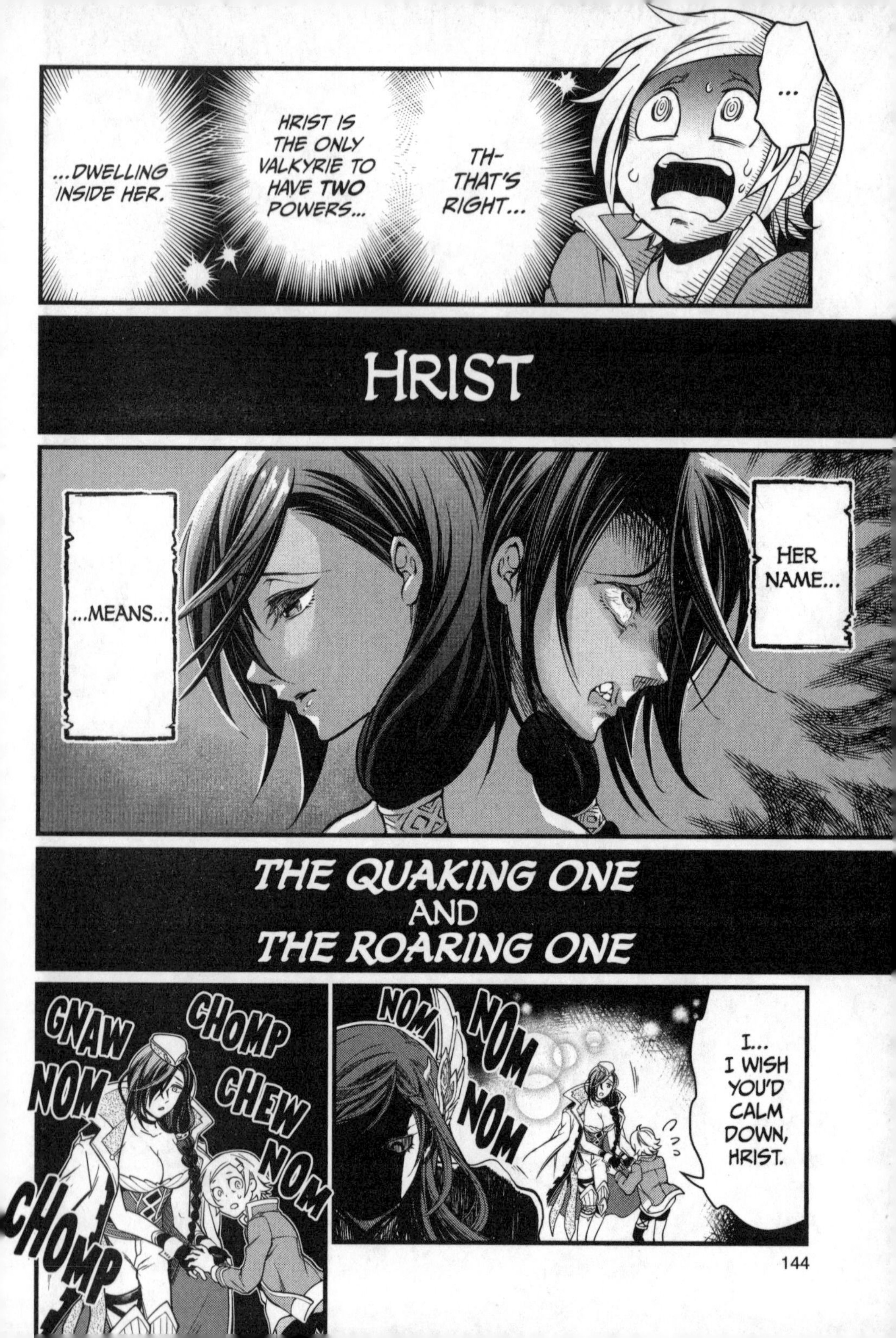
...
TH- THAT'S RIGHT...
HRIST IS THE ONLY VALKYRIE TO HAVE TWO POWERS...
...DWELLING INSIDE HER.
HRIST
HER NAME...
...MEANS...
THE QUAKING ONE AND THE ROARING ONE
I... I WISH YOU'D CALM DOWN, HRIST.
NOM NOM NOM NOM
CHOMP CHEW NOM
GNAW NOM
CHOMP

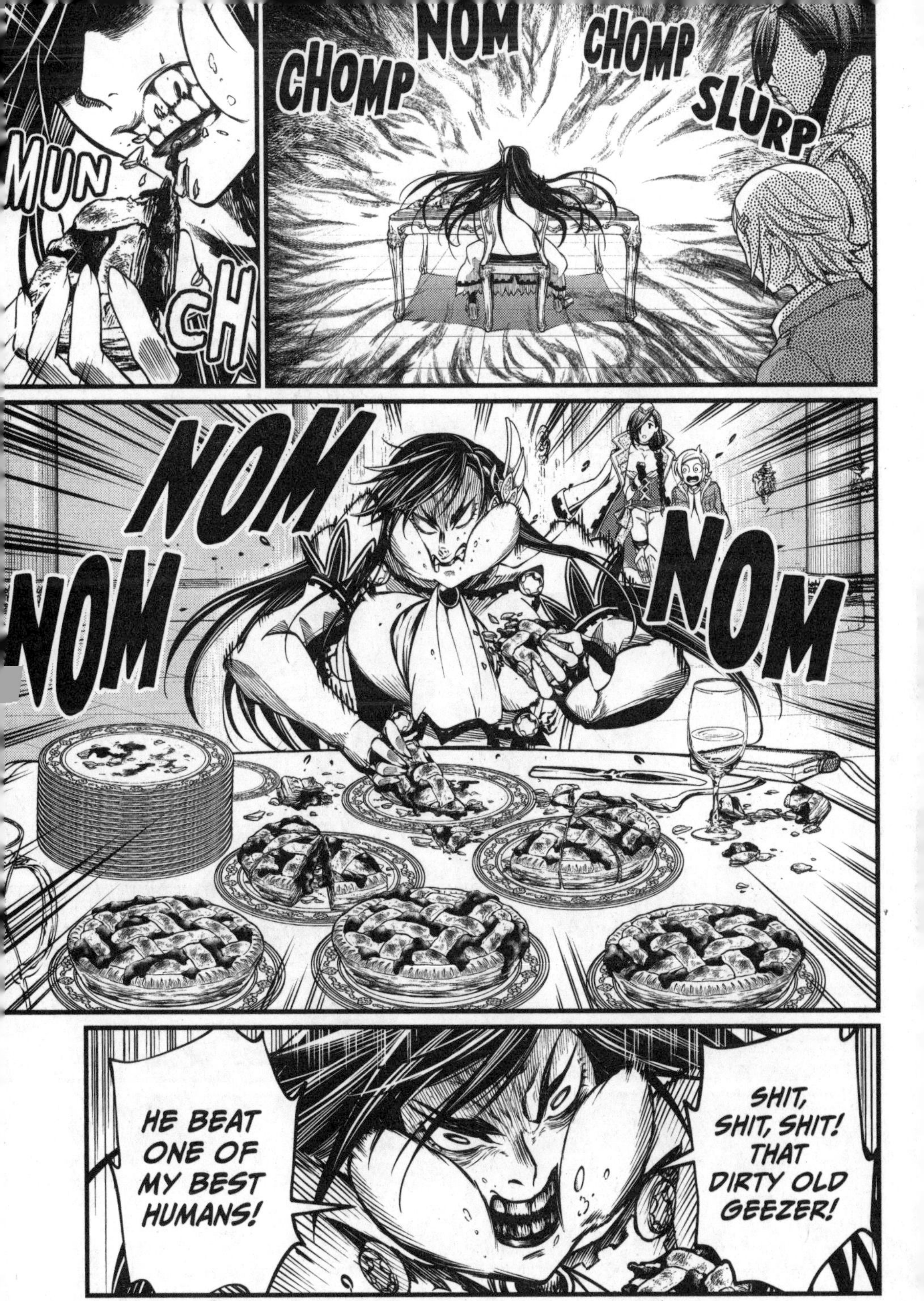
SLURP
CHOMP
NOM
CHOMP
MUNCH
NOM
NOM
NOM
NOM
SHIT, SHIT, SHIT! THAT DIRTY OLD GEEZER!
HE BEAT ONE OF MY BEST HUMANS!

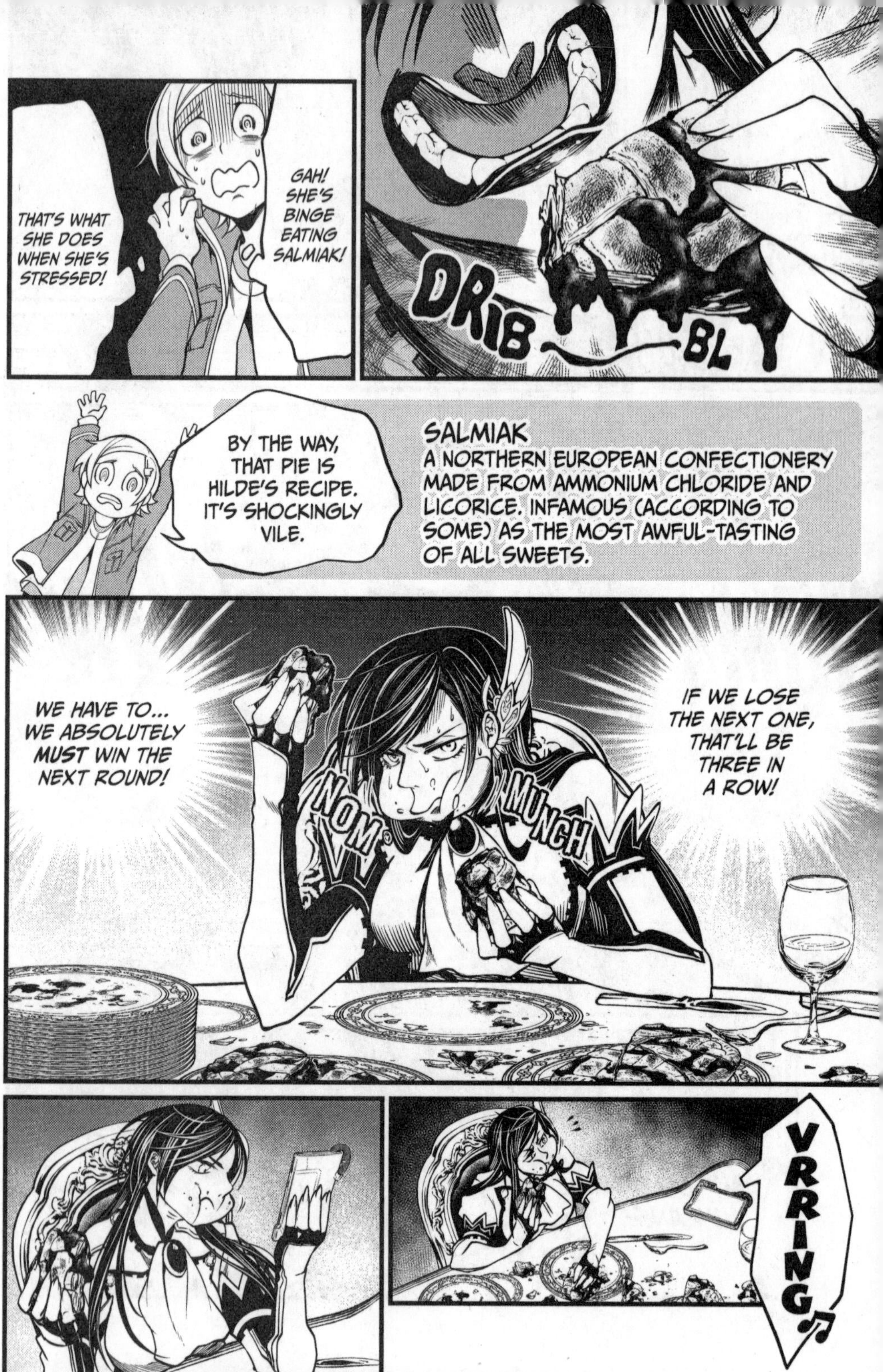
DRIB
BL
GAH! SHE'S BINGE EATING SALMIAK!
THAT'S WHAT SHE DOES WHEN SHE'S STRESSED!
SALMIAK
A NORTHERN EUROPEAN CONFECTIONERY MADE FROM AMMONIUM CHLORIDE AND LICORICE. INFAMOUS (ACCORDING TO SOME) AS THE MOST AWFUL-TASTING OF ALL SWEETS.
BY THE WAY, THAT PIE IS HILDE'S RECIPE. IT'S SHOCKINGLY VILE.
IF WE LOSE THE NEXT ONE, THAT'LL BE THREE IN A ROW!
WE HAVE TO... WE ABSOLUTELY MUST WIN THE NEXT ROUND!
MUNCH
NOM
VRRING

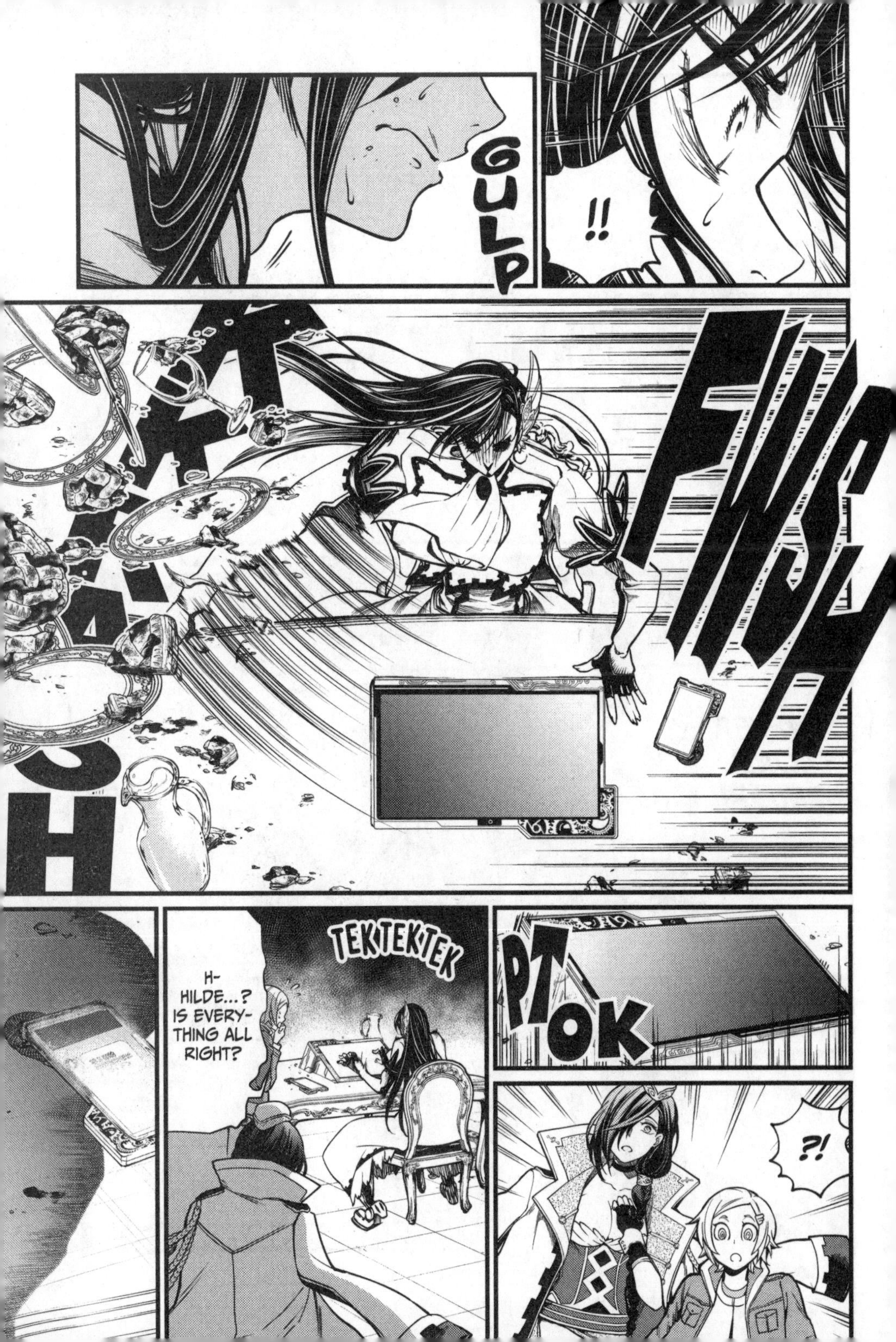
!!
GULP
PTOK
?!
TEKTEKTEK
H-HILDE...? IS EVERYTHING ALL RIGHT?

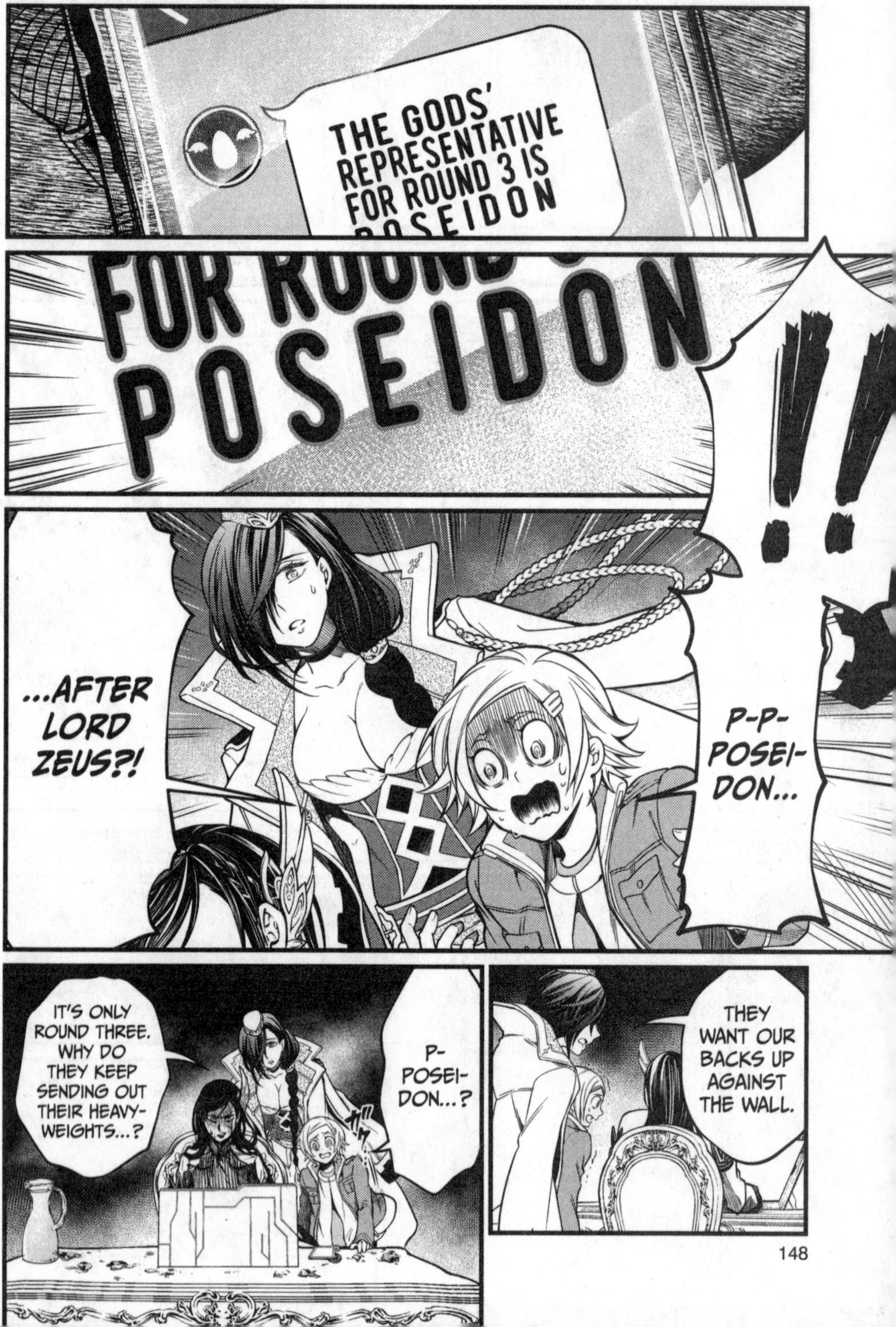
THE GODS' REPRESENTATIVE FOR ROUND 3 IS POSEIDON
FOR ROUND
POSEIDON
!!
P-P-POSEI-DON...
...AFTER LORD ZEUS?!
THEY WANT OUR BACKS UP AGAINST THE WALL.
P-POSEI-DON...?
IT'S ONLY ROUND THREE. WHY DO THEY KEEP SENDING OUT THEIR HEAVY-WEIGHTS...?

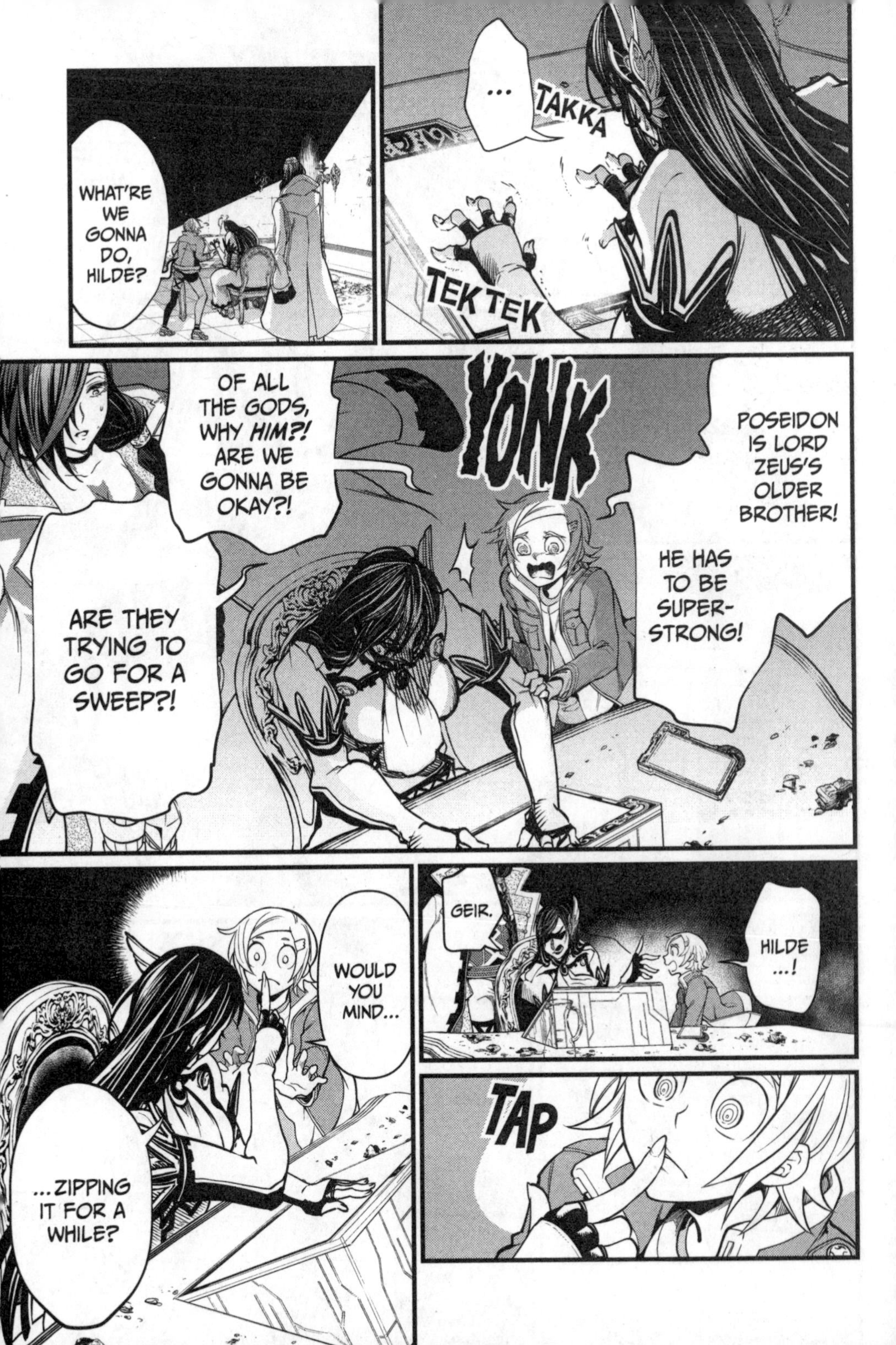
...
TAKKA
TEKTEK
WHAT'RE WE GONNA DO, HILDE?
POSEIDON IS LORD ZEUS'S OLDER BROTHER!
YONK
OF ALL THE GODS, WHY *HIM*?! ARE WE GONNA BE OKAY?!
HE HAS TO BE SUPER-STRONG!
ARE THEY TRYING TO GO FOR A SWEEP?!
HILDE ...!
GEIR.
TAP
WOULD YOU MIND...
...ZIPPING IT FOR A WHILE?

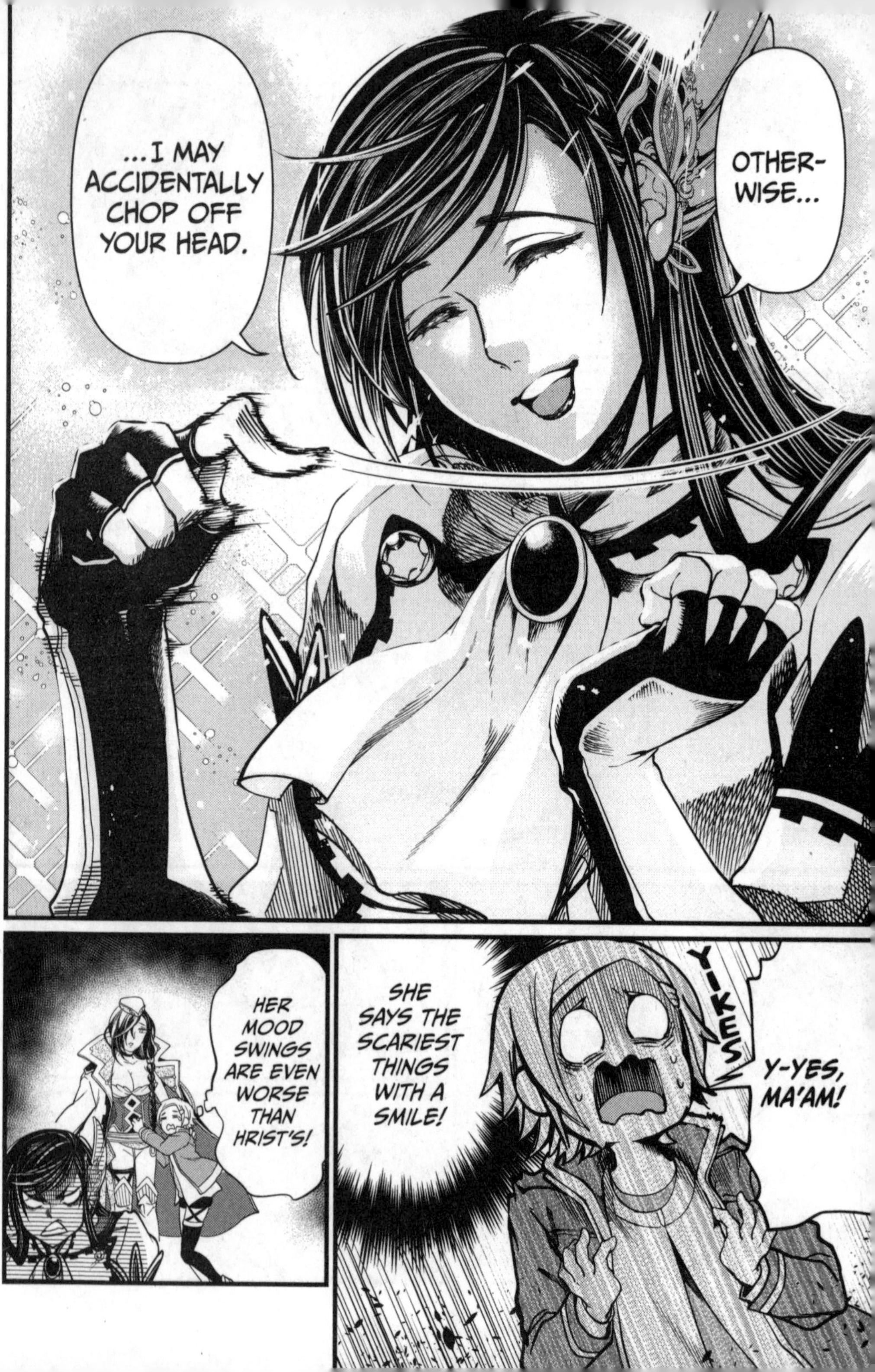
OTHER-WISE...
...I MAY ACCIDENTALLY CHOP OFF YOUR HEAD.
YIKES
Y-YES, MA'AM!
SHE SAYS THE SCARIEST THINGS WITH A SMILE!
HER MOOD SWINGS ARE EVEN WORSE THAN HRIST'S!

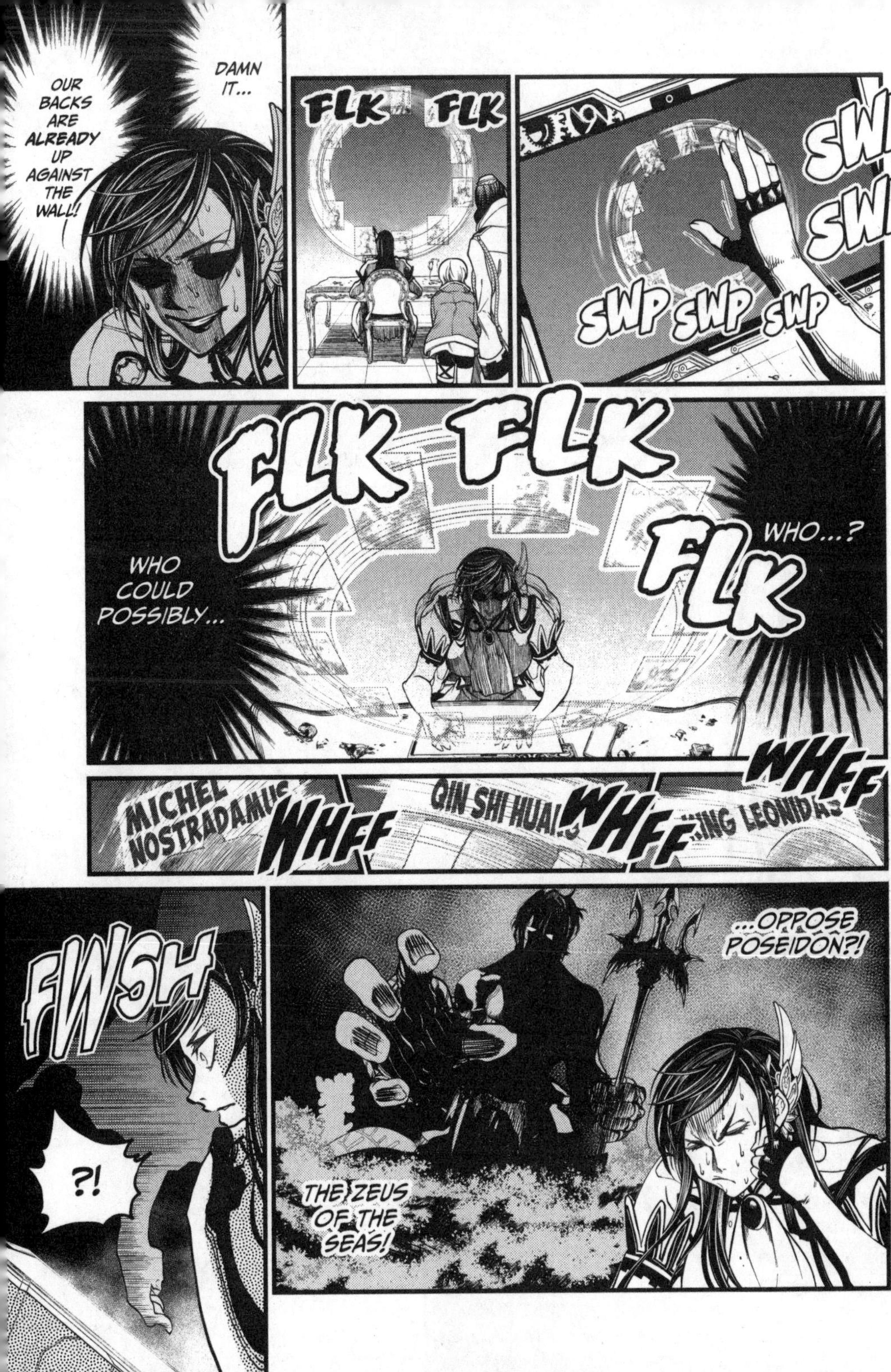
SWP SWP
SWP SWP SWP
FLK FLK
DAMN IT...
OUR BACKS ARE ALREADY UP AGAINST THE WALL!!
FLK FLK
WHO...?
FLK
WHO COULD POSSIBLY...
WHFF
ING LEONIDA
WHFF
QIN SHI HUA
WHFF
MICHEL NOSTRADAMUS
...OPPOSE POSEIDON?!
THE ZEUS OF THE SEAS!
FWSH
?!

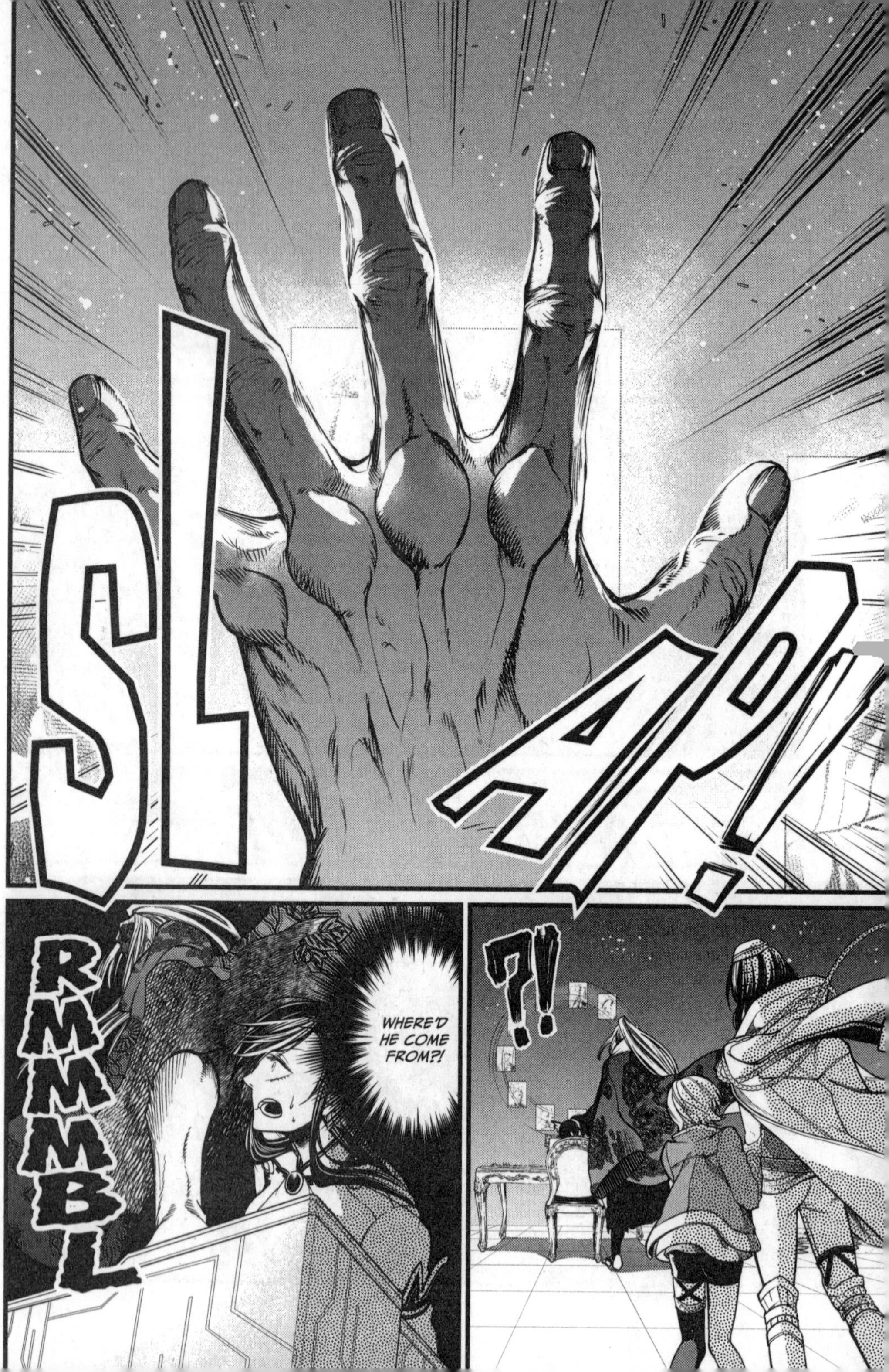
SLAP!
?!
RMMMBL
WHERE'D HE COME FROM?!

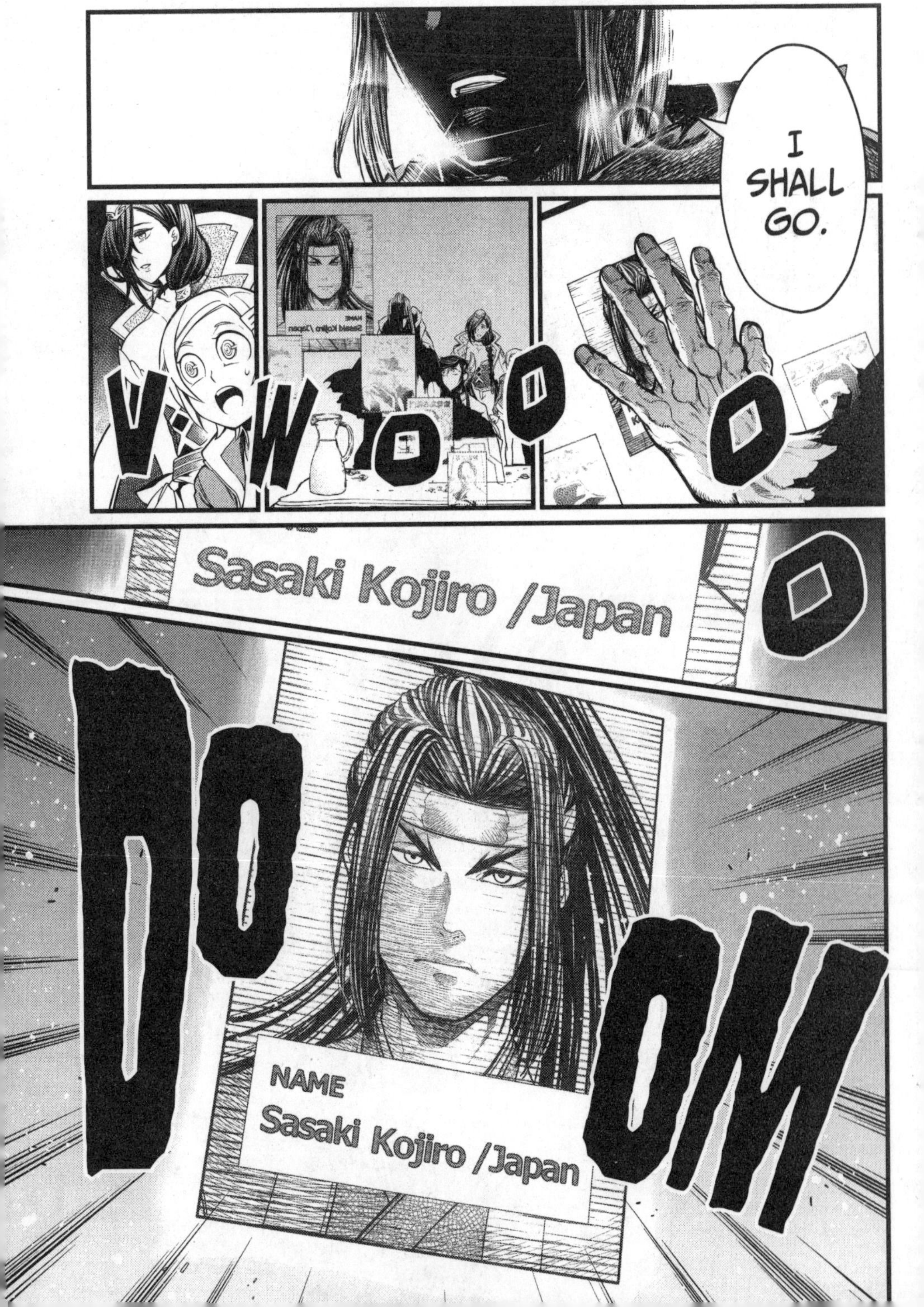
I SHALL GO.
VWOOOOO
Sasaki Kojiro /Japan
NAME
Sasaki Kojiro /Japan
DOOM

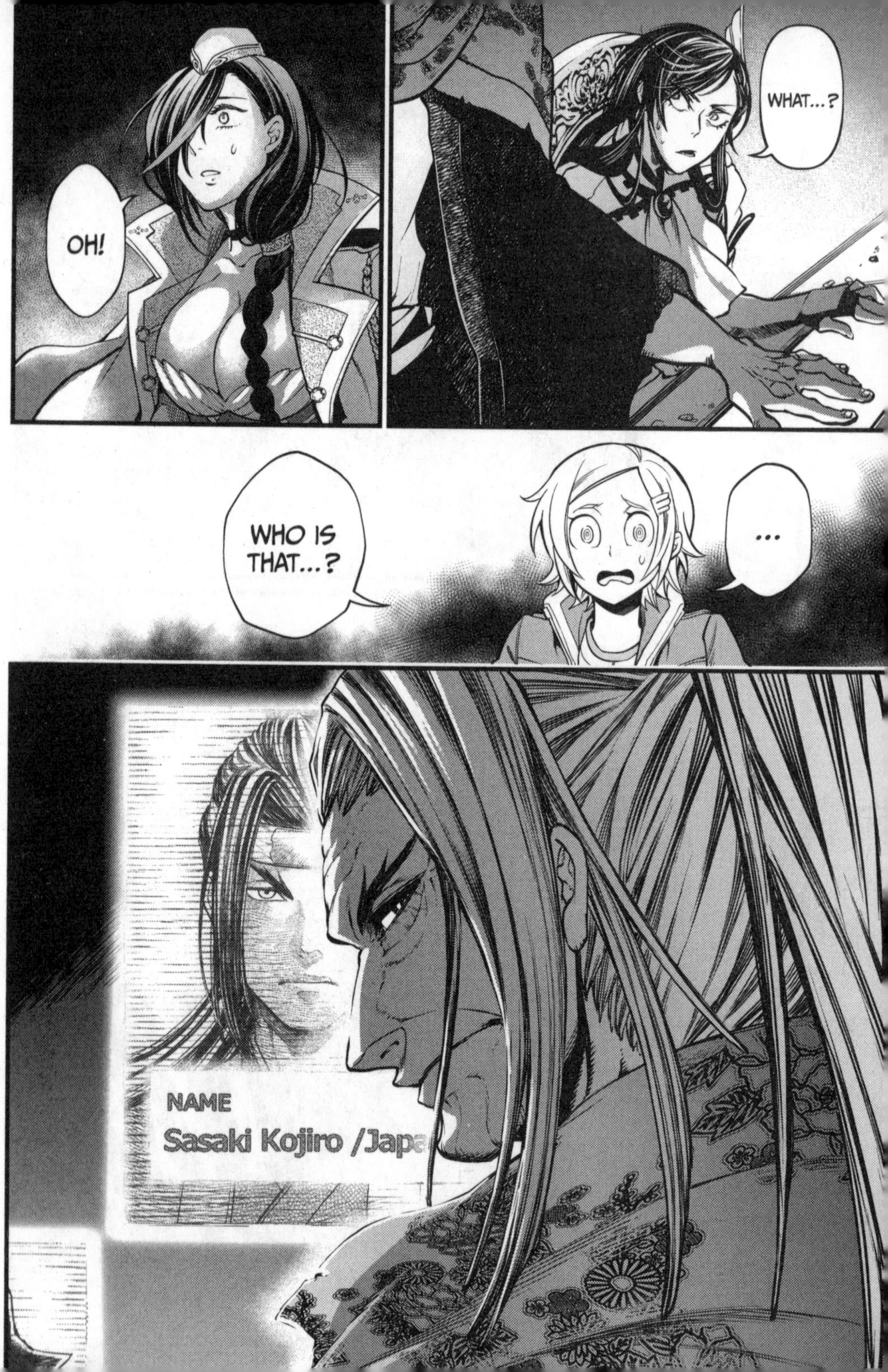
WHAT...?
OH!
...
WHO IS THAT...?
NAME
Sasaki Kojiro /Japa

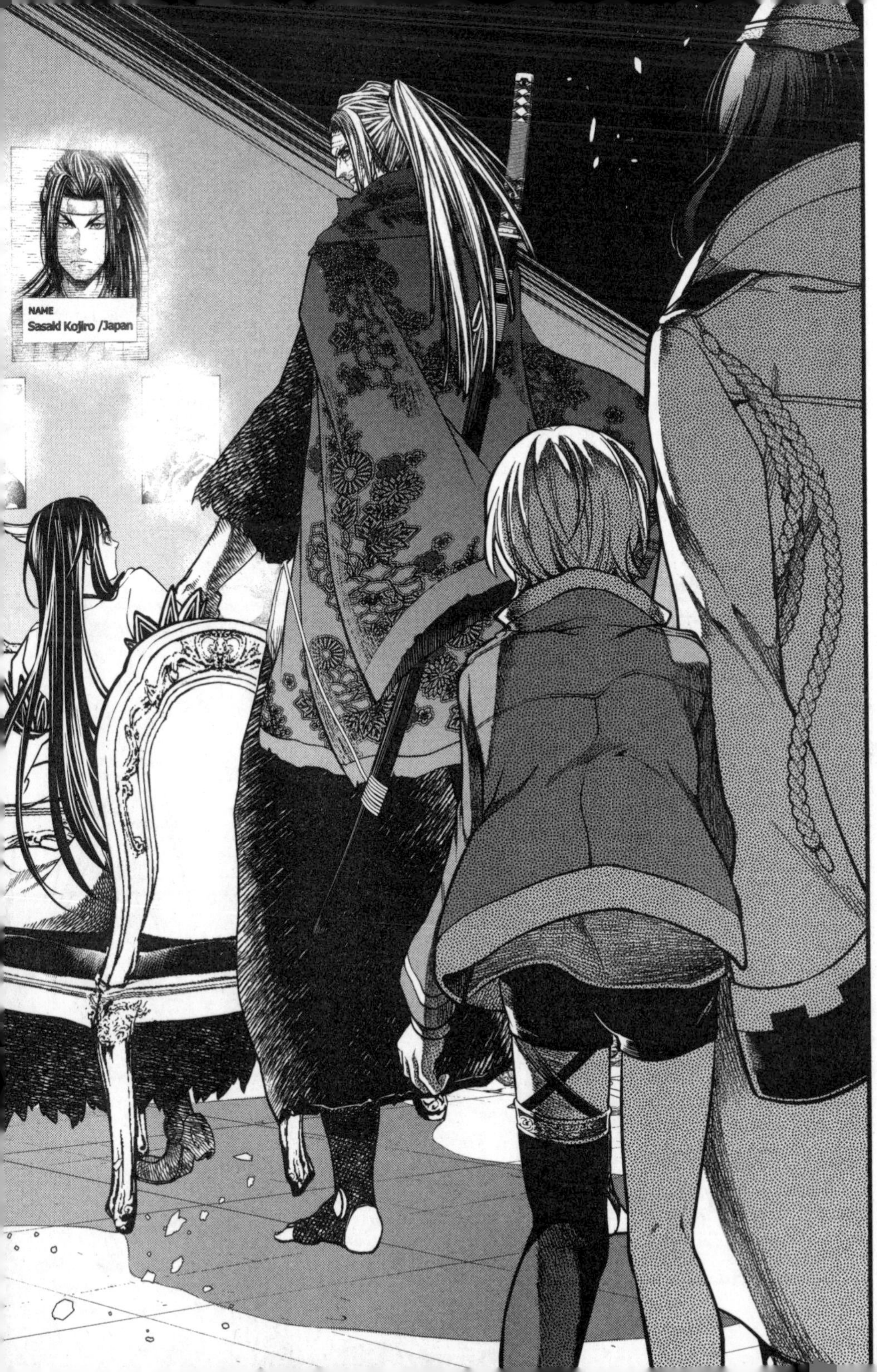
NAME
Sasaki Kojiro /Japan

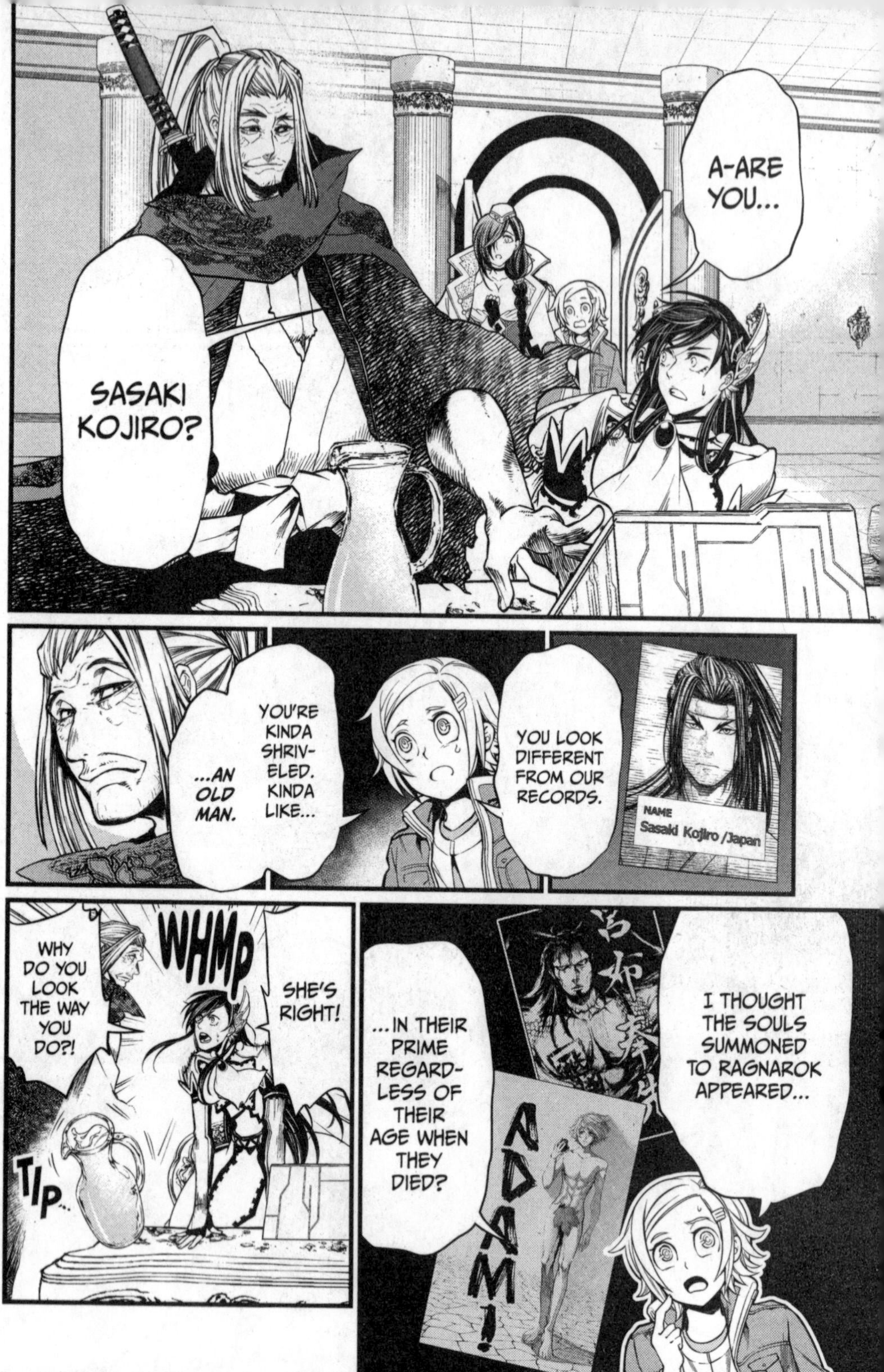
A-ARE YOU...
SASAKI KOJIRO?
NAME
Sasaki Kojiro /Japan
YOU LOOK DIFFERENT FROM OUR RECORDS.
YOU'RE KINDA SHRIVELED. KINDA LIKE...
...AN OLD MAN.
I THOUGHT THE SOULS SUMMONED TO RAGNAROK APPEARED...
...IN THEIR PRIME REGARDLESS OF THEIR AGE WHEN THEY DIED?
ADAM!
WHMP
SHE'S RIGHT!
WHY DO YOU LOOK THE WAY YOU DO?!
TIP...

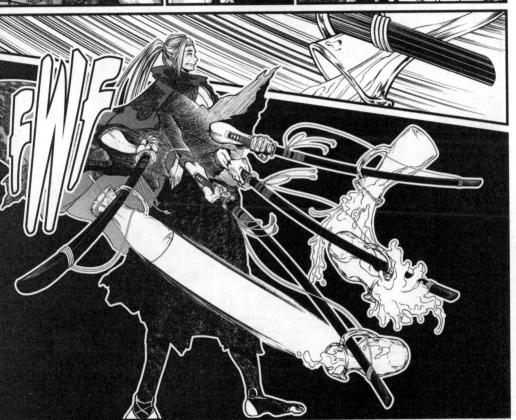

FWF

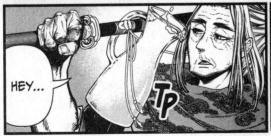

HEY...

TP

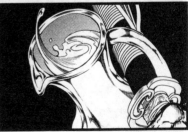

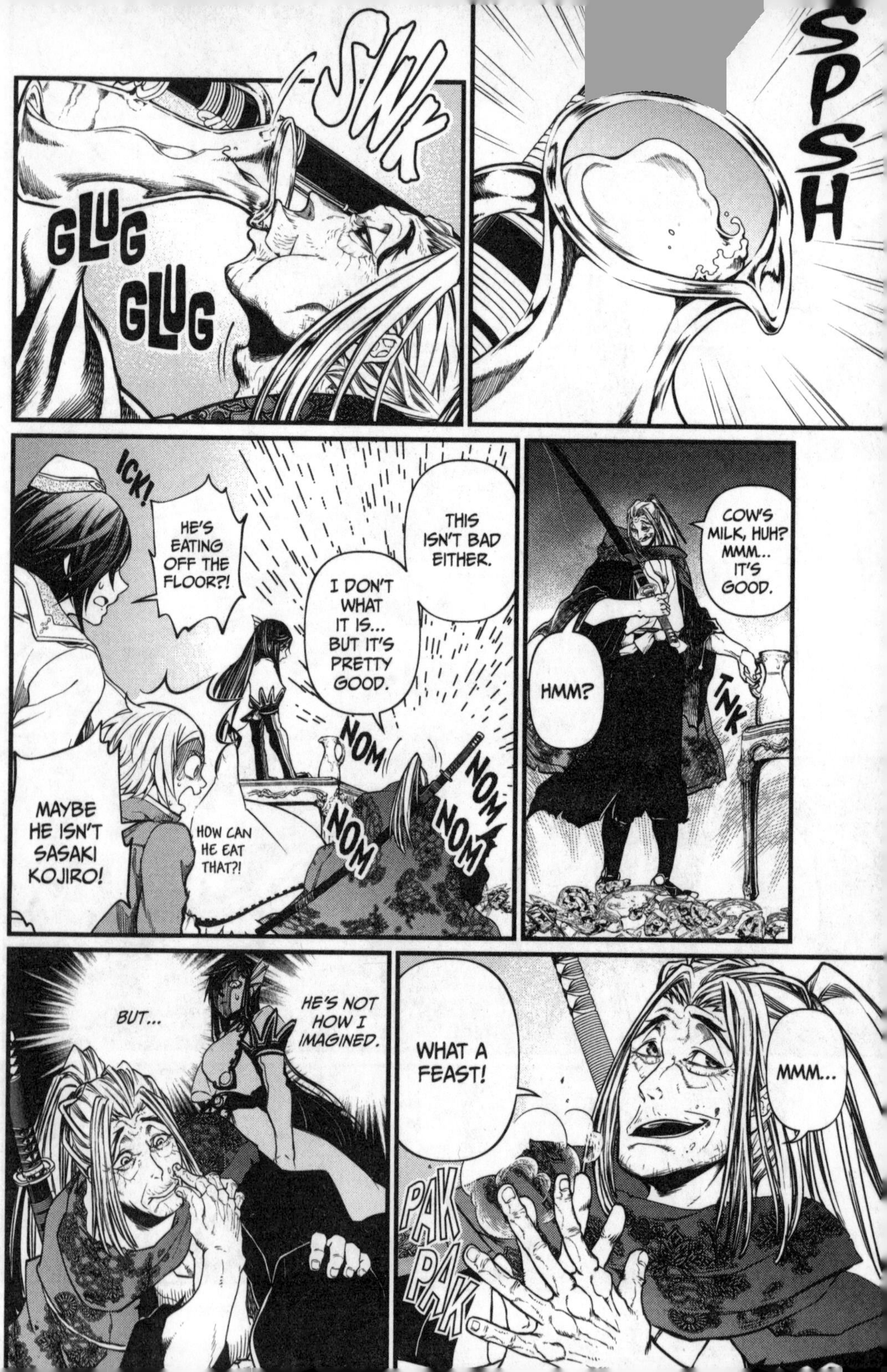
SPSH
SWIK
GLUG
GLUG
COW'S MILK, HUH? MMM... IT'S GOOD.
TNK
HMM?
THIS ISN'T BAD EITHER.
I DON'T WHAT IT IS... BUT IT'S PRETTY GOOD.
ICK!
HE'S EATING OFF THE FLOOR?!
NOM
NOM
NOM
NOM
HOW CAN HE EAT THAT?!
MAYBE HE ISN'T SASAKI KOJIRO!
MMM...
WHAT A FEAST!
PAK
PAK
HE'S NOT HOW I IMAGINED.
BUT...

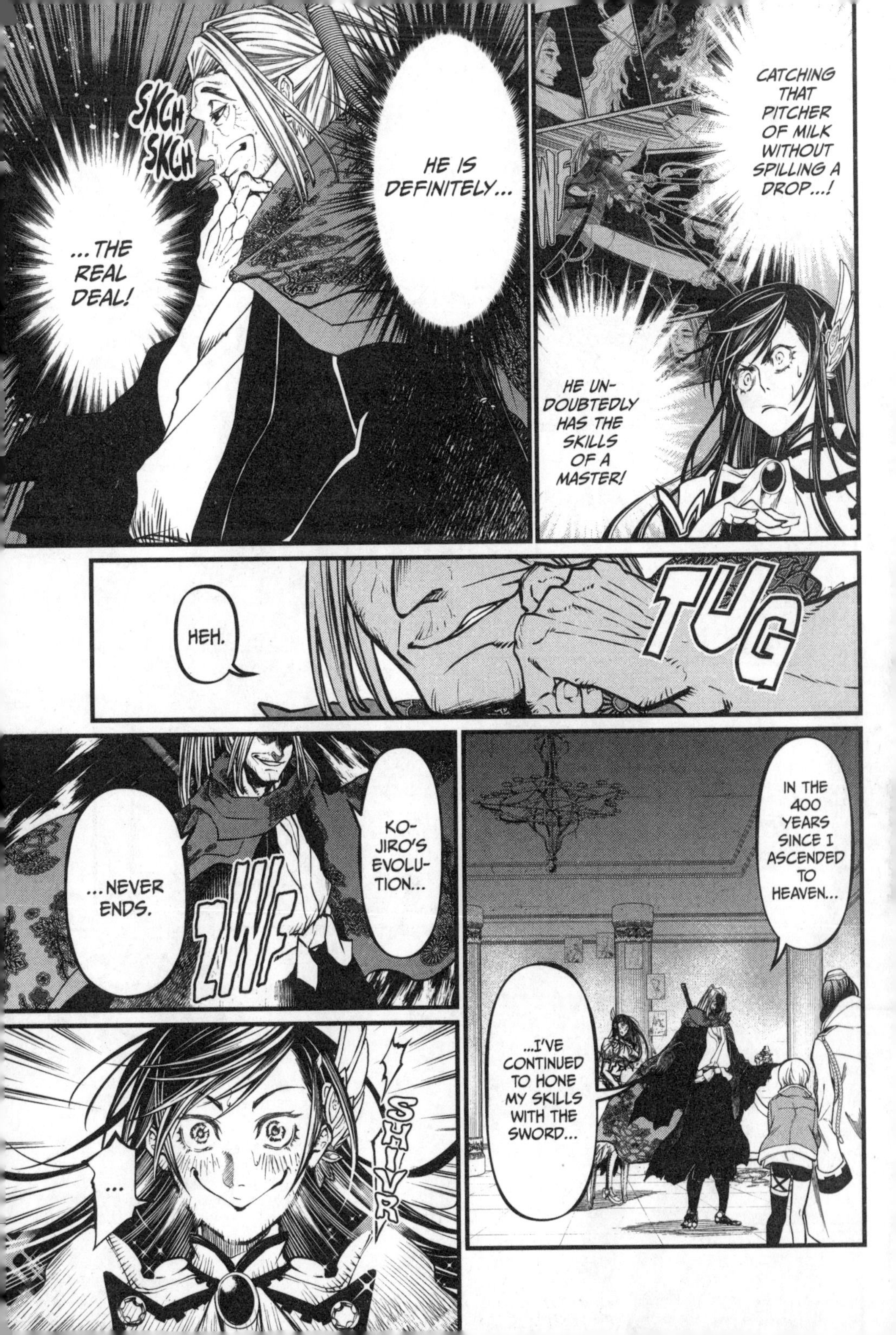
CATCHING THAT PITCHER OF MILK WITHOUT SPILLING A DROP...!
ZWF
HE UN-DOUBTEDLY HAS THE SKILLS OF A MASTER!
HE IS DEFINITELY...
SKCH SKCH
...THE REAL DEAL!
TUG
HEH.
IN THE 400 YEARS SINCE I ASCENDED TO HEAVEN...
...I'VE CONTINUED TO HONE MY SKILLS WITH THE SWORD...
KO-JIRO'S EVOLU-TION...
ZWF
...NEVER ENDS.
SHIVR
...

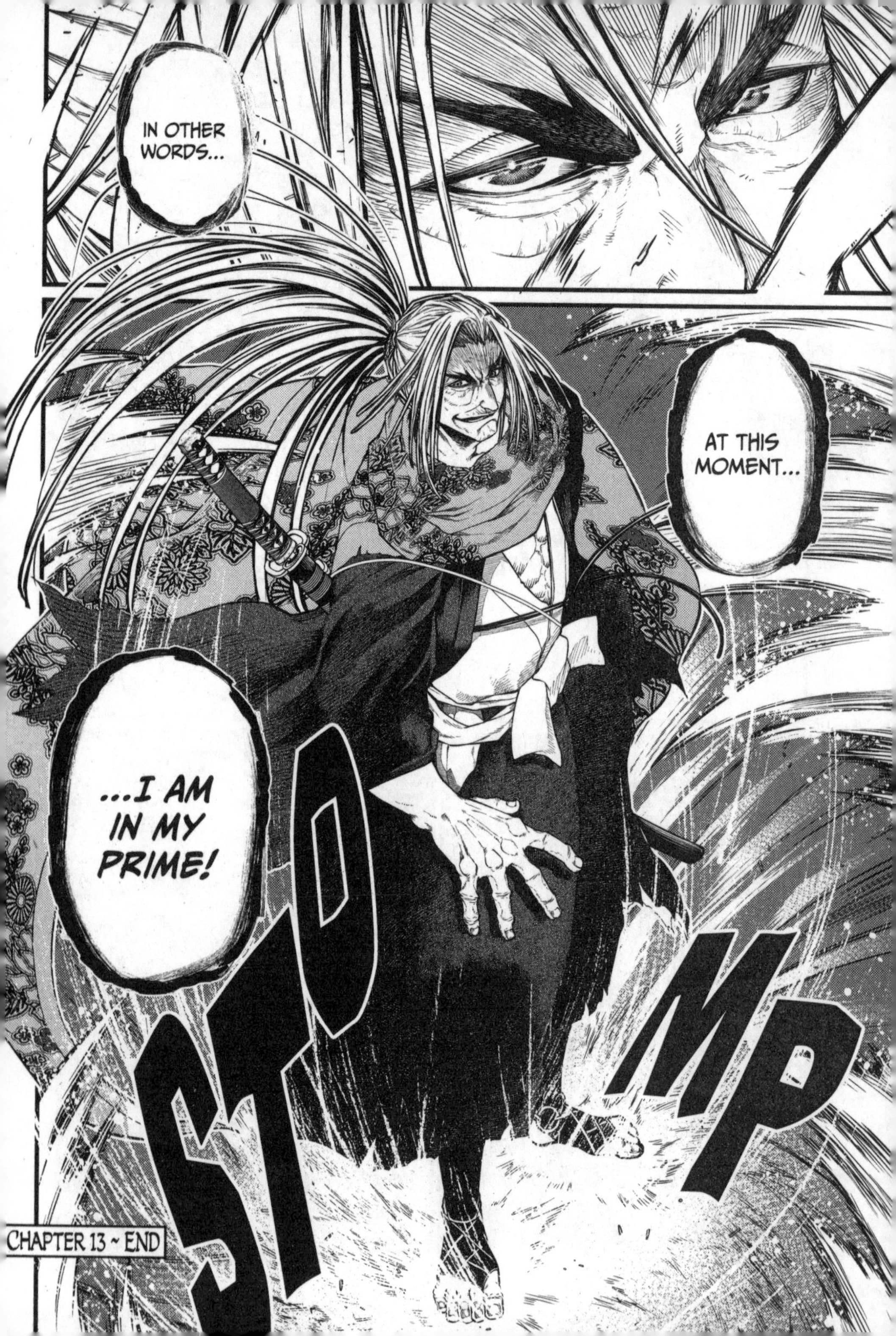

IN OTHER WORDS...
AT THIS MOMENT...
...I AM IN MY PRIME!
STOMP
CHAPTER 13 ~ END

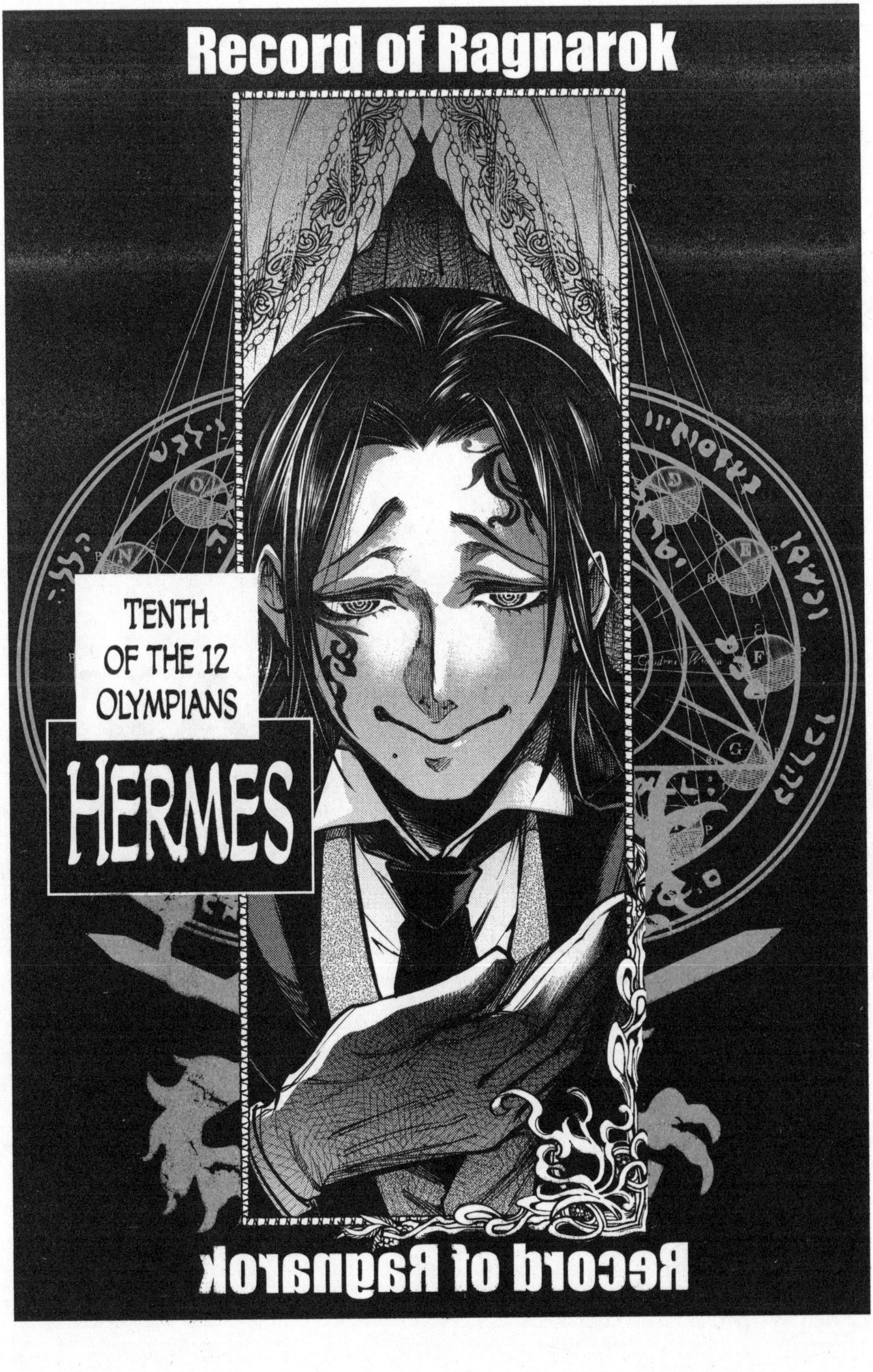
Record of Ragnarok
TENTH
OF THE 12
OLYMPIANS
HERMES
Record of Ragnarok

RECORD OF
RAGNAROK

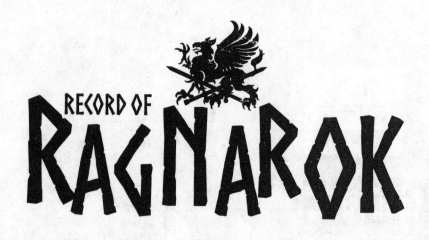

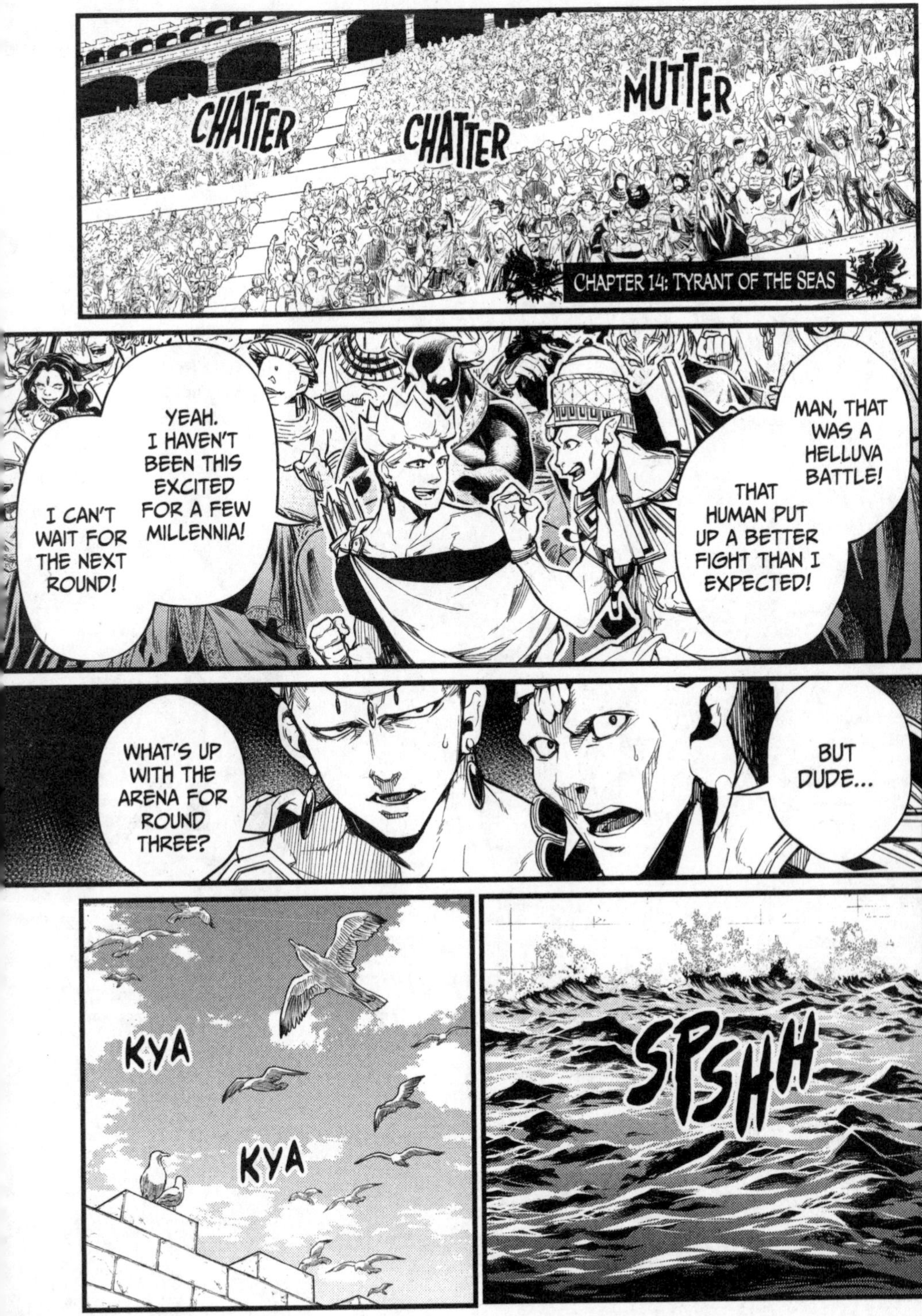
MUTTER
CHATTER
CHATTER
CHAPTER 14: TYRANT OF THE SEAS
MAN, THAT WAS A HELLUVA BATTLE!
THAT HUMAN PUT UP A BETTER FIGHT THAN I EXPECTED!
YEAH. I HAVEN'T BEEN THIS EXCITED FOR A FEW MILLENNIA!
I CAN'T WAIT FOR THE NEXT ROUND!
BUT DUDE...
WHAT'S UP WITH THE ARENA FOR ROUND THREE?
SPSHH
KYA
KYA

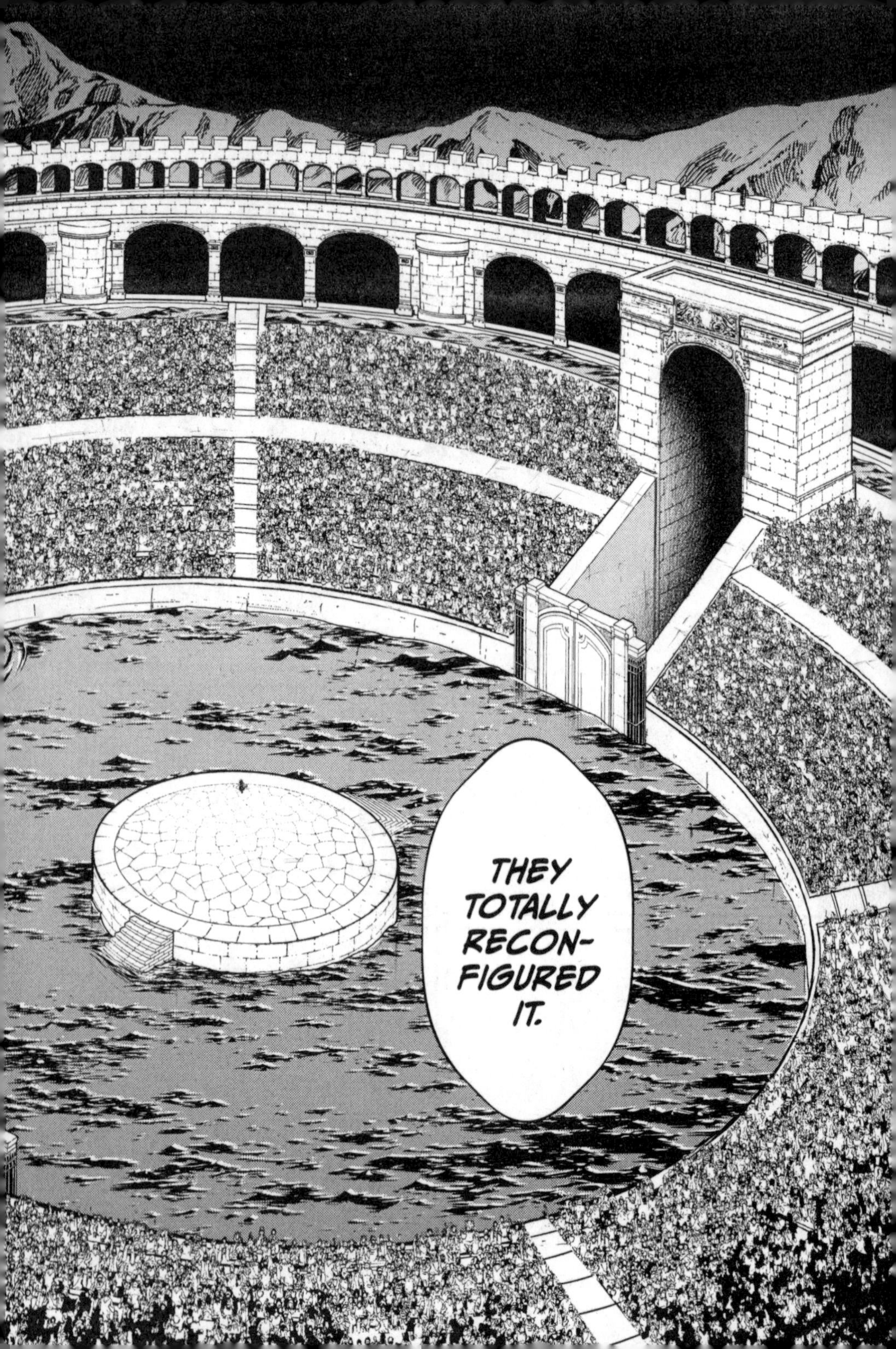
THEY TOTALLY RECON- FIGURED IT.

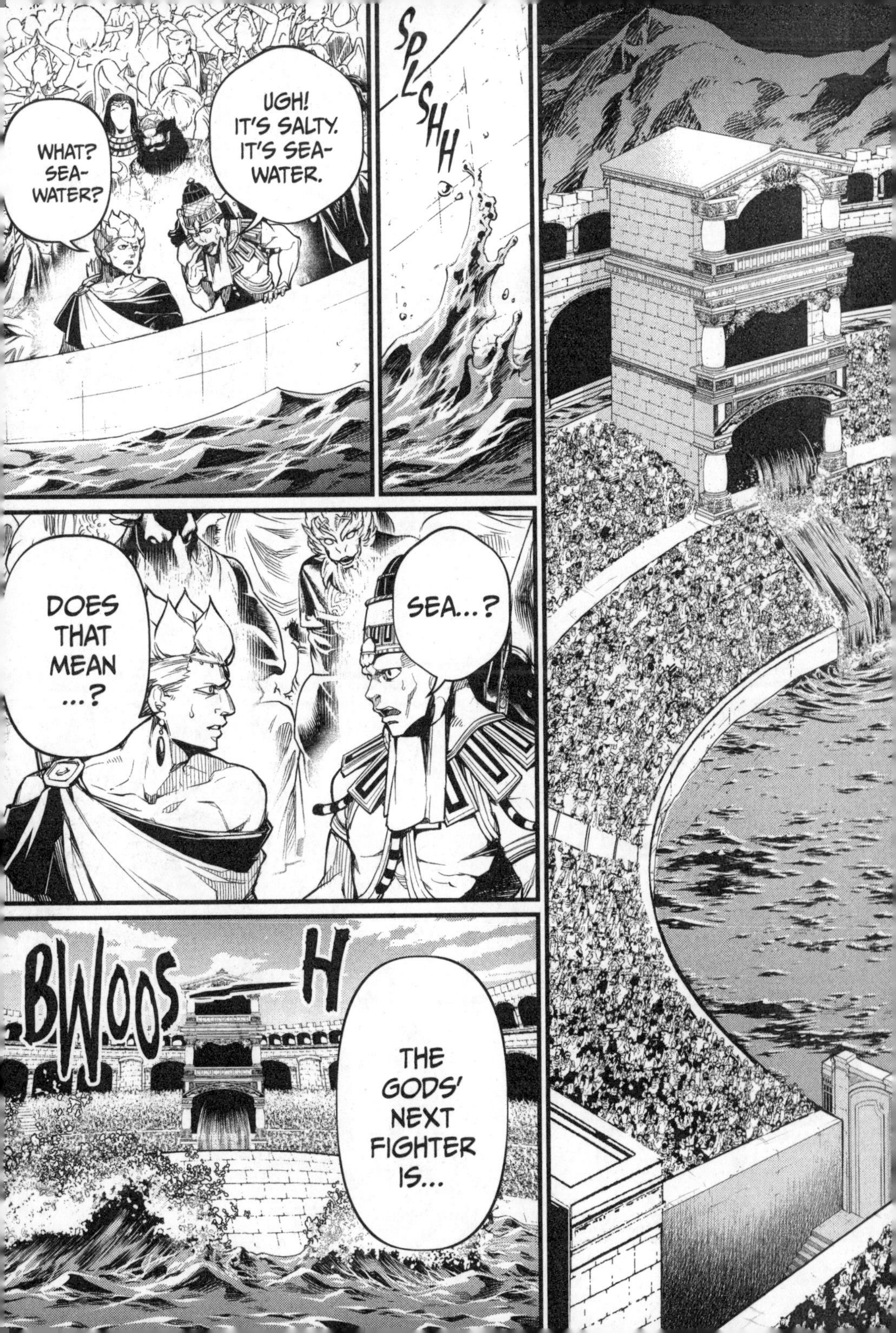
SPLSHH
UGH! IT'S SALTY. IT'S SEA-WATER.
WHAT? SEA-WATER?
SEA...?
DOES THAT MEAN ...?
BWOOSH
THE GODS' NEXT FIGHTER IS...

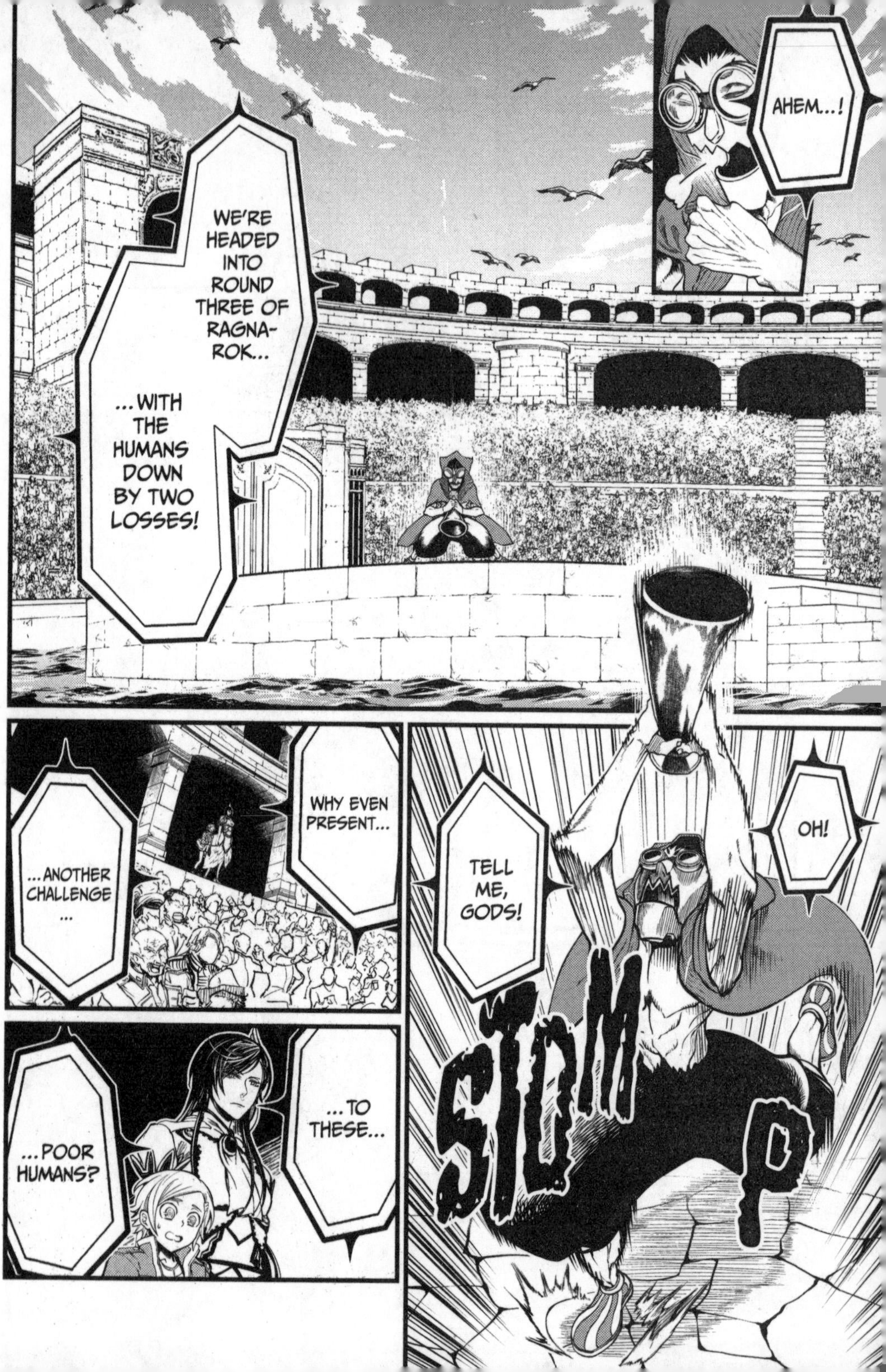
AHEM...!
WE'RE HEADED INTO ROUND THREE OF RAGNA-ROK...
...WITH THE HUMANS DOWN BY TWO LOSSES!
OH!
TELL ME, GODS!
STOMP
WHY EVEN PRESENT...
...ANOTHER CHALLENGE...
...TO THESE...
...POOR HUMANS?

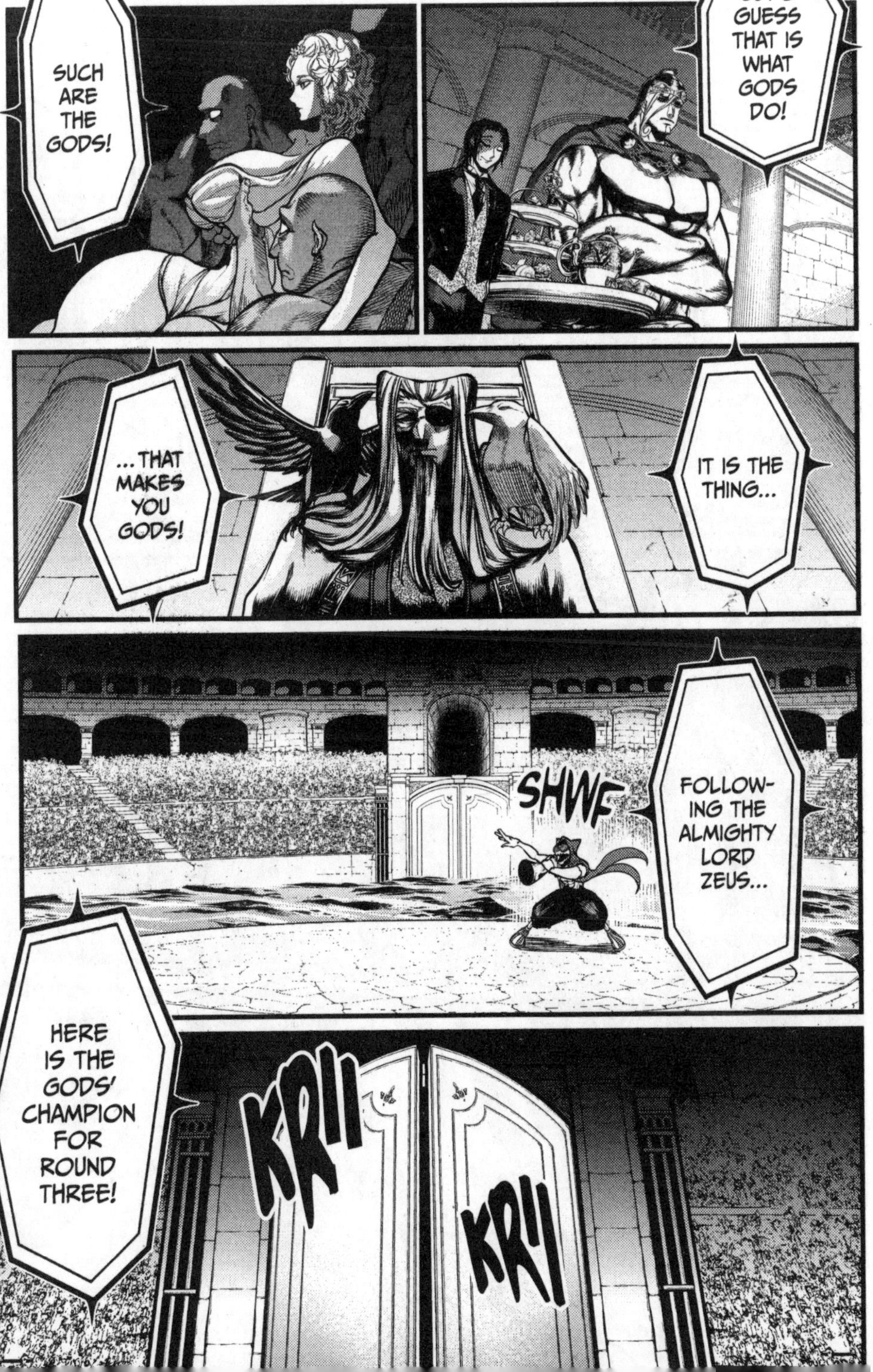
BUT I GUESS THAT IS WHAT GODS DO!
SUCH ARE THE GODS!
IT IS THE THING...
...THAT MAKES YOU GODS!
FOLLOW-ING THE ALMIGHTY LORD ZEUS...
SHWF
HERE IS THE GODS' CHAMPION FOR ROUND THREE!
KRII
KRII

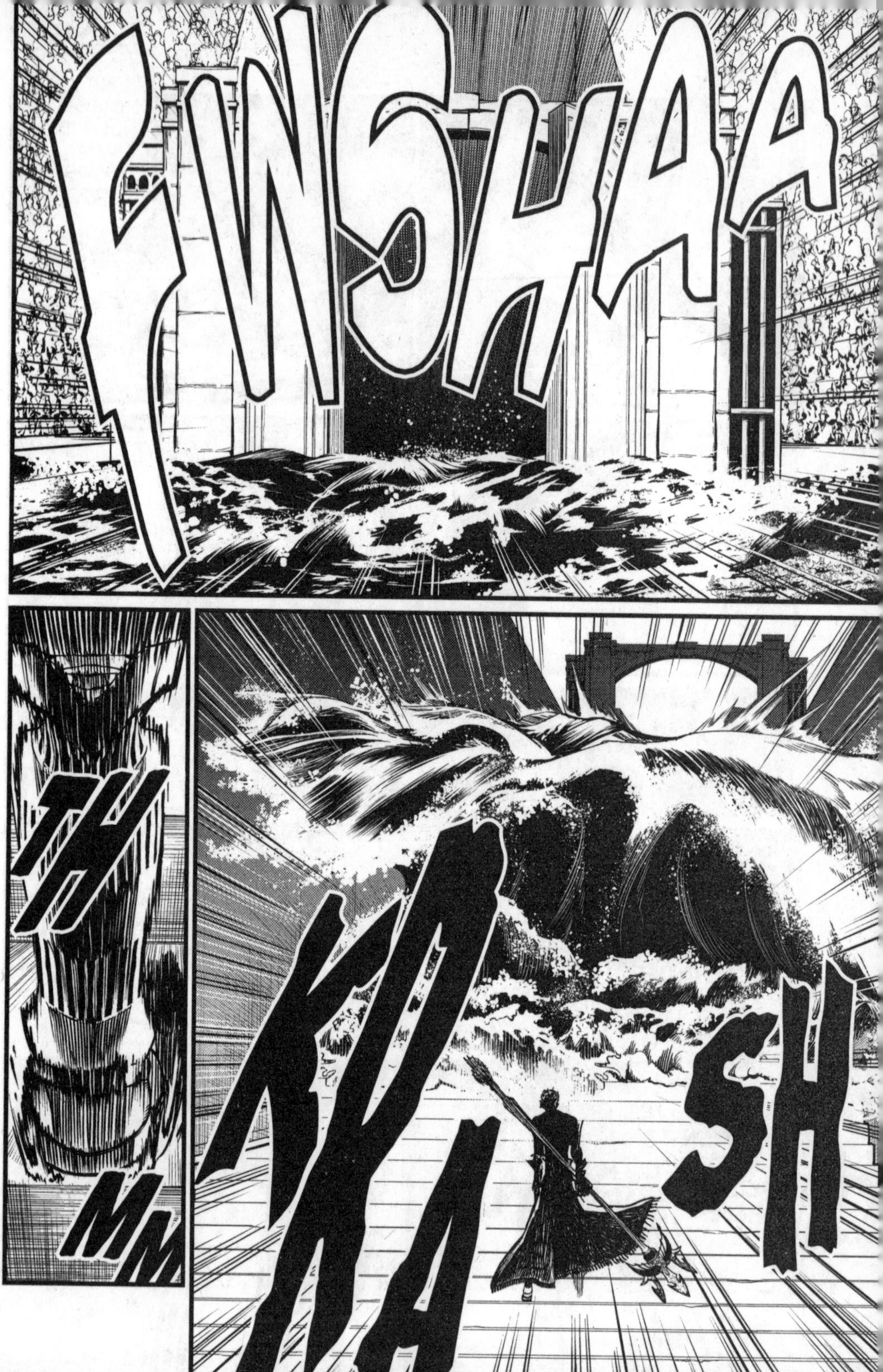
FWSHAA
KWASH
TH
MM

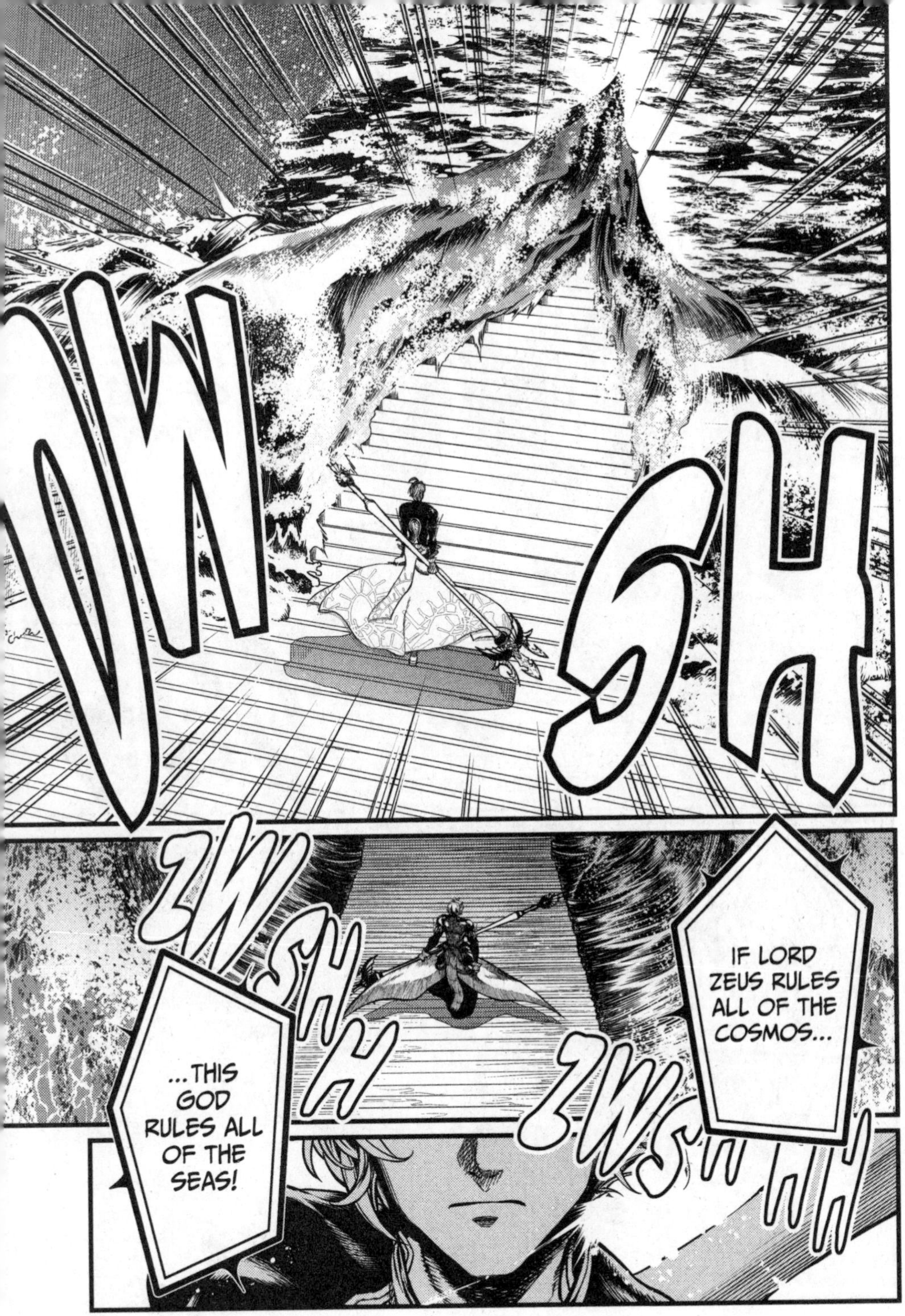

ZWSHHH
IF LORD ZEUS RULES ALL OF THE COSMOS...
ZWSHH
...THIS GOD RULES ALL OF THE SEAS!

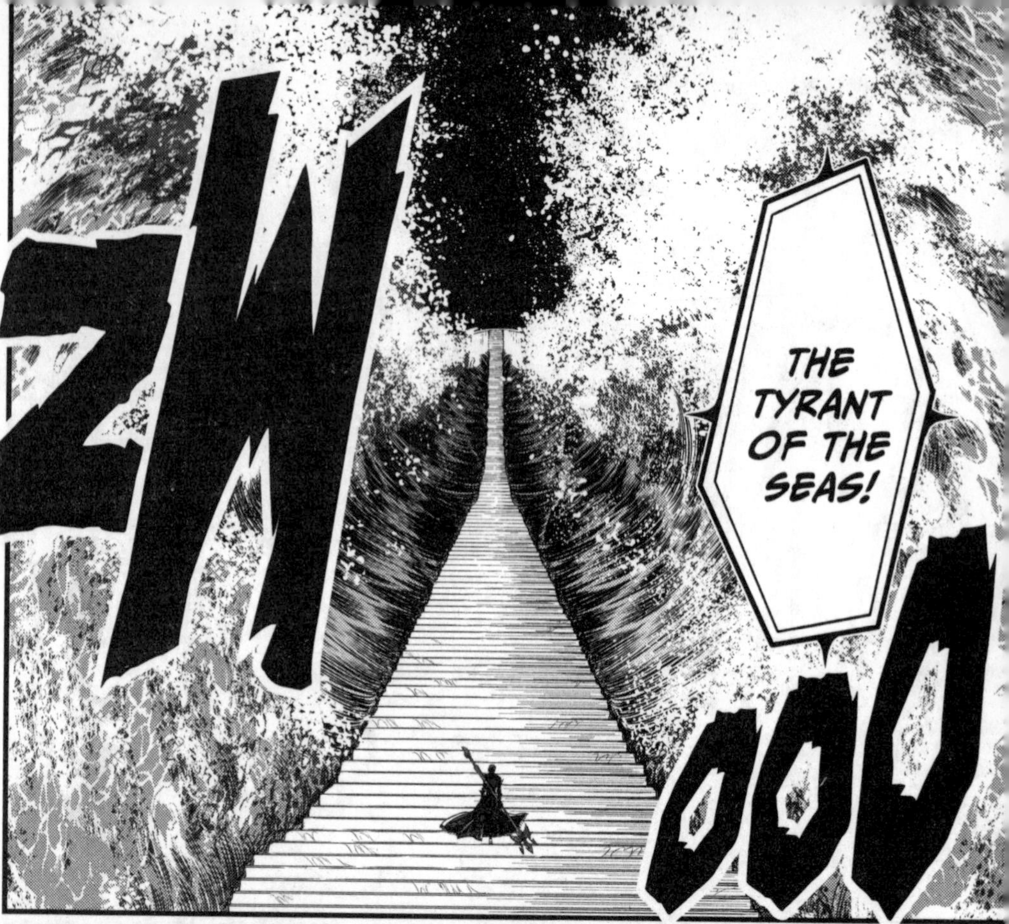
THE TYRANT OF THE SEAS!
ZWOOOO

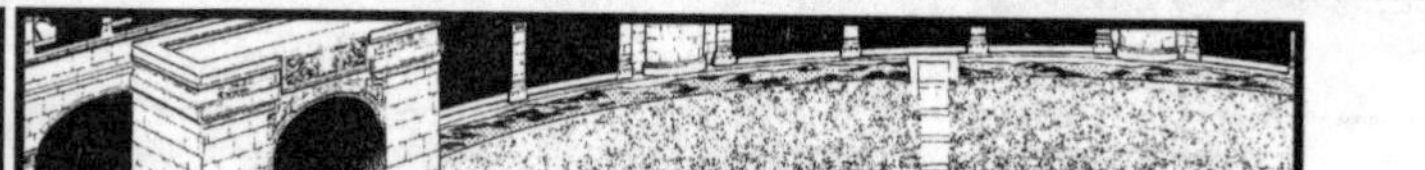
ZSHHHHH

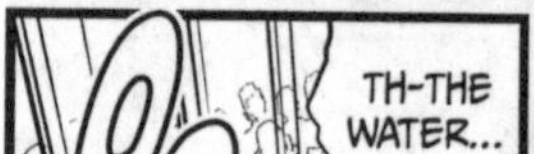
OOOOH
TH-THE WATER...
...IS PARTING!

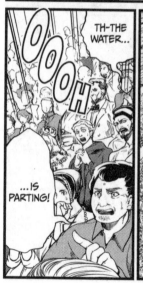

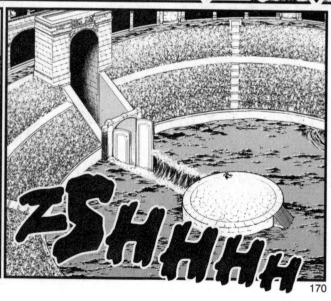

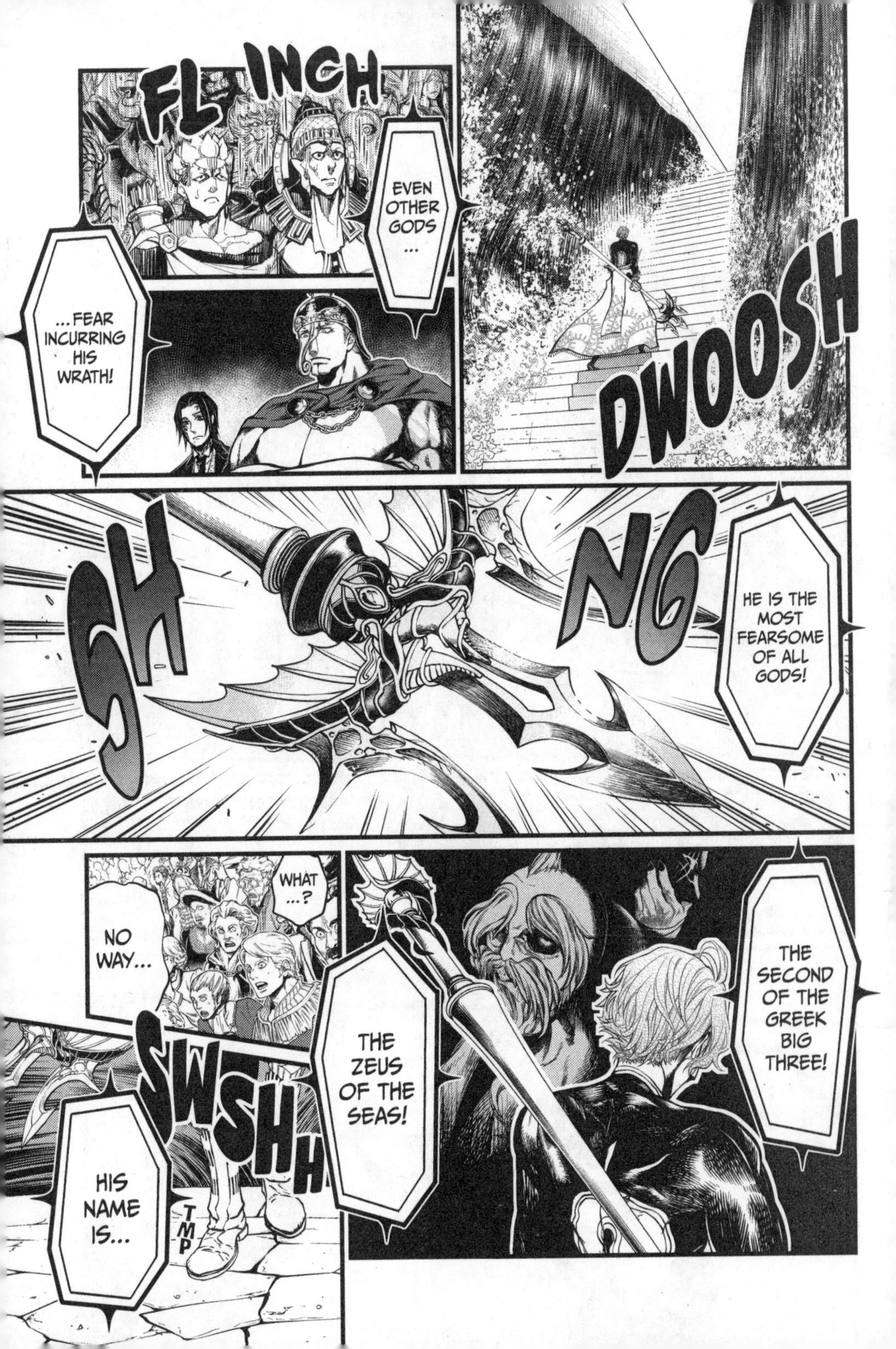
DWOOSH
FLINCH
EVEN OTHER GODS ...
...FEAR INCURRING HIS WRATH!
SH
NG
HE IS THE MOST FEARSOME OF ALL GODS!
THE SECOND OF THE GREEK BIG THREE!
THE ZEUS OF THE SEAS!
WHAT ...?
NO WAY...
SWSHH
HIS NAME IS...
TMP

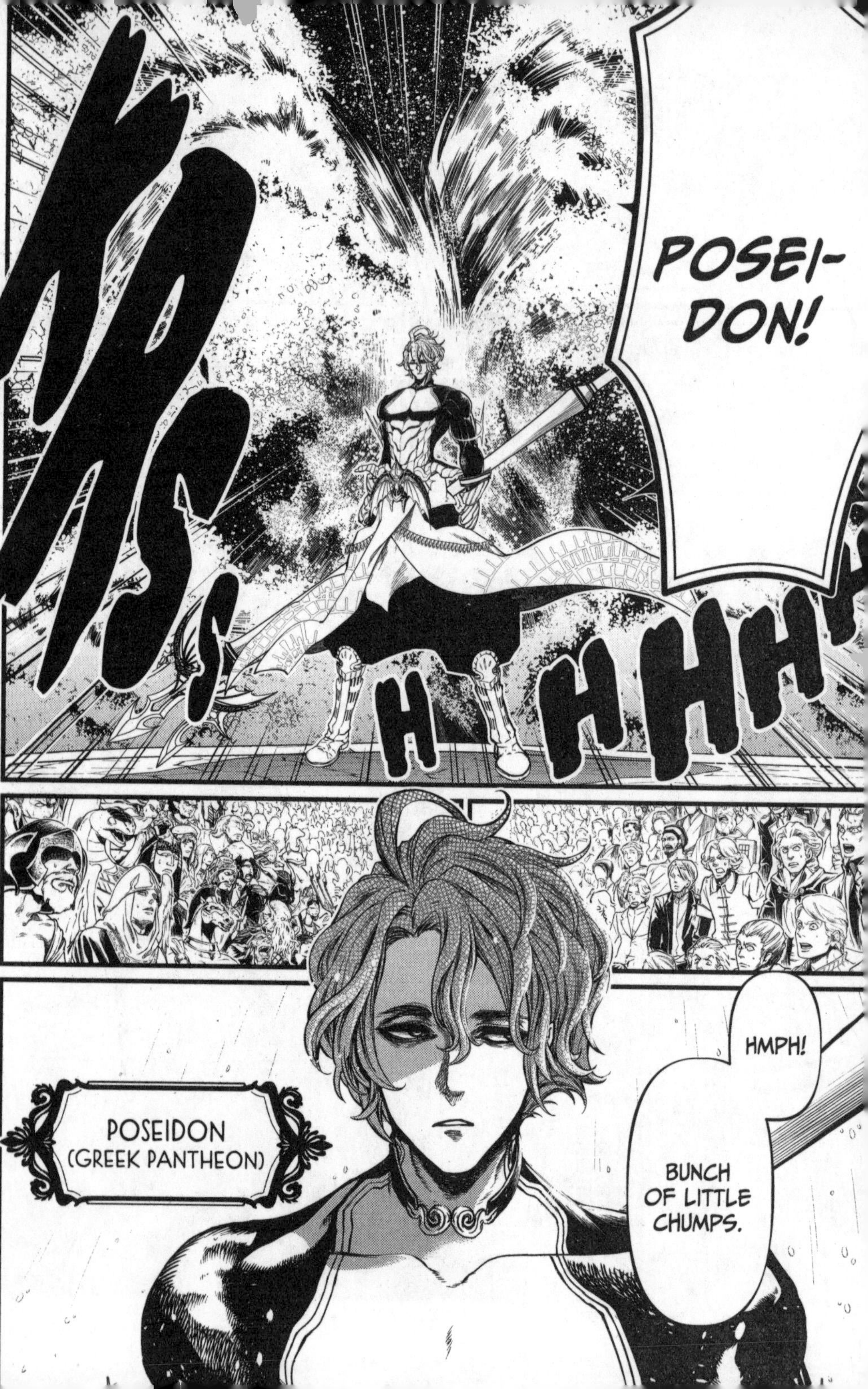
POSEI-
DON!
HMPH!
BUNCH OF LITTLE CHUMPS.
POSEIDON
(GREEK PANTHEON)

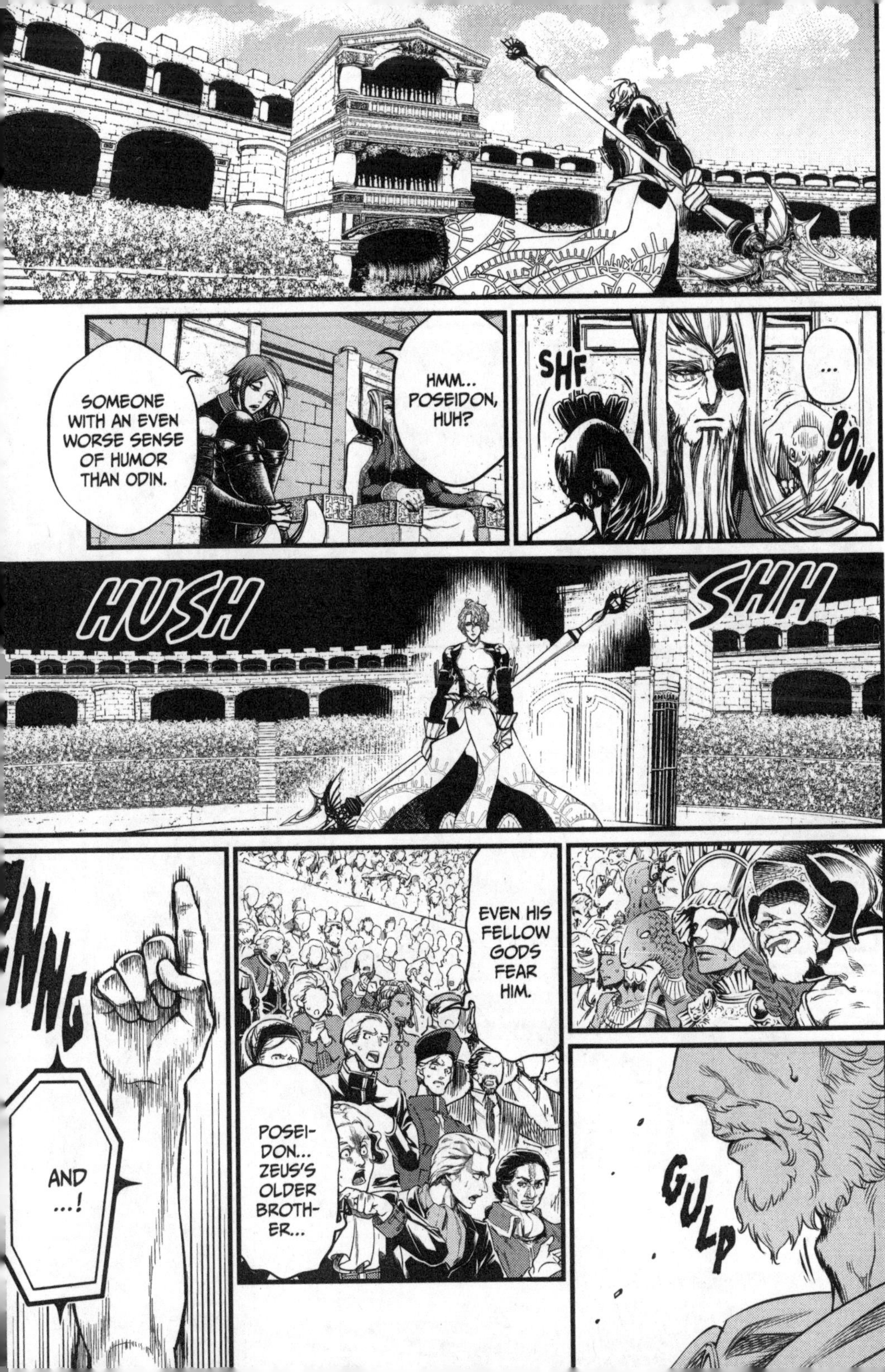

...
SHF
BOW
HMM... POSEIDON, HUH?
SOMEONE WITH AN EVEN WORSE SENSE OF HUMOR THAN ODIN.
SHH
HUSH
GULP
EVEN HIS FELLOW GODS FEAR HIM.
POSEI-DON... ZEUS'S OLDER BROTH-ER...
AND ...!

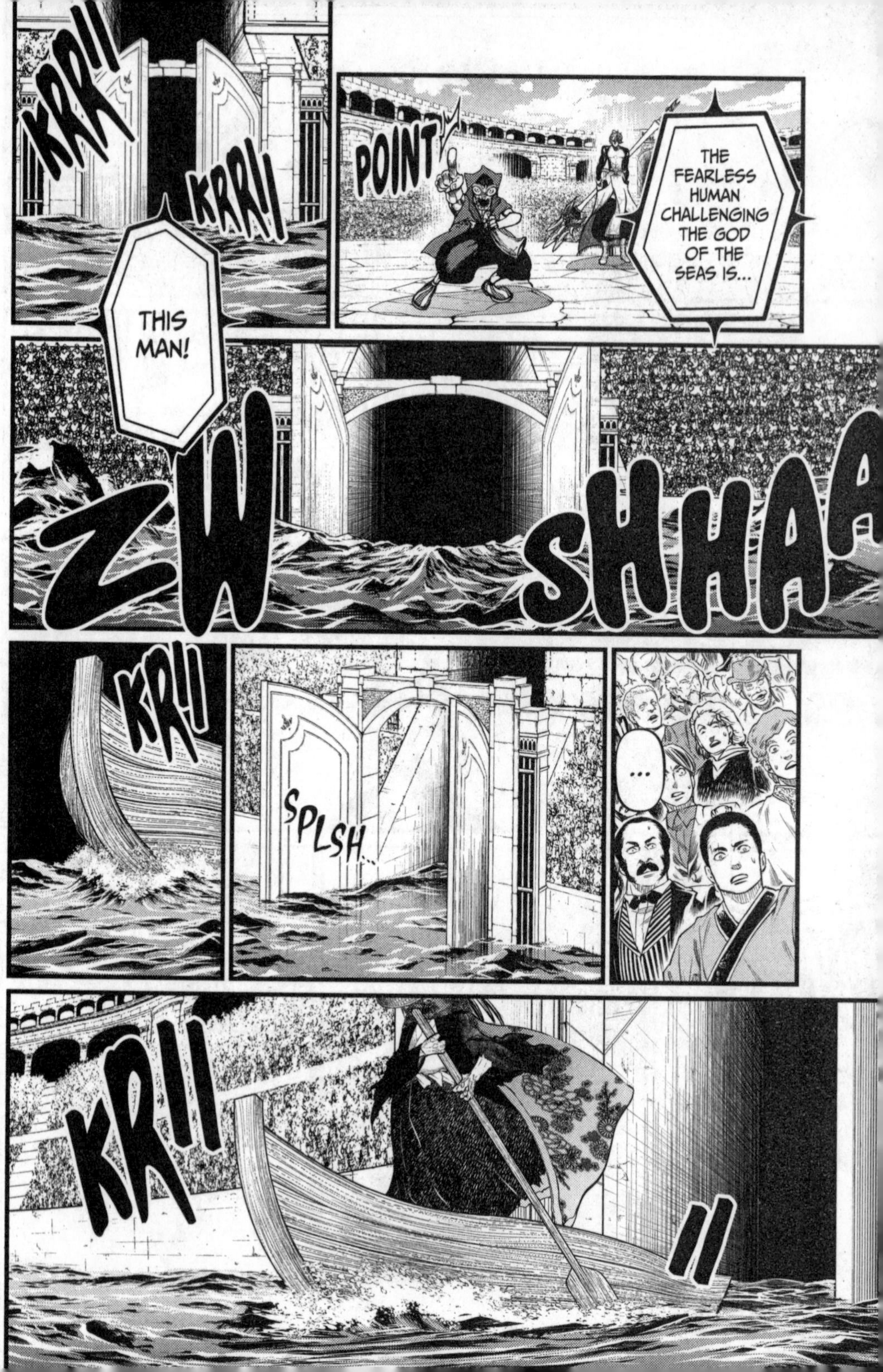
POINT
THE FEARLESS HUMAN CHALLENGING THE GOD OF THE SEAS IS...
KRRII
KRRII
THIS MAN!
ZW SHHAA
...
SPLSH...
KRII
KRII

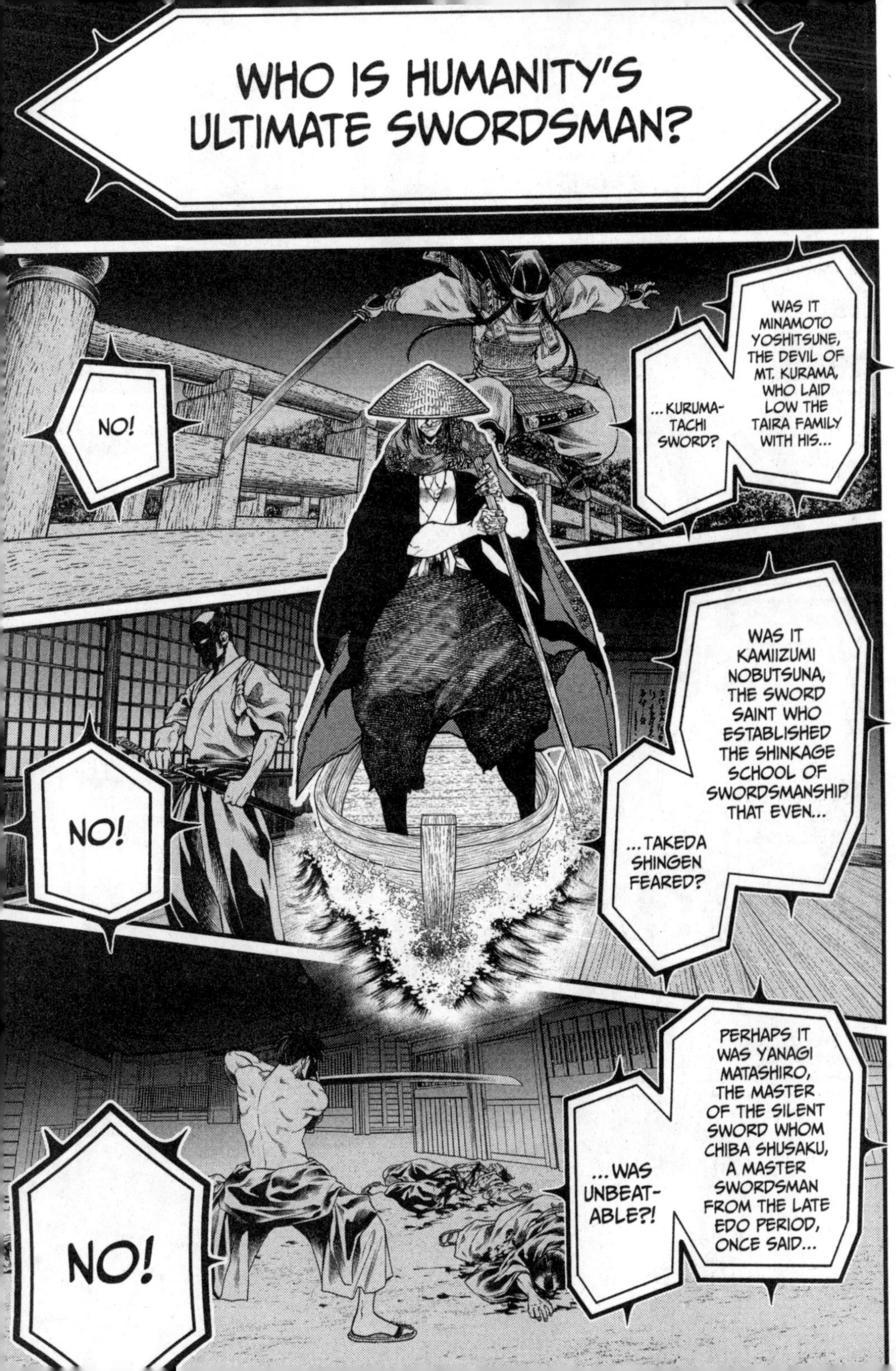
WHO IS HUMANITY'S ULTIMATE SWORDSMAN?
WAS IT MINAMOTO YOSHITSUNE, THE DEVIL OF MT. KURAMA, WHO LAID LOW THE TAIRA FAMILY WITH HIS...
...KURUMA-TACHI SWORD?
NO!
WAS IT KAMIIZUMI NOBUTSUNA, THE SWORD SAINT WHO ESTABLISHED THE SHINKAGE SCHOOL OF SWORDSMANSHIP THAT EVEN...
...TAKEDA SHINGEN FEARED?
NO!
PERHAPS IT WAS YANAGI MATASHIRO, THE MASTER OF THE SILENT SWORD WHOM CHIBA SHUSAKU, A MASTER SWORDSMAN FROM THE LATE EDO PERIOD, ONCE SAID...
...WAS UNBEAT-ABLE?!
NO!

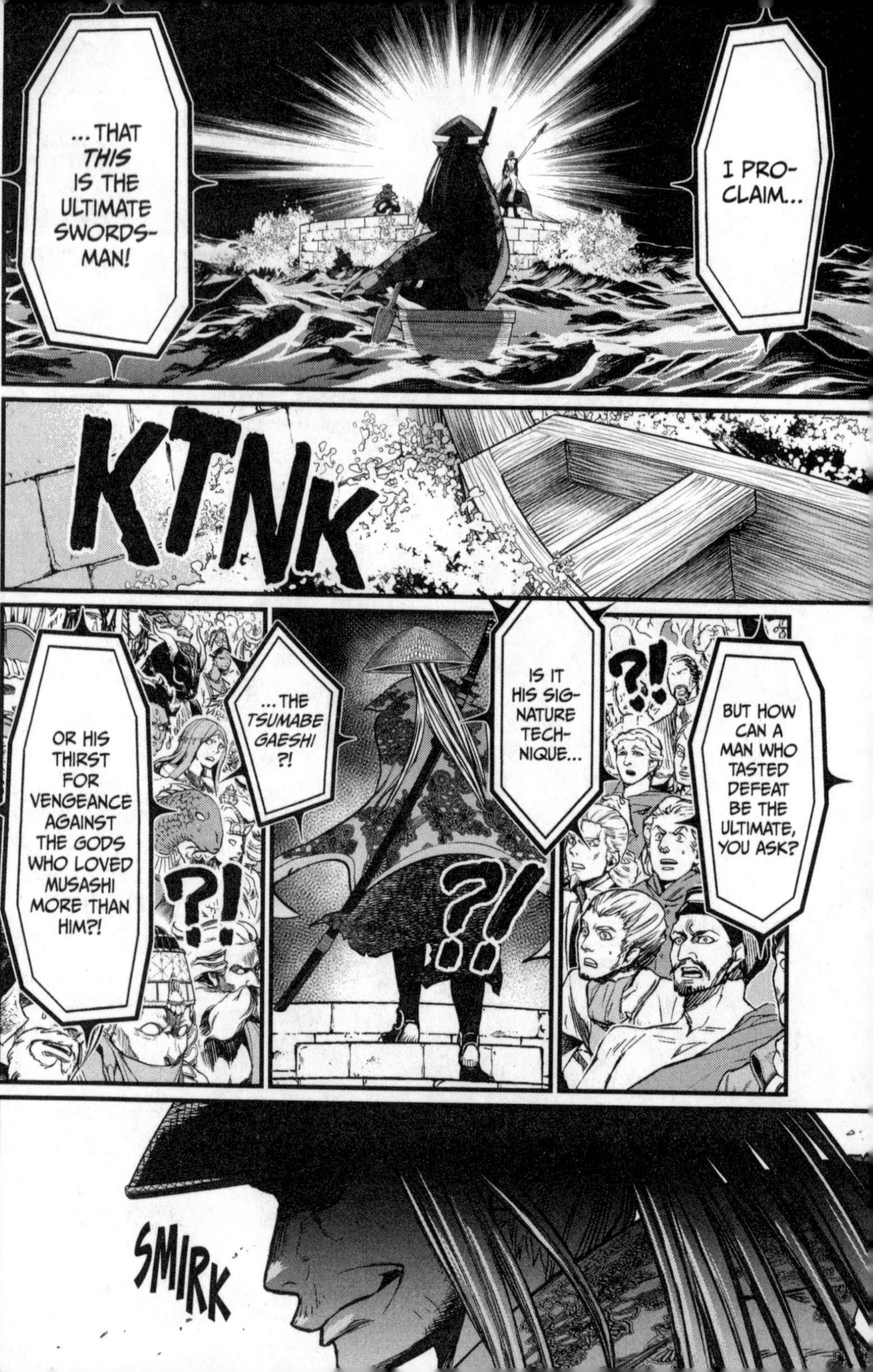
I PRO-CLAIM...
...THAT *THIS* IS THE ULTIMATE SWORDS-MAN!
KTNK
BUT HOW CAN A MAN WHO TASTED DEFEAT BE THE ULTIMATE, YOU ASK?
?!
IS IT HIS SIG-NATURE TECH-NIQUE...
...THE *TSUMABE GAESHI* ?!
?!
OR HIS THIRST FOR VENGEANCE AGAINST THE GODS WHO LOVED MUSASHI MORE THAN HIM?!
?!
SMIRK

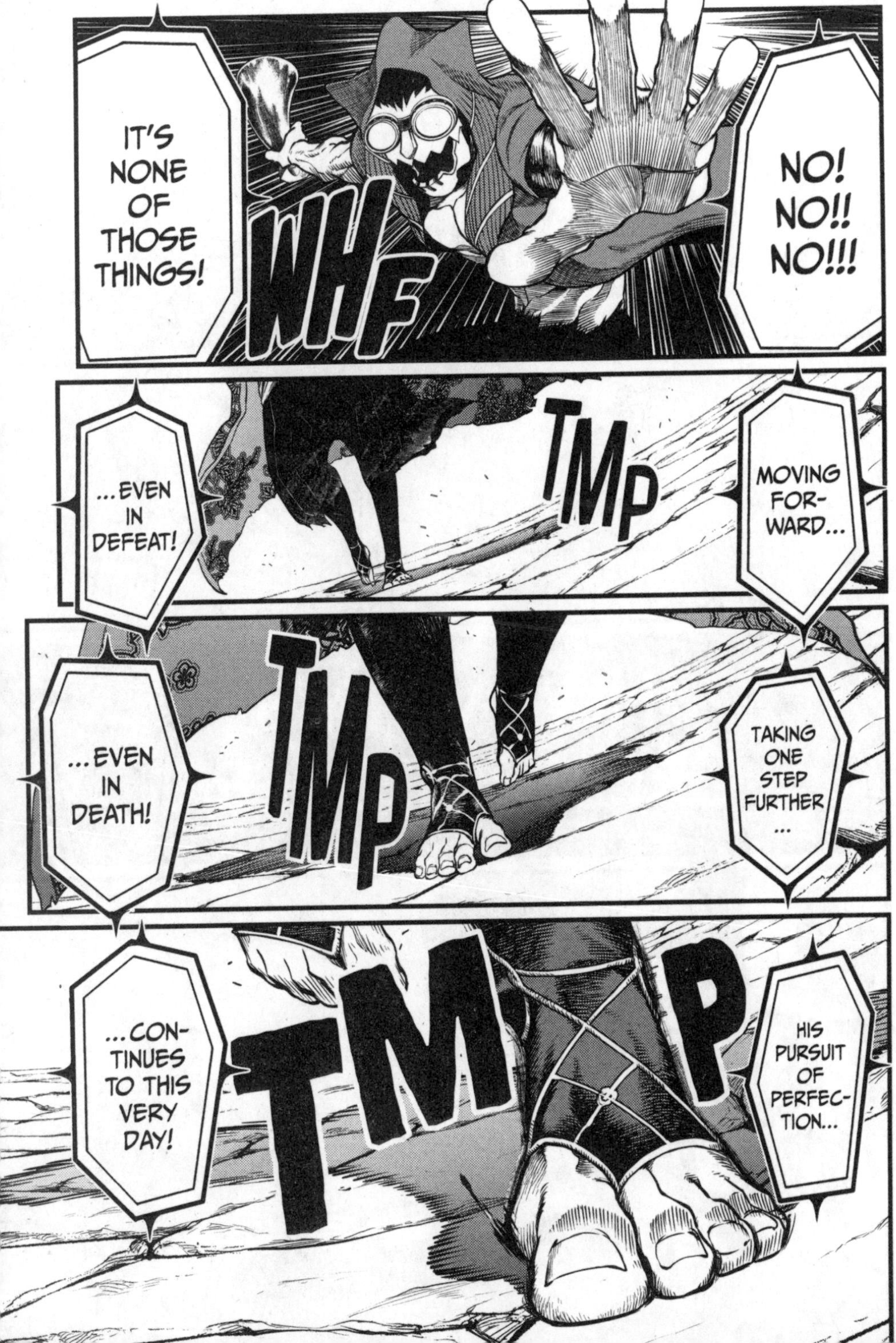
NO! NO!! NO!!!
WHF
IT'S NONE OF THOSE THINGS!
MOVING FORWARD...
TMP
...EVEN IN DEFEAT!
TAKING ONE STEP FURTHER...
TMP
...EVEN IN DEATH!
HIS PURSUIT OF PERFECTION...
TMP
...CONTINUES TO THIS VERY DAY!

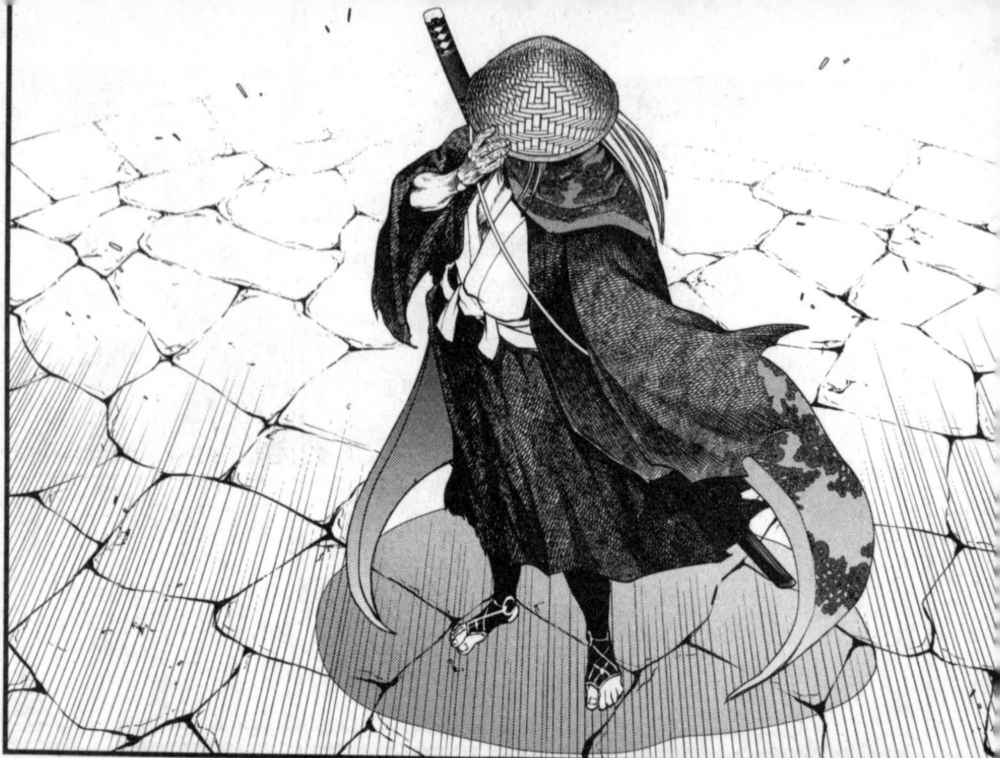

HUMANITY'S GREATEST LOSER

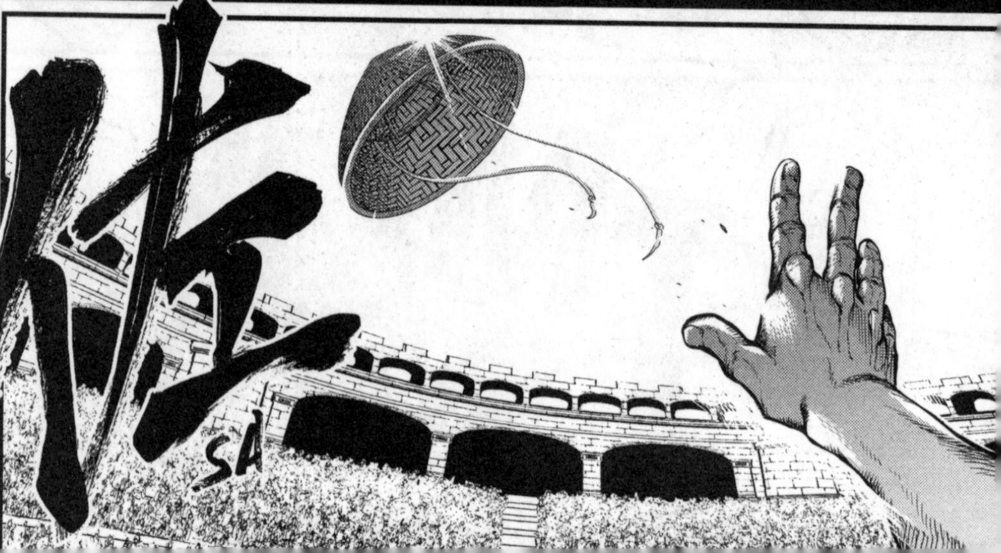
SA

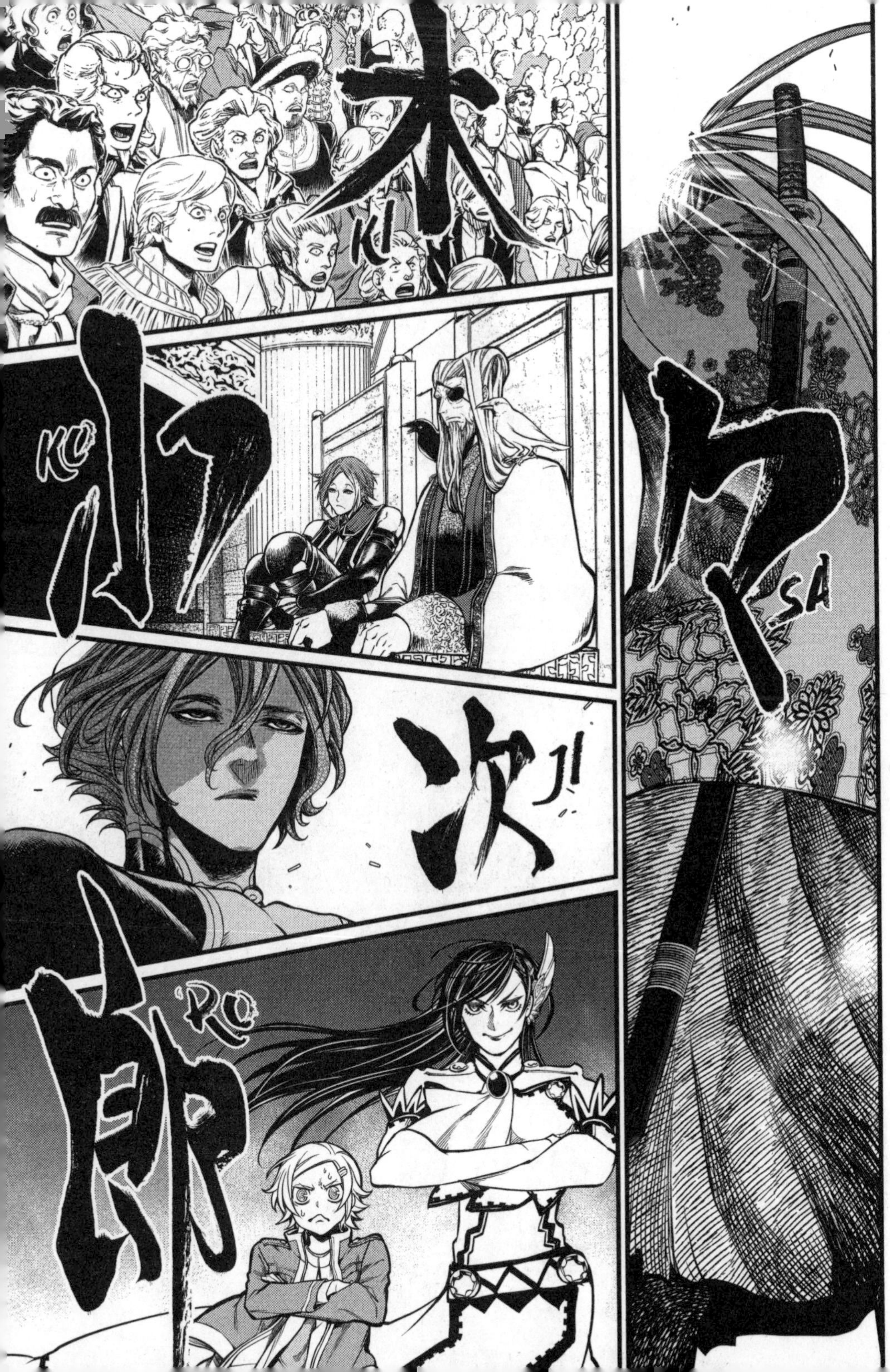
SA
木
KI
小
KO
次
JI
郎
RO

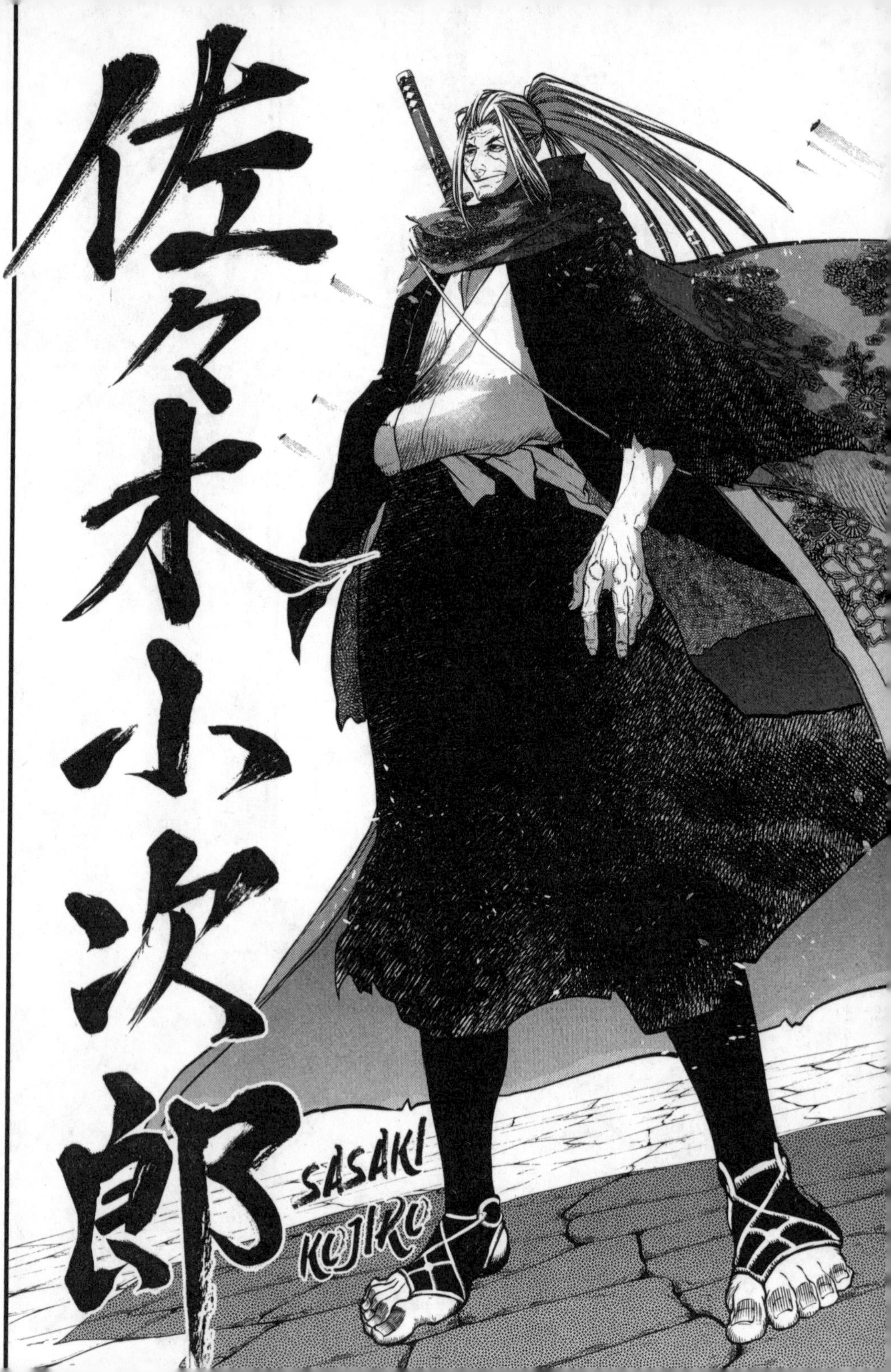
佐々木小次郎
SASAKI KOJIRO

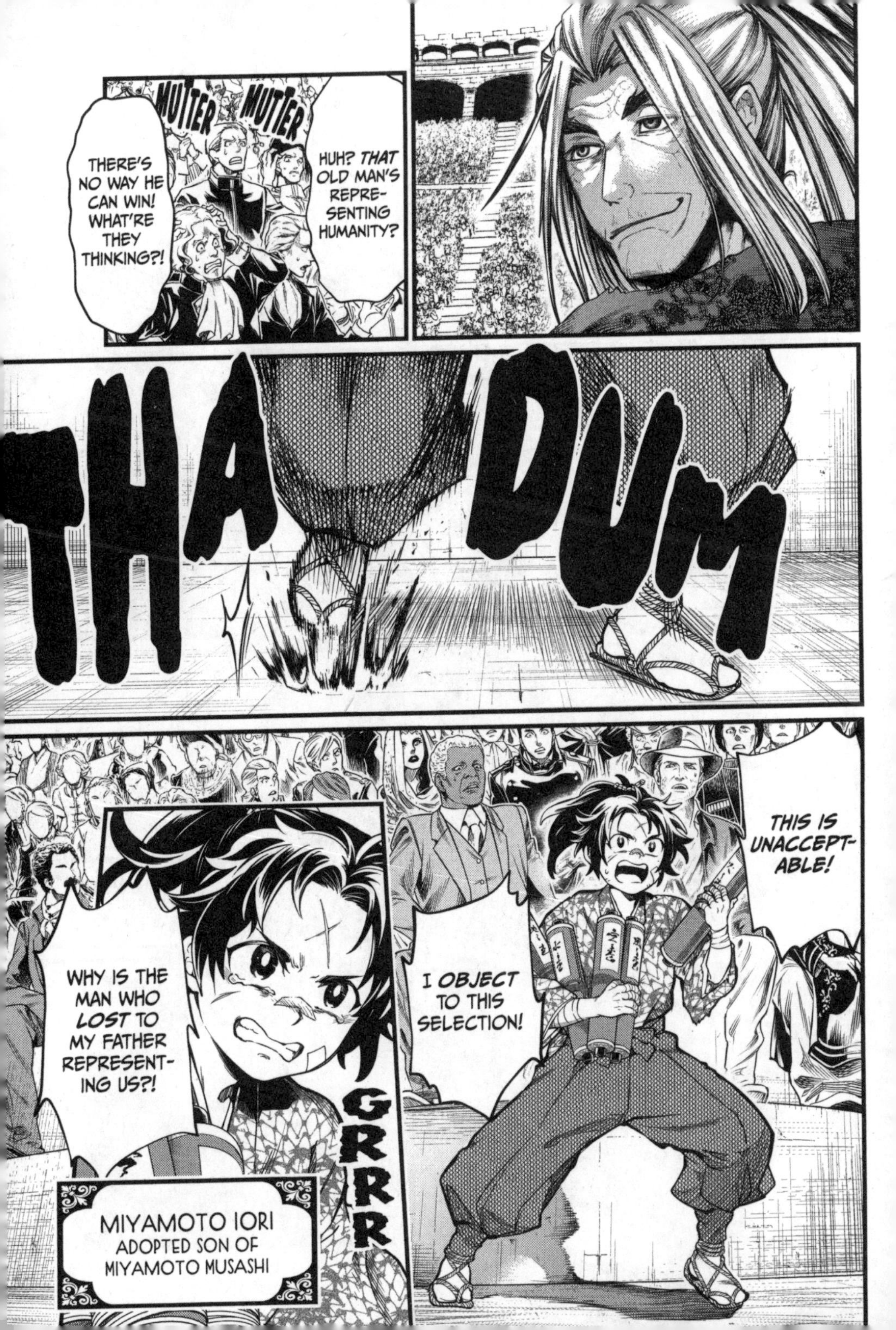
MUTTER MUTTER
HUH? THAT OLD MAN'S REPRESENTING HUMANITY?
THERE'S NO WAY HE CAN WIN! WHAT'RE THEY THINKING?!
THA DUM
THIS IS UNACCEPTABLE!
I OBJECT TO THIS SELECTION!
WHY IS THE MAN WHO LOST TO MY FATHER REPRESENTING US?!
GRRR
MIYAMOTO IORI
ADOPTED SON OF MIYAMOTO MUSASHI

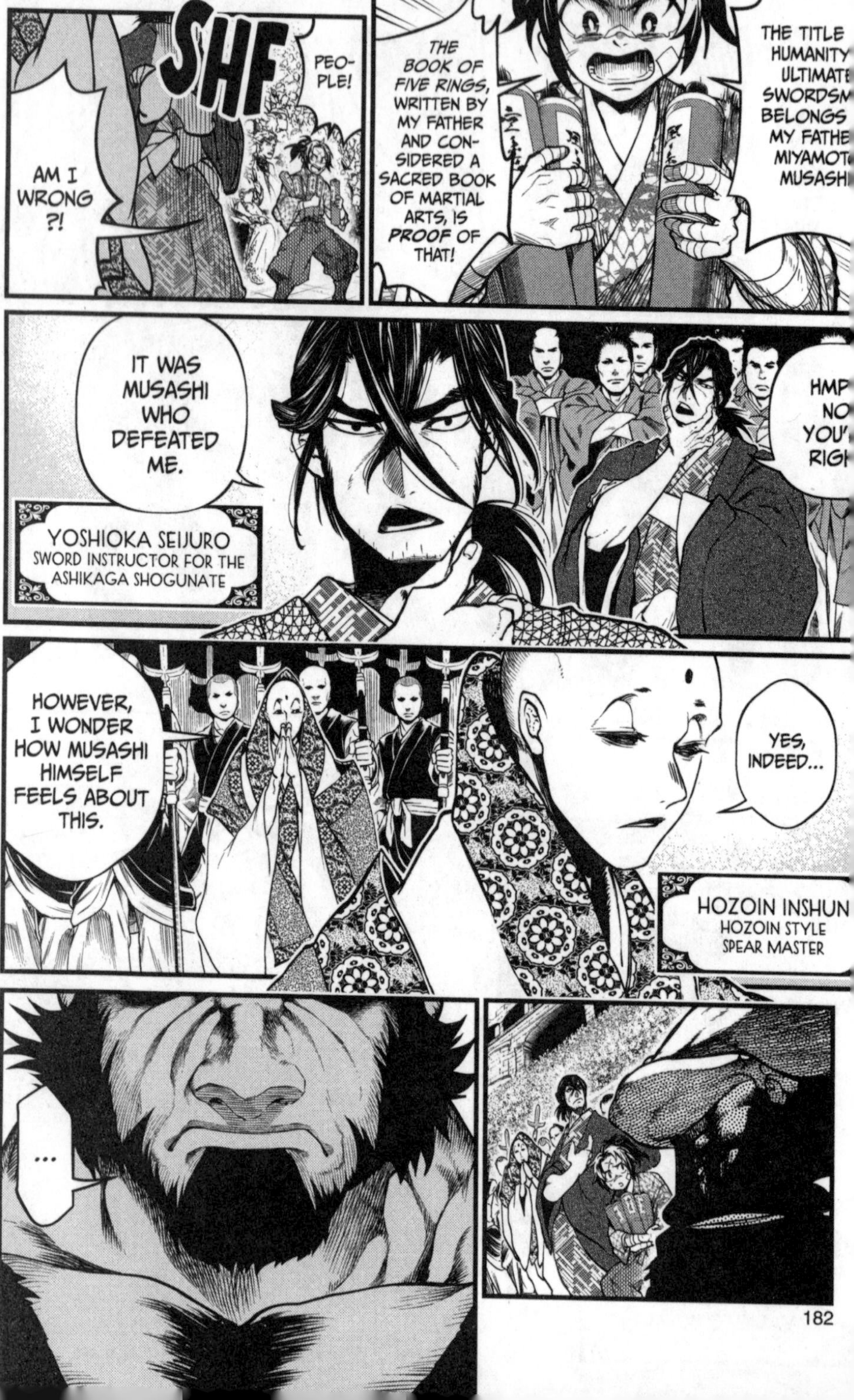
THE TITLE HUMANITY ULTIMATE SWORDSM BELONGS MY FATHE MIYAMOTO MUSASH
THE BOOK OF FIVE RINGS, WRITTEN BY MY FATHER AND CONSIDERED A SACRED BOOK OF MARTIAL ARTS, IS PROOF OF THAT!
PEO-PLE!
SHF
AM I WRONG ?!
HMP NO YOU' RIGH
IT WAS MUSASHI WHO DEFEATED ME.
YOSHIOKA SEIJURO
SWORD INSTRUCTOR FOR THE ASHIKAGA SHOGUNATE
YES, INDEED...
HOZOIN INSHUN
HOZOIN STYLE SPEAR MASTER
HOWEVER, I WONDER HOW MUSASHI HIMSELF FEELS ABOUT THIS.
...

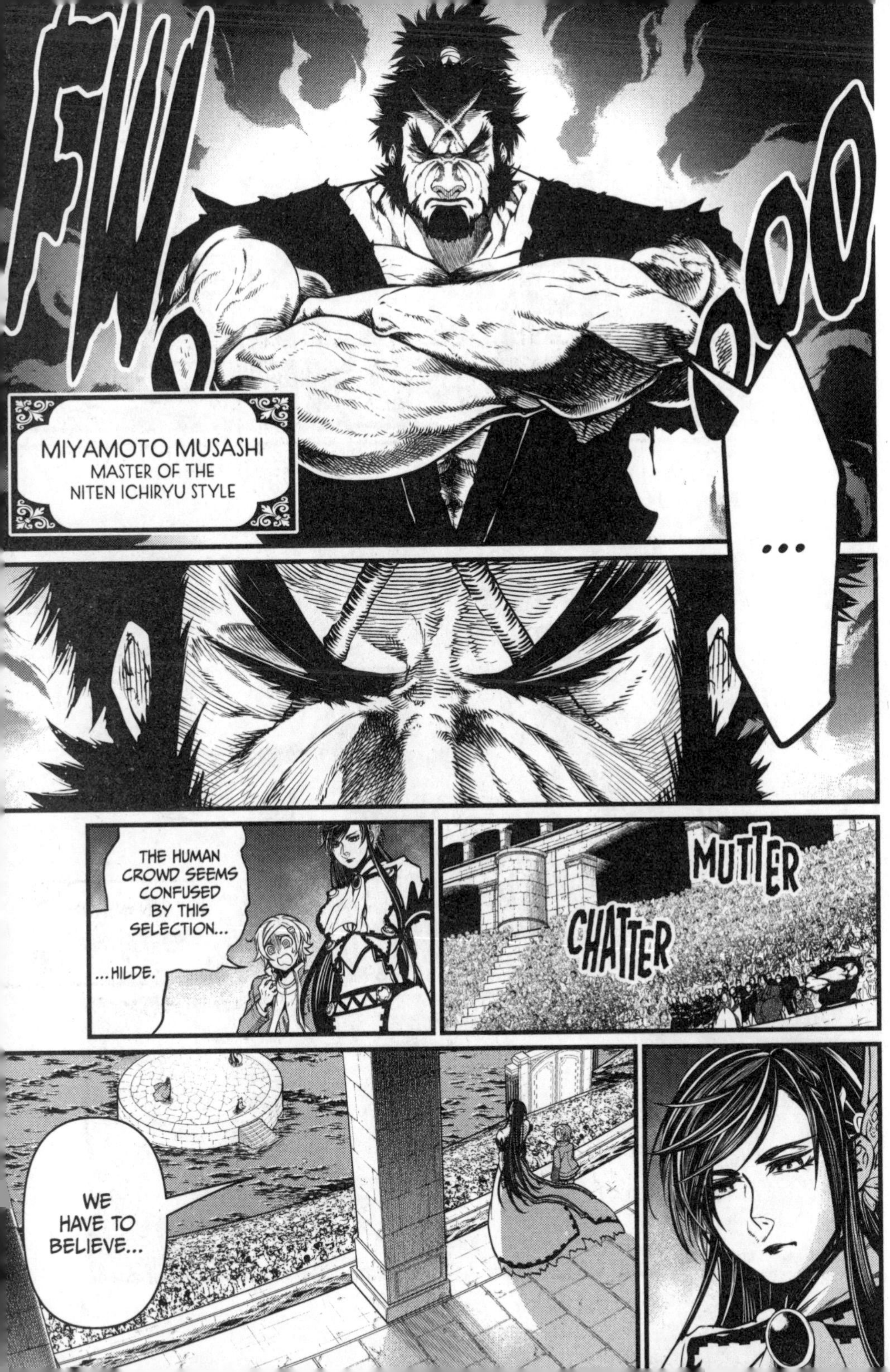
FWOOOO
...
MIYAMOTO MUSASHI
MASTER OF THE NITEN ICHIRYU STYLE
MUTTER
CHATTER
THE HUMAN CROWD SEEMS CONFUSED BY THIS SELECTION...
...HILDE.
WE HAVE TO BELIEVE...

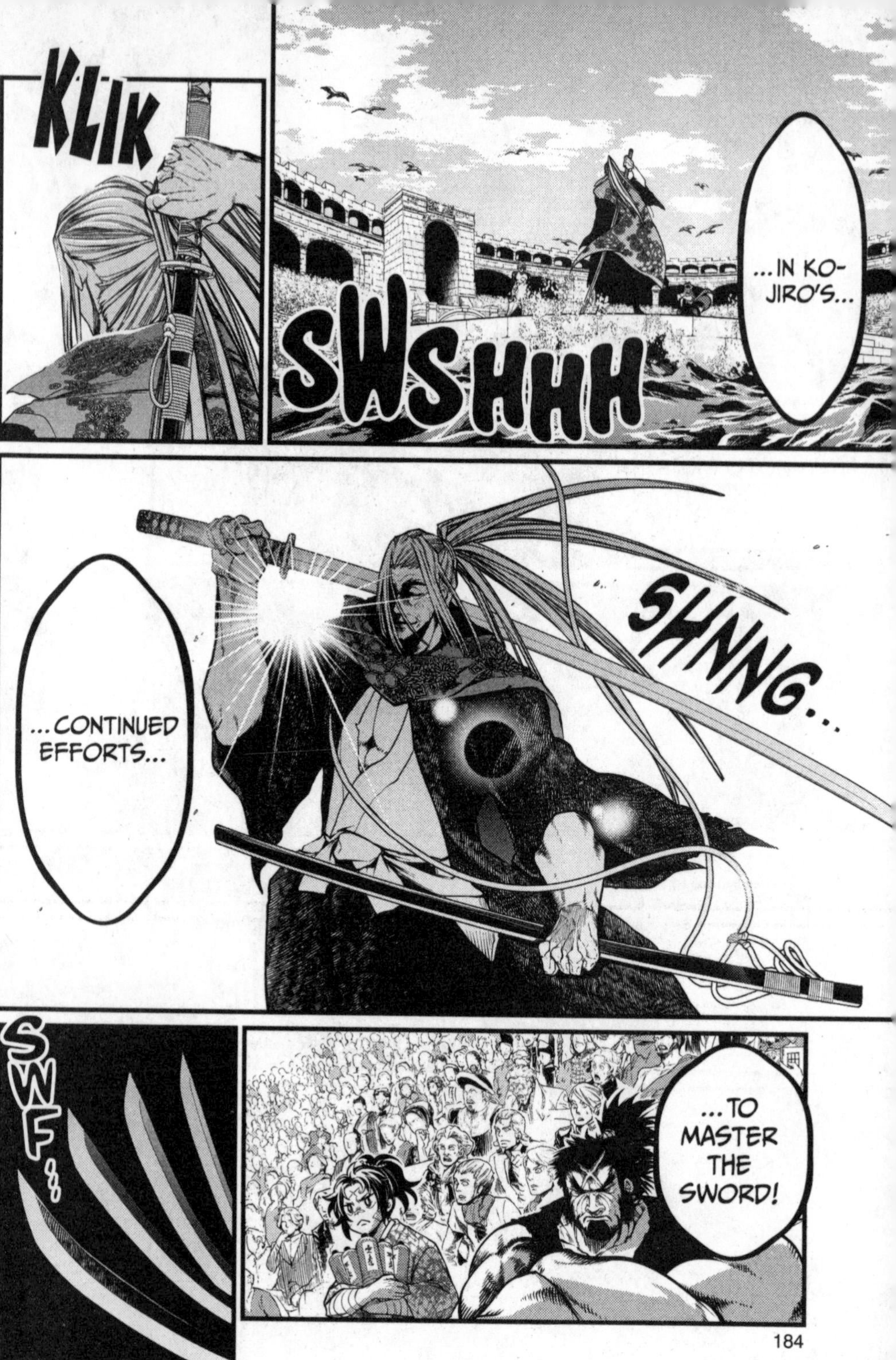
...IN KO-JIRO'S...
SWSHHH
KLIK
SHNNG...
...CONTINUED EFFORTS...
...TO MASTER THE SWORD!
SWF

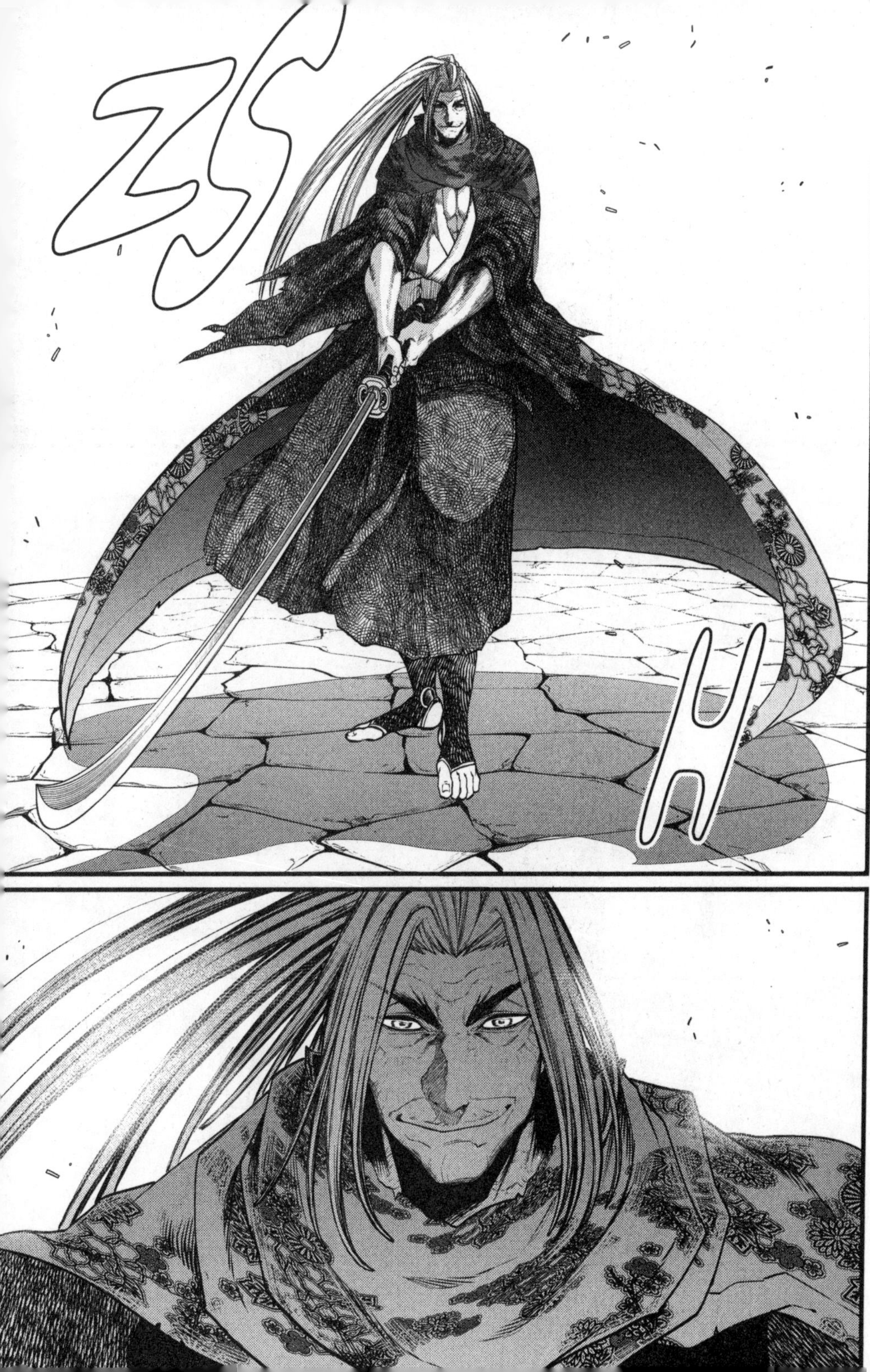
ZS
H

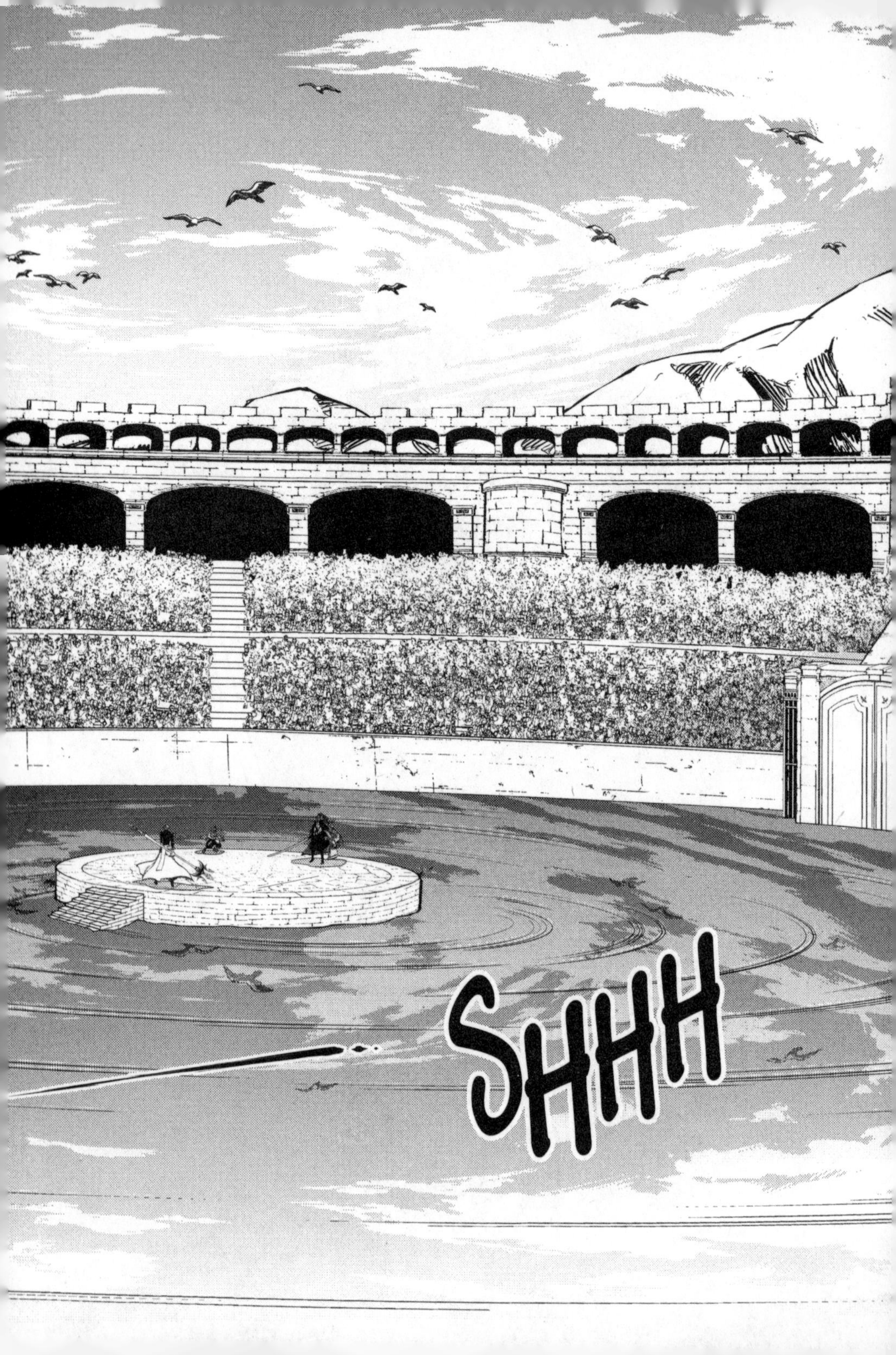
SHHH

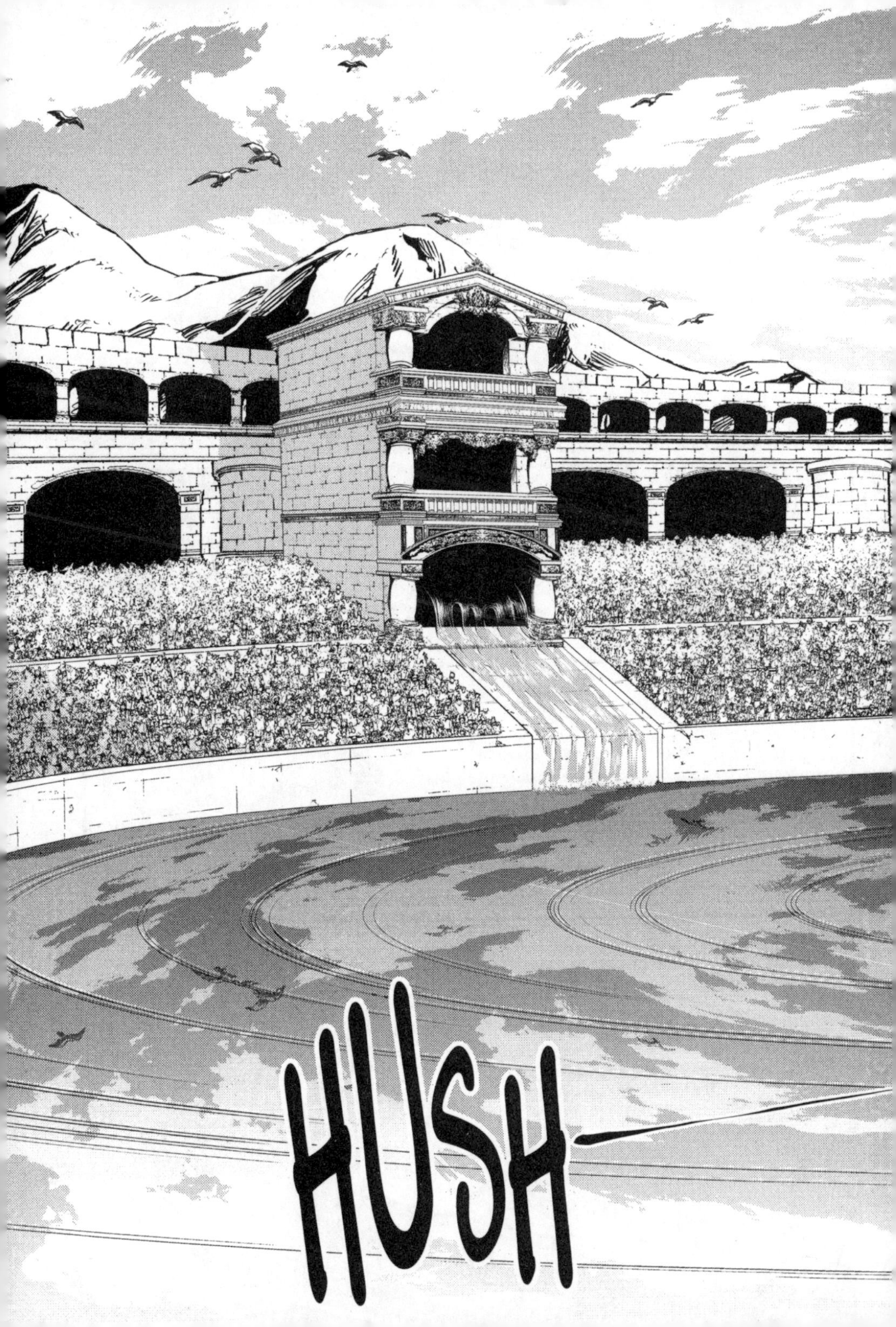
HUSH

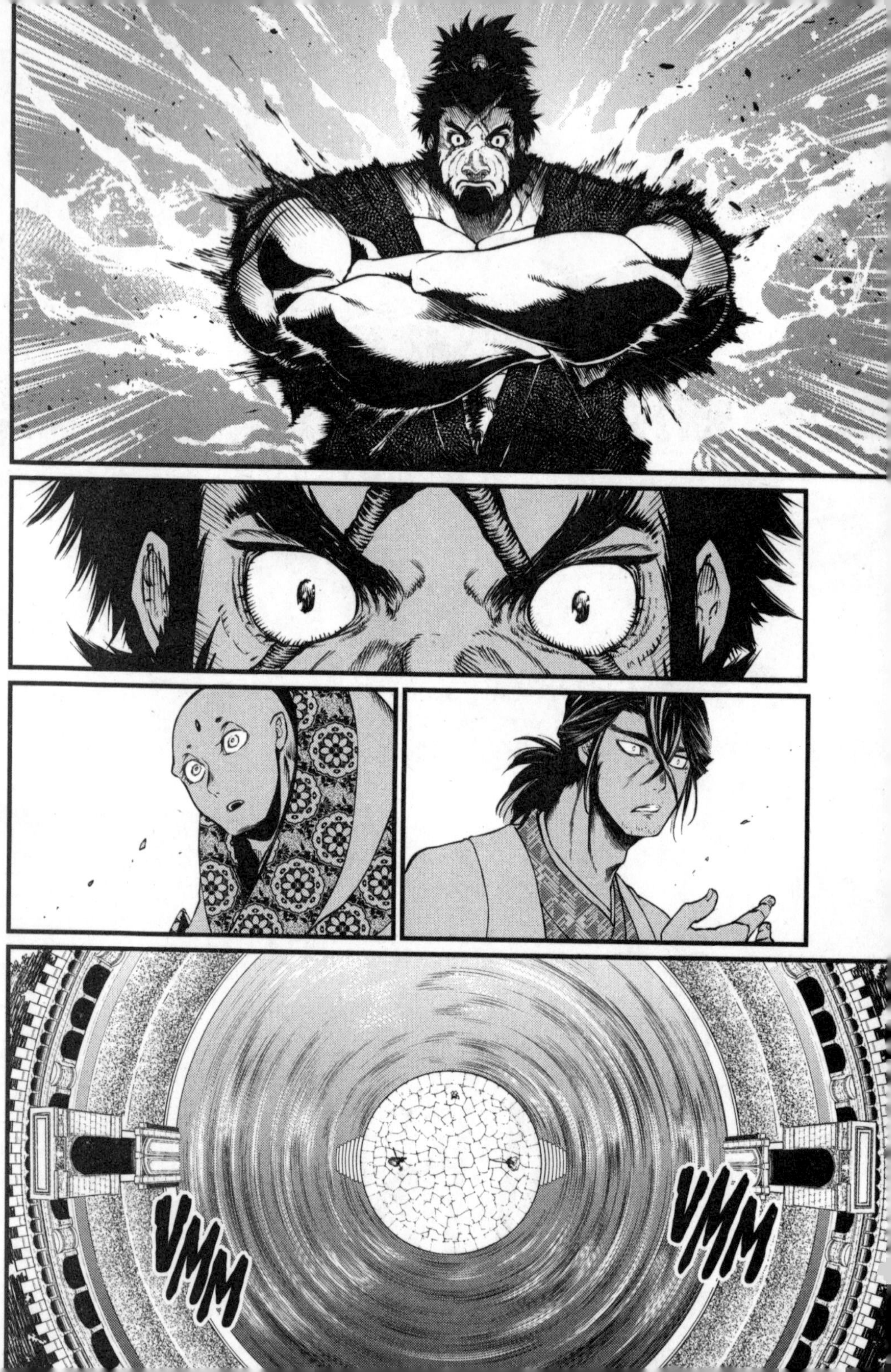
VMM
VMM

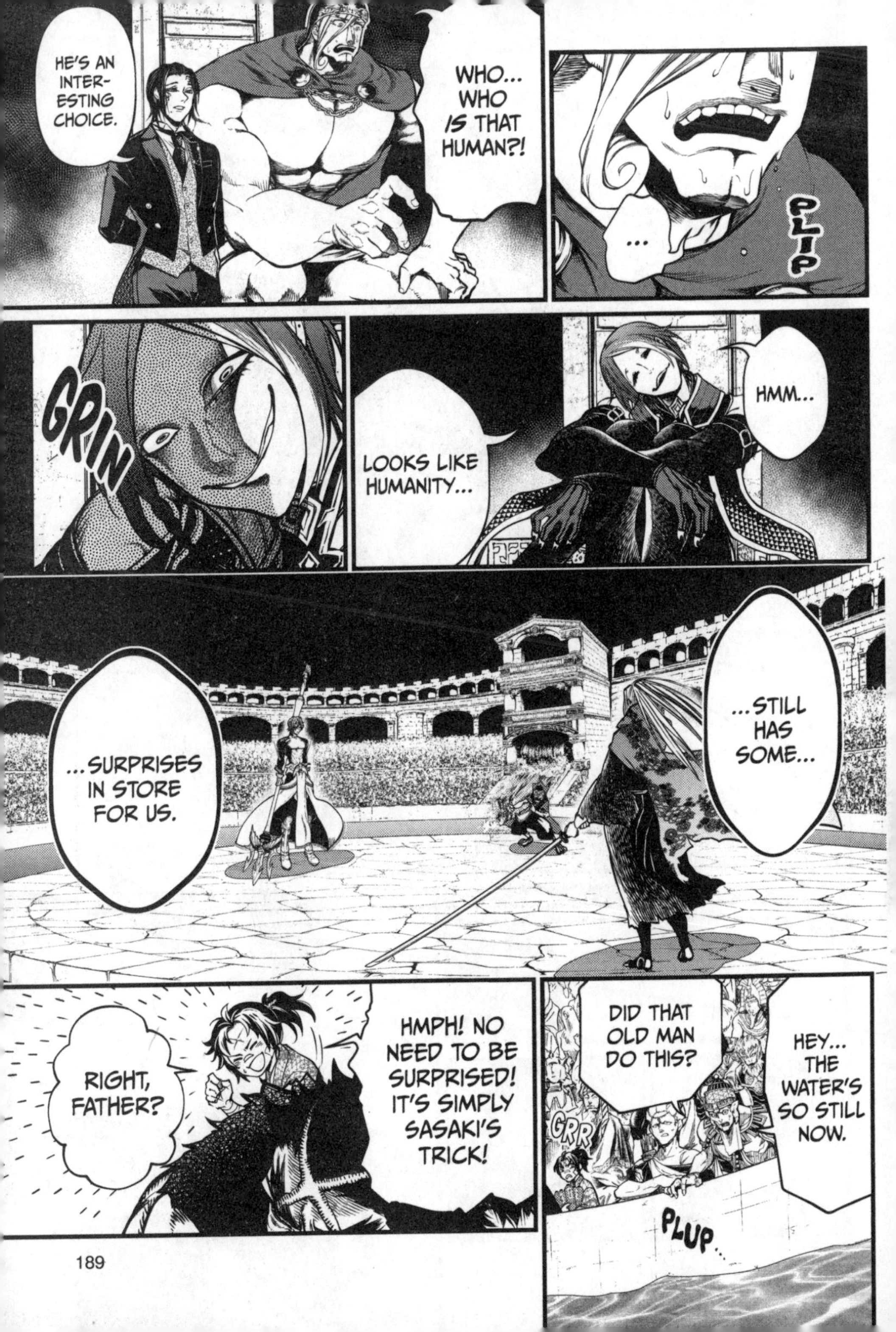
...
PLIP
WHO... WHO *IS* THAT HUMAN?!
HE'S AN INTERESTING CHOICE.
HMM...
LOOKS LIKE HUMANITY...
GRIN
...STILL HAS SOME...
...SURPRISES IN STORE FOR US.
HEY... THE WATER'S SO STILL NOW.
DID THAT OLD MAN DO THIS?
GRR
PLUP...
HMPH! NO NEED TO BE SURPRISED! IT'S SIMPLY SASAKI'S TRICK!
RIGHT, FATHER?

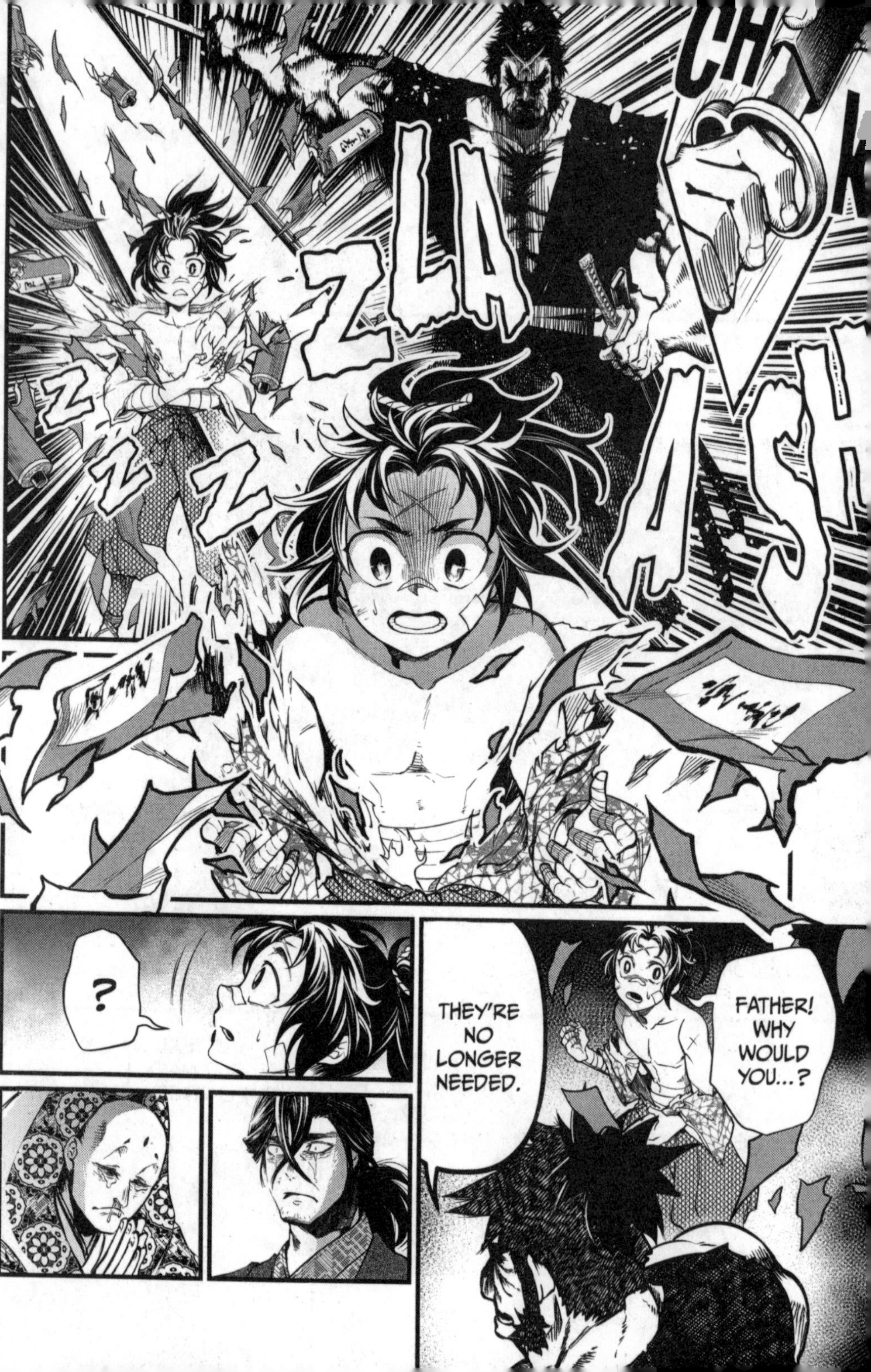
CHK
ZLASH
Z Z Z
FATHER! WHY WOULD YOU...?
THEY'RE NO LONGER NEEDED.
?

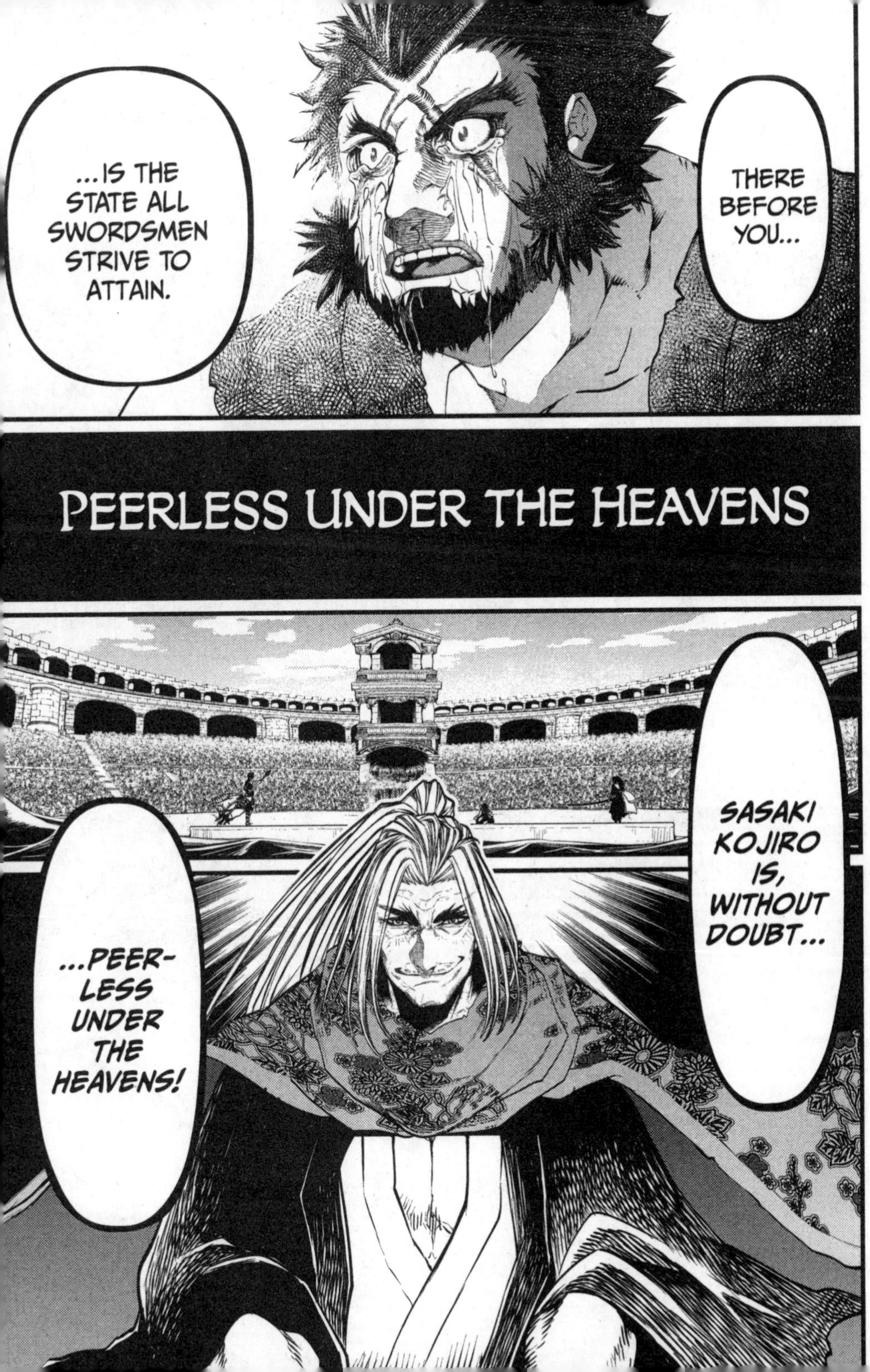
THERE BEFORE YOU...
...IS THE STATE ALL SWORDSMEN STRIVE TO ATTAIN.
PEERLESS UNDER THE HEAVENS
SASAKI KOJIRO IS, WITHOUT DOUBT...
...PEER-LESS UNDER THE HEAVENS!

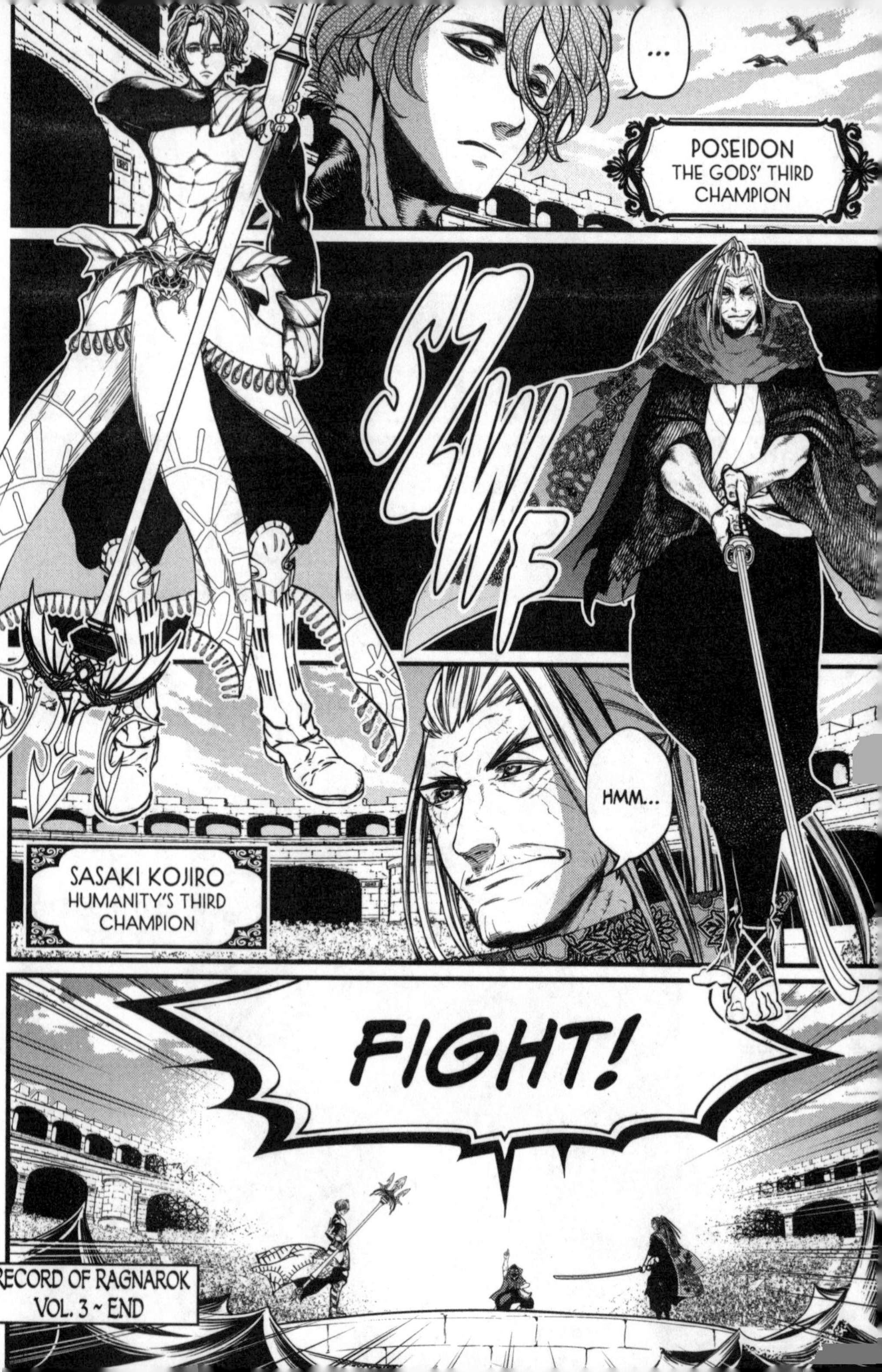
...
POSEIDON
THE GODS' THIRD
CHAMPION
HMM...
SASAKI KOJIRO
HUMANITY'S THIRD
CHAMPION
FIGHT!
RECORD OF RAGNAROK
VOL. 3 ~ END

RECORD OF

RAGNAROK

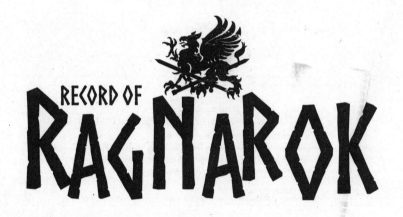

RECORD OF RAGNAROK

VOLUME 3
VIZ Signature Edition

Art by **Azychika**

Story by **Shinya Umemura**

Script by **Takumi Fukui**

Translation / Joe Yamazaki
English Adaptation / Stan!
Touch-Up Art & Lettering / Mark McMurray
Design / Julian (JR) Robinson
Editor / Mike Montesa

Shumatsu no Walkure
©2017 by AZYCHIKA AND SHINYA UMEMURA AND TAKUMI FUKUI/COAMIX
Approved No. ZCW-123W
First Published in Japan in Monthly Comic ZENON by COAMIX, Inc.
English translation rights arranged with COAMIX Inc., Tokyo
through Tuttle-Mori Agency, Inc., Tokyo

The stories, characters, and incidents mentioned in this publication are entirely fictional.

Printed in Canada

Published by VIZ Media, LLC
P.O. Box 77010
San Francisco, CA 94107

10 9 8 7 6 5 4 3 2 1
First printing, July 2022

viz.com

PARENTAL ADVISORY
RECORD OF RAGNAROK is rated T+ for
Older Teen and is recommended for ages
16 and up. Contains graphic violence.

VIZ SIGNATURE

vizsignature.com

IN THE ORIGINAL CLASSIC MANGA set in a postapocalyptic wasteland ruled by savage gangs, a hero appears to bring justice to the guilty. This warrior named Ken holds the deadly secrets of a mysterious martial art known as Hokuto Shinken—the Divine Fist of the North Star!

FIST OF THE NORTH STAR

Story by **BURONSON** Art by **TETSUO HARA**

VIZ

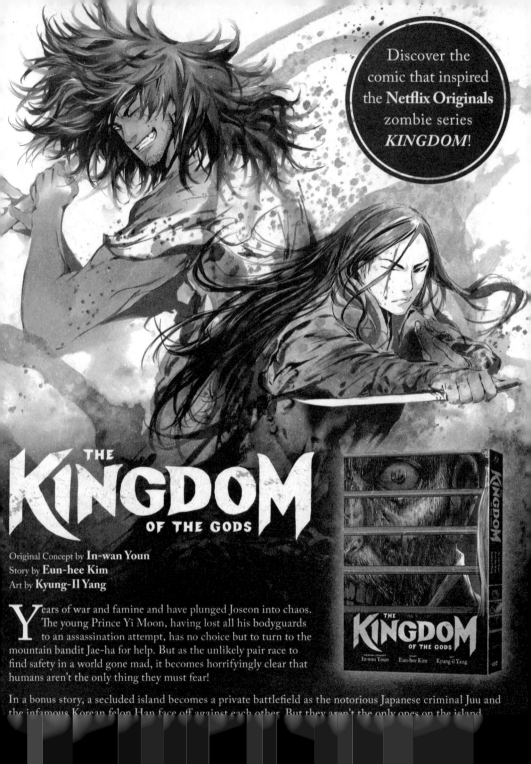

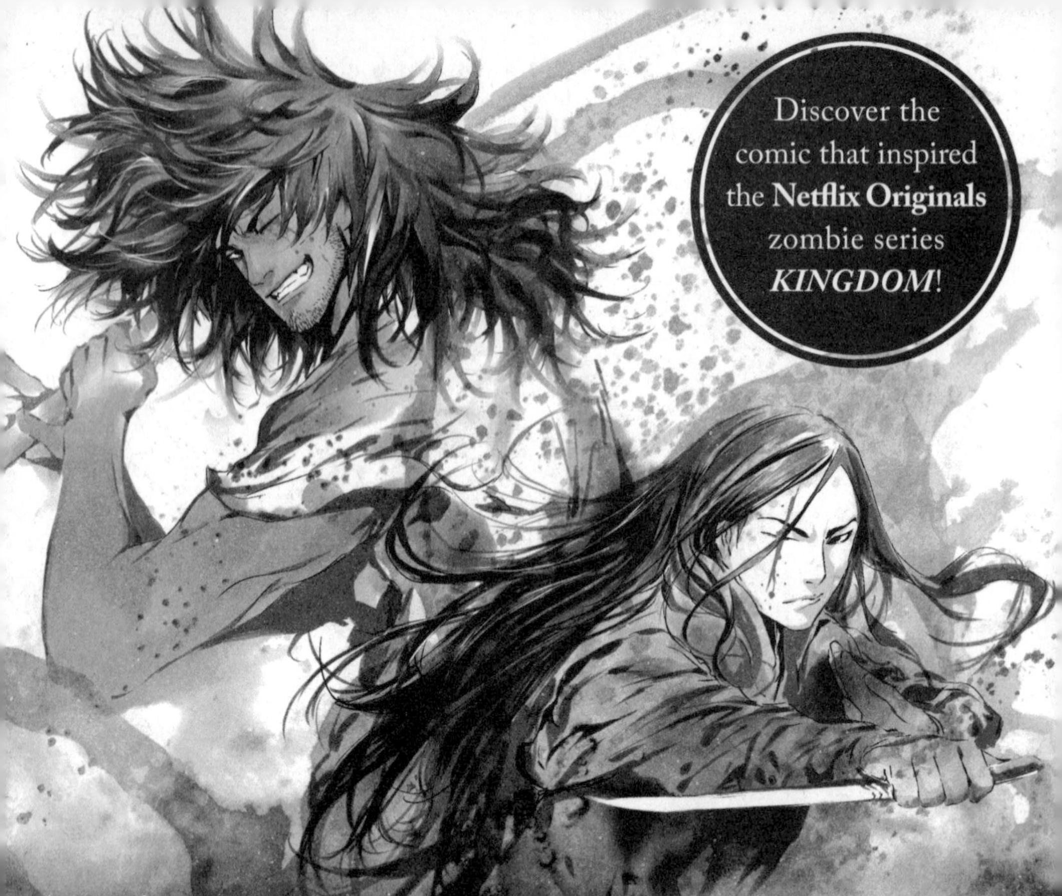
Discover the comic that inspired the **Netflix Originals** zombie series *KINGDOM*!

THE KINGDOM OF THE GODS

Original Concept by **In-wan Youn**
Story by **Eun-hee Kim**
Art by **Kyung-Il Yang**

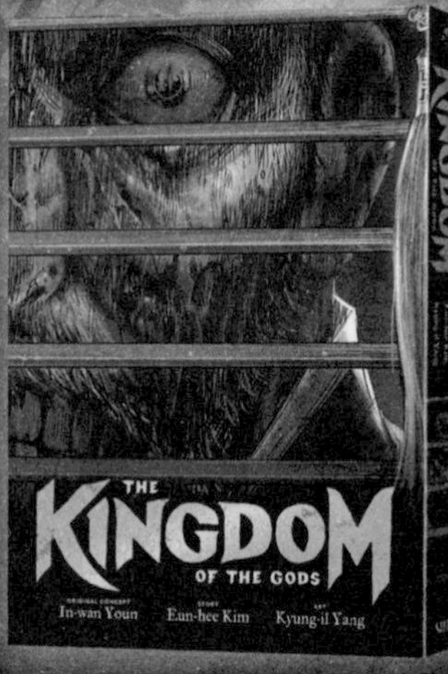
THE KINGDOM OF THE GODS
In-wan Youn
Eun-hee Kim
Kyung-il Yang

Years of war and famine and have plunged Joseon into chaos. The young Prince Yi Moon, having lost all his bodyguards to an assassination attempt, has no choice but to turn to the mountain bandit Jae-ha for help. But as the unlikely pair race to find safety in a world gone mad, it becomes horrifyingly clear that humans aren't the only thing they must fear!

In a bonus story, a secluded island becomes a private battlefield as the notorious Japanese criminal Juu and [redacted]

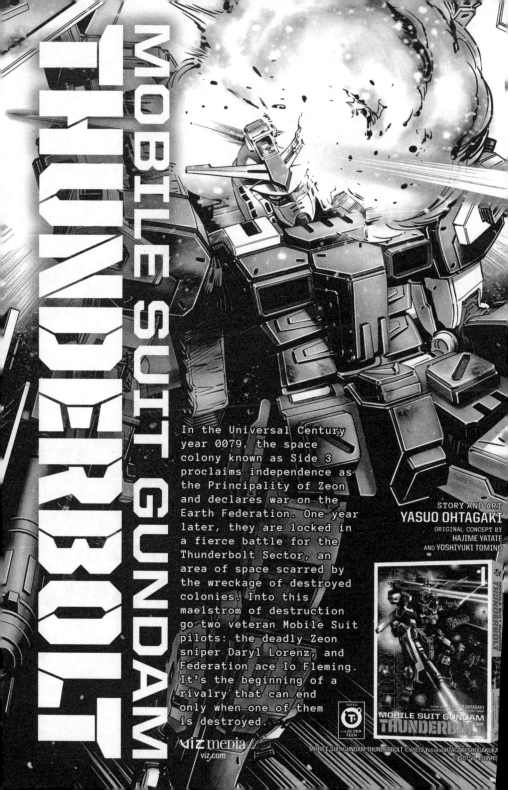

MOBILE SUIT GUNDAM THUNDERBOLT

In the Universal Century year 0079, the space colony known as Side 3 proclaims independence as the Principality of Zeon and declares war on the Earth Federation. One year later, they are locked in a fierce battle for the Thunderbolt Sector, an area of space scarred by the wreckage of destroyed colonies. Into this maelstrom of destruction go two veteran Mobile Suit pilots: the deadly Zeon sniper Daryl Lorenz, and Federation ace Io Fleming. It's the beginning of a rivalry that can end only when one of them is destroyed.

STORY AND ART
YASUO OHTAGAKI
ORIGINAL CONCEPT BY
HAJIME YATATE
AND **YOSHIYUKI TOMINO**

RATED
T
FOR OLDER
TEEN

viz media
viz.com

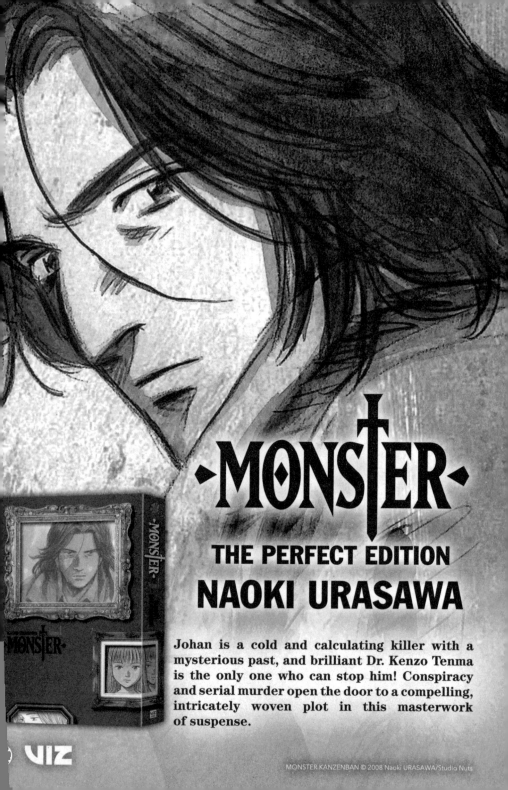

·MONSTER·

THE PERFECT EDITION
NAOKI URASAWA

Johan is a cold and calculating killer with a mysterious past, and brilliant Dr. Kenzo Tenma is the only one who can stop him! Conspiracy and serial murder open the door to a compelling, intricately woven plot in this masterwork of suspense.

YOU'RE READING IT WRONG!

RECORD OF RAGNAROK

reads right to left starting in the upper-right corner. Japanese is read from right to left, meaning that action, sound effects, and word-balloon order are completely reversed from English order.

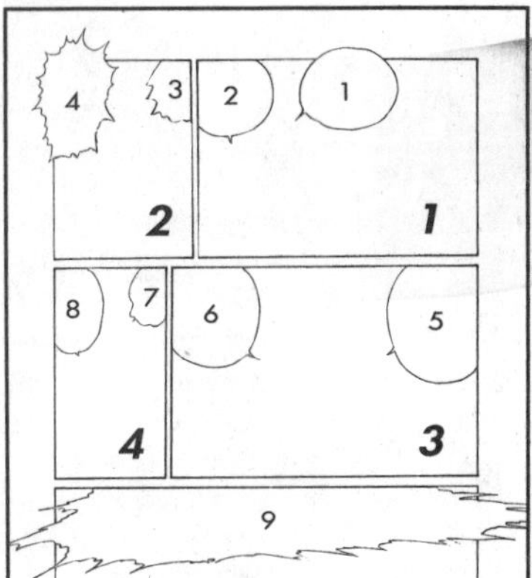
1
2
3
4
1
2
5
6
7
8
3
4
9
5
142

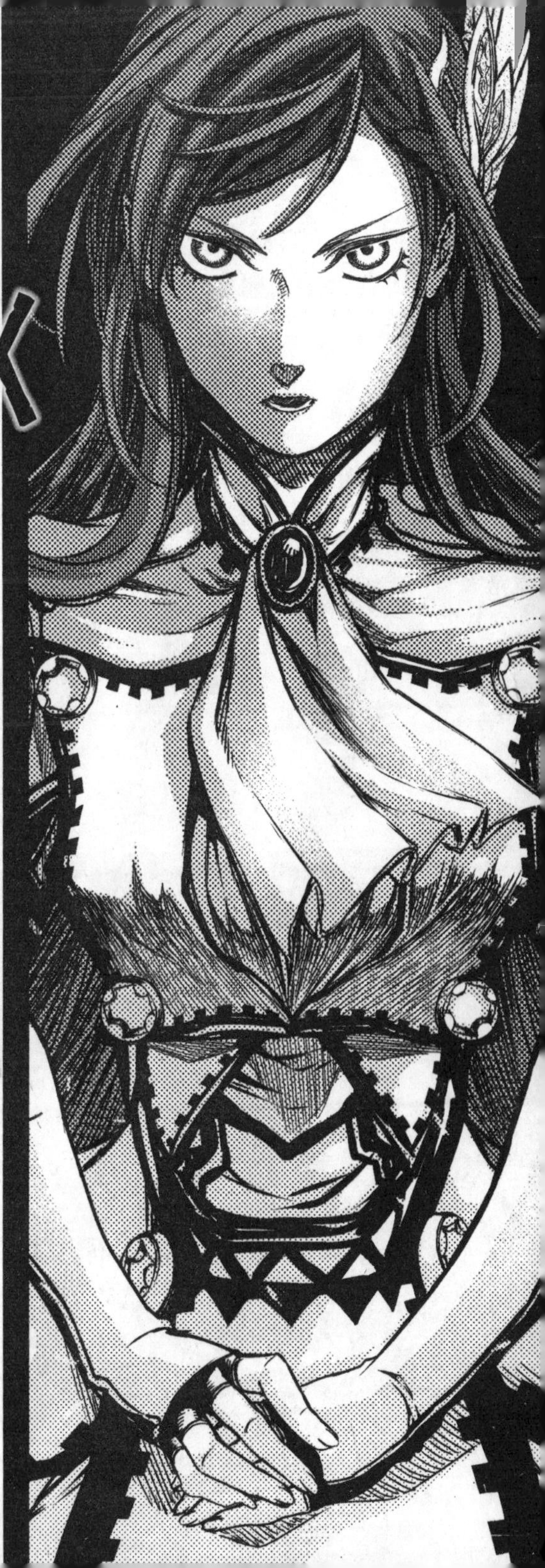

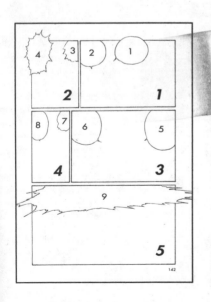

REMINA

JUNJI ITO'S CHILLING SCI-FI MASTERWORK *REMINA*
PITS THE CHAOS OF THE COSMOS AGAINST THE CRUELTY
OF HUMANITY IN THIS DELUXE HARDCOVER.